China in
The
National
Interest

China in
The
National
Interest

Owen Harries, editor

Transaction Publishers
New Brunswick (U.S.A.) and London (U.K.)

First paperback printing 2003

New material this edition copyright © 2003 by Transaction Publishers, New Brunswick, New Jersey. Originally published in *The National Interest*.

Library of Congress Catalog Number: 2002029106
ISBN: 0-7658-0157-4 (cloth); 0-7658-0561-8 (paper)
Printed in the United States of America

Library of Congress Cataloging-in-Publication Data

China in the National interest / Owen Harries, editor.
        p. cm.
    ISBN 0-7658-0561-8 (alk. paper)
    1. China—Politics and government—1976- 2. China—Social conditions—1976- 3. China—Economic conditions—1976-2000. I. Harries, Owen. II. National interest.

DS779.26 .C473517 2002
951.05—dc21   2002029106

Contents

Introduction

During the first years of *The National Interest's* life, the foreign country that occupied most of the magazine's attention was the Soviet Union, initially as a still formidable rival and then as a superpower engaged in a spectacular process of self-destruction. Then for a brief period it was Japan that held center stage. But even as it was being described as an unstoppable "juggernaut", Japan's economy stalled and it became evident that the country lacked the assertive will and confidence to become a full-blown world power.

From the mid-1990s on there has been near universal agreement that the main contender for the world heavy weight title, currently firmly in the hands of the United States, is going to be China. This has been reflected in the pages of *The National Interest*. Between 1995 and 2001, the magazine published no fewer than 28 articles dealing with some aspect of that country, and it is a significant subset of these essays that now make up this volume.

Collectively, they present a picture of that country in the round: not only of its place in the international system and its interaction with the United States—though these aspects are dealt with in depth—but also China's history, its culture, its society and economy, its polity and military. Written by leading scholars, analysts and policymakers, these articles certainly reflect the prevailing consensus concerning the looming importance of China. But just as certainly they also serve to remind us—by what they say about past American attitudes and assumptions, by the currently prevailing views they feel obliged to contest, and not least by their frequent sharp differences with each other—that China has been and is a particularly difficult subject for Americans. It arouses strong and conflicting emotions, and creates deep divisions concerning high policy.

Robert Zoellick reminds us that America's dealings with China reflect two strong and conflicting traditions, one stemming from an extended missionary experience and one representing a realist concept of interest and power. The result of this conflict, he argues, has been a pendulum swing of alternating attitudes, now romanticizing now demonizing China. Bruce Cummings observes merely that "To say 'China' is instantly to call up a string of metaphors giving us the history of Sino-American relations", and he proceeds to rattle off a list of very diverse examples ranging from boxes within boxes, to open door, to the good earth, to sick man, to little red book, to Ping-Pong, to playing card, to butcher—and so on and on.

Zoellick's image of a swinging pendulum is if anything too sedate to convey the erratic and violent swings of the American attitude. Many of those Americans who insisted on treating China as a paragon and model during the hideous years of the "Cultural Revolution" are now its most severe critics on human rights, despite the fact that its performance concerning those rights, though still bad, has improved enormously in the meantime. Conversely, in the 1970s American leaders who for years had insisted on treating China as a pariah suddenly decided to cozy up and deal with it, and did so at a time when that country's internal affairs were about as bad as they could be. Circumstances—ones that as often as not have little to do with what is happening in China itself and a great deal to do with what is happening in the rest of the world, and the internal politics and prevailing moods of the United Sates—have certainly altered cases dramatically in Sino-U.S. relations.

Another aspect of American dealings with China that suggests a degree of confusion and emotionalism is the tendency, both exhibited and discussed in these pages, to demand of the Chinese a standard of behavior that the United states itself does not meet. This has been especially evident in recent years, when the United States has complained bitterly of Chinese espionage while engaging in widespread espionage itself, including most egregiously and incompetently the bugging of the Chinese president's aircraft; and when outrage has been expressed at Chinese interference in the American electoral process, something that the United states has long practiced with respect to other countries. It is most notable of all in complaints about China's military build-up, at a time when the United States outspends the rest of the world combined; and about the iniquity of China's arms sales to other countries at a time when the United States itself is the world's main exporter of arms. As Robert Ross says in these pages:

> No moral equivalence is intended or required. But the United States should avoid the conceit that a given mode of behaviour can be wrong for every country in the world but still right for the United States because of the purity of its motives. Obviously, when other countries develop similar policies to pursue similar objectives, interest rather than morality is the appropriate standard of judgment.

"Moral equivalence" is a charge that has to be resorted to with great care if it is not to become an obscurantist device for stifling discussion. And in practical terms, if the world's leading rule-setter does not observe its own rules, it will inevitably lose credibility and effectiveness.

While this collection of essays raises many questions, three interrelated ones are central: Must China inevitably be a rival and a threat to the United States in coming years? What are the prospects concerning China's internal evolution? And, critically, what is America's best option in terms of dealing with China?

As for the first of these, the case for inevitable rivalry and hostility has been based on very little empirical evidence. Apart from a half-hearted and ineffectual effort to establish a presence in Africa over three decades ago, China has been singularly unambitious beyond its region. Even within its region its assertiveness has in recent years been modest, and as its ideological ardor has diminished almost to the vanishing point, it has ceased supporting local insurrections. Leaving aside the special case of Taiwan for the moment, its ambitions currently manifest themselves mainly in the form of claims to a number of small uninhabited or sparsely inhabited islands in the East and South China Seas whose ownership is the cause of dispute among several countries. While these islands have some strategic value, this hardly amounts to a country that seeks "relentlessly to expand its reach" (Charles Krauthammer, back in 1995) or is pursuing a foreign policy that puts it on a "collision course" with the United States (Karen Elliott House, writing in the same year).

The "collision" conclusion, widely subscribed to, is based rather on the belief that in a system of sovereign states the number one and number two powers *must* be rivals. The example nearly always cited to make the point is that of Willhelmine Germany's determination to contest Great Britain's hegemonic status a century ago. But while it is undeniably true that there is always the likelihood of a degree of rivalry and friction between the two leading powers, that falls far short of an inevitable "collision." Besides, there are substantial differences between the pre-1914 Germany, with its arriviste mentality and vain, insecure Kaiser, and a China that is the oldest state on earth. One might also recall that at the beginning of the last century there existed another challenger to British supremacy—the United States—and that, far from becoming deadly enemies, in that case hegemon and challenger became close allies, even as they swapped positions in the international hierarchy.

As to whether China will have the military means realistically to challenge the United States in the foreseeable future, even if it should wish to do so, opinions are divided, and opposing views on the subject are canvassed in these pages. What there does seem to be general agreement on is that at least for the next couple of decades the United States will continue to enjoy a huge military advantage. As against that, however, it has been true in the past that in some circumstances (for a very well remembered example, those pertaining in Vietnam three decades ago) superior intensity of commitment can go far toward compensating for technical inferiority; and a greater capacity to absorb punishment can sometimes effectively balance an inferior capacity to inflict it. Whether in the case of China these truths will still hold in the future, given the revolution in military affairs, we can only hope that we shall not have the opportunity to find out any time soon.

Moving to the second question—on the prospects for China's internal evolution—many aspects of China's domestic life are discussed in these pages. By general consent, however, the central issue is whether rapid economic growth, based on an increasing application of market principles, is compatible with the continued existence of a political regime that is authoritarian and still repressive.

In one view, widely subscribed to and put most forcibly here by Henry Rowen, rapid economic growth virtually ensures the emergence of a democratic polity in China, as it has done elsewhere. Rowen points to the development of elected local councils, the strengthening of the legal system, and a growing degree of freedom in the media. But the kernel of his argument is the striking global correlation between GDP growth and the move to a democratic system. Without being quite as certain, precise and optimistic, several other contributors essentially concur, believing that the divergence and tension between the existing political structure and the economic trends make stability unsustainable for long—that, as Zbigniew Brzezinski briskly puts it, "commercial communism is an oxymoron." Something will have to give, and the current rulers in Beijing know it. There is at least a chance that the outcome will be the kind of more liberal, democratic political system that has accompanied capitalism in the West.

Others are skeptical. They argue that as long as the economy continues to grow rapidly and deliver the goods, and as long as living standards keep rising, the regime will be strengthened not weakened—and that is how China's leaders calculate. John Fitzgerald eloquently emphasizes the intense Chinese concern with dignity, both personal and national, which raises the question as to whether a concern with standing and prestige may take precedence over a demand for individual rights. David Zweig emphasizes the entrenched power of a huge bureaucracy and the ingrained habits of a rent-seeking economic culture, and predicts a corporatist rather than a liberal outcome. The sociologist Grace Goodell, commenting on the experience of the four Little Dragons—like China, Confucian in their culture—observes that "these four societies reverse many basic tenets of the common traditional western understanding of capitalism", in that "during the period of their most spectacular growth none supported the theory that capitalism needs a free press, democracy, and the substantive rule of law to curb the arbitrary powers of a dictator." The pressure for democracy is not preordained; it will depend on whether a powerful middle class emerges that presses hard for democracy. But whether *that* happens will depend as much on culture as on economics.

Last, and crucially, there is the question of U.S. policy toward China. It is a measure of the emotionalism that clouds American thinking on the subject that this question is often discussed essentially in terms of a single one-to-one relationship between the two countries, with scant attention to context and third parties. Indeed, and even worse than that, the complexity of the bilateral relationship is to all intents and purposes frequently reduced to the Taiwan question. It is a great virtue of the discussion of U.S.–China relations in this volume—by, among others, one who played a principle role in laying its foundations (Zbigniew Brzezinski), and two who are currently playing significant parts in implementing and updating it (Paul Wolfowitz and Robert Zoellick)—that great attention is paid to placing it firmly in both a regional and global context.

In recent years, discussion of America's options has often been reduced to a stark choice between "engagement" and "containment." What is made clear here is that there is no such simple choice, that—insofar as these simple terms apply at all—the United States will have both to engage and contain. The real questions concern what content should be given these terms—what "engagement" should and should not mean (bearing in mind that not too long ago it was taken to include "strategic partnership"), and how "containment" should be interpreted both in relation to more traditional terms like "balance" and to China's growing weight and economic importance.

While the Taiwan question is discussed at length, there is full recognition that it is only one facet of a complex relationship, and that it can not be allowed to dominate all aspects of America's dealings with China. There is consensus that in the case of an unprovoked attack on the island the United States would certainly come to its defense. But as to what the obligations of the United States would be in the case of a Taiwan-initiated attempt to alter the status quo by a unilateral move from *de facto* to *de jure* independence is more complicated. There is an interesting and important divergence of opinion between Brzezinski, who stresses the continuing utility of ambiguity concerning the nature and extent of America's commitment to protecting the island, and Paul Wolfowitz, who argues that the time has come when clarity on the matter—that is, guaranteeing support in virtually any circumstance—would now better serve U.S. interests.

In pondering the best options for the United States in its dealings with China, it is not necessary to rely entirely on abstract speculation. We have half a century of dealing with this regime to draw on. That experience falls into two very distinct periods: the first two decades, from 1949 to the early 1970s, during which to the best of our abilities we strove to isolate and contain China; and the last three decades, during which we have developed extensive political, strategic and economic relations with it. The first period was one of the most disastrous in Chinese, and indeed human, history. Millions of Chinese were killed by the regime or died as a consequence of its insane policies. The second period is one that has seen the political system in China change from a genuinely totalitarian one to something much more moderate. It still is no thing of beauty, and it gives its intellectuals and some of its religious and ethnic minorities a hard time, but living standards have risen appreciably, there is much less government intrusion into the daily lives of ordinary people, and overall life is better in the country than it has been for over a century and a half. While one cannot, of course, draw a simple causal connection between all this and the shift in American policy from one period to the other, it is almost certainly true that the shift was at least a necessary condition for the improvements.

All but two of the articles reprinted here were written before September 11, 2001. Given the emotional impact of that event, and the initial assumption that everything was changed, changed utterly, by it, I believe that the analyses of U.S.-China relationship and policy contained in this volume are of particular importance. At a time when, for perfectly understandable reasons, one issue dominates this country's thinking about the world, they provide a necessary and forceful reminder of the continuing and intractable elements that must be taken into account in shaping America's foreign policy. China must not of necessity be America's enemy in the coming decades, but it will certainly be an even more important player than it is today. This volume is in no way dated by 9/11; if anything, it is even more relevant as the United States makes its reluctant return to history.

Owen Harries
Editor Emeritus, *The National Interest*

Part 1

China, Asia, and America

1

Living With China

*Zbigniew Brzezinski**

Eurasian politics have replaced European politics as the central arena of world affairs. Once European wars became evidently threatening to America, there was no choice for America but to inject itself into European politics in order to prevent new conflicts from erupting or a hostile European hegemony from emerging. Thus America's engagement in world affairs was precipitated during the twentieth century by European politics. Today, it is the interplay of several Eurasian powers that is critical to global stability. Accordingly, America's policy must be transcontinental in its design, with specific bilateral Eurasian relationships woven together into a strategically coherent whole.

It is in this larger Eurasian context that U.S.-China relations must be managed and their importance correctly assessed. Dealing with China should rank as one of Washington's four most important international relationships, alongside Europe, Japan and Russia. The U.S.-China relationship is both consequential and catalytic, beyond its intrinsic bilateral importance. Unlike some other major bilateral relationships that are either particularly beneficial or threatening only to the parties directly involved (America and Mexico, for example), the U.S.-China relationship impacts significantly on the security and policies of other states, and it can affect the overall balance of power in Eurasia.

More specifically, peace in Northeast and Southeast Asia remains dependent to a significant degree on the state of the U.S.-China relationship. That

* Zbigniew Brzezinski, former national security adviser to the president, is counselor and trustee of the Center for Strategic and International Studies and Professor of American Foreign Policy at the School of Advanced International Studies, the Johns Hopkins University, Washington, D.C.

This essay first appeared in *The National Interest*, No. 59 (Spring 2000).

relationship also has enormous implications for U.S.-Japan relations and Japan's definition—for better or worse—of its political and military role in Asia. Last but not least, China's orientation is likely to influence the extent to which Russia eventually concludes that its national interests would best be served by a closer connection with an Atlanticist Europe; or whether it is tempted instead by some sort of an alliance with an anti-American China.

For China, it should be hastily added, the U.S.-China relationship is also of top-rank importance, alongside its relations with Japan, with Russia and with India. In fact, for China the Beijing-Washington interaction is indisputably the most important of the four. It is central to China's future development and well-being. A breakdown in the relationship would prompt a dramatic decline in China's access to foreign capital and technology. Chinese leaders must carefully take into account that centrally decisive reality whenever they are tempted to pursue a more assertive policy on behalf of their national grievances (such as Taiwan) or more ambitious global aspirations (such as seeking to replace American "hegemony" with "multipolarity").

In essence, then, in the complex American-Chinese equation, Beijing should be prudent lest its larger ambitions collide with its more immediate interests, while Washington must be careful lest its strategic Eurasian interests are jeopardized by tactical missteps in its handling of China.

It follows that the United States, in defining its longer term China policy and in responding to the more immediate policy dilemmas, must have a clearly formulated view of what China is, and is not. There is, unfortunately, enormous confusion in America on that very subject. Allegedly informed writings regarding China often tend to be quite muddled, occasionally even verging toward the hysterical extremes. As a result, the image of a malignant China as the inevitably anti-American great power of the 2020s competes in the American public discourse with glimpses of a benign China gently transformed by U.S. investors into an immense Hong Kong. Currently, there is no realistic consensus either among the public or in the Congress regarding China.

In recent years, inconsistency has also characterized the attitude of the U.S. government. It is unfortunately the case that the Clinton administration has been guilty of "vacillation and about-faces on China, often in response to popular and congressional pressure", that the President himself was "not willing to protect U.S.-China relations from tampering by Congress", and that "some in Congress would destroy the relationship if given the opportunity to do so."[i] The presidential mishandling in late spring 1999 of the World Trade Organization (WTO) negotiations with the Chinese and the persisting inclination of Congress to grandstand on the China issue validate that indictment.

In addition, public perception of China tends to be defined by spectacular symbols that allegedly encapsulate the essence of today's and tomorrow's China. Thus, for many Americans Tiananmen Square and Tibet have come to reflect the central reality of enduring communist oppression and of intensifying national chauvinism. For others, the Chinese economic "miracle", dramatized by the skyscrapers of Shanghai, and by China's growing free-market openness to the world through the Internet, travel, and foreign investment, symbolizes a transforming nation that is progressively shedding its communist veneer. Which China, then, is the real China, and with which China will America clash or cohabit in the years to come?

Having digested much of the available literature on Chinese political, economic and military prospects, and having dealt with the Chinese for almost a quarter of a century, I believe that the point of departure toward an answer has to be the recognition of an obvious but fundamental reality: China is too big to be ignored, too old to be slighted, too weak to be appeased, and too ambitious to be taken for granted. A major and ancient civilization—encompassing 20 percent of the world's population organized in a historically unique continuity as a single nation-state, and driven simultaneously by a sense of national grievance over perceived (and, in many cases, real) humiliations over the last two centuries, but also by growing and even arrogant self-confidence—China is already a major regional player, though not strong enough to contest at this time either America's global primacy or even its preponderance in the Far Eastern region.

China's military strength, both current and likely over the next decade or so, will not be capable of posing a serious threat to the United States itself, unless China's leaders were to opt for national suicide.[ii] The Chinese nuclear force has primarily a deterrent capability. The Chinese military build-up has been steady but neither massive nor rapid, nor technologically very impressive. It is also true, however, that China is capable of imposing on America unacceptable costs in the event that a local conflict in the Far East engages vital Chinese interests but only peripheral American ones. In this sense, China's military power is already regionally significant, and it is growing.

Nonetheless, unlike the former Soviet Union, the People's Republic of China (PRC) is not capable of posing a universal ideological challenge to the United States, especially as its communist system is increasingly evolving into oligarchical nationalist statism with inherently more limited international appeal. It is noteworthy that China is not involved in any significant international revolutionary activities, while its controversial arms exports are driven either by commercial or bilateral state interests. (As such, they are not very different from those of France or Israel, with the latter actually exporting weapons technology to China.)

Moreover, in recent years China's international conduct has been relatively restrained. China did not exercise its veto to halt UN-sanctioned military actions against Iraq over Kuwait. Nor did it block the Security Council's approval of the international protectorate in Kosovo. It approved the deployment of UN peacekeepers in East Timor, and—unlike India in the case of Goa, or Indonesia when it seized East Timor—it peacefully re-acquired Hong Kong and more recently Macau. China also acted responsibly during the Asian financial crisis of

1998, for which it was internationally applauded. Last but not least, its current efforts to gain membership of the WTO, whatever the merits or demerits of China's negotiating stance, signal the PRC's growing interest in global multilateral cooperation.

Internal Contradictions

The picture becomes more mixed when the domestic scene in China is scrutinized and when current Chinese views of the United States are taken into account. China is basically unfinished business. Its communist revolution has run out of steam. Its post-communist reformation has been partially successful, particularly at the urban-industrial-commercial levels, but this has required major doctrinal concessions and compromises. The result is that the Chinese system is a hybrid, with strong residues of communist dogmatism in the industrial sectors and in the state bureaucracy coexisting uneasily with dynamic, capitalist entrepreneurship driven by foreign investment. China's future systemic orientation is thus yet to be fully defined, but it is already evident that the cohabitation within it of communism and commercialism is inherently contradictory.

The trajectories of China's economic change and of its political evolution are thus parting. At some point, the distance between them will become too wide to sustain. Something, then, will have to give. Moreover, the existing political elite—itself not so young—will soon be replaced by a generation that came to political maturity neither during the Great Leap Forward nor during the Cultural Revolution, both epiphenomena of communist doctrinal exuberance. The emerging political elite matured during Deng Xiaoping's pragmatic upheaval in the Chinese economy, and hence may be more inclined to correct the political trajectory of China's evolution, bringing it closer to the economic trajectory.

The issue of human rights is thus likely to become more acute as the political regime seeks one way or another to close the gap between itself and its evolving socioeconomic context. The constraints on personal political liberty, the denial of religious freedom, and the suppression of minorities—most notably in Tibet—cannot be sustained in a setting of growing social and economic pluralism. The recent efforts to suppress the Falun Gong movement testify to the regime's sense of ideological and political vulnerability. Accordingly, the issue of freedom is bound to become both more critical and more difficult for the existing regime to manage. Indeed, it is almost safe to predict that in the near future—probably within the coming decade—China will experience a serious political crisis.

In any case, whatever its political prospects, China will not be emerging as a global power in the foreseeable future. If that term is to have any real meaning, it must imply cutting-edge superiority of a truly global military capability, significant international financial and economic influence, a clear-cut technological lead, and an appealing social lifestyle—all of which must combine to create worldwide political clout. Even in the most unlikely circumstance of continued rapid economic growth, China will not be top-ranked in any of these domains for many decades to come. What is more, its backward and debilitated social infrastructure, combined with the per capita poverty of its enormous population, represents a staggering liability.

One should note here that some of the current scare-mongering regarding the alleged inevitability of China's emergence as a dominant world power is reminiscent of earlier hysteria regarding Japan's supposedly predestined ascendancy to superpower status. That hysteria was similarly driven by mechanical projections of economic growth rates, without taking into account other complex considerations or unexpected contingencies. The Japanese purchase of Rockefeller Plaza became at one point the symbol of the paranoiac, one-dimensional glimpse into Japan's future.

Be that as it may, China's unsettled domestic scene is likely to reinforce an inherently ambivalent and occasionally antagonistic attitude toward the United States. Though Chinese leaders recognize that they need a stable and even cooperative relationship with the United States if their country is to continue developing, China is no longer America's strategic partner against a threatening Soviet Union. It became so after the Shanghai breakthrough of 1972 and, even more so, after the normalization of relations in 1980, which dramatically transformed a three decade-long adversarial relationship into a decade of strategic cooperation.[iii] Today, with the Soviet Union gone, China is neither America's adversary nor its strategic partner.[iv] It could become an antagonist, however, if either China so chooses or America so prompts.

Accentuating the Negative

Currently, Chinese policy toward the United States is a combination of functional cooperation in areas of specific interest and of a generally adverse definition of America's world role.[v] The latter has prompted Chinese diplomatic initiatives designed to undercut U.S. global leadership. Chinese policy toward Russia is ostentatiously friendly on the rhetorical level, with frequent references to "a strategic partnership." Such is also the case (perhaps not surprisingly) with Sino-French relations, with both sides proclaiming (as, for example, during the October 1999 Paris summit between Presidents Chirac and Jiang) their passionate fidelity to the concept of global "multipolarity"—not a very subtle slam at the disliked American "hegemony."

Indeed, the word "hegemony" has become the favorite Chinese term for defining America's current world role. Chinese public pronouncements and professional journals that deal with international affairs regularly denounce the United States as an overreaching, dominant, arrogant and interventionist power, increasingly reliant on the use of force, and potentially tempted to intervene even in China's internal affairs.

The NATO action in Kosovo precipitated especially a massive outpouring of Chinese allegations that America has embraced the concept of interventionism at the expense of respect for traditional national sovereignty, with dire implications for China. As one alarmed Chinese expert put it:

> Suppose serious anti-Communist Party or anti-government domestic turbulence erupts in China which cannot be quickly brought under control, and, at the same time, the international community commonly joins the anti-China stream. In this case, the hegemonists (perhaps jointly with their allied nations) could launch a military invasion of China.[vi]

The above was neither an extreme nor an isolated assertion. Such charges have been accompanied by growing concern that the United States is accelerating and intensifying its efforts to construct an anti-Chinese coalition in the Far East, embracing what is represented as a dangerously rearming Japan, South Korea and also Taiwan, a coalition "that resembles a small NATO of East Asia."[vii] American, Japanese and South Korean discussions of possible collaboration against theater missile attacks have intensified these Chinese suspicions. Occasional American and Taiwanese press speculation that Taiwan might be included in such a collective effort has also further aggravated the Chinese, who see it as additional evidence that the United States is increasingly inclined to make permanent the current separation of Taiwan from China.

Perhaps the most striking example of the current Chinese inclination to stress the negative dimensions of the U.S.-China relationship is the attempt to provide a deeper intellectual or cultural rationalization for the seemingly intensifying antagonism. The Chinese-owned Hong Kong daily, *Ta Kung Pao*, published a major editorial entitled "On the Cultural Roots of Sino-U.S. Conflict" in September 1999, advancing the thesis that "the conflict between Chinese and American civilizations is at a deeper level one between sacred and secular lifestyles." Amazingly for a nominally communist regime, it is China that is said to represent the former: "Chinese civilization has always stressed an integration of heaven with man." This identity is said to contrast sharply with "the consumerist and hedonist mode of behavior that grew out of American Civilization", making Americans "look down on Oriental Civilization, holding that it is backward and ignorant." The policy inference that was drawn from the foregoing was stark: "in China-U.S. relations, it will be absolutely impossible to permanently resolve conflicts of political views in areas such as human rights, democracy, and freedom."[viii]

To be sure, the foregoing views are in part instrumental, for they are also meant to serve the current Chinese efforts to put America on the ideological defensive. They do not define for Beijing the overall character of the U.S.-China relationship. Since China seeks to reduce the scope of America's global preponderance (and its resulting leverage on China), it needs some sort of a doctrinal legitimation for controlled antagonism; yet China also wants to retain for itself, for obvious reasons of domestic self-interest, the vital benefits of collaboration with America. Striking a balance between the two is not easy, especially given the fact that China's communist leaders have not found an effective substitute for their previous Marxist world-view. That central reality imposes a severe restraint on Chinese anti-American proclivities.

Hence, U.S.-China military links are being preserved, economic ties enhanced and political relations kept relatively congenial—even while "multipolarity" is hailed and "hegemony" condemned in joint declarations with Moscow, Paris and whoever else cares to join. The result is a confused amalgam, involving communist terminology and Chinese nationalist sentiments. That mishmash reflects the ambivalent position in which the Chinese leadership finds itself both at home and at large, given the unresolved ambiguities of Chinese domestic and foreign policy.

Doubtless, China's leaders, generally intelligent and hardheaded, sense that inherent ambiguity. They must realize that Paris, rhetoric aside, will not join in some fanciful Beijing-Moscow-Paris anti-American coalition. They have to know that Russia does not have much to offer to China, except perhaps some technologically not very advanced military equipment. Ultimately, they have to understand—and their conduct reflects that they do—that at this historical juncture the relationship with the United States is central to China's future. Outright hostility is simply not in China's interest.

The foregoing points toward a further observation. China today, in relationship to the wider international system, is neither the militarist Japan of the 1930s nor the ideologically and strategically threatening Soviet Union of the 1950s–70s. Though all analogies, by definition, are partially misleading, there are some important parallels between China's current situation and imperial Germany's circa 1890. At that time, German policy was in flux, while Germany itself was a rising power. Like today's China, Germany's ambitions were driven by a resentment of a perceived lack of recognition and respect (in the case of Germany, especially on the part of a haughty British Empire, and in the case of today's China, on the part of an arrogant America), by fears of encirclement by a confining and increasingly antagonistic coalition, by rising nationalistic ambitions on the part of its predominantly young population, and by the resulting desire to precipitate a significant rearrangement in the global pecking order.

One will never know with any certainty whether the European war of 1914, a quarter of a century later, could have been avoided by wiser policy in the 1890s. Similarly, one cannot be certain about which direction China will head over the next quarter of a century. However, already at this stage it should be self-evident which prospect is to be avoided. For America, that requires a strategically clearheaded management of the sensitive issue of Taiwan and, even more so, of the longer range task of fitting China into a wider and more stable Eurasian equilibrium.

The Taiwan Question

For America, Taiwan is a problem; China is the challenge. Taiwan complicates U.S.-China relations, but it is U.S.-China relations that will determine in large measure the degree of stability or instability in the Far East and, more generally, in Eurasia. Admittedly, how the Taiwan issue is handled will influence—and in some circumstances could even determine—the evolution of U.S.-China relations. But, except for its impact on those relations, the status of Taiwan itself is not a central international concern.

Still, it is important to take both history and strategy into account when addressing the sensitive and volatile issue of Taiwan's relationship with the mainland. That issue is a direct legacy of China's civil war. It is also an unresolved legacy, for Taiwan's separate existence reminds that neither side involved in the civil war succeeded in totally eliminating the other. Though one side won by gaining control over the mainland, and thus over the vast majority of the Chinese population, the losing side still preserved itself not only as a political entity but also as a potential political alternative, even though entrenched on a relatively small island inhabited by only 2 percent of China's people.

That Taiwan succeeded in preserving its independence from the side that emerged victorious in the Chinese civil war has been due mainly to the United States. America, though indirectly, continued to be involved in that war even after its termination on the mainland in 1949. It both protected and bolstered Taiwan. Episodic military clashes in the Taiwan Strait occurred until the de facto suspension of the civil war in the 1970s—a suspension attained by direct U.S.-China talks initiated under President Nixon and later formalized through the normalization of U.S.-China relations under President Carter.[ix] The resulting arrangement was genuinely creative, for it enabled the winning side to acquiesce to the de facto partition of China as the transitional outcome of the civil war without accepting it as a permanent *de jure* reality.

That sensible accommodation was made possible by the acceptance on both sides of the intricate formula whereby (1) the United States acknowledged that in the view both of the mainland and of Taiwan there is only one China; and (2) the United States affirmed that it expects the issue of reunification to be resolved peacefully (and that U.S. national interest would be engaged if it should be otherwise); whereas (3) the Chinese reiterated that reunification is an internal Chinese matter, to be attained by whatever means China deems appropriate, though their preference is also for a peaceful resolution.

Once that hurdle had been traversed it followed that the officially recognized government of China had to be the one that governs 98 percent of the Chinese people. And it also followed that Taiwan could not be recognized as a separate "sovereign" state, though the United States could maintain practical and functional ties with it. Such ties were then formally legislated by the U.S. Congress in the "Taiwan Relations Act" of 1980, which regularized U.S. relations with Taiwan without defining it as a sovereign state. In effect, the outcome of the great bargain preserved the formal unity of China while practically respecting the current reality of a separate status for Taiwan.

That arrangement has proven to be a blessing for Taiwan, while simultaneously permitting the development of extensive U.S.-China ties. Taiwan's resulting prosperity hardly needs documenting. It has blossomed both as an economic miracle and as a democracy in the more secure setting of abated Sino-American tensions, of continued U.S. arms sales, and of the openly proclaimed U.S. stake in a peaceful Taiwan Strait. Taiwan's success has also provided stunning and encouraging evidence for the proposition that democracy and Chinese culture are compatible, an example that has significant long-term implications for the future evolution of mainland China.

Taiwan has not only prospered economically and flowered politically but has become a respected and active participant in various international organizations. For example, it is a full member of the Asian Development Bank, APEC and the Central American Bank for Economic Integration, and is currently seeking access to the WTO. It maintains regular economic, technological and cultural ties with more than 140 states with which it does not have formal diplomatic relations.

An even more impressive testimonial to the benefits accruing from the U.S.-China normalization of relations has been the actual pacification of the Taiwan Strait. In contrast to the sporadic clashes that used to occur prior to normalization, there has been a massive flow of capital and people across the hitherto separating water.[x] These socioeconomic ties, in turn, have permitted the emergence of an informal but serious dialogue between representatives of the respective authorities.

Lee's Unilateralism

That informal accommodation was jeopardized in the second half of 1999 by the unilateral redefinition of Taiwan's relationship to the mainland, abruptly launched by the Taiwanese authorities. In a highly publicized interview, President Lee Teng-hui of Taiwan suddenly abandoned the "One China" formula, redefining the Taiwan-mainland relationship as involving "state-to-state relations." The import of the new formulation was self-evident: one China was brusquely redefined as two separate states. Moreover, Lee in a subsequent statement insisted that the inhabitants of Taiwan have acquired a "fresh national identity based on the New Taiwanese consciousness."[xi]

Lee's initiative was launched without any prior consultations with the United States. It was immediately followed, however, by stepped-up efforts by Taiwanese supporters in the United States, encouraged by a well-financed Taiwan lobby, to induce the U.S. government, through congressional pressure, to take a stand in support of Taiwanese "sovereignty."[xii] Various supporters of Taiwan also launched a public campaign alleging a growing Chinese military threat to Taiwan, urging particularly the Republican presidential candidates to support the so-called "Taiwan Security Enhancement Act", introduced earlier in the year in the U.S. Congress. That proposed act aimed at nothing less than the de facto revival of the 1955 Mutual Defense Treaty with the Republic of China (terminated following the U.S. recognition of the People's Republic of China), with its specific and non-discretionary provisions designed to restore Taiwan as a U.S. military ally against China.

It should be noted that these alarmist pressure tactics disregarded the fact that the PRC currently lacks, and in the foreseeable future will not have, the airlift and sealift capability to effect a successful 120-mile, cross-strait amphibious invasion. One need only recall the enormous difficulty of the Normandy landings in 1944 across the narrower English channel, in spite of overwhelming allied air and naval supremacy as well as the relative weakness of the German forces. In contrast, the Taiwanese ground forces that would be resisting any landing communist forces are relatively better armed and more mobile. Taiwan also has the means to contest PRC efforts to assert air and naval superiority in the Taiwan Strait.

It is also noteworthy that the U.S. secretary of defense, in an assessment issued in February 1999, concluded that only "by 2005, the PLA [People's Liberation Army] will possess the capability to attack Taiwan with air and missile strikes which would degrade key military facilities and damage the island's economic infrastructure."[xiii] Even then, the acquisition of such a capability would not mean that the PRC could execute an effective invasion. One must also take into account Taiwan's capacity to retaliate effectively by striking or mining China's major ports, thereby cutting China's trade links with the entire world.

In any case, whatever may have been Mr. Lee's motives in publicly venting the formula of "state-to-state relations", there was no pressing security need for his unilateral initiative. Hence the question: cui bono? Since the Taiwanese leadership had to know that it would complicate U.S.-China relations and generate new tensions in the Taiwan Strait, one has to assume that the initiative was taken (at least in part) on the calculation that any U.S.-China military confrontation, even if provoked by Taiwan, would work to Taiwan's political advantage.

For the United States, acquiescence to the new formulation and passage of the proposed "Taiwan Security Enhancement Act" would mean that Taiwan has been granted nothing short of a carte blanche to redefine its status as it wishes, with the United States obligated to defend the island, come what may. It would amount to a de facto unconditional guarantee of U.S. protection for whatever provocative step Taiwan might take, including even a formal secession from China, and thus it would be a repudiation of prior U.S.-China undertakings. It is also important to note that in any ensuing hostilities in the Taiwan Strait, the United States would find itself altogether isolated internationally.

For China, the proposed U.S. legislation would signal America's re-engagement in the Chinese civil war, while Beijing's acquiescence to the new "state-to-state" formulation would mean the formal acceptance of the permanent partition of China. Neither is a palatable choice for Beijing. It would also mean that, in the eyes of the Chinese, the grand bargain with the United States had been exploited by Washington, first to consolidate Taiwan, and then to transform a separatist Taiwan into a permanent U.S. protectorate. No current Chinese leader could accept such an outcome and normal relations between the United States and the PRC would thereby be jeopardized.

The Clinton administration was, therefore, fully justified in repudiating the new Taiwanese formula and in reassuring Beijing that previous U.S.-China understandings remained in force. For some time to come, Washington will have no choice but to navigate carefully between the risk inherent in any unconditional assurances to Taiwan's security and the obligation to discourage any Chinese attempt at coercive unification. Perhaps an additional bilateral Washington-Beijing clarification regarding Taiwan might be helpful if it were to involve a clear-cut Chinese commitment (expressed, naturally, as a unilateral Chinese decision) never to use force in order to achieve national unity, matched by a simultaneous—and similarly "independent"—U.S. commitment to terminate all arms sales to Taiwan if it should formally declare itself to have seceded from China. However, even then, the U.S.-China relationship would still remain vulnerable to disruption because of the unresolved and always sensitive issue of Taiwan's future. That is why it is unlikely that either side would be willing to exchange such mutual assurances.

Democracy: The Essential Condition

Ultimately, the issue of Taiwan will be determined primarily by what happens in China itself. A China that fails to evolve politically, or that flounders socially—not to speak of a China that regresses ideologically—will not attract Taiwan. Nor will it intimidate Taiwan, for the United States will continue to have a tangible national interest in the prevention of warfare in the Taiwan Strait. It follows that Taiwan will, and should, continue to have prudently measured access to the necessary U.S. military wherewithal for self-defense.

In contrast, a successfully developing and progressively democratizing China may eventually be able to reach some practical arrangement with Taiwan. It might do so by enlarging the "one country, two systems" formula (currently applied to Hong Kong) to "one country, several systems."

The "one country, two systems" formula was unveiled, with considerable publicity, by Deng Xiaoping during my meeting with him in Beijing in 1984. It was explicitly designed to accommodate Taiwan. In 1997, during a visit to Taiwan, I used the phrase "one country, several systems", having in mind—in addition to China—Hong Kong, Macau and perhaps eventually Taiwan. In an interview with the London Times (October 18, 1999), President Jiang tantalizingly observed, in speaking of "the main objectives for China *by the middle of the next century*", that, "We will ultimately resolve the question of Taiwan and accomplish the great cause of national reunification by adhering to the policy of '*peaceful reunification* and one country, two systems' after the successful return of Hong Kong and Macao." (The italicized passages [my emphasis] clearly hint at historical patience.)

At this stage, it is not possible to be more precise, but Taiwanese spokesmen are generally correct in postulating that China's democratization is the practical precondition for any arrangement that may approximate (and eventually become) reunification. It thus follows that the real strategic challenge for the United States—more important than the issue of Taiwan—pertains to China's evolution, both in its domestic politics and especially with regard to the global mindset of its ruling elite.

That evolution can be subtly influenced from the outside, even if a democratic transformation of China cannot be so imposed. Positive change in China will come, in the main, from socioeconomic pressures, unleashed (in part, unintentionally) by the ruling elite's otherwise rational economic reforms. Their cumulative effect, especially because of modern mass communications, is inherently incompatible with enduring political repression. In that context, the cause of human rights can be, and should be, deliberately supported from the outside, even at the cost of some friction with China's rulers.

China, however, is not America's client state. Nor does it pose a global ideological challenge like the former Soviet Union, in which case it was useful to put that country on the defensive by making human rights into a major issue. Indeed, a policy of sustained ideological confrontation with China is more likely to delay desired changes by stimulating more overt regressive reactions from an increasingly insecure political elite. Given the ongoing changes within China, including its evident trend toward more openness to the world, the promotion of human rights in the country is likely to be more effective if pursued with deliberate indirection.

For example, extensive programs to assist the Chinese in embracing the rule of law are bound to have a significant democratizing impact. Indeed, as the negative experience of post-Soviet Russia shows, loud emphasis on electoral democracy can prove to be self-deceptive. In contrast, the institutionalized spread of the rule of law can create enduring foundations for genuine democratization while enhancing the prospects for a functioning market economy. Since the ruling elite finds the latter to be in its interest, the propagation of the rule of law is both politically easier and in the long run more effective.

Similarly, the development of functional assistance to local officials, who in increasing numbers are subject to election, should be a major focus of an enlightened but not strident program on behalf of human rights. The stronger and more democratic the local government, the weaker the central controls. Yet here, too, the top political elite is susceptible to seductive co-optation since it realizes that an effective local government is necessary for successful modernization. Human rights can thus be piggybacked onto China's own domestic ambitions. The U.S. Congress would be well advised to bear the above strictures in mind, while providing more support for various non-governmental organizations engaged in helping the Chinese to develop a genuine civil society.

The matter of Tibet is more intractable, especially since a strategy of indirection is not responsive to the more immediate grievances of the Tibetan people. Hence, on this issue a public stance of disapproval is unavoidable. At some point, the Chinese government may conclude that the costs to China's reputation are too high, and that some creative application of the "one country, several systems" formula would provide a more constructive solution to what is clearly a major violation of established international norms for the treatment of ethnic minorities. Direct talks with the Dalai Lama would represent a significant step in the right direction, and continued U.S. support for the Tibetan people is thus in order.

The Japan Factor

Effective management of these delicate issues is more likely if the United States sustains a policy that progressively enhances the Chinese stake in a peaceful Northeast Asia and in a constructive Chinese role in a stable Eurasian power equilibrium. Only in that larger context can the salience of the Taiwan issue eventually be subsumed and the formula of a democratic and prosperous China as "one country with several systems" become reality. Moreover, just as the United States could not have conducted a successful policy toward the Soviet Union without simultaneously calibrating most carefully its relations with Europe, so American policy toward China must also be, almost by definition, a triangular policy, shaped with Japan very much in mind.

China is especially sensitive to anything pertaining to Japan and its changing international role. China views Japan both as a historic rival and as an extension of U.S. power. The character and scope of the U.S.-Japan alliance is hence a matter of the utmost importance to Beijing. And, not surprisingly, the Japanese are similarly preoccupied with China and its relationship with the United States. Particularly striking was the observation by Democratic Party of Japan President Yukio Hatoyama that, "We should make more efforts to reinforce China's confidence in Japan because we are not certain what the future holds for U.S.-China relations." Hatoyama added: "It cannot completely be ruled out that Washington and Beijing will not compete with each other over hegemony. Thus, it is potentially somewhat dangerous to consider it safe to always side with the United States." It is no exaggeration to say that whether Japan remains primarily allied with America, or instead arms itself and acts largely on its own in Asia, will be predominantly determined by how well or badly the United States handles its relations with China.[xiv]

The consequences of this triangular reality cut two ways. For China, the key implication is that Beijing would be wise to exercise self-restraint in its anti-American "hegemony" campaign. It could backfire badly for China. Overheated Chinese rhetoric about an anti-American coalition with Russia (and perhaps also with India) might prompt even stronger pressures in America on behalf of an anti-Chinese, U.S.-led alliance embracing not only Japan and South Korea but even Taiwan. Some in America might also advocate a strategic counter toward India, on the grounds that India is wary of China and that it shares America's democratic credentials. The Chinese should also be aware that latent but ingrown anti-Chinese sentiments, once given the opportunity, could quickly come to dominate Japanese politics.

In fact, anti-Chinese sentiments in Japan, especially in its foreign policy establishment, are visibly on the rise. In the words of Nobuo Miyamato, the Director of the Nomura Research Council, even though a joint declaration by Japan and China talks about a 'friendly and cooperative partnership', Japan and China will not be able to extricate themselves from a relationship of political and strategic competition for the next 50-100 years.[xv] Open Sino-American hostility would most likely spur an intense arms race between Japan and China, to the detriment of both the stability of, and the American position in, the Far East. Though neither America nor Japan can exclude the possibility that China may, indeed, become a threat—and hence their alliance is also a form of insurance—it is neither in America's nor in Japan's interest to precipitate that threat. Hence an anti-Chinese alliance with a rearmed Japan should be America's last, and not first, strategic option.

Accordingly, for America the key implication is that the United States has to be very deliberate in balancing the inevitable readjustment in U.S.-Japan defense cooperation, pointing toward an enhanced international security role for Japan, with the imperative of sensitivity for Chinese concerns. The Chinese are convinced that Japan is irrevocably committed to significant remilitarization and that its sharp edge is pointed at China. The Chinese press very deliberately plays up any Japanese statements that can be construed as anti-Chinese. Thus even the most authoritative Chinese newspaper went into paroxysms of anger when the newly elected governor of Tokyo, Ishihara Shintaro—known also for his attacks on the United States—referred to Taiwan as Japan's "peripheral state."[xvi] The United States, therefore, must be especially careful to make certain that a more militarily powerful Japan is fully integrated into a larger cooperative security system in Northeast Asia and is not poised primarily as America's anti-Chinese ally.

It follows also that increasing U.S.-Japan security cooperation in the Far East should be designed in a manner that does not mimic NATO's originally overt focus on the Soviet Union's aggressive intentions. For the present, China does not have the capacity for genuinely serious regional aggression. Accordingly, ongoing U.S.-Japan-South Korea defense planning as well as joint exercises should avoid an overtly anti-Chinese cast. In addition, China should be included, as much as possible, in the emerging multilateral dialogue regarding regional security. It has taken years, and much American effort, to precipitate serious three-way U.S.-Japan-South Korea military discussions. Some four-way U.S.-Japan-China-South Korea defense consultations have also been initiated, and these may become gradually more formal. The key point to bear in mind here is that regional security in Northeast Asia is not a zero-sum game; how China is treated might well become a self-fulfilling prophesy.

The politically sensitive issue of Theater Missile Defense (TMD) is very germane to the above comments. Handled well, a TMD system could be regionally stabilizing; handled badly, it could spark intense U.S.-China hostility while setting off in Japan a polarizing and destabilizing debate over Japan's relations with the United States and with China. Accordingly, two important precautions are in order. The first is that no regional U.S.-Japan-South Korea TMD should include Taiwan either formally or through direct deployment. Taiwan can be de facto covered by a TMD located on U.S. naval platforms, thereby avoiding the Chinese charge that the United States is reverting by the back door to a formal defense arrangement with Taiwan. Secondly, consultations with the Chinese regarding any eventual missile system should be held on the same basis as proposed to Russia. There is no compelling reason to treat China differently.

More generally, it is also important to make the utmost effort to stimulate a comprehensive strategic dialogue with China regarding not only the security of Northeast Asia but of Eurasia more generally. Whenever possible, it should be a triangular dialogue, involving also the Japanese. Appropriate subjects should include the future of Russia (a topic rarely discussed in depth with the Chinese—yet of vital importance to China, given its far larger population, rapidly growing economy, and the emptiness of the neighboring Russian Far East[xvii]), the status of the Central Asian states (with their energy resources being of great interest to both China and Japan), stability in Southeast Asia, and the unstable relationship between nuclear-armed India and Pakistan. Developing and institutionalizing such a dialogue, and especially making it truly trilateral, will require a major effort and much time, but promoting it should be viewed as a high U.S. strategic priority.

Over time, a successful three-way dialogue, as well as a cooperative (and not unilateral) approach to the TMD issue, may foster a greater Chinese inclination to resolve peacefully the division of Korea. That division, the last major unresolved territorial-political legacy of the Cold War, is increasingly anomalous. However, its constructive resolution requires not only China's assent but its actual participation. That participation will become more likely when China begins to view itself as part of a larger security scheme in the Far East in which America and Japan are not perceived as its potential adversaries.

A three-way strategic dialogue could in turn pave the way for a broader Eurasian security forum, spanning America, Europe, Russia, China and Japan. The west of the Eurasian continent is already highly organized through NATO and the EU, and these integrated structures overlap with Eurasia's volatile "middle zone" through the fifty-four member Organization for Security and Cooperation in Europe (OSCE), which includes Russia and the Central Asian states. In the east, institutionalized security cooperation involves only the formal U.S.-Japan and U.S.-South Korea treaties as well as the informal Japan-South Korea consultations. China is not formally engaged, and there is no equivalent to the loosely cooperative OSCE. At the very least, a serious five-way strategic dialogue might prompt the redefinition of the letter e in OSCE from "European" to "Eurasian" through the inclusion in an expanded and redefined OSCE of a dozen or so Asian states.

Dealing China In

The task of assimilating China into a wider Eurasian equilibrium has to be pursued on other fronts as well. In addition to shaping a more sustained triangular relationship with China and Japan, China's accession to the WTO and the regularization of normal trade relations between the United States and China would be significant steps in the gradual integration of China into the world economy. Much the same applies to the question of China's inclusion in the G-8 (which I have been advocating for more than three years). The G-8 summit has become a hybrid, neither a forum for the democracies nor a conclave of the most advanced economies. That dual formula was compromised by the politically expedient decision to include Russia, hardly an advanced economy and questionably a democracy. Similar political expediency, therefore, should dictate the inclusion of the economically much more dynamic China, with the G-9 thereby becoming a more genuine global power forum. That would propitiate China's quest for status while also enhancing its stake in the emerging global system.

In some respects, China's international behavior is already no worse, and may be even better, than India's. New Delhi over the years backed various forms of Soviet aggression, went to war with its neighbors more often than China, flaunted its disregard for nuclear non-proliferation, used force to resolve some colonial legacies such as Goa, has been careless of human rights in Kashmir, and has proved no less obstreperous than China in the WTO negotiations. Yet no leading presidential candidate in America has labeled India as America's major "competitor", as was the case with China in late 1999. Obviously, India's democratic credentials give its external ambitions a more benign cast, but the comparison with India—like China a very poor, developing, but also politically aspiring power—should help to place in perspective the somewhat over-heated fears of China.

Still, it is important to reiterate that China is unlikely to become America's strategic partner again in the manner that it was during the decade starting with the late 1970s. The most that can reasonably be expected, barring a serious domestic or international crisis, is that China will gradually become an increasingly cooperative player in the international "game", in which the major participants play according to shared rules even while each keeps his own score. As a major regional player, China will occasionally collide with the United States, but it is also likely to find that its long-run interests are better served by observing common standards. China may thus become neither a formal ally nor a declared enemy of America but an important participant in the evolving international system, increasingly meeting and grudgingly accepting more and more of that system's conventions.

Such an internationally more cooperative China will have an important geostrategic effect on Eurasia. Given Russia's evident fears of China's larger economy and population, such a China will be much more likely to push Moscow toward the Atlanticist Europe than a China that is antagonistic toward the United States. At the same time, such a China will reinforce Japan's stake in a stable alliance with America without frightening Tokyo either into rapid rearmament or into divisive tensions with the United States.

It follows that the central strategic task of U.S. policy toward China should be nothing less than the attainment of a fundamental, truly historic shift in the mindset of the Chinese elite: to view China no longer as the self-isolated Middle Kingdom, or as the Celestial Empire, or as the aggrieved victim, or as the world's revolutionary center—but, more prosaically, as a vested partner in Eurasian stability and as a key player in the global system.

NOTES

[i] Kenneth Lieberthal, "A New China Strategy", *Foreign Affairs* (November/December 1995). Lieberthal has been a member of the Clinton NSC staff.

[ii] See the conclusion drawn by Z.M. Khalilzad et al., "The United States and China: Strategic and Military Implications" (Santa Monica, CA: RAND, 1999), p. 59.

[iii] The full story of the productive U.S.-China cooperation directed against the Soviet Union (especially in regard to Afghanistan), initiated by the Carter administration and continued under Reagan, still remains to be told.

[iv] It has, of course, become a significant economic partner—the United States' fourth-largest trading partner, in fact. China's bilateral trade with the United States amounted to exports of $62.6 billion and imports of $12.9 billion in 1997. That same year, U.S. foreign direct investment in China was just over $5 billion.

[v] Some top Chinese leaders have even speculated about the possibility of a U.S.-China military collision. In an address to senior PLA cadres, Zhang Wannian, the vice chairman of the Central Military Commission, bluntly stated in early 1999 that, "The possibility that a limited war may break out between China and the United States does exist." *Cheng Ming* (Hong Kong monthly), April 1, 1999.

[vi] Shi Yinhong, "Scholar on Hegemonistic Interference", *Ta Kung Pao*, July 2, 1999, trans. by Foreign Broadcast Information Service (FBIS). More specifically, he warned that "the hegemonists could possibly

intervene in China's affairs on the following issues: the Taiwan issue, the Tibet and Xinjiang issue, the South China Sea islands issue, China's internal political system or China's strategic weapons."

[vii] Ding Sheng, "The New Clinton Doctrine", *Xiandai Guoji Guanxi*, August 20, 1999, trans. by FBIS. An authoritative discussion of the alleged American plans to dominate Eurasia strategically, and to exploit to that end its various ethnic problems, is contained in an analysis of U.S.-Russia relations by Lu Zhongwei, "International Security Environment Goes Through Changes", *Beijing Review*, August 23, 1999.

[viii] "On Cultural Roots of the Sino-U.S. Conflict", *Ta Kung Pao,* September 21, 1999, trans. by FBIS.

[ix] An unusually candid presidential account of how normalization was effected is provided in Jimmy Carter, "The Real China Story", *Foreign Affairs* (November/December 1999).

[x] It is estimated that up to 200,000 Taiwanese businessmen now work in the PRC, with Taiwanese investments in mainland China now well in excess of $20 billion, and another $25 billion planned. The PRC is now Taiwan's third-largest trade partner, following the United States and Japan.

[xi] Lee Teng-hui, "Understanding Taiwan", Foreign Affairs (November/December 1999).

[xii] The notion of a "sovereign" Taiwan was explicitly postulated in a public statement issued by a group of conservative foreign policy experts, some of whom play an active role in the ongoing presidential campaign. (Heritage Foundation press release, August 24, 1999.)

[xiii] William S. Cohen, "The Security Situation in the Taiwan Strait", Report to the Congress pursuant to the FY99 Appropriations Bill (Washington, DC: Department of Defense, 1999).

[xiv] For a revealing discussion of Japan's relationship with China and the United States conducted by leading Japanese officials, see "Seeking True Independence, et al." (in Japanese), *Yomiuri Shimbun*, January 11, 2000.

[xv] Chuo Koron (February 1999), p. 247, trans. by FBIS.

[xvi] See "Ishihara's Antics Worth High Vigilance", *Renmin Ribao*, November 17, 1999, trans. by FBIS.

[xvii] Both the Russians and the Chinese are very sensitive to the demographic realities prevailing in Eurasia's eastern extremities. The population of Manchuria alone is 102.3 million and the density per square kilometer is 168. The total population of the four adjacent Russian regions is 6.1 million, with a population density of only 5.3 per square kilometer.

2

Remembering the Future

Paul Wolfowitz*

Even though it has been ten years since the Berlin Wall came down, we still have no better name for the period in which we live than "the post-Cold War era." True, many have aspired to play the role of the next George Kennan—defining American strategy for this new era that does not yet have a name—but so far none has succeeded. Moreover, given the rate at which many politicians and commentators have been revising their recollections of their own stances during the period 1946–91, it may not be too long before someone disputes Kennan's authorship of the original containment strategy. For it seems that now, safely after the event, we have all become cold warriors.

In his maiden speech on foreign policy, presidential candidate Bill Bradley declared that, "For 50 years after the end of World War II and until the fall of the Berlin Wall in 1989, we were sure about one thing: We knew where we stood on foreign policy." The former senator from New Jersey went on to rue the fact that today we face a more difficult challenge:

> When it comes to foreign affairs, things are not so clear. The world's a more complicated place and it's no longer divided like it once was into good and evil, clear enemies,

* Paul Wolfowitz was dean of the Paul H. Nitze School of Advanced International Studies, Johns Hopkins University. He currently serves as Deputy Secretary of Defense.

This essay first appeared in *The National Interest*, No. 59 (Spring 2000).

obvious friends. The choices are no longer so stark, and stark choices are always the easy ones.

This nostalgia for the supposedly easier choices of the Cold War is not confined to Bradley. President Clinton, too, routinely echoes the lament about the lost clarity and clear choices of the recent past.

It is astonishing to hear the Cold War era so described. For in reality, it was a time when the country was deeply divided over issues of foreign policy—most bitterly over the war in Vietnam, but also over the commitment of U.S. troops to Europe and Korea, the Strategic Defense Initiative and arms control, Central America and nuclear weapons, and over almost every year's budget request from the Defense Department.

Descriptions of the long conflict as being clear-cut and simple are particularly astounding coming from leaders of the party of George McGovern. During the 1970s and 1980s, the Democratic Party ceased to be the party of Harry Truman or "Scoop" Jackson and became instead the party that supported the Mansfield Amendment to remove U.S. troops from Europe; that reflexively opposed many of the weapons systems that were critical in the American competition with the Soviet Union; and that advocated a "nuclear freeze" at a time when the Reagan administration was trying to convince NATO to proceed with the deployment of intermediate-range nuclear forces. Far from believing that the Cold War was a clear struggle between good and evil, the leaders of the Democratic Party attacked President Reagan as a war-mongering ideologue when he declared that the Soviet Union was an "evil empire."

Then, too, rarely were the country's leaders so sharply divided as they were in 1991 over the decision to evict Saddam Hussein's forces from Kuwait. Voting on largely partisan lines, it was only by slender majorities that both houses of Congress granted President Bush the authority to use force. Although Senator Bradley has lately discovered that "Iraq, 1991" exemplifies one of those times and places when "the national interest is clear", at the time he joined the majority of congressional Democrats in voting against the President. And for Governor Clinton the issue was not so clear either. In a characteristically hedged statement he said: "I guess I would have voted for the majority if it was a close vote. But I agree with the arguments the minority made.''

All of this forgetfulness might merely be a matter for amusement were it not for the fact that much of what is being forgotten is crucially relevant to our immediate future.

Reflections on Consensus

In 1992 a draft memo prepared by my office at the Pentagon, which proposed a post-Cold War defense strategy, leaked to the press and sparked a major controversy. The draft suggested that a "dominant consideration" in U.S. defense strategy should be "to prevent any hostile power from dominating a region whose resources would, under consolidated control, be sufficient to generate global power." Those regions were specified as Western Europe, East Asia, the territory of the former Soviet Union and Southwest Asia.

The New York Times, having published the leak, editorialized violently against the document, as did some prominent members of Congress. Senator Edward Kennedy said that the Pentagon plans "appear to be aimed primarily at finding new ways to justify Cold War levels of military spending." Senator Robert Byrd commented that, "We love being the sole remaining superpower in the world and we want so much to remain that way that we are willing to put at risk the basic health of our economy and well-being of our people to do so." Senator Joseph Biden ridiculed the proposed strategy as "literally a Pax Americana. . . . It won't work."

Just seven years later, many of these same critics seem quite comfortable with the idea of a Pax Americana. They have supported or urged American military intervention in places like Haiti and Rwanda and East Timor, places never envisaged in my 1992 memorandum. Moreover, they seem very comfortable that all of this can be accomplished, and our commitments to our European and Asian allies maintained, with a greatly reduced defense burden and without risking the "basic health of our economy." Today the criticism of Pax Americana comes mainly from the isolationist right, from Patrick Buchanan, who complains that "containment, a defensive strategy, had given way to a breathtakingly ambitious offensive strategy—to 'establish and protect a new order.'"

One would like to think that this new consensus—Buchanan apart—reflects a recognition that the United States cannot afford to allow a hostile power to dominate Europe or Asia or the Persian Gulf; that the safest, and in the long run the cheapest, way to prevent this is to preserve the U.S.-led alliances that have been so successful—to paraphrase Lord Ismay in more diplomatic language—at keeping Americans engaged, allies reassured, and aggressors deterred. But in reality today's consensus is facile and complacent, reflecting a lack of concern about the possibility of another major war, let alone agreement about how to prevent one.

Still, one should not look a gift horse in the mouth. There is today a remarkable degree of agreement on a number of central points of foreign policy. No one is lobbying to withdraw troops from Korea, as was the case as recently as the late 1980s. No one is arguing that we should withdraw from Europe. American forces under President Clinton's command have been bombing Iraq with some regularity for months now, without a whimper of opposition in the Congress and barely a mention in the press. Even on ballistic missile defense there is today an emerging consensus that something needs to be done—although no agreement on precisely what.

Partly, this consensus is the result of a seemingly benign international environment. Thus, we have been told that the really important problem is "the economy, stupid", or the environment, or, as the vice president most recently announced, aids in Africa. What is wrong with these claims is not that aids in Africa and the environment are not serious problems; rather, it is the implication that conventional security is no longer something we need to worry much about.

Perhaps, indeed, we have seen the last of the Napoleons and the Kaisers and Hitlers and Stalins and Tojos. In a world where American primacy seems so overwhelming, it is hard to imagine how threats of that magnitude could come about. But if we contemplate the last century we find abundant evidence that even a decade can bring about enormous transformations in world affairs. (Consider the changes from 1905 to 1915, or from 1929 to 1939, or from 1981 to 1991.) And if that was true in earlier decades, how much truer is it today when the tempo of change has increased so dramatically? Further, even if the chances of another assault on world peace are remote, what is at stake is too great to permit complacency or neglect of America's responsibility as the world's dominant power.

Wars in Faraway Places

Ultimately, we are placing bets on the shape of an uncertain future—a task which will prove that much more difficult if we cannot get the past right. The experience of Munich has provided a cautionary lesson for the second half of the last century—even if a somewhat overused one—and it should not be forgotten in this one. Addressing the British people by radio two days before his departure for Munich in 1938, Prime Minister Neville Chamberlain made the case for appeasement in stark terms:

> How horrible, fantastic, incredible it is that we should be digging trenches and trying on gas masks here because of a quarrel in a far-away country between people of whom we know nothing. . . . I am myself a man of peace to the very depths of my soul. . . . But if I were convinced that any nation had made up its mind to dominate the world by fear of its force, I should feel that it must be resisted; . . . but war is a fearful thing, and we must be very clear, before we embark on it, that it is really the great issues that are at stake, and that the call to risk everything in their defense, when all the consequences are weighed, is irresistible.

As it turned out, it was precisely "the great issues" that were at stake. Chamberlain's failure to come to the aid of those faraway Czechs meant that Britain would shortly face a much more terrible war and on much more disadvantageous terms.

As a result, this "lesson" was seared into the consciousness of the Western democracies and their leaders. It contributed to the resolve of President Truman to resist communist aggression in such "faraway" places as Korea, Iran, Turkey, Greece and Berlin, and of President Kennedy to resist Soviet pressure in Berlin and Cuba. But let us remember that it was also with Munich in mind that British Prime Minister Anthony Eden and French Prime Minister Guy Mollet took the unfortunate decision to oppose with force Nasser's takeover of the Suez Canal in

1956, and that a few years later, with even worse consequences, Presidents Kennedy and Johnson decided that Vietnam was a similar case of aggression that had to be opposed.

With the end of the Cold War, the United States and its allies and partners are again confronted with a series of wars in faraway places, and many repeat Chamberlain's counsel that we have no business intervening in conflicts among people we do not understand, where, in the current idiom, "we have no dog in the fight." Of course, the fact that the arguments have a similar ring to them does not mean that those who echo Chamberlain today are necessarily wrong, any more than those who argue for intervening in messy civil wars or ethnic conflicts for moral purposes are necessarily repeating the mistakes of Vietnam. History does not tell us what to do, but it does offer us some options to ponder.

Imagine, counterfactually, that England and its allies had successfully resisted Hitler in the Rhineland in 1936 or at Munich in 1938. Germany would then have been "contained." In that case we would certainly have been treated—would we not?—to learned discourses about how the resulting "cold war" with Germany was the unnecessary product of unwarranted Western suspicion and hostility toward a country that—chafing under unjustified Western impositions—had only been seeking its rightful "place in the sun." Or, to take a more recent example, we will never know what might have happened if Saddam Hussein's occupation of Kuwait had not been reversed: would he have, as seems entirely probable, brought the governments of the Arabian Peninsula under his control and, with the wealth that provided, built up his arsenal of conventional and nuclear weapons in preparation for a much bigger war with Iran or with Israel? If so, then what President Bush achieved was much more than just the liberation of Kuwait; but that achievement will never be as clear as Chamberlain's failure.

Even actions that seem like mistakes at the time may be rescued by the twists and turns of history. The failure to do more to deter Saddam Hussein from attacking Kuwait in 1990 seemed like a mistake at the time and is still treated as such in most discussions of that crisis. But consider: we shall never know what might have happened if Saddam Hussein had been deterred at that point—only to confront the world with a crisis several years later, but now armed with nuclear weapons.

When the consequences of alternative courses of action are so uncertain, even in hindsight, who in their right mind would defy Yogi Berra's famous advice that "it's a mistake to try to make predictions, especially about the future"?

Lessons of the Cold War

The refusal to remember the deep divisions and sharp debates over policy that took place during the Cold War is in some cases part of an effort to deny that there are any lessons to be learned from that long struggle, to put it all behind us. On the other side, some seem to believe that, since the policies that won the Cold

War clearly worked, every effort should be made to keep them in place indefinitely. In the face of such advice we would do well to remember Lord Salisbury's advice that "The commonest error in politics is sticking to the carcass of dead politics." What is true, I believe, is that while policies must change as circumstances change, there are still valid lessons to be learned from the Cold War. Here are some of them:

Democracy Matters

At the beginning of the Reagan administration, when Congress refused to confirm the administration's first nominee as assistant secretary of state for Human Rights, some saw this as an opportunity to do away entirely with the State Department's Office of Human Rights. Fortunately, and due in large measure to the intervention of Reagan's personal friend and then-Deputy Secretary of State William Clark, the office was preserved and human rights and the promotion of democracy became enshrined as major features of the Reagan administration's foreign policy. There can be little doubt that this contributed in an important way to the triumph of democracy in the Cold War. Perhaps more surprising to Reagan's numerous critics, his administration also witnessed and supported an enormous advance of democracy in countries on "our" side of the Cold War, not only in Latin America but in some surprising places in Asia such as South Korea, Taiwan and the Philippines.

Nothing could be less realistic than the version of the "realist" view of foreign policy that dismisses human rights as an important tool of American foreign policy. There are no doubt examples of human rights policies that can damage other U.S. interests, but often these are policies that are bad for human rights and democracy as well—for example, the notion that undermining the Shah's regime would have been a great advance for the Iranian people, or the belief that weakening South Korea's ability to defend itself from the North was necessary in order to advance human rights. What is more impressive is how often promoting democracy has actually advanced American interests.

Democratic change not only weakened our enemies, but helped strengthen our friends. This became clear to me when I was involved in drafting U.S. policy toward the Philippines in the mid-1980s, during the last years of the Marcos regime. As the United States put pressure on Marcos to reform, we were asked whether doing so would simply pave the way for a regime that would in retrospect make Marcos look good, as the Ayatollahs in Iran had done for the Shah. In fact, it was Marcos who was in the process of paving the way to victory for a particularly vicious communist insurgency, and there was available a true democratic alternative in the Philippines. Political change did indeed jeopardize American bases in the Philippines, but it seemed more important to have a healthy ally without American bases than a sick ally with them.

History has amply vindicated that judgment. Similarly, the transition to democracy in South Korea has not only been good for the Korean people but has significantly strengthened U.S.-Korean relations. As one contemplates the enormous problems of Indonesia today, one can only wish that the transition to a more representative government there had begun ten years earlier.

Promoting democracy requires attention to specific circumstances and to the limitations of U.S. leverage. Both because of what the United States is, and because of what is possible, we cannot engage either in promoting democracy or in nation-building simply by an exercise of will. We must proceed by interaction and indirection, not imposition. In this respect, the post-World War II examples of Germany and Japan offer misleading guides for the present. What proved feasible following total victory and prolonged occupation—in societies that were economically advanced but, at the same time, had profoundly lost faith in their own institutions—does not offer a model that applies in other circumstances.

One of the important lessons of the Cold War is that some regimes are more open to change than others, that there is indeed a difference between authoritarian and totalitarian governments. The Soviet Union itself was not ready for change until it became clear that it was losing the Cold War. Our ally South Korea was a very different matter, even though severe criticisms could be leveled at the Chun Doo Hwan regime of the 1980s. Reagan's willingness to receive Chun as his first foreign visitor at the White House was criticized by human rights groups, but it secured the reprieve of Kim Dae Jung's death sentence and his release from prison. Reagan's own visit to Korea two years later was also criticized, but it secured Chun's pledge to honor the Korean constitution and step down at the end of his term of office.

Harking back to Marcos again, it is important to recall that he only proved willing to heed advice that he step down when his own people had made his position completely untenable. Thus, another lesson that we should remember from our Cold War successes in promoting democracy is that such efforts require indigenous support to be effective. The chances of success without such support—say, in North Korea today—are small. It is the difference between pushing on a locked door and pushing on a balanced scale.

In the former cases, as in Afghanistan, our strongest weapon may be the oppressed people themselves. But we have an obligation to deliver the support we promise them. Kennedy's failure to make good on his pledges to the Cubans at the Bay of Pigs, like Clinton's abandonment of the Iraqi opposition in 1996, was a moral failure that was also costly to American power and credibility. Even when the promises are vague, or only implicit—as with Eisenhower encouraging the Hungarians in 1956 or Bush the Iraqis in 1991—we must remember that our reputation will be determined by what people believe we promised rather than what we intended. This is a reason to promise carefully and deliver on the promises we make—but it should not become an excuse for refusing our help to those who need it, like the Iraqi opposition today.

Deterrence Works

It is surprising, after not only the Cold War experience but the earlier history of the twentieth century, that we still hear echoes of "Why die for Berlin?" or "Why die for Danzig?"

The purpose of extending security guarantees, such as the ones recently extended to NATO's newest members, is not to have to fight wars on behalf of others, but precisely to avoid having to do so. It is impressive how often American clarity during the Cold War worked, and how often ambiguity led to trouble. This is not to say that showing resolve will always suffice to ensure peace. But we should not entertain the illusion that a refusal to extend guarantees will enable us to avoid war. Chamberlain not only sacrificed Czechoslovakia at Munich, but brought on the wider war that he was trying to avoid. When Acheson implied that Korea was outside our defense perimeter he not only invited a North Korean attack but could not then keep the United States out of war when it came.

Here there seems to be a persistent difference between democracies, which look constantly for pragmatic solutions to resolve concrete problems in isolation, and those more ruthless and avaricious leaders who see every such effort as a sign of weakness and whose real goal is to change power relationships in a fundamental way. Henry Kissinger has observed that British Prime Minister Harold Macmillan's "exploration" of pragmatic concessions to resolve the Berlin crisis in 1959 was seen by Khrushchev "as another confirmation of a favorable tilt in the balance of forces and the augury of even better things to come", as were subsequent American efforts. It was only with the frustration of Khrushchev's final attempt to raise the ante—by placing missiles in Cuba—that he was finally forced to stop testing the West on Berlin.

America's Alliance Vocation

Perhaps no Cold War lesson is more important than what can be learned from the remarkable record of the United States in building successful coalitions. This includes lessons about the importance of leadership and what it consists of: not lecturing and posturing and demanding, but demonstrating that your friends will be protected and taken care of, that your enemies will be punished, and that those who refuse to support you will live to regret having done so. It includes lessons about the difference between coalitions that are united by a common purpose, and collections of countries that are searching for the least common denominator and for easy ways out of a problem. And it includes important lessons that the "enemy of our friend" does not always have to be our enemy as well—whether dealing with Egypt and Israel, Israel and Saudi Arabia, Greece and Turkey, Russia and Ukraine, or China and Taiwan, the United States has demonstrated a remarkable capacity to work both sides of the street.

The Importance of Principle

There is much else to be learned from the experience of the Cold War: conflicts breed arms races, and not the other way around; it is far better to equip others to fight for their country than to send Americans to fight for them; conversely, refusing to arm our friends, whether in Bosnia, or Cambodia or elsewhere, is a strategic as well as a moral mistake; and force, when used, should be used decisively—bluffing or "signaling" with military power should not be done without a careful calculation of what comes next.

As important as any other lesson, however, is that in international relations, as in other human activities, principles count. This is a practical as well as a moral point, because principle is a powerful force in politics, particularly in democratic politics. It cannot be an absolute because it must be applied to specific cases, requiring judgments about the facts and the stakes of each one. Even in the case of Munich, Churchill acknowledged that,

> No case of this kind can be judged apart from its circumstances. The facts may be unknown at the time, and estimates of them must be largely guesswork, coloured by the general feeling and aims of whoever is trying to pronounce. Those who are . . . ready to fight whenever some challenge comes from a foreign Power, have not always been right. On the other hand, those whose inclination is to bow their heads, to seek patiently and faithfully for peaceful compromise, are not always wrong. On the contrary, in the majority of instances they may be right, not only morally but from a practical standpoint.

There is, however, Churchill continued,

> one helpful guide, namely, for a nation to keep its word and to act in accordance with its treaty obligations to allies. . . . An exaggerated code of honour leading to the performance of utterly vain and unreasonable deeds could not be defended, however fine it might look. [At Munich], however, the moment came when honour pointed the path of duty, and when also the right judgment of the facts at that time would have reinforced its dictates.

China, Past and Future

There is no issue facing us today in which the past weighs more heavily on the present and on future prospects than that of our relationship with the People's Republic of China (PRC). China is an emerging major power, but it has not yet become one. Persuading an emerging power that the status quo should be changed only peacefully has always been a challenge historically, and the failure to do so with Germany and Japan in the last century had catastrophic consequences. That failure serves as a reminder of the stakes involved, but does not constitute a reason to be pessimistic about the outcome in the case of China.

Almost surely, China will not become an ideological threat like the old Soviet Union or try to conduct ideological crusades and campaigns of subversion as it did in the 1950s and 1960s. Not only is the ideological fervor gone in China, but also the ideology has no appeal internationally. However, China does have deep historical grievances, much more legitimate than those voiced a century ago by Germany or Japan. It remains to be seen whether China will come to accept that a peaceful status quo in the Western Pacific—albeit one in which the principal countries around the Pacific Rim are America's allies or friends—best serves its own interests.

Clearly China's growing strength will pose challenges to the United States, its allies and its friends, but on balance it is probably better to face the challenges of a strong China than a weak one. Certainly it would be a mistake to treat China like the Soviet Union, restricting its trade in order deliberately to weaken it or to use human rights as leverage. A weaker China might take longer to become a military competitor, but what we would gain in time we would lose in enmity. Moreover, a collapsed China would not be in our interest, quite apart from the fact that it would involve enormous human suffering.

The most important reason, however, for treating China differently from the old Soviet Union is because an evolution is taking place in the People's Republic, one that bears some resemblance to the earlier development of the Asian "tigers." Today's China is no longer a completely closed society in which the party and government dominate everything. There is a substantial private sector whose scope and sphere are growing. It is in the U.S. interest—and in that of Taiwan and Hong Kong and the region as a whole—to encourage such growth, which is heavily dependent on trade with the West. That is the most fundamental and important reason for continuing normal trade relations with China and encouraging Chinese membership of the WTO.

The U.S. interest in supporting democratic trends in China is more than "international social work." Although our capacity to influence the process is limited, the United States has a fundamental strategic interest in encouraging greater openness. Even though democracies are not as irenic as the extreme proponents of "democratic peace" like to argue, a China that governs its own peoples by force is more likely to try to impose its will on its neighbors. And in turn, China's neighbors and the United States will be more likely to trust it and accept its growing influence if it becomes a democracy. A government whose legitimacy rests on valid claims to be representative has less need to make dangerous appeals to nationalism. Finally, and not insignificantly, a democratic China would have a far better chance of coming to terms with Taiwan peacefully. I have even been told by a Chinese Communist Party member that what "terrifies those old men in Beijing" is the demonstration by Taiwan that Chinese can manage democracy successfully.

Is Taiwan an obstacle in U.S.-China relations or might it actually be an opportunity? For the last twenty-five years, U.S.-China differences over the issue have been successfully managed within a framework that has two essential premises: first, these differences must be addressed peacefully; second, they must be resolved by agreement of both parties, without a unilateral declaration of independence by Taiwan. This is called the "One China" policy, although the policy rests on a fundamental ambiguity concerning its very name: both sides have different views of what "One China" means and the United States has never advanced a view of its own (although President Clinton's adoption of the PRC's "Three No's" formulation during his visit to Shanghai in 1998 was interpreted as a substantial tilt toward the PRC's view). "One China" is supposed to be open to any interpretation the two sides can agree on.

Although today's circumstances are vastly different from those that prevailed when the Shanghai Communiqué was signed in 1972, the "One China" policy remains the best available framework for handling a difficult and sensitive issue. It is a framework that preserves freedom, democracy and prosperity in Taiwan, even as it denies the island the formal independence that many of its citizens desire. At the same time, by avoiding a direct affront to mainland China's sovereignty, it helps to avoid military conflict. Yet it will be more difficult to sustain this framework in the post-Cold War period, because of the enormous changes that have occurred on both sides of the Taiwan Strait.

The most important of these changes has been the establishment of genuine democracy in Taiwan. As recently as twenty years ago—another example of the rapidity of change—the island was still ruled by a brutal dictatorship. As welcome as it is, democratization complicates Taiwan's dealings with the mainland. The government in Taiwan must now answer to its people, the great majority of whom are native Taiwanese with little attachment to China. In the post-Cold War period, when flimsy mini-states such as Macedonia, the Kyrgyz Republic and East Timor have acquired independence, it is difficult to explain why a prosperous democracy of more than twenty million people is not so entitled.

From the PRC side, fear that pro-independence sentiment might lead to a de jure assertion of independence by Taiwan has apparently strengthened the view in some quarters that the aim of reunification must be pressed more rapidly. It may also be that Jiang Zemin, like some other world leaders, has an eye toward his personal legacy and believes that, following on Hong Kong and Macau, he can somehow complete reunification in his lifetime. Nor can one discount the possible influence of the kind of strategic thinking found in Chinese military circles that Taiwan is the "crucial point in the first chain of islands", the key to realizing Admiral Liu Hua-qing's assertion that "the Chinese navy should exert effective control of the seas within the first island chain", defined as comprising the Aleutians, the Kuriles, Japan (including the Ryukyus), Taiwan, the Philippines and most of Indonesia.

The stiffening of the PRC's approach to Taiwan also reflects the changed geopolitical situation since the end of the Cold War. China no longer needs the United States to balance a threatening neighbor and may instead revel in the prospect of its own growing power. Not that the United States ever used its leverage very well in any case. All the talk about China as a "card" to be played in U.S.-Soviet relations obviously increased China's own sense of its bargaining power with the United States. George Shultz—who described his own attitude as "a marked departure from the so-called China-card policy"—observed at the time he became secretary of state that,

> When the geostrategic importance of China became the conceptual prism through which Sino-American relations were viewed, it was almost inevitable that American policymakers became overly solicitous of Chinese interests, concerns, and sensitivities. . . . On the basis of my own experience, I knew it would be a mistake to place too much emphasis on a relationship for its own sake. A good relationship should emerge from the ability to solve substantive problems of interest to both countries.

"You owe us a debt", Deng Xiaoping said to Kissinger in one negotiating session in 1974, referring to the American use of the "China card" in its dealings with Moscow. Yet in this case, as in so many others, China managed to convince the United States—or to help Americans convince themselves—that we needed the relationship more than they did, when the situation was more nearly the reverse. It is a mystery why the United States needed China's help to reach two Strategic Arms Limitation Treaties that conceded large advantages to the Soviet Union—the second of which, indeed, was so deeply flawed that it never gained Senate ratification. It is much more obvious what China gained from the relationship during a period when the Soviet Union was threatening preventive war against China.

Most amazingly of all, it was we Americans who sought a hasty conclusion of the normalization negotiations in late 1978. If any side urgently needed normalization then it was China, which was preparing to invade Vietnam, a country that had just signed a Treaty of Friendship and Cooperation with the Soviet Union. But again, the United States acted as though the U.S.-China relationship was more important to us than to China. The result was easy to predict: an opportunity to achieve clarity on the crucial issue of arms sales to Taiwan was lost. Instead, the United States agreed to a moratorium on arms sales during the first year after normalization, mumbling an explanation that afterwards "the sale of selected, defensive arms . . . would continue in a way that did not endanger the prospects for peace in the region", while taking "note of China's continuing opposition to arms sales." This led directly to the crisis that culminated in the August 1982 communiqué on arms sales, an ambiguous resolution of the issue that rests on conflicting interpretations by the two sides.

Clarity is not always a virtue, and often ambiguity is a practical way to achieve an agreement with which both sides can live. The very term "One China" is ambiguous and the United States should leave any attempts at clarification to the parties themselves. By adopting the PRC's "Three No's" when he was in Shanghai in 1998, President Clinton foreclosed some possible avenues of agreement. More dangerously, he undermined the confidence of the Taiwanese in earlier U.S. assurances. Taiwanese anxiety was further heightened by the justifiable impression that the United States was surrendering to PRC pressure, as reflected in Assistant Secretary of State Stanley Roth's talk about an agreement on "interim measures", or China specialist Kenneth Lieberthal's proposal, shortly before joining the NSC, for a fifty-year interim agreement.

The more we seem to be pressing Taiwan to negotiate with China, the more fearful Taiwan becomes and the more we encourage the PRC to intensify its pressure. The United States needs to encourage maximum patience on this issue. For the status quo is quite satisfactory, and serious movement can only come if the PRC offers inducements to Taiwan, not pressure. Indeed, the record strongly suggests that the PRC and Taiwan—not unlike the Arab states and Israel—deal best with one another when they have to take responsibility for their own negotiating positions, with U.S. encouragement but without U.S. pressure. Under these conditions they negotiated joint membership of the Asian Development Bank in 1985 and of APEC in 1991.

The record further suggests that Taiwan-PRC relations improve when Taiwan—like so many others who have been dependent on the United States—feels secure in its reliance on America. Despite repeated warnings from various experts that strong U.S. demonstrations of support for Taiwan—the Taiwan Relations Act of 1979, Reagan's 1982 refusal to terminate arms sales, the Indigenous Defense Fighter project in 1985, the sale of F-16s in 1992—would disrupt the relationship between Beijing and Taipei, a period of convivial relations followed each of these events. When trouble has arisen, it has been the product of mixed signals, as with the administration's shifting positions on the question of a visa for Lee Teng-hui in 1995, which indicated to both sides that U.S. policy might very well bend under pressure.

While ambiguity on the definition of "One China" is desirable and on the subject of arms sales is probably necessary, there are two areas involving American intentions where ambiguity serves no purpose. The first concerns the U.S. attitude toward the use of force to resolve the Taiwan issue, the second our attitude toward Taiwanese independence.

A senior Clinton defense official reportedly told the Chinese that America's response to the use of force against Taiwan would "depend on the circumstances." At the same time, many in Taiwan believe that U.S. support remains unconditional. We have indulged misleading impressions on both sides. It would be a strategic as well as a moral mistake for the United States to let China have its way with Taiwan. No matter how much other countries in the region might criticize Taiwan for having contributed to the crisis, and no matter how much they might try to distance themselves from the United States, they would also view the U.S. response as a test of America's strategic will. At the same time, while making it clear to Taiwan that the United States will not abandon it or force it to negotiate under pressure, we should also convey that we expect reasonable behavior in return—which would include avoiding a unilateral declaration of independence.

There are some who wish that the Chinese civil war had ended with a more complete communist victory, so that we would not have to deal with the Taiwan "obstacle." One of my predecessors as assistant secretary of state for the Asia-

Pacific region is reported once to have wished in jest that a tidal wave might literally wash the problem away. But this view is as unrealistic as it is morally blind. Once we accept the hand we have been dealt, obstacles can be turned into opportunities. We will not have peace in the Taiwan Strait if this promising democracy is made to disappear. We will only have peace when it is accepted as a fact of life. Only then will the friends of Taiwan be able to see why it is genuinely better for Taiwan to be joined with China, pointing the way to the kind of government that the great Chinese people deserve.

While far from perfect, the only means available to us of anticipating what may lie ahead is to reflect as best we can on what has gone before. China is just one example of where reflecting on our Cold War experiences provides us a road map for the future. It is to be hoped that the next century will be one of great opportunity for the improvement of life on this planet and the expansion of human creativity, not one scarred by the deep tragedies that marked much of the last century. But we will have a far better chance of achieving that aim if we remember how we got to where we are today, rather than burying the divisions of the past in a warm and fuzzy nostalgia.

3

Asia in the 21st Century: Power Politics Alive and Well

Rajan Menon and S. Enders Wimbush[*]

After decades of Cold War-induced predictability, Asia today is rapidly transforming into something new and unrecognizable. The very term "Asia" has lost its clarity. As a consequence of a revolution in communications and the frenetic pace of globalization, parts of Asia that have traditionally been distinguished by their geography—East Asia, Southeast Asia, South Asia, Central Asia—tend increasingly to blur and merge. Developments in one region shape the strategies of distant states in another with unprecedented rapidity. This new "Asia" really sweeps from the Pacific to Russia's western border and from the Arctic to the Indian Ocean.

The region's breadth is equaled only by its volatility. Russia, the long-dominant Eurasian power, is in decline, and its very territorial integrity is in question. In contrast to much of the last century, Russia's weakness—rather than its strength—will have a determining influence on Asia. Along its vast periphery new coalitions are forming and new competitions are taking shape. China and India, for example, both view themselves as emerging powers destined to shape the region's future. And Japan—for half a century the most dynamic presence in Asia, the key American outpost there and the principal prism through which the United States assesses its interests throughout the region—has languished in the

[*] Rajan Menon is Monroe J. Rathbone Professor of International Relations at Lehigh University and Director of Eurasia Policy Studies at the National Bureau of Asian Research. S. Enders Wimbush is Vice President for International Strategy and Policy at Hicks and Associates.

This essay first appeared in *The National Interest*, No. 59 (Spring 2000.)

doldrums for the better part of a decade. Today it faces significant challenges and the prospect of a possible American retreat from the Pacific Rim.

As the hierarchy among Asian states has changed, so too have the political orders within them. Many are plagued by political turmoil, ethnic and religious strife, and economic collapse. Some may even disintegrate or disappear: Russia, Indonesia, Pakistan and Afghanistan seem poised for reconfiguration, if not extinction. From some of these upheavals, new states and confederations with distinctly new interests and strategic alignments will surely emerge.

Compounding these familiar sources of instability are threats of an unfamiliar kind. In Asia today, the very meaning of national economic policy is becoming unclear. Forces beyond the control of individual states have prompted capital to flee, currencies to plummet, and prices to soar. The costs of staying competitive in an unforgiving global marketplace are reforms that invariably worsen the lot of already impoverished citizenries. Social unrest looms as an ever present danger as budgets are slashed and subsidies eliminated; those who rule appear rudderless while those who are ruled grow ever more resentful. Some regimes will survive the storm, while others will watch as their already tenuous legitimacy crumbles around them.

In addition, the fragile consensus in Asia against the proliferation of weapons of mass destruction is beginning to disintegrate. States such as China and Russia have sought to improve their strategic leverage by transferring nuclear and missile technology to allies. Within a decade, accurate, long-range missile systems will be available to most of the region's players, as will a variety of other weapons that may dramatically alter the current balance of power.

Power Transitions and New Alignments

The key determinant of the Asian balance of power in the next century will be China. If it remains stable and maintains the impressive rate of economic growth it has achieved since 1978, China's influence on the Asian order will rapidly increase. In a way that is characteristic of rising powers—democratic or authoritarian—it will seek to refashion the received order, one that was forged when it was weak, and to dominate its neighbors in the process. China's long economic tentacles already extend into Southeast Asia, Central Asia and, increasingly, the Russian Far East. An unstable or weak China could—some would say is likely to—pursue similar objectives, but in a different, more dangerous manner. Such a China would be more inclined to project military force beyond its borders to achieve the same results more quickly, if only to prop up the failing communist regime's legitimacy.

China's power will in turn likely expand in equal or greater proportion to the decline in the power of the United States. Here we should note that a unified Korea is a virtual certainty; the only questions remaining are how and when. Whatever the modality of Korean unification—a benign and peaceful one analogous to Germany's, or a violent affair with war, internal disorder and massive outpourings of refugees that shake surrounding countries—once it does happen, the continued presence of U.S. forces on the Korean Peninsula will likely be deemed unnecessary. China, which will undoubtedly participate in managing reunification, will almost certainly make the phased withdrawal of American troops a condition for its cooperation. The departure of U.S. forces from the peninsula may in turn generate pressure for an American military withdrawal from Japan as well. The Japanese would not wish to be the sole remaining platform for American troops and materiel in Northeast Asia, and the misgivings of Japanese citizens over U.S. bases on their soil would only be strengthened by the demise of the Pyongyang regime.

Even apart from the fate of Korea, political support for the U.S.-Japan alliance appears likely to erode in both countries unless a persuasive new rationale can be created for it. The incantation that Japan is the key bilateral partner of the United States is a bromide that will not prevent the weakening of an alliance that is bereft of a compelling mission, and in which the truly dangerous responsibilities are unevenly distributed. Absent such a new rationale, the Asian balance of power could well be recast by a radical change in Japanese defense policy. Japan already has the world's third-largest defense budget, and "Self-Defense Force" is a euphemism for what is, in fact, a small but state-of-the-art military machine.

Though Japanese military power has for the past half a century been maintained at a level far below that of which it is financially and technologically capable, the continuation of this moderation should not be taken for granted; certain features of the Northeast Asian balance of power underpin it, and Japanese defense strategists have already begun to anticipate changes that will reduce Japan's security and increase its vulnerability—with such taboo topics as military forces capable of significant power projection and even nuclear weapons now part of the discussion. The American view that Japan is frozen in a posture of military restraint is, in any case, ahistorical. The country's history since the Meiji Restoration of 1868 is characterized by dramatic and rapid shifts in both its domestic politics and foreign policy, usually set in motion, although not determined, by events beyond Japan's borders.

While a rearmed and more assertive Japan is a distinct possibility, Japan's aging population will be increasingly strained to meet the financial demands of both social entitlements and military expansion. A population that is projected to be approximately half of its current size within a century is unlikely to wish to hasten its demise by engaging in war with powers possessing highly lethal weaponry. Hence, the pressure of what the Japanese call their "strategic demography" may impel Japan to accommodate itself to, or enter into an alliance with, a powerful and assertive China.

Japan is also likely to seek other defense alignments that could alter dramatically the Asian strategic equation. It could make common cause with Russia because each is a flanking power for the other against China. If Korea unifies and tacks toward an increasingly powerful China, and the United States disengages from the Pacific, Japan could seek such allies in several directions. It might arm Taiwan, including with nuclear weapons. Or it might pursue a looser strategic alignment with India, again in order to flank China, but also to bolster the security of the sea lanes and straits that constitute Japan's energy lifeline. Japan could well pursue all three of these options simultaneously.

India is less certain about its geopolitical ambitions, and the reach of its military forces is limited. But India is stirring, and its strategic thinkers are looking beyond nearly half a century of introspection and self-reliance at a variety of new challenges and opportunities—in the Persian Gulf, Central Asia, Southeast Asia and Northeast Asia—that will afford their country geopolitical prominence. India's economic prospects have brightened as well. Its economy has grown at the annual rate of 6.5 percent since 1992, while the population growth rate, now at 1.8 percent per year, has been slowing.

Much has been written about the possibility that India—which, with its unwieldy size and heterogeneity, conjures up memories of the old Habsburg Empire—could come unglued. Yet the country has in fact proven remarkably stable. Its politics has remained democratic (if imperfectly so), with national elections now established as the means for acquiring and transferring power. The political system has weathered the assassination of its founding father and two prime ministers. The army has stayed out of power (a miraculous achievement considering the prevailing pattern in the Third World). Upheavals have been contained, whether they involve ethno-religious violence in Kashmir or the Punjab, or between Muslims and Hindus elsewhere, or between opponents and proponents of making Hindi the national language. Ironically, what many perceive to be the Achilles' heel of India may in fact be its major strength: its size and chaotic character. Because of its relatively decentralized political order and its breathtaking ethnic and linguistic diversity, India's crises are localized and seldom spread through the system. It is difficult for people living in, say, Kerala in the deep south, to get exercised by what happens in the Punjab or Kashmir.

Though a remarkably durable polity, India, unlike China, has yet to remove the many impediments that have prevented it from realizing its economic potential. But it clearly has some of the prerequisites for breaking into the ranks of the great powers. It has a vast pool of scientists and engineers; a thriving high-tech industry; and an advanced and promising missile program complemented by advances in the design of its nuclear warheads. Still, poverty, illiteracy and an entrenched bureaucracy continue to weigh India down. And for all of its pretension, India's foreign policy seems often to be little more than a Pakistan policy.

Change in the subcontinent will not come easily, but there are encouraging signs. While no national consensus has been achieved, much of India's elite now dismisses the Nehruvian emphasis on self-reliance and self-sufficiency, no doubt because it has become painfully evident that India can achieve neither. In particular, the demise of the Soviet Union, and with it the Soviet-Indian strategic alignment, has left India strategically anchored. India cannot tackle challenges such as those in the Gulf, Central Asia, the Bay of Bengal and Southeast Asia alone, for it has neither the military reach nor the economic resources to do so. Most Indian strategists do not take Moscow's current offer of an India-Russia-China alliance seriously, seeing it as exactly what it is: a failing Russia's desperate attempt to be more than it can be.

By contrast, an India-Japan alignment would make strategic sense for both countries. Such an alliance would require China to spread its military forces as widely as possible, and would secure the oil routes from the Persian Gulf to Northeast Asia. Taiwan, too, might become a party to such a coalition, if it were to decide to resist unification and opt for independence. Other states wary of China's new-found assertiveness, including Vietnam and Russia, might be attracted as well. But the principal partners—the bookends—will be India and Japan.

If the growing power of India and China shapes the emerging Asian order, Russia will be central to that order because of its declining power. Once a superpower, Russia now faces a situation in which not a single index of power is moving in a favorable direction. During the Cold War, the overriding preoccupation of the West and its allies was whether the Soviet Union would expand beyond its borders. Today, Russians worry that others, and particularly China, will expand into Russia. The two countries share a 2,666-mile border, and the low density of population on the Russian side stands in marked contrast to the masses of Chinese on the other. Moreover, the economic contrast between the shopworn Russian Far East and the rapidly developing Chinese northeast makes for an imbalance of power as well as population.

Russia's decline is welcomed by some states in Asia. Experience has taught them that there is an inverse relationship between Russian power and their own security. Yet the progressive weakening and disunity of Russia will have some pernicious consequences. The strength of Russian organized crime and the scope of its transnational operations will expand. The danger of nuclear accidents and environmental pollution (such as the dumping of nuclear waste into the oceans) will increase. Weapons of mass destruction and missile technologies will be more available to those with money to spend. Refugees fleeing violence or economic hardship will strain the capacity and, even more quickly, the hospitality of neighboring countries. Disease will overwhelm Russia's already failing public health system, and epidemics such as aids are all but inevitable. Having ceased to be Asia's superpower, Russia is fast becoming its sick man.

There are now four nuclear powers in this part of the world: Russia, China, India and Pakistan. The first two are rivals and potential adversaries, their current talk of a strategic partnership notwithstanding; the latter two have fought three wars since becoming independent. In the summer of 1999, having recently tested their nuclear weapons, India and Pakistan embarked on yet another round of fighting in Kashmir, casting doubt on the common assumption that nuclear weapons make even stubborn enemies retreat from the brink of war.

Taiwan, North Korea, South Korea, Iran and Japan are also candidates to acquire nuclear weapons. Even Turkey, which has Asian ambitions, will be hard pressed not to acquire nuclear weapons once Iran or Iraq does so. The motives and events that might induce these states to obtain nuclear arms vary considerably. For Taiwan—particularly if it continues down the path of independence—it will be the cold reality of a friendless world in which, when push comes to shove, few if any can be counted on to counterbalance Chinese power. For North Korea, the motive may be the calculation that nuclear weapons provide the only leverage to blackmail rich states. For Iran, the inducement will be that, as the examples of India and Pakistan demonstrate, nuclear weapons confer lasting respect and only temporary condemnation. For Japan, the nuclear option will be attractive if any of three conditions come to pass. The first is a belief among Japanese leaders that, for one reason or another, the United States is no longer a reliable protector. The second is the rise of an increasingly powerful and assertive China. The third is the advent of nuclear weapons on the Korean Peninsula.

In the twenty-first century, chemical and biological weapons will also become part of the region's arsenals. The hope that these weapons will never be used because they are inhumane is naive and unrealistic. They lack the lethality of nuclear bombs when measured by the number of immediate fatalities a single weapon can cause, but they are inexpensive, easy to manufacture, and will be fairly simple to deliver on target by widely available means.

Energy, too, will be a key concern for Asian states, as Asia will become the world's largest energy consumer within the first two decades of the twenty-first century. China, which became a net importer of energy in 1993, will dominate Asian demand. Its onshore production is declining, and the search for offshore oil has proved to be expensive and disappointing. Nor has the energy bonanza anticipated from the Tarim River Basin in Xinjiang been realized. Thus, China has moved with determination into Central Asia, the Bay of Bengal, Iraq and much of the rest of the energy-producing world in search of oil and gas. To reduce its dependence on sealanes, China plans to build and link a long, expensive pipeline from Kazakhstan to the centers of consumption in eastern China.

All of these options, if successfully exploited, will ease China's energy problems, but the overwhelming share of its oil will still come from the Middle East. This dependence will cause China to expand its naval power to protect the sea lanes that connect it to that region through Southeast Asian waters. China's commitment to building a powerful navy will accelerate if Indonesia continues to be wrecked by disorder. Japan, which is entirely dependent on imported oil—and India, which also draws heavily on the Gulf—would then expand their own naval power. Japan may have to do so not only because of what China does, but because there may no longer be a stable, united Indonesia guarding the shipping routes that convey Japan's oil supplies. The stage is then set for rivalries in which the anticipation of hostilities proves more decisive than malign motives and unfriendly acts.

The competition for energy is also likely to extend to oil-rich Central Asia, especially Kazakhstan and Kyrgyzstan. If Central Asia turns out to be an unstable region, China will forge alliances and possibly establish military bases there to protect investments, pipelines and friendly governments. Russia will have few means with which to resist such moves. But Russia will not be the only state unhappy with a Chinese sphere of influence in Central Asia: India sees the region as a promising market, a source of energy, as well as an area in which Pakistan's influence and the threat of militant Islamic movements pose serious threats. India regards Central Asia as its "extended strategic neighborhood." And it would be profoundly disturbed by an enhanced Chinese presence there. For those Central Asians seeking to contain an increasingly assertive Chinese policy in their region that is met by only meager Russian resistance, India may offer an increasingly attractive counterbalance.

Sources of Internal Upheaval

While a balance of power may be established in Asia over time, the continent will continue to experience civil unrest created by separatist and irredentist nationalism, ethnic strife, and mass movements with the capacity to overwhelm fragile political institutions. Asia is rife with such disorders. Russia's troubles in the Caucasus and Central Asia have been well documented. Afghanistan continues to be torn by the latest variant of the civil war that has plagued it since 1978. Pakistan's calculation that it will gain from a friendly and dependent Afghanistan (as distinct from the unfriendly and pro-Indian governments that have held power in Kabul since 1945) may be misplaced. Should the Taliban consolidate its power there, it could reactivate irredentist claims against Pakistan's northwest frontier province, which is separated from Afghanistan by a nineteenth-century demarcation, the legality of which has been challenged by successive Afghan governments. Tajikistan has disappeared as a functioning state and is now an arena for drug smugglers, private armies and assassins, with the Russian army providing what passes for order. Separatist sentiments are running strong in Xinjiang, Tibet, Kashmir, Sri Lanka, Burma and Indonesia, and they will alter the shape and size of states throughout Asia.

The Chinese province of Xinjiang provides a glimpse of what may be in store for much of the region. The Chinese leadership has finally acknowledged what outsiders have long known, namely, that Uighur nationalism, rebellion and violence persist in Xinjiang. Protests and bombings have increased since the fall of the Soviet Union and the establishment of predominantly Turkic countries in Central Asia that share borders with Xinjiang. The Chinese determination to expand communications and commerce with Central Asia will only further inflame Uighur passions. The traffic of weapons, political literature and insurgents has prompted the Chinese to increase surveillance in Xinjiang and, intermittently, to close its border with Pakistan.

Nationalist rebellions could, of course, be quelled by violence, and the danger of losing public support would be much smaller than if the government's guns were turned against ethnic Chinese protestors. Yet even if it could be accomplished in short order, repression of ethnic minorities would hardly be compatible with China's desire to attract foreign investment. Under Deng Xiaoping China opted to pursue economic development and national power by engaging the global economy and leaving behind the days of autarchy, Red Guards and millenarianism. Thus far it has stayed the course. But to succeed, it must maintain the confidence of investors, assistance from international financial organizations, and good relations with the world's leading economic powers. Accordingly, as China's integration with the world's economy proceeds, its leadership will find that its choices for dealing with domestic unrest have narrowed.

Globalization—the rapidity and multiplicity of ways in which "here" is hostage to "there"—is commonly portrayed as a stern disciplinarian, a foe of particularism, inefficiency and waste. It punishes unwise economic policies and forces states that seek advancement in the global marketplace to get their economic houses in order. It promotes aspirations, values and fashions that transcend borders and cultures. But globalization has another side. Under its sway states are subject to swift and sharp economic downturns that can reduce the legitimacy of governments. Individuals are exposed to new ideas from abroad that call into question outlooks and interpretations propagated by their governments. The disparities in wealth and power between "us" and "them" are transmitted immediately, vividly and viscerally. The freedom and ferocity with which governments—at least those that want to participate in the global economy—can resort to repression is reduced dramatically. This increases the freedom to maneuver and the publicity available to disgruntled national minorities. States in which ethnic minorities are geographically concentrated, and politically and culturally disenfranchised, find that coercion is more costly because it is more easily observed and publicized by the outside world.

Globalization can promote integration among states. But it can also foster conflict and disintegration within them by exposing the limitations and ineptitude of governments, by generating traditionalist backlashes against alien values that present themselves as universal, and by creating huge disparities of wealth and power among nationalities, regions and classes. These effects will prove especially burdensome for the states that have risen from the detritus of the Soviet Union, as well as for the many other states of Asia—including China, Pakistan, Afghanistan and Indonesia—that share such traits. Identity based on myth, language, religion and culture may not be strong enough to hold these states together, or, if they do remain territorially intact, to provide them with adequate political stability. China, which has a more cohesive populace, may be better suited to weather the shocks of globalization. But the Chinese leadership will learn that not all effects of globalization are benign. As levels of investment, access to information through email and the Internet, and travel and residence abroad increase, the tension between China's economy, society and polity will surely grow.

Implications for American Policy

This portrait of the emerging Asia is at least as plausible as, and perhaps more so than, that of the Asia that most American policymakers seem to see unfolding incrementally, on the basis of linear projections of today's observable trends. Admittedly, the intellectual enterprise of extracting lessons from the past to predict the future is by its very nature an imprecise one, but it takes little to imagine that the new Asia of the early twenty-first century will not follow projected or preferred paths. Events there will cascade and generate many second and third-order consequences. Key states and groups will acquire new capabilities and pursue new objectives through new strategies. "Wild card" occurrences—such as natural catastrophes or accidents—will yield rapid and unexpected consequences. In the face of all this, alliances that have served America well for half a century in Asia may slowly disintegrate. Maintaining political commitments to, and a military presence in, Asia will become much more difficult once the requisite network of bases is no longer available. New centers of power—China, Japan and India—will emerge, and they and the United States will participate in a new balance of power contest with alignments that bear little resemblance to those of the latter part of the twentieth century.

Yet in the United States one cannot detect any inclination to develop new strategic partners in Asia. Few U.S. policymakers seem to appreciate that new strategic partners are likely to be found among former adversaries—India, Iran or Vietnam, for example. Instead they are quick to embrace short-term measures for short-term gains—sanctions against India or Iran, for example—that will make it harder to find and develop such partners.

Then, too, a growing number of states and groups in the new Asia will soon have access to weapons of mass destruction, despite U.S. efforts to prevent their spread. In such a world, it does not make sense to remain blindly committed to the aim of non-proliferation, when in fact the selective spread of these weapons to states whose interests converge with those of the United States might advance our aims. Preaching non-proliferation to the Indians, whose determination to establish a nuclear deterrent is logical and understandable, simply verges on the comical—especially when the preacher is standing on a mountain of his own nuclear weapons. America's refusal to adjust to the reality—in its rhetoric and its policy—of a nuclear India will simply breed anti-American sentiment in that country, and prevent the necessary shift from an outdated adversarial relationship.

Those Asian states that look to the United States for reassurance are clearly less assured today than they were during the Cold War, unipolarity notwithstanding. American military interventions in the Clinton years—in Somalia, Haiti, Bosnia and Kosovo—characterized as they have been by a gap between threats and action, unseemly exits, and the application of force from beyond the horizon and well above the clouds, have done little to dispel these doubts. Asian states that have traditionally relied upon the United States discern little evidence that Washington understands its own interests in Asia, let alone theirs. And they wonder whether the American public will continue paying in blood and treasure for the protection of distant (and now prosperous) allies.

How can the United States contribute to stability and security in Asia? Military power will continue to be important in the new balance of power contest. A more fluid presence and a greater reliance on sea power and impermanent basing rights will be required. But non-traditional threats less easily dealt with through deterrence or the application of force will become even more pronounced. These include transnational criminal and drug networks, nuclear and other environmental accidents, the fragmentation of states, the increasing salience of groups with significant military resources, the movement of peoples across state boundaries because of economic crises and civil unrest, and the dislocations created by globalization. With new uncertainties generated by new rivalries and new threats, and with the relative decline in American power, the cooperation needed to draw states together to address such common problems will prove even more difficult than it is now. To maintain the balance of power, the United States will have to use methods other than the ones that worked so well during the Cold War.

If the Asia of the twenty-first century bears a significant resemblance to that described here, the United States will find itself in an environment qualitatively different from that of the final years of the twentieth century. But who among key policymakers—or among foreign policy advisers in the presidential campaigns—thinks this way? Discussions of what Asia might look like and how it might challenge U.S. interests invariably suggest that the future will bear a strong resemblance to the past; the conventional wisdom rules. Few are willing to consider that Asia could present threats that are truly different. The first and most important challenge that the emerging Asia poses, then, is to prevailing thinking.

4

China: What Engagement Should Mean

*Robert B. Zoellick**

The United States enjoyed a united policy toward China for two decades. That unity ended with Tiananmen Square. But the challenge of an ascendant China now requires a consistent, steady, long-term view. The United States must rebuild a bipartisan policy toward China based on a strategy that can be supported by successive presidents and Congresses, Republicans and Democrats.

Past U.S. policies toward China have reflected two very different national traditions. One has drawn images of China, its people, and its future salvation from America's missionary experience. The other approach has viewed China in light of the realist's concepts of power, national interest, and balancing relationships among great states. At times, the United States has managed to fuse these two traditions in an unlikely amalgam, although the compound has usually displayed cracks created by countervailing forces.

Missionaries, Heretics, and Romantics

America has had a special relationship with China. We have romanticized, and then demonized, China and its people, time and again, in a pendulum of alternating attitudes, which led in turn to swings in policy. America's missionary experience with China helped shape these views. Our first widespread public contact with China came from efforts in the nineteenth century to convert the

---

* Robert B. Zoellick was an undersecretary of state and White House deputy chief of staff during the George H.W. Bush administration. He currently serves as United States Trade Representative

This essay first appeared in *The National Interest*, No. 46 (Winter 1996/97).

Chinese to Christianity, to rescue them from their condition, to educate them, to make them like us.

It was an effort that tapped some of the best American impulses. The missionary movement reached deep into Christian churches across the United States, certainly far beyond the elite seaboard groups that considered themselves the guardians of U.S. foreign policy. Millions of children learned about China at Sunday school, or from evening programs with returning missionaries who brought home pictures and stories, and then asked for nickels and dimes to help the Chinese.

The missionaries' influence also extended to more select company. After all, many were trained at Yale, Princeton, Oberlin, and other leading schools, and their children returned to become political leaders, scholars, and foreign service officers. They became the American interpreters of China. The children of missionaries also wrote books that influenced America's attitude toward China. The most famous and influential of these writers was Pearl Buck, whose book *The Good Earth* received the Pulitzer Prize, sold 1.5 million copies, became a Broadway play, and was transformed into a movie seen in the United States by an estimated 23 million people. Nor was this a singular example of the infatuation with China in America's popular culture. For later generations, the popular film *The Sand Pebbles* portrayed the confusing experience of the U.S. Navy and missionaries in a bewildering China caught between the old ways and the new, while *The Last Emperor* pictured Pu Yi's and China's twentieth-century journeys.

The images of China created by the missionaries were reinforced by America's trading ties. The romantic stories of China clippers, exotic lands, and vast fortunes to be made—or lost—captured America's imagination. Unlike Europeans, Russians, and Japanese who grasped territories from disintegrating Qing China, U.S. Secretary of State John Hay stood for an "Open Door" that would allow all to prosper from the "great China trade."

The romantic, missionary view of China has had important implications for U.S. policies. When the Chinese have embraced the United States and its ways, Americans have been smitten. So Americans admired and committed themselves to Sun Yat-sen, Chiang Kai-shek, the Soong family, the Flying Tigers, the YMCA and YWCA in China, Christian schools, the stoic dignity of enduring peasants, and, in a later era, ping-pong diplomacy and the modernizer Deng Xiaoping.

But when China refused to be as Americans imagined it, or worse, rejected America, the United States responded with the combination of fury and hurt reserved for heretics. Whether Taiping rebels, Boxers, "Red" Chinese, "human wave" assaults in Korea, or the gray old men who crushed the young demonstrators in Tiananmen Square, America could not understand why these Chinese would not be like the United States or would even attack it. So the pendulum of attitudes would swing, from embrace to rejection and back again. Meanwhile, the Chinese, who for centuries viewed themselves as living in the

"Middle Kingdom", a place above the rest of the earth if still short of heaven, must have had a terrible time figuring out the all-too-earthy Americans.

Thucydides, Napoleon, and the Realists

There is another view of China—that of the realist. Realists have been concerned with China's power, not its soul. They trace their perspective to Thucydides, the great historian of the Peloponnesian War. Thucydides wrote that the war among the great city-states of his day was the inevitable result of the growth of Athens' power, and of the fear it inspired in Sparta. Centuries later, another student and practitioner of power, Napoleon, noted that China was a sleeping giant, and that the world would quake when it awoke.

During the Second World War, the United States hoped to arm and train huge Chinese armies to help fight the Japanese invaders; regardless of the ideologies of Chinese Nationalists or Communists, these realists concluded that America's interest would be served by a unified Chinese effort against imperial Japan. After 1949, when the Communists established control over mainland China, some American realists recognized that China posed a new force with which the United States must reckon. This power appeared allied with the Soviet Union by reason of a shared ideology, and the Korean War then led to a bloody encounter with this Chinese enemy. But President Eisenhower and General Omar Bradley sought to avoid an expanded ground war with China because of the priority they placed on defending Europe from the Soviet Union. According to General Bradley, a military contest on the Asian mainland would be "the wrong war, at the wrong place, at the wrong time, and with the wrong enemy."[i] This assessment of ends and means prevailed.

It took President Nixon and Secretary of State Kissinger, however, to recognize that China's power might be balanced against that of the Soviet Union. Ignoring America's fundamental differences with China's political system, Nixon and Kissinger applied the realist's dictum: The enemy of my enemy is my friend. The strategic rapprochement between the United States and China that began in 1971 was based on a common interest in countering the power of the Soviet Union.

Over the past ten years, however, the Soviet Union's collapse and China's amazing economic development have presented a new challenge for realists. China is no longer a "card" to be played in a global game against the Soviets. In a sense, the "card" has become the new game. Napoleon's prophecy is coming true: China is now stirring, shaking established foundations for policies in Asia and the world.

In some respects, China today is analogous to Germany at the end of the last century. As rising regional powers with potentially global influence, Germany then and China now are characterized by a mixture of arrogance and insecurity. Germany expected, and China expects, to be taken seriously. The challenge, now as then, is to demonstrate to the rising power that it will benefit from integration within regional and global systems, but also that it must accept the rules of those systems or face negative consequences. The failure to deal effectively with Germany's rise led to seventy years of conflict, followed by the forty-five year division of Europe just recently overcome. America needs a strategy toward China that avoids similar mistakes. In the words of Senator Sam Nunn, "History should teach us that established powers must provide consistent and credible signals about their expectations and set forth reasonable terms on which they are willing to incorporate the rising power into the international system."[ii]

It is time to stop the pendulum of policy positions toward China. We need to recognize China for what it is—a huge, complex country, heir to an ancient civilization, in the midst of enormous transformations. At the same time, we need an approach that recognizes America for what it is—and what it stands for. We need the wisdom of realpolitik, wedded to the goals of America's exceptionalist tradition.

Ad Hoc Engagement Isn't Enough

As the Clinton administration struggled to rework its policy toward China, it turned to the label "engagement" to describe its strategy. Engagement points in the right direction, but it is not enough. Indeed, ad hoc engagement between the United States and China, without an integrated strategy to manage the inevitable problems, is likely to lead to a short-term and short-sighted policy of merely coping with crises, which will lead to increased political friction in both countries.

Consider, for example, the prospects for economic engagement. China's ongoing transformations are likely to create problems in the Sino-American economic relationship. China still lacks an effective system to protect property rights. It must deal with the problems of reforming a large state-owned sector. Because its macroeconomic policy instruments are only now being developed, China has lurched through stop-go growth cycles, with concomitant surges of inflation. Given its Mandarin heritage, the Chinese state also remains far too willing to interfere by changing the rules (even retroactively) if it does not like a result.

Even absent these problems, China's very size would make it a challenging economic partner. When the Chinese economic elephant changes course, those in the way may easily get trampled. For example, China is already the world's largest importer of sugar and cooking oil, and before long it could become the biggest importer of wheat, corn, barley, and cotton. Governmental actions, or even market disruptions, affecting these imports could throw global markets into turmoil. Similarly, imagine the ramifications of a Mexico-style financial crisis in China, or a breakdown in Hong Kong that triggers capital flight.

The point of citing these possibilities is not to denigrate China's amazing movement toward market economics, its astounding record of growth, or its positive potential. Indeed, the United States can benefit significantly from trade and investment with China. Much of China's import demand is a good match for sectors in which the United States has a comparative advantage—such as capital goods, machinery and equipment, chemicals, and aircraft. China's exports to the United States, in turn, enable the United States to pay less for products—such as light manufactures, toys, footwear, and apparel—that in significant part it would import from other third countries.[iii] In addition, the economic reform process is likely to increase pressure to develop the rule of law in China, expand the scope of private sector activity, and enhance freedoms associated with both those developments.

Nevertheless, ad hoc economic engagement, in the context of China's difficult adjustment process, is likely to trigger a host of highly specific complaints from U.S. interests, and, as usual, the "squeaky wheels" will get the most attention. The standard U.S. government response, absent an integrating strategy, will be to make narrow case-by-case demands through bilateral channels. This combination is likely to lead to a series of public, acrimonious disputes in one-on-one face-offs, leaving all parties frustrated and angry. Ongoing conflicts could have larger consequences: If two of the largest economies fail to get along, the effects are likely to be damaging both to one another and to the rest of the world.

The United States and China face similar risks in the area of security. China can influence security issues as diverse as the proliferation of weapons of mass destruction and missiles, North Korea, regional security arrangements, territorial disputes over land and sea in Asia, the effective working of the UN Security Council, Mideast conflicts and peace processes, and global climate change—to name just a few topics. But a policy of security engagement is likely to produce conflict if it just takes the form of a long laundry list of actions the United States would like China to take.

A Strategic Approach

The United States needs a strategy for engagement that will integrate China within regional and global security, economic, and political systems. This strategy should have two elements at its core. First, the United States, China, and others need to maintain a stable security context in the Asia-Pacific so that states do not resort to armed conflict or threats of force to resolve disputes with peaceful countries. Second, the United States and others need to demonstrate to China the mutual advantages that flow from full participation in world market arrangements. In effect, the security objective is to maintain the peaceful balance that has been a prerequisite for achieving dynamic economic growth, which in turn can strengthen the development of common interests, broaden networks of private ties, and promote a civil society premised on basic rules of behavior. Over time, the economic connections may create political and private ties that establish a basis for moving beyond a security balance toward cooperation and partnership. In the meantime, however, the balance in security relations meets everyone's baseline interests.

To reach an understanding with China on the nature of security and stability in the Asia Pacific, the United States needs discussions with China that differ from the interactions of recent years. The United States should initiate this dialogue by explaining its security interests and strategy in the region and by inviting China to do likewise. More specifically, the United States should explain its interest in avoiding the domination of East Asia by any power or group of powers hostile to the United States. We also want to preserve the freedom of maritime and air transit across, around, and beyond the Pacific.

The United States should explain to China that it has entered into defensive treaty obligations with Japan, South Korea, the Philippines, Thailand, and Australia to support this interest in stability, not to pursue aggressive ends. To be able to carry out its obligations as a Pacific power, the United States has maintained a naval and military presence in the region for almost a century. Over time, China may expect the United States to seek to increase the mutual commitment of, and to share the responsibilities with, allies and other friendly states. America welcomes efforts by other Pacific nations, such as the ASEAN (Association of Southeast Asian Nations) Regional Forum, to encourage cooperation, reduce suspicions, and resolve disputes.

The United States should point out to China that U.S. commitments to Japan are designed to assure Japan that its security is linked to that of the United States. The U.S.-Japan alliance precludes a need for Japan to develop a unilateral approach to its security. The United States expects to work closely with Japan as that country increases its contribution to the security system from which it benefits.

The United States should reiterate to China that U.S. security arrangements with the Republic of Korea have been, and remain, defensive. One of America's current challenges is to promote cooperative relations between the Republic of Korea and Japan, China, and Russia, so that if there should be a crisis in North-South relations, the international context would be conducive to a constructive response.

China's interests should not be threatened by this security strategy. A flexible policy of balancing provides the conditions for cooperation; it is vastly different from a rigid effort at containment, which would not succeed. Indeed, as China concentrates on its internal development, it should welcome regional stability and the avoidance of contests for dominance.

The prerequisite for China, however, will be a continuation of the American "one China" policy. China's fundamental interest is its territorial integrity, including Taiwan, Tibet, and Hong Kong. The United States should reassure China on this key point, as long as China acts peacefully. With Taiwan in particular, the United States will meet its obligations and will want to continue peaceful economic and private ties. These contacts are not a threat to China, and in fact provide an assurance that enables China and Taiwan to pursue a closer relationship.

The United States should also address its concern about the proliferation of weapons of mass destruction, especially to countries threatening their neighbors. To the degree the United States can demonstrate multilateral support for its proliferation policies, China is more likely to be receptive, as it has been with the nuclear test ban treaty. Where the United States is compelled to act alone, it should brief China privately as to why it is doing so. The habit of serious consultation will minimize the likelihood of Chinese miscalculations about American purposes. A pattern of serious, high-level security discussions also grants China the respect it believes it deserves. By paying attention to China, the United States will be better positioned to indicate to it which security matters are especially important and which Chinese actions will trigger a strong American response.

This strategy for security engagement with China depends principally on bilateral contacts, although it has multilateral dimensions. It should be complemented by a strategy for economic engagement that relies principally on multilateral diplomacy, supported by certain bilateral actions. The United States should work with Europe, Japan, and others in the Asia Pacific to bring China and Taiwan into the institutions and regimes of the international market economy. We want China to accept the rules. We want China to perceive that adherence to norms of behavior will benefit it as well as others. And we want China to recognize that these requirements are not a form of American political *diktat*, but rather are the principles of a system designed for mutual advantage.

China's acceptance of these rules and norms will also shape its internal development, including the advancement of the rule of law. By linking self-interest to certain policies, the United States and others might strengthen the arguments of China's reformers. China's membership in the International Monetary Fund, the World Bank, and the Asian Development Bank has already helped it to move toward a market economy. Opening up the world to more of the Chinese people will have the effect of enabling more Chinese to see the advantages of liberty and tolerance.

At the same time, the terms of China's entrance into the international economic system need to recognize China's protracted transition. As Americans have learned through bilateral agreements with China on market access and intellectual property, the United States will be best able to affect long-term policies there by working with China to accept both core principles and an ongoing system to apply those principles. The targets of attention will evolve as its economy adapts, as we learn more about impediments to trade, and as it develops internal constituencies with interests in the application of the principles. Given this ongoing process, it would be prudent to have terms of accession to international organizations that reasonably phase in China's participation and benefits. In effect, the United States and others in the world need a series of mutually beneficial "executory contracts" with China, so that all sides have interests in performance, adaptation, and the custom of working out responses to the inevitable bumps in the road.

China and G-7 Summits

The United States can draw together the security, economic, and political dimensions of its strategy by promoting China's phased membership in the G-7 summit process. This overture would signal America's strong commitment to integrating China into the global system as long as it accepts international economic and security norms. China would welcome the acknowledgment of its genuine accomplishment and status, especially since Russia has already had a special seat at the summit tables.

Indeed, China's participation with the G-7 might strengthen the hand of the reforming modernizers who want to ease it into a cooperative relationship with the rest of the world. In contrast, the recent pattern of conflicts has played to the advantage of Chinese leaders who are stirring the pot of fiery nationalism as substitute fare for the legitimacy that communism no longer offers. These leaders assume that China can set its own rules, or at least play a good game of global power politics by manipulating the interests of others against U.S. demands. China's gradual introduction to the G-7 might be employed both to convince the Chinese that World Trade Organization (WTO) membership really does require a commitment to meet basic trading system standards, and to maneuver Europe and Japan into a unified presentation on WTO requirements. If the United States, Europe, and Japan sit down together with China regularly, the democratic threesome is more likely to develop a united position and stick to it.

The nature of China's relationship with the G-7 would depend on its degree of cooperation and commitment. For example, initially it might participate with Russia in the political discussions by heads of governments. Once China and the WTO worked out terms of accession, it might also participate in the economic discussions at the summits. As it approaches world financial and trade standards, it might take part in the more extensive G-7 finance ministers' process.

Adding China would also have the benefit of making the G-7 less of a Eurocentric gathering. Not surprisingly, the presence of Germany, Great Britain, France, Italy, and the European Commission at summit meetings leads to a European bias in a group that is supposed to be examining world economic—and frequently political—problems. China's participation might prod Europeans to broaden their outlook and weigh the implications of their actions—or inaction—for regions outside their continent.

China, Taiwan, and the WTO

The United States also should adjust its approach toward the accession of China and Taiwan to the WTO to fit this overall strategy. All parties would benefit from China's accession to the WTO if the parties could determine acceptable "executory" terms. Unfortunately, it appears that the United States has unintentionally transformed WTO accession into a bilateral Sino-American conflict. Moreover, the tension has been exacerbated by trading partners who have emphasized their support for China's early accession, instead of focusing on the standards that China needs to meet. Even Chinese economic reformers now maintain that WTO accession is a "political", not an economic, question. They believe that the United States alone is keeping China out of the organization in order to secure political leverage or to punish China. These misconceptions have created dangerous possibilities for miscalculations on all sides, as well as for widening fault lines among current WTO members.

Working with the WTO's leadership, the United States should reach agreement with the European Union, Japan, other North Americans, and ASEAN and other APEC (Asia Pacific Economic Cooperation) members on a core set of principles that China must accept in order to accede to the WTO. These might include, for example, transparency of the trade regime, uniform nondiscriminatory application of trade rules, national treatment (applying the same rules to both foreigners and nationals), the minimum international protections for investment, reasonable opportunities for market access, adequate and effective protection of all forms of intellectual property, and use of dispute resolution mechanisms. If China accepts such a core set of principles, the WTO can be more flexible in phasing in China's obligations. In the meantime, the WTO would need to have processes in place to work with China to identify and address problems of implementation. The WTO might maintain certain provisions that have been used with non-market economies, which could be phased out as China's reforms enabled it to adhere effectively to the principles.

The United States should not let itself become the sole advocate of this accession regime. On the contrary, we should be the catalyst for organizing ongoing common efforts. American diplomacy should make clear to allies and partners that this effort has significant strategic implications, and that therefore the United States values and expects cooperation.

This effort should also seek to bring Taiwan into the WTO as a developed economy. There is ample precedent for membership in economic groups by both China and Taiwan as "an economy." Both belong to the Asian Development Bank. In 1991, with U.S. help, Korea managed to negotiate the APEC membership of China, Taiwan, and Hong Kong. Obviously, this effort can succeed only if the United States assures Beijing that it is not seeking to dismantle China and that it stands behind the commitments of the three communiqués and the Taiwan Relations Act. Again, the United States would be wiser to pursue this approach to China and Taiwan in concert with others, and on a systematic rather than episodic basis.

APEC and ASEAN

The APEC group, first convened in 1989, is a fledgling body that is still developing cohesion and a sense of purpose. Nevertheless, it offers another forum for the United States and its economic partners to engage China on the benefits and responsibilities of integration in international economic systems. As a promoter of "open regionalism", APEC should encourage China to develop internal and external reforms in a multilateral context. APEC's message should reinforce other communications about the WTO accession process. And until China joins the WTO, APEC could serve as the primary vehicle for introducing China to the norms of the multilateral market economy.

The United States will need to work, preferably discreetly, with the other APEC nations to persuade them to take on these tasks. Most APEC nations are looking to accommodate China, which they perceive as the rising power in the region. But many Asians also recognize the strategic importance of persuading China to accept security and economic rules. Moreover, these nations would like the United States to remain as the "balancing wheel" in the Pacific, and at least some could be persuaded that the integrationist approach outlined here serves mutual purposes—especially in contrast to the recent pattern of Sino-American conflict.

ASEAN's Regional Forum (ARF), recently initiated by ASEAN to discuss security issues with other nations in the region, offers a means of engaging China on collective security topics. This approach can be useful for the United States in three respects.

First, the discussions can communicate to China the benefits of abiding by the core security norms that underpin the U.S. strategy of engagement in the region; alternatively, China may see firsthand that aggressive actions are likely to generate group condemnation and perhaps even opposition. Second, ARF may usefully press others in the region to recognize that security, including that involving China, is a mutual responsibility—necessitating their contributions as well as that of the United States. Over time, for example, the United States may persuade ASEAN and others in ARF to address the dangers of proliferation, creating a regional multilateral context that could encourage China's cooperation as a member. Third, ARF offers a vehicle for gradually involving Japan in security questions to a greater degree and in an open fashion.

Bilateral Battles

Instead of catalyzing multilateral efforts to draw China into international economic groups, the United States has drifted into a campaign of bilateral battles. The United States is bearing alone the burden of contentious disputes with China, even though the issues are of interest to many countries. Even when America's leverage is great, this approach can be risky and counterproductive because China's leadership, jostling in the succession struggle, is vulnerable to nationalistic pressure against yielding to American demands. What is worse, if the United States makes threats it is unwilling to carry out, China will sense weakness and be emboldened to confront America.

In 1993-94, the linkage of most favored nation (MFN) status to human rights improvements fell into this trap, and the administration then had to crawl out. The United States has now granted annual extensions of MFN in 1995 and 1996. The president and Congress should reconsider whether this annual excoriation continues to serve U.S. interests. Despite the appellation "most favored nation", this status is in fact not a favor at all; it is the baseline trade relationship accorded to virtually all countries. A debate each year on whether to terminate this status certainly does not accord with a long-term strategy of engagement with China. It draws America away from the more promising multilateral approach, and the reality is that even when the United States has objections to some of China's policies, it is highly unlikely to terminate MFN status. Moreover, the Jackson-Vanik Amendment on which this exercise is based only requires presidential certification that a non-market economy is not impeding emigration. (Deng Xiaoping once offered to permit ten million Chinese to emigrate to the United States in order to prove the absence of restrictions.) In sum, as a practical matter the annual MFN exercise produces ineffective criticism of China and serves as a stark reminder that the United States is not willing to take the extreme step of ending MFN to address its concerns.

If the U.S. government wants to end this diversionary exercise, there are several options available. First, the president could certify that China does not restrict emigration. Second, the president could certify China as a market economy, perhaps as part of the phase-in process with the WTO. Third, Congress could change or repeal the Jackson-Vanik Amendment, recognizing that while it played an honorable role during the Cold War, that conflict is now over and the old formulation no longer suits our interests.

There are, however, forms of bilateral engagement with China that could help the United States achieve its goals. The U.S.-China Joint Economic Committee, chaired by the Treasury Department, could play a more active role in providing technical assistance for China's reforms. In the past, this committee has stressed mutual interests in China's integration into the world economy. It has helped reformers learn from international experience, stimulated constituencies for reform, and identified impediments within China in a non-adversarial context.

Many Chinese recognize that the establishment of the effective rule of law is in their economic interest. This is the field Americans should cultivate in order to plant and nourish the seeds of economic and political liberalization. In doing so, the United States must clarify, by words and deeds, that legal developments should be in our mutual interest, and not interpreted solely as a Western imposition.

America's bilateral actions in other areas—intellectual property rights, market access, human rights, prison labor exports, corruption, and exchange-rate practices—are likely to be more successful if they are designed to accord with the strategy outlined here:

- Seek to develop an international coalition to promote international standards.
- Stress China's self-interest in adhering to the rules.
- Find and help develop internal constituencies.
- Learn how the issues are handled within China (including within different provinces) so as to tailor solutions to specific problems.

And while pursuing these approaches, continually stress to Chinese officials that their credibility is also an asset that China should value. China must keep its word and abide by agreements it has made.

Facing Facts

In considering the future course of Sino-American relations, we should keep in mind the distance already traveled. China has moved far toward developing a market economy, although this particular "long march" still has many mountains to climb.[iv] As capitalism has spread through China, living conditions have improved for hundreds of millions of people. The Chinese enjoy more freedom, choice, and opportunity to learn about the world than they did when the United States re-established ties with China a quarter century ago.

The United States should also acknowledge the effect of its own changeable role over time. As the pendulum of policies toward China has swung toward, away, and now again toward China, Americans need to learn from their experience. The United States should recognize China for what it is, not what Americans imagine it to be.

The China of today is rushing toward economic development while its government struggles to reconcile momentous tensions: between Beijing and the provinces; mainland China and Hong Kong and Taiwan; urban and rural citizens; private and state-owned enterprises; decayed political legitimacy and an increasingly pluralistic public; and different generations looking to a new era of leadership. China's leaders are highly sensitive to the risk that these tensions could spin out of control, because they have witnessed—and many have suffered through—times of turmoil. They also resent China's past humiliation—and territorial dismemberment—when it was weak. It is particularly important to recognize this history and present reality if the United States is to pursue its interests effectively. Most important, the United States needs a long-term strategy—and outlook—appropriate for dealing with a China that will be in a condition of flux for decades, not just years.

The pursuit of a realistic policy toward China can and should also include the promotion of principles that are based on America's special national identity. The advancement of these principles will be most effective if the United States faces facts, instead of proceeding in terms of romanticized images of China that mirror American images. The United States will accomplish more if it employs the power and attractiveness of its capitalist economy and free market ideas in order to integrate China into regional and global groups—groups that have already helped extend core U.S. principles.

The recent failure of communism in Eastern Europe and the Soviet Union itself is a reminder of the tremendous force of the political and economic freedom that America represents. Yet the effectiveness of that force as an agent of change in the rest of the world is not automatic and guaranteed. The United States must be smart as well as confident and proud. America must employ its advantages and influence to shape the future it wishes to achieve.

NOTES

[i] U.S. Senate Committee on Armed Services and Committee on Foreign Relations, hearings on the military situation in the Far East (Washington, DC: U.S. Government Printing Office, 1951), pt. 2, p. 732.

[ii] Senator Sam Nunn, "The Relationship Between the United States and China", speech to the floor of the U.S. Senate, Feb. 23, 1996, p. 1.

[iii] Marcus Noland, "U.S.-China Economic Relations", Institute for International Economics, working paper on Asia Pacific Economic Cooperation, pp. 3, 7, 16-19.

[iv] See Henry Rowen's "The Short March: China's Road to Democracy", *The National Interest* (Fall 1996).

5

Why Our Hardliners Are Wrong

*Robert S. Ross**

Critics of U.S. China policy have been enjoying unprecedented attention lately. Between those who want to get tough with China and those who want to be more accommodating, the Clinton administration's second-term project to consolidate and expand cooperative Sino-U.S. relations has been vastly complicated. Advocates of nearly every stripe have had a hand in distorting China's impact on American interests and Washington's policy record since the late 1980s, which, despite its bad press, has had important successes. Character assassination has been so rampant and policy critiques so politicized that the normal rules of evidence used to evaluate a serious, complicated set of policy choices have been among the first casualties. Lost, too, in many cases, has been any sense of the geopolitics of the problem—that cool-headed assessment of capabilities and motives that ought to be our first task, not an emotionally exhausted afterthought.

Particularly egregious have been many of the claims of those neo-cold warriors in their efforts to persuade Americans to abandon engagement and follow a policy of "containing" the "China threat." As an example of the hostile hyperbole that has become quite common, consider this statement of June 9 from the Washington-based William J. Casey Institute of the Center for Security Policy: "The nature of the threat posed by China is in key respects of a greater magnitude

---

* Robert S. Ross is professor of political science at Boston College and research associate at the John King Fairbank Center for East Asian Research at Harvard University. He is co-author of *The Great Wall and the Empty Fortress: China's Search for Security* (W.W. Norton, 1997).

This essay first appeared in *The National Interest*, No. 49 (Fall 1997).

and vastly greater complexity than that mounted by the Soviet Union at the height of the Cold War." It is a rousing statement, to be sure, but by no reasonable or objective measure is it even remotely true.

If we step back and evaluate the issues fairly, two truths come clear: China is not a "rogue state", and U.S. policy has made important gains in affecting Chinese behavior over a wide range of issues bearing on important American interests. Both points may be demonstrated by looking at military and economic dimensions of the bilateral relationship, as well as at the heated debate over China's human rights practices.

Security Conflicts and Accommodations

The most serious Chinese challenge to the United States is its potential military power. The Chinese economy is growing and Beijing's ability to increase defense spending is growing with it. But advocates of containing China vastly overestimate Chinese power and underestimate our own.

A larger Chinese economy will not necessarily lead to greater military power. China can import weaponry, but sustained improvement in military capabilities will require indigenous defense modernization. China still cannot manufacture a reliable 1970s-generation fighter plane, much less anything like a U.S. F-16. The need of the People's Liberation Army to import Russian equipment is telling. Buying from Russia is a quick and relatively inexpensive way for China to equip its forces with materiel far superior to indigenous products. But this should not be particularly upsetting to U.S. planners, whose forte is the destruction of Soviet equipment with remarkable speed and skill. Moreover, China lacks the basic ability to maintain Russian equipment. It now requires extensive Russian assistance to repair many of its recently acquired SU-27s and its Kilo submarines.

China has developed a limited number of more modern destroyers, but it is decades away from being able to manufacture and deploy a first-generation, limited capability aircraft carrier. The PLA lacks the ability to conduct sustained military operations more than 100 miles from the Chinese shoreline. China is a formidable land power, but in maritime Southeast Asia, where U.S. interests are most at stake, China is militarily inferior even to such countries as Singapore and Malaysia.

In the end, China may succeed in modernizing its military. But it may fail, too—economic and technological modernization is a precarious enterprise. As an export processing zone for the advanced industrial countries, China has succeeded in raising living standards and its GNP, but this is a far cry from developing the economic and technological capabilities to field a twenty-first century military force.

U.S. military supremacy is so overwhelming that Washington has the luxury of being able to observe Chinese technology development and weapons production before adopting countervailing policies. As Secretary of Defense

William Cohen recently observed, Washington has global superiority in every phase of warfare, and while China is trying to catch up, the United States is not standing still. Not only is the U.S. defense budget greater than the combined defense budgets of the next six largest competitors, but U.S. technology and weapons modernization are advancing so rapidly that, in all probability, with each passing day and despite its strenuous efforts, China's technological and military capabilities are losing ground rather than catching up with those of the United States.

Politically, too, the American alliance system in Asia is superior to anything the Chinese can hope to have. Logistically, the U.S. alliance with Japan and its access to basing facilities throughout the region give the United States an enormous advantage. Diplomatically, China is increasingly viewed in the region as a problem to be managed, while the United States is seen as a relatively disinterested power-broker whose aims are compatible with regional peace and prosperity for all. A potential Chinese alliance with Burma can hardly offset the U.S. relationship with Japan, South Korea, Australia, and the maritime states of Southeast Asia (including, still, the Philippines). With such logistical and diplomatic superiority to bring to bear, current U.S. defense spending and weapons acquisitions are already more than sufficient to hedge against China's potential development of advanced military capabilities.

It is true, nevertheless, that despite China's limited military capabilities the PLA can use force effectively and is not shy to do so. The PLA has been part of every major crisis in East Asia since 1949. It has the ability to disrupt regional stability and inflict considerable costs on U.S. interests. Clearly, the most serious security conflict in U.S.-China relations remains the Taiwan issue, and it is in principle unresolvable. Beijing wants unification under PRC rule and reserves the right to use force to bring it about. The United States insists on Taiwan's right to make its choices free from military pressure.

Even if the Taiwan issue is intractable in principle, it can be managed so that U.S.-China conflicts of interest do not disrupt cooperative relations; this has clearly been the U.S. experience from the early 1970s to the early 1990s. U.S. policy has guaranteed Taiwan's security and, as important, has provided an environment in which Taiwan developed a prosperous economy and a flourishing democracy. These successes form the bedrock of Taiwan's diplomatic autonomy, and the only concession Washington had to make to help Taiwan achieve them was to refrain from actions that could be interpreted as support for formal Taiwanese independence.

Equally important, Washington's multifaceted assistance to Taiwan did not make improved relations with China impossible. Diplomatically, what seemed a zero-sum game between Taiwan and the mainland turned out not to be zero-sum at all for American policy. The main reason for this was China's strong desire to cooperate with the United States against the Soviet Union, but it was not the only reason. Mutually beneficial economic relations and cooperation in maintaining regional stability on a wide range of issues were also important, and they remain so despite the fact that the Soviet Union is no longer there as a common enemy. Indeed, a good deal less has changed than is often assumed. China today no less than before wants to avoid heightened U.S.-China adversarial relations, much less a literal fight with the United States over Taiwan. That being so, Washington can continue to protect Taiwan's most vital interests—security from mainland power and continued economic and political development—and avoid great power conflict and escalation of regional tension by employing more or less the same Taiwan policy that has worked well over the past twenty-five years. The United States can fulfill its moral obligations to Taiwan and assure its "realist" objectives toward both Taiwan and the mainland without having to do either more against the mainland or less in favor of Taiwan.

Chinese weapons exports have drawn much attention from critics of U.S. China policy. It has now become common knowledge that, as Gary Bauer pronounced recently in the *Wall Street Journal* (June 26), "The Chinese have treated pariah states such as Iran and Iraq as their 'most favored nation' trading partners. They have been doing a land-office business in chemical weapons, including poison gas, and nuclear materials." It is true that Chinese commercial enterprises have exported chemical weapons materiel. But it is also true that its weapons proliferation policy is in substantive compliance with all international arms control agreements.

Since the end of the Cold War, and with the partial exception of its strategic relationship with Pakistan, China has not exported a single missile, transferred any nuclear technology, or engaged in proliferation of chemical weapons raw materials in violation of any international arms control regime. Contrary to several reports, China has not exported the M-9 missile to Syria. Its missile exports to the Middle East have consisted solely of short-range missiles that are not covered by the Missile Technology Control Regime (MTCR). Its cooperation with Algeria in nuclear energy, which dates back to the mid-1980s, has been under the continuous inspection of the International Atomic Energy Agency. In 1995 Beijing canceled its nuclear energy project with Iran. Its 1996 ring magnet transfer to Pakistan did not violate the Nuclear Non-Proliferation Treaty (NPT). China's policy on chemical weapons proliferation has been equally compliant. Although in May 1997 Congress imposed sanctions on Chinese firms for exporting chemical weapons materiel to Iran, these exports did not violate the Chemical Weapons Convention.

China's most serious proliferation activities have been its nuclear assistance to Pakistan in the 1980s and its missile transfers to Pakistan in the 1990s. But just as post-Cold War U.S. weapons and technology transfers to Britain and Japan reveal that Washington engages in nuclear and missile proliferation when it suits its interests, Chinese transfers to Pakistan reflect its security interests. In some respects China's Pakistan policy may fairly be compared to American indulgence toward Israel's nuclear weapons. While the United States was never the principal supplier of Israeli nuclear technology or know-how, Washington and Beijing both prefer that their respective allies be able to deter attacks from more powerful adversaries on their own. It is safer that way, and avoids complicating their own relations with other countries. Just as Washington does not want its support for Israel needlessly to jeopardize its relations with Arab countries, Beijing does not want its support for Pakistan to derail its efforts to improve relations with India.

This is not to equate Pakistan with Israel, Japan, and Britain, which have well deserved reputations for prudence. No moral equivalency is intended or required. But the United States should avoid the conceit that a given mode of behavior can be wrong for every country in the world but still right for the United States because of the purity of its motives. Obviously, when other countries develop similar policies to pursue similar objectives, interest rather than morality is the appropriate standard of judgment. Washington does not turn an occasional deaf ear toward proliferation because it believes that proliferation is morally good, but because there are occasions when it is a necessary and a lesser evil. There is no reason to assume that China's motives in its relations with Pakistan turn on a different sort of reasoning—and every reason to think, by the way, that had the United States acted as a truer ally to Pakistan, much of what China provides that country would have been rendered unnecessary.

Overall, Chinese policy has supported the development of the global non-proliferation order. China has progressively joined international arms control agreements. In 1992 it formally joined the NPT. In 1996, despite the implications for its unreliable nuclear deterrent and grumbling from the PLA, Beijing signed the Comprehensive Test Ban Treaty. Over PLA objections, it has also signed and ratified the Chemical Weapons Convention, and agreed to the Land Mine Protocol to the Convention on Inhumane Weaponry. Recently, Chinese leaders have expressed interest in joining the Zangger Group, the export control arm of the NPT. Chinese participation in these regimes reflects American success at pressuring Beijing to accept global responsibility for controlling proliferation, even at a cost to China's own interests.

There are important arms control regimes from which China is shut out, including the MTCR and the Wassenaar Group, which oversees conventional weapons exports. It is America that has blocked Chinese participation. Chinese absence from the MTCR is most troubling. Washington can have but limited confidence that Beijing will refrain from missile proliferation when it was party neither to the original negotiations nor to subsequent adjustments to the MTCR. Even in these circumstances, Chinese exports to Pakistan stand as its only violation of the MTCR, and these—particularly the 1992 transfer of M-11 missiles—were only made in direct retaliation for the U.S. sale of 150 F-16s to Taiwan, itself an unambiguous violation of the August 1982 U.S.-China communiqué. As in any bilateral relationship, contemporary or historical, China is inclined to retaliate when American violations of U.S.-China agreements undermine its interests. This is not roguish but realist.

In the non-nuclear realm, the United States does not oppose proliferation of missiles because they are "weapons of mass destruction", but because they are the only delivery system against which the United States has no defense. But for most countries, U.S. F-16s, which Washington sells freely, are more threatening and more destructive than a Chinese m-11 missile. It is not at all clear that U.S. arms exports are any less "destabilizing" than Chinese exports.

Obviously, Chinese exports of weapons not covered by arms control regimes could undermine U.S. interests. But thus far the impact has been minimal. Exports of low technology short-range cruise missiles and chemical weapons precursors to Iran do not enhance Iran's ability to contend with the U.S. Navy or Air Force as much as they undermine American diplomatic efforts to enforce dual containment. But here China's record is not much different from that of many other countries, including several U.S. allies. The most flagrant challenge to Washington's dual containment policy with respect to Iraq comes not from China but from France, Turkey, and Russia, all of whom have strained to lighten the sanctions regime for financial reasons. Meanwhile, Japan and the members of the European Union trade with Iran as they do with any other country, and greatly resent U.S. efforts to stop them from doing so. German dual-use technology exports to Iran continue unchecked. This commerce is more important to Tehran than anything that China provides.

China's record is far from perfect when it comes to arms dealing, but it is not the flagrant violator it is often represented as being. Its more controversial exports reflect legitimate security interests rather than predatory political or opportunistic commercial interests. Moreover, some Chinese violations reflect not central government policy but rather Beijing's limited control over economic enterprises and its inability to establish an effective export control regime. Political and economic decentralization best explain the 1996 Chinese export to Pakistan of ring magnets and the export to Iran of chemical weapons materiel. In these circumstances, the appropriate response is not to carry out "feel-good diplomacy" and sanction Beijing for policies it does not control, thus increasing tension without hope of practical benefit, but to assist its effort to develop a more effective regulatory system. Indeed, Washington's restrained response to the export of ring magnets to Pakistan reflected such a sober analysis; this did not, of course, prevent it from being savaged in much op-ed commentary.

With specific reference to the Middle East, the most sensitive area in which Chinese behavior has been criticized, China has for the most part respected U.S. interests, and it has not done so without cost to itself. China has no inherent reason to refrain from proliferation to regions outside East Asia; since such countries cannot harm China directly, it might simply have allowed economic interests to drive its export policy. Instead, China has accommodated U.S. policy because both the Bush and Clinton administrations have effectively combined coercive threats with constructive diplomacy. Since China's first missile exports to the Middle East in 1988, the systematic application of limited and well targeted sanctions has persuaded Chinese leaders that Washington pays close attention to these PRC exports, and that exports that violate international regimes or harm U.S. interests risk disrupting U.S.-China cooperation. At the same time, the continuation of engagement in other areas has worked to convince Chinese leaders that cooperation with the United States is still feasible and worthwhile. The net result is that U.S. policy has compelled Beijing to comply with international arms control regimes and cooperate with U.S. interests more generally than might have been expected.

Economic Conflicts and Costs

The most important economic conflicts between the United States and China concern Chinese piracy of intellectual property rights (IPR), the large and growing U.S. trade deficit with China, the terms for Chinese admission to the World Trade Organization (WTO), and prison-labor exports. But as is the case concerning security conflicts, the attention given to Chinese economic policy is disproportionate to its impact on U.S. interests. Similarly, criticism of U.S. trade policy fails to acknowledge American success in bringing China's behavior into greater compliance with those interests.

Chinese IPR piracy has been the focus of periodic U.S.-China tensions. Seeking Chinese cooperation in reducing financial losses to U.S. entertainment and software industries, Washington has threatened economic sanctions if China does not change its domestic policies. But while Chinese piracy of IPR is certainly a problem, the extent of losses both in absolute and comparative terms is much exaggerated. The widely used figure of $2 billion is an industry estimate premised on an inelastic demand curve. That is, estimates of losses are calculated on the basis of the profits that would have been earned if the hypothetical quantity of licensed sales were to equal actual pirated sales. Obviously, this is very unrealistic; no one expects fully above-board retailers to sell the same number of products at seven or ten times the black market price. The actual profits from licensed sales would have been but a small fraction of $2 billion. U.S. financial losses are not irrelevant, and it is true that a matter of principle is involved, but these losses are negligible given the scale on which Hollywood and the American computer software industry operate.

Equally important, critics fail to apply a comparative perspective on Chinese IPR piracy. Piracy is a worldwide phenomenon and no country is fully effective at stopping it. Indeed, industry groups have targeted not China but Greece, Paraguay, and Russia as priority countries for U.S. IPR policy. Nor is China among the eleven countries that these groups have recommended be placed on the special 301 "priority watch list." According to industry estimates, losses to U.S. firms from piracy in Japan are nearly double those from piracy in China. In absolute terms, the greatest losses to American industries occur in the United States itself. Further, if industry estimates used assumptions based on more realistic elastic demand curves, then estimates of relative losses to Chinese IPR piracy would be even smaller.

Moreover, in contrast to losses from other markets, Chinese enforcement abilities are relatively weak; indeed, IPR piracy in China affects domestic manufacturers on a wide range of name-brand consumer goods, including computer software products, more than it affects U.S. industries. It also harms the legitimacy of the Chinese government. Its inability to prevent the manufacture and sale of inferior imitations of popular name-brand consumer goods has earned it a reputation among its own people for ineffective protection of consumer interests. To a large extent, lax PRC enforcement of intellectual property rights is not by design, but reflects the government's general inability to develop effective regulatory and legal systems.

But despite the chaos in Chinese society, American policy has succeeded in encouraging reforms that meet the interests of U.S. manufacturers. Beijing has fundamentally fulfilled its 1992 agreement with the United States to enact domestic legislation protecting the intellectual property rights of foreign companies. The 1995 U.S.-China agreement on the implementation of Chinese domestic legislation has also scored important successes. Between May 1996 and March 1997, due in part to Chinese government offers of rewards for information, Beijing shut down thirty-seven illegal compact disc factories, and Chinese courts have begun to sentence IPR violators to significant prison terms.

The American trade deficit with China is large and growing, but the relevant policy issue is the impact of the deficit on the U.S. domestic economy. It is, in fact, very small, largely because Chinese exports to the United States primarily consist of goods that American workers no longer make, such as low-cost textiles, shoes, toys, and inexpensive low technology electronic goods. The United States stopped making such things over twenty years ago when Japanese products captured the American market. Subsequently, as Japanese labor costs increased, products from Taiwan, South Korea, and Hong Kong dominated the U.S. market. Now, as labor costs in Taiwan, South Korea, and Hong Kong have increased, Chinese consumer goods are in turn taking their places. Chinese export success has primarily affected the overall trade deficits and labor conditions of Taiwan, South Korea, and Hong Kong, not those of the United States. The proof is in the data: The cumulative U.S. trade deficit with China, Hong Kong, Taiwan, South Korea, and Japan has not appreciably grown since 1988; only the distribution of the U.S. deficit among these markets has changed.

America's response to a trade imbalance should reflect the extent to which that imbalance is the result of a trading partner's conscious policy choices as opposed to other factors. In the case of Japan, Washington confronted this issue in the 1980s and the lesson of that experience should be clear: The U.S. deficit with Japan declined not in response to changing Japanese trade policy, but in response to changes in exchange rates and in the Japanese economy itself. The trade deficit with China also reflects economic conditions. China's national savings rate is far higher than that of the United States, and the Chinese are much poorer per capita than Americans. Thus, the United States can readily import inexpensive Chinese consumer goods, while there is a limited market in China for America's expensive high technology goods. Contrasting economic conditions guarantee that the United States will have a large trade deficit with China regardless of how much pressure the United States applies and how much Chinese trade policy changes. As Henry S. Rowen put the matter in these pages in summer 1997, "The Sino-American bilateral trade balance reflects market behavior far more than official manipulation."

Regardless of the economic causes of trade deficits, it is generally in the American interest to minimize the obstacles to doing business in China, so long as doing so does not obviously prejudice American strategic interests. But American businesses widely agree that despite the corruption that exists there and the fact that its laws and regulations are largely unenforceable, it is already far easier to do business in China than in Japan or South Korea. Thus, in sectors in which the United States has a global comparative advantage—including civilian aircraft, grain export, computers, high technology electronic goods such as cellular telephones, and industrial machinery—it does well in the Chinese market. As in the case of IPR piracy, American attention to the trade deficit is disproportionate to the impact of that deficit on U.S. interests and to the role that U.S. and Chinese government policies can play in affecting it.

Nevertheless, U.S. trade policy has achieved some important successes in improving access to China's market. In response to the threat of punitive tariffs advanced by the Bush administration in 1992, Beijing agreed to make transparent its trade regulations. By 1995 Beijing had substantively complied with this agreement, making it easier for foreign businesses to operate in China. In response to pressure from the Clinton administration, Beijing agreed this year for the first time to liberalize foreign access to its textile market. While these developments will not fundamentally affect the trade balance, they do promote America's objective in expanding market access and promoting fairer U.S.-China trade. They also show that, contrary to established opinion on American op-ed pages, the Chinese are not intrinsically duplicitous; they will implement negotiated agreements to maintain U.S.-China cooperation.

Another important issue concerns China's admission to the WTO. This problem is frequently portrayed as having been made difficult by China's refusal to accept the norms of the international liberal trade order. The Chinese have indeed resisted U.S. proposals, but the conflict is one of interest, not principle. Admission to the WTO is based on individually negotiated agreements reflecting the economic interests of both the applicant and the existing WTO membership. As was the case with Japan, South Korea, Hong Kong, and Singapore at earlier stages of their development, China's leaders seek an agreement that will protect its infant industries from international competition. This is Hamiltonian in character, not Stalinist. But the size of China's market and its potential economic influence require Washington to adopt a more demanding posture toward Chinese protectionism than that which it had earlier adopted toward the protectionism of the smaller Asian economies.

The solution to this conflict is not Chinese isolation from the WTO. At present, China protects its domestic industries and still enjoys many WTO benefits indirectly from the MFN status it receives from the advanced industrial economies. Without U.S. concessions to Chinese interests, China will remain outside the WTO, its protectionist policies will continue to influence the global economy, and it will bear no obligation whatsoever to liberalize those policies. It is in the U.S. interest to create Chinese obligations to liberalize its trade by bringing China into the WTO. This may require a prolonged liberalization schedule as well as granting the PRC permanent MFN status. Such concessions would be politically controversial, but they promote our interests. Not only would they commit China to eventual trade liberalization, but Chinese membership in the WTO would replace often counterproductive unilateral American pressure with more politically acceptable multilateral pressure that could, additionally, reinforce the efforts of pro-reform Chinese politicians.

Toward the end of 1996 the Clinton administration adopted a more flexible policy on China's admission to the WTO. But the flap over campaign finance irregularities and sensitivities over the return of Hong Kong to China raised domestic political temperatures to the point that the risks of compromising with China fell before the less costly path of deferral. It may well be that Beijing will refuse to compromise and seek an agreement that will allow China to "free-ride" indefinitely on the WTO regime, in which case the United States should block Chinese membership. But until the United States is willing to consider serious changes in current policy and negotiate an agreement that takes into account both Chinese and U.S. interests, we will never find out if a mutually acceptable agreement is possible.

The final trade issue concerns Chinese export of goods made by so-called slave labor in Chinese prisons. On this issue, American hypocrisy and obfuscation frame the debate. The issue is not whether there are political prisoners in China. Of course there are. Nor is the issue whether the Chinese government compels its prisoners to work and then exports the goods to gain an unfair trade advantage. It does. But so does the United States. American prisoners are frequently compelled to work, making license plates or clothing, or in chain-gangs doing road construction, and there is no American law prohibiting export of prison-made goods. By U.S. standards, too, the conditions in Chinese prisons are horrendous, but they have to be if Beijing is not to make prisons more comfortable than villages in the impoverished Chinese countryside. Finally, there is no evidence that China has exported to the United States goods made by human rights prisoners.

Human Rights: Not Whether But How

China's human rights violations are numerous and grave. The United States has a moral imperative and a mandate from its people to include human rights diplomacy in its China policy. The issue is not whether to try to change China for the better, but how most effectively to go about it.

The focus of American debate these days is over the wisdom of having normal trade relations with China and conducting regular high level U.S.-China diplomatic exchanges while Chinese leaders imprison political dissidents. Congressional pressure on the White House has tried to hold U.S.-China cooperation hostage to the fate of Chinese dissidents and has thus turned these dissidents into bargaining chips. Chinese leaders care little if a dissident remains in jail or is released to the constant supervision of a hoard of security police. Our making clear to China that the release of dissidents is the quid pro quo for improved U.S.-China relations gives Beijing a vested interest in keeping dissidents in jail until it can secure a payoff for releasing them.

In the past, China released dissidents prior to the congressional MFN vote, and then cracked down on them immediately afterwards. China seemed prepared to release a prominent dissident, Wang Dan, prior to Vice President Gore's 1997 visit to Beijing, but changed its plans when it became clear that releasing dissidents would not at that time achieve any relaxation of America's China policy, which had become hostage to the then-raging campaign finance scandal. It is unseemly and self-indulgent for the United States to reduce China's democracy activists to political pawns in U.S.-China relations and increase their jail time by so doing. Yet that is exactly the effect of current U.S. policy in this sphere.

It is difficult to see how punishing Beijing's imprisonment of dissidents by downgrading political and economic relations will promote political liberalization in China. Should the United States stigmatize China by sanctioning its human rights violations, it will most likely encourage the Chinese leadership to adopt more repressive domestic policies; hostile U.S.-China relations, after all, can only intensify Beijing's concern with subversion and domestic instability. Overt American diplomatic pressure has not encouraged China to loosen its restraints on political speech; and sanctions, while they may make their American sponsors feel better, will only make the situation in China worse.

The harsh criticism of U.S. human rights policies by congressional critics and human rights groups fails—or refuses—to recognize American successes. Part of the problem is one of definition. By limiting the definition of human rights to the freedom of public dissent, human rights activists obscure a wide range of activity that should also be free from government interference. A broader, and better, benchmark is the extent to which people can live their lives free from government harassment and intimidation. By this standard, China has made considerable and rapid progress, for which the United States and its democratic allies can rightly claim significant credit.

As is the case with all one-party authoritarian systems, the Chinese government monitors a wide range of public activity. Within the constraints of one-party rule, however, the Chinese people increasingly enjoy unprecedented access to Western entertainment programs on television, in cinemas, and on stage. The Chinese consumer market is flourishing, with production determined by consumer demand for Western-style clothing, make-up, entertainment magazines, and fast food. The most popular movies are produced in Hollywood, and the most popular pop music comes from Hong Kong, Taiwan, and the United States. American basketball players are superstars in China, too.

These developments are not trivial. Through them Chinese society has developed values antithetical to those of its leadership. Increasing interaction has meant that Western cultures are penetrating China's society and have started to create the conditions for political cleavages between government and society, and ultimately for political change. The weakening of government authority is already apparent in Chinese universities. In the sciences, engineering, and humanities, and even in many of the social sciences, government interference has significantly diminished. Scholars with doctorates from the United States and other countries are teaching in Chinese universities and are transforming courses across the curriculum. Domestic and international migration is practically unrestricted. Most significant, in recent years there has been an expansion of multiple-candidate competitive free elections in rural China.

Chinese leaders continue to direct abhorrent human rights abuses, including torture of Tibetan independence activists and imprisonment of leaders of unapproved religious activities. But compared to many countries in the Middle East and Southwest Asia—in which the sale and lifetime servitude of child brides is commonplace, religious tolerance is nearly nonexistent, women suffer intolerable abuse, and Western popular culture is barred—and to the one-party dictatorships of sub-Saharan Africa, where even slavery is tolerated and degrading and harmful tribal customs brook no challenge, China's performance, and particularly its recent record of positive change, does not cry out for special censure. South Asian countries, even including democratic India, tolerate slavery, and the horrid abuse of women in India is especially disturbing. The point is not that China's human rights record is good, but that abhorrent violations occur throughout the Third World and that, as in both security and economic issues, U.S. attention to China's human rights situation is disproportionate to China's violations when viewed comparatively and in the context of its improving situation.

Much of the impetus behind recent positive changes comes from the collapse of Communist Party control and the continuing decentralization of economic power in China. But Western involvement with China's economy and society has also been influential. Mere interaction with Americans, whether through educational exchanges, travel, or business, has exposed the Chinese people to Western values and to what is for them the novel notion that people can be free from the fear of their own government. It has clearly stimulated demands for similar freedoms in China; there would never have been a democracy movement in the spring of 1989 without Western interaction with the Chinese economy.

Economic interaction has also impressed the Chinese with the superiority of capitalism, which has already contributed not only to higher standards of living but also to the economic independence required for genuine social autonomy. Such interaction has underscored the value—increasingly, the necessity—of an institutionalized legal system to protect both enterprises and individuals from arbitrary authority. The determined independent development of the Chinese legal profession and the widespread demand for impartial law enforcement clearly reflect a highly positive Chinese exposure to Western ways.

Both the Western success at contributing to change in China through broad-based personal ties, and the Western failure to change appreciably the lot of Chinese dissidents by threatening to limit those ties, underscore the importance of resisting demands that the United States reduce its level of engagement with China. Some of the most successful foreign activities in China, including programs in legal training and for the promotion of democracy, have been funded by the U.S. government and American philanthropic organizations. The record of Western interaction with post-Mao China is overwhelmingly positive. It suggests that we should put an end to the detrimental politicization of human rights policy, and expand U.S.-China cooperation wherever practicable.

There are no unmanageable U.S.-China conflicts. The Taiwan problem raises the most sensitive and dangerous issues, yet even here Beijing and Washington have established a way to satisfy their respective interests without undermining cooperative relations. In both economic and security relations, conflicting interests are amenable to negotiation and mutually satisfactory outcomes. As in any negotiation between great powers, solutions will require mutual compromise. But through negotiations with China, the United States can further a wide range of bilateral and regional interests and maintain regional and global stability, while simultaneously promoting change in China that reflects American values.

It is fashionable to argue that the end of the Cold War has undermined the strategic foundation for U.S.-China cooperation. This is true, but the removal of one support is not a reason to go about destroying all the rest. Cooperation is still important, and an adversarial relationship between the United States and China will only become inevitable if one of the two sides insists on it. Given the consequences that would flow for all of East Asia, it would be disastrous if it were Americans who so insisted.

6

China: Getting the Questions Right

*Thomas J. Christensen and Richard K. Betts**

The challenge presented by a rising China is the principal issue facing American foreign policy. This is not always obvious to most Americans or even to many of our leaders. Since the end of the Cold War, defense policy has been absorbed in second-order problems of deterring or defeating mid-level powers such as Iraq, North Korea and Serbia, and in third-order problems of peacekeeping and humanitarian intervention. Over the long term, however, the first priority of a serious foreign policy is to handle challenges from discontented, nuclear-armed, major powers.

It is hardly inevitable that China will be a threat to American interests, but the United States is much more likely to go to war with China than it is with any other major power. Other current or emerging great powers either are aligned with the United States (NATO countries and Japan), are struggling against crippling decline (Russia), or, while having a tense diplomatic relationship with Washington, have no plausible occasion for war with America (India). China, by contrast, is a rising power with high expectations, unresolved grievances and an undemocratic government.

Debate about whether and how China might threaten U.S. security interests has often been simplistically polarized. Views range from alarmist to complacent:

* Richard K. Betts is director of the Institute of War and Peace Studies at Columbia University, and a senior fellow at the Council on Foreign Relations. Thomas J. Christensen is associate professor of political science and a member of the Security Studies Program at the Massachusetts Institute of Technology.

This essay first appeared in *The National Interest*, No. 62 (Winter 2000/01).

from those who see China emerging as a hefty and dangerous superpower, to those who believe the country's prospects are vastly overrated; and from those who see its economic growth as an engine for building threatening military capabilities, to those who see that growth as a welcome force for political liberalization and international cooperation.

Most strategic debate about China still focuses on a few simple questions. With respect to capabilities, these revolve mainly around whether the Chinese armed forces will develop to the point that they rival U.S. military power, and whether the economic surge—with its implications for military transformation—will continue indefinitely or stall. With regard to intentions, China watchers want to know how thoroughly and how soon the country will integrate into a global economy that allegedly constrains conflict; whether Beijing will adopt aggressive aims as its power grows; and whether political liberalization will occur as its wealth grows. Concern also zeroes in on whether the People's Republic of China (PRC) has the ability to take Taiwan by force.

These are relevant questions at the most basic level, but they are the wrong ones to generate progress in a mature debate. The most worrisome possibilities are those that lie beyond the answers to these questions, and between alarmist and complacent viewpoints. The truth is that China can pose a grave problem even if it does not become a military power on the American model, does not intend to commit aggression, integrates into a global economy, and liberalizes politically. Similarly, the United States could face a dangerous conflict over Taiwan even if it turns out that Beijing lacks the capacity to conquer the island.

Will China's Military Power Rival America's?

There is little disagreement that the People's Liberation Army (PLA), a generic designation for all the Chinese armed forces, remains a threadbare force, well below Western standards. Pockets of excellence notwithstanding, most personnel are poorly educated and trained. Weapons systems are old, and even those acquired most recently are inferior to those in Western arsenals. Many units spend a good deal of time in non-military activities; staffs do not practice complex, large-scale operations; exercises and training regimens are limited; and equipment is not well maintained. Even according to the highest estimates, defense spending per soldier is low by First World standards, indicating the dominance of quantity over quality in the Chinese forces.

The main disagreement among Western analysts of China's military is about whether the PLA is poised to move out of its unimpressive condition and into a new era of modernity, efficiency and competitiveness, as anticipated economic reform and growth translate into military improvement. Arguments to that effect are supported by a number of PLA writings about a prospective Chinese "revolution in military affairs" (RMA).[i] The current backwardness of the PLA reflects its low priority in the country's modernization efforts since the 1970s, and the diversion of the energy of the military into business activities (which are now supposed to be curtailed). In this view, the military potential of the PLA will be liberated when the political leadership decides to give it significantly more of the resources generated by economic development.

For China to develop a military on the model of the United States would be a tremendous stretch. The main issue is not whether Beijing will have high defense budgets or access to cutting-edge technology. A rich China might well be able to acquire most types of advanced weaponry. Deeply ingrained habits of threat assessment in the U.S. defense community encourage focusing on these factors. Unfortunately, however, basic "bean counts" of manpower and units and the quality of weapons platforms are poor measures of truly modern military capability. More fundamental to that assessment is whether the PLA establishment is capable of using whatever increase in resources it might receive to build the complex supporting infrastructure necessary to make Chinese forces competitive in combat. The PLA's current mediocrity—like that of many armed forces in the world—may be rooted in a history, ideology and culture that are incompatible with the patterns of organization and social interaction necessary to rival the best First World militaries. This does not mean that the PLA can never break out of this box. It does mean that it will not be easy to do, and will not occur quickly.

Modern military effectiveness has become more a matter of quality than of quantity, and less a matter of pure firepower than of the capacity to coordinate complex systems. The essence of the American RMA lies in the interweaving of capacities in organization, doctrine, training, maintenance, support systems, weaponry and the overall level of professionalism. These factors are harder to measure, but they are what make it feasible to assimilate and apply state-of-the-art weapons effectively. Those capacities require high levels of education throughout a military force, a culture of initiative and innovation, and an orientation toward operating through skill networks as much as through traditional command and obedience hierarchies. Few militaries have developed these capabilities. Indeed, experience in the Persian Gulf and Kosovo indicate that the United States is in a class by itself in these respects. If the PLA has the resources to integrate complexity and a willingness to delegate authority to overcome its mediocrity, it is a well-kept secret. As yet it is not obvious that PLA effectiveness is likely to be closer to that of the American military than to that of, say, Iraq.

If the PLA remains second-rate, should the world breathe a sigh of relief? Not entirely. First, American military power is not the only relevant standard of comparison. Other armed forces in Asia that the PLA could come up against are much closer to the Chinese standard than to the American. (This is true even of Taiwan's technologically sophisticated military, whose long isolation has eroded its quality.[11]) Second, the United States has global interests and often finds itself distracted or pinned down in other regions. Third, the Chinese do not need to match U.S. capabilities to cope with them. Rather than trying to match an American revolution in military affairs, they might do better to develop a counter-revolution by devising asymmetrical strategic options on various parts of the technological spectrum that can circumvent U.S. advantages.

One such example could be "cyberwar" attacks on the complex network of information systems that stitches American military superiority together. Another could be the use of new weapons like land attack cruise missiles or lower tech weapons such as naval mines to impede American access to the region. Still another could be the modification of China's no first-use policy on nuclear weapons, making an exception for repelling an invasion of Chinese territory. Although it is almost unimaginable that China would use nuclear weapons in an effort to gain political concessions from Taiwan, it might threaten their use to deter U.S. military action on behalf of the island. As Disarmament Ambassador Sha Zukang said in 1996, "As far as Taiwan is concerned it is a province of China. . . . So the policy of no-first-use does not apply."[iii] Even though the Foreign Ministry subsequently repudiated the statement, nothing makes a future adaptation of doctrine in that direction unthinkable.

Pundits on defense policy commonly observe that China lacks power projection capabilities—the ability to send and sustain combat forces far from home. By U.S. standards this is true. Talk about obtaining aircraft carriers has produced nothing deployable, the navy and air forces lack the requisite assets for "lift" (transporting and supplying large units for operations abroad), and Chinese forces have negligible logistical capacity as we know it. For those worried about facing a Chinese force on the American model, these are all good grounds for optimism. Indeed, there is general agreement that Beijing lacks the capability at present to invade Taiwan and that it could take decades to overcome the obstacles. But China does not need to match American standards to reshape the Asian strategic environment. This becomes especially clear when one considers where power projection will be an issue.

Taiwan is both the most dangerous and most likely instance of Chinese power projection (more on which below), but it is not the only one. China has conceivable points of conflict in several places that would not require its forces to cross large bodies of water, and where it would not be facing opposition as potent as Taiwan's military. Although less likely than conflict over Taiwan, an imbroglio in Korea would be scarcely less dangerous if the Pyongyang regime were to collapse and South Korean or American forces were to move into the vacuum without Beijing's agreement. Far too little attention has been focused on the odds of miscalculation in a confused situation of this sort. The PLA does not have the American army's logistical capacity, but even a half century ago it managed to project a force of hundreds of thousands of men deep into Korea.

While the Chinese navy is weak, some of its neighbors' navies are weaker still. Two of these neighbors, Vietnam and the Philippines, have outstanding sovereignty disputes with China and have not fared well in naval skirmishes in the past three decades. We also cannot rule out the possibility of a land attack. The PLA did poorly in its invasion of Vietnam over twenty years ago, but the

Vietnamese army is now less than half the size it was then, and the Vietnamese economic base is far more inferior to China's than it was in 1978. Logistical limitations would hamper, but not preclude, PRC action in Mongolia, or in the Russian Far East, if that region were to fall out of Moscow's effective control. Granted, conflict over these places is improbable. The problem is that the same could have been said of most wars before they happened.

Will China Become the World's Leading Economy?

Military potential grows out of economic capacity. China's economy, like its military, is neither to be envied nor denigrated. In recent years it has been the fastest growing major economy in the world. Until strains became evident in the late 1990s, it was common to project high growth rates straight into the future and to see China's GNP surpassing America's early in the twenty-first century.[iv] But China's economy faces daunting challenges. And even if it solves many of its problems, the central government may not have sufficient control over the fruits of growth to use them for military coercion.

Even if China achieved the highest GNP in the world, low per capita wealth would persist, limiting disposable income that could be reallocated to the military. In any case, the fantastic economic surge of the last two decades has sputtered. Although China's economy seems to be recovering, it has just completed three years of deflation, and this despite dangerous levels of government deficit spending on infrastructure projects. Such deficits, and the high ratio of unrecoverable bank loans to GNP, risk exposing the economy to the same dangers experienced in Southeast Asia and Korea in 1997.

Straight-line projections in the negative direction would, of course, be as naive as the excessive expectations of the 1990s. One common and rather condescending mistake made by some foreign analysts of China is to offer a long list of problems and then forget to mention that Chinese elites are smart enough to do something about them. Under the economic leadership of Premier Zhu Rongji, the Chinese Communist Party has tried to reform the financial sector, force the military to abandon much of its commercial empire (including its lucrative smuggling operations), and meet the stringent demands of China's accession to the World Trade Organization (WTO).

Still, most of the methods available to spur growth involve politically risky measures, such as reform of the financial sector and state-owned enterprises, that threaten to leave tens of millions of additional urban residents jobless.[v] These would join the ranks of the floating population of more than 100 million already in search of work. Similar problems affect the military, as cutbacks in the overall size of the PLA (needed for modernization and professionalization) create yet more disgruntled citizens. To maintain comfortable lifestyles, especially for officers, the military became dependent on business activities and large-scale smuggling of goods otherwise subject to high tariffs. If able officers and soldiers are to stay in uniform, then, the military units need to be subsidized at a high rate in order to implement successfully the plan to get the PLA out of commercial activities and back into the barracks.

All in all, there are no easy ways out for Beijing. Even if all growth-spurring measures work and the Communist Party maintains stability during the transition, the process of doing so will be expensive—especially for a central government that takes in a far smaller percentage of GNP than do Western governments. As China grows through capitalist reforms, Beijing must scramble to find new ways to tax private wealth. However inefficient they may have been, large state-owned enterprises provided a large portion of government revenues. The soft loans that officials forced government-owned banks to give to these enterprises functioned as an indirect tax on families, which, before Chinese membership of the WTO, had no alternatives to the state banks. If the Party is successful in demolishing both the monopoly of state-owned banks and the sturdy safety net for state-owned enterprises, it will need to raise money elsewhere for the government operating budget. That budget, in turn, will be strained by increases in welfare spending needed to maintain social stability—pensions for the unemployed and retired, and compensations to the military for its lost sources of legal and illegal revenue.

What is left over will be available to invest in education (critical to creating sustained growth in high-tech areas) and in military modernization. However, even if China's economy and high-tech sectors were to grow rapidly, it is not clear that Beijing will be able to channel resources effectively to create armed forces that could rival those of the United States, even in the region. For one thing, it is doubtful that the state will be able to channel young technical talent into defense research and development. China's turn to Russia and Israel for military technology is worrisome, but if it continues it will say more about China's inability to close the technological gap with the West than anything else.

Will China Be Pacified by Globalization?

To pessimists steeped in realpolitik, a rich China will necessarily be a threat, because economic power can be translated into military power and power generates ambition. To optimists impressed with the revolutionary implications of globalization, however, a more powerful China will not be a threat because it will have too much to lose from disrupting international trade and investment. The latter view is more common in the West than the former, which seems to many to reek of old thinking.

The notion that a web of commercial ties discourages war, however, is itself quite old, if not exactly venerable. It was popularized by Henry Thomas Buckle in the 1850s, by Norman Angell just a year before World War I erupted, and again in the 1970s, when interdependence was said to have reduced the utility of force. Most recently, at a White House rally for permanent normal trade relations, Al Gore quoted his father as saying, "When goods do not cross borders, armies will."

The argument this time around is that the proposition is finally true because the nature of interdependence has changed in a crucial way. A century ago it was characterized by vertical trade between imperial centers and colonies, trade in final products between wealthier nations, and portfolio investments. Today there is much more direct investment and transnational production of goods, which fosters "a growing interpenetration of economies, in the sense that one economy owns part of another."[vi] With the PRC, Taiwan, Japan and the United States all owning pieces of each other, how can they fight without destroying their own property? As the Chinese elite make more and more money from bilateral investments with Taiwan, simple greed will prevent huffing and puffing from crossing the line to war. If development thoroughly enmeshes the PRC in the globalized economy, therefore, peace will follow.

There are at least two problems with this latest version of interdependence theory. One is that both sides in a political dispute have a stake in not overturning profitable economic integration. The PRC might not want to kill the golden goose, but neither would Taiwan or the United States. Why, then, should Beijing be any more anxious to back down in a crisis than Taipei or Washington? Mutual dependence makes a political conflict a game of chicken, in which each side expects the other to bow to the stakes, and in which collision may result rather than concession.

The second problem is that there is little reason to assume that sober economic interest will necessarily override national honor in a crisis. A tough stand by Beijing may be viewed from the inside as essential for regime survival, even if it is not seen by detached observers as being in China's "national interest." In an imbroglio over Taiwan, which capitals will feel the strongest emotional inhibitions against backing down? Beijing and Taipei both have a greater material, moral and historical stake in the outcome than does the United States.

The global economy does indeed change logical incentives to compromise in political conflict, but not to the degree that it makes Beijing likely to be more "reasonable" than anyone else. Economic globalization does not eliminate the high priority that nations place on their political identity and integrity. Drawing China into the web of global interdependence may do more to encourage peace than war, but it cannot guarantee that the pursuit of heartfelt political interests will be blocked by a fear of economic consequences.

Will China Become Aggressive?

Whether China has aggressive motives is what most policymakers want to know about Beijing's strategic intentions. Optimists say the answer is no, because the PRC is ideologically anti-imperialist and seeks only respect as a status quo great power. Pessimists say the answer is yes, because a seething set of Chinese grudges and territorial ambitions are on hold only for a lack of confidence in capability, or simply because all great powers tend to become aggressive when they get the chance.

But such focusing on the unlikely odds of deliberate aggression diverts attention from possibilities that are both much more likely and almost as dangerous. Most countries viewed as aggressors by their adversaries view their own behavior as defensive and legitimate. Whether Beijing is a tiger in waiting, about to set out deliberately on a predatory rampage, is not the most relevant question. No evidence suggests that Chinese leaders have an interest in naked conquest of the sort practiced by Genghis Khan, Napoleon Bonaparte or Adolf Hitler. The model more often invoked by pessimists is Kaiser Wilhelm's Germany. Like Germany a century ago, China is a late-blooming great power emerging into a world already ordered strategically by earlier arrivals; a continental power surrounded by other powers who are collectively stronger but individually weaker (with the exception of the United States and, perhaps, Japan); a bustling country with great expectations, dissatisfied with its place in the international pecking order, if only with regard to international prestige and respect. The quest for a rightful "place in the sun" will, it is argued, inevitably foster growing friction with Japan, Russia, India or the United States.

Optimists do not have a hard time brushing off this analogy to a state of a different culture on a different continent at a different time, a long-gone era when imperialism was the norm for civilized international behavior. Their benign view, that economic development and trade will inevitably make China fat and happy, uninterested in throwing its weight around, strikes them as common sense. It could turn out to be true. It is more an article of faith, however, than a prediction grounded in historical experience. The United States, for example, is quite interested in gaining the goodies from globalization, yet on the world stage it sometimes throws its weight around with righteous abandon.

Indeed, the most disturbing analogy for China's future behavior may not be Germany but the United States. If China acts with the same degree of caution and responsibility in its region in this century as the United States did in its neighborhood in the past century, Asia is in for big trouble. Washington intervened frequently in Mexico, Central America and the Caribbean for reasons most Americans consider legitimate, defensive, altruistic and humane. The United States and its allies in Asia, however, would see comparable Chinese regional policing as a mortal threat. Even if China does not throw its weight around, the fact that there are others who can respond to the growth of Chinese power sets up the possibility of a classic spiral of tense actions and reactions. China faces alliances involving the United States, Japan, Australia and South Korea, and potential alliances in Southeast Asia.

Would Chinese Liberalization Guarantee Peace?

Many assume that as long as democratization accompanies the growth of Chinese power, China will not necessarily pose a security challenge. This would hold true even if China proves able to maintain high levels of economic and technological growth, a healthy degree of government accumulation of the increasing national wealth, and, thereby, military modernization. This theory of the democratic peace—that developed democracies virtually never fight one another—is currently the most influential political science theory among American foreign policy elites.

Even if we accept the democratic peace theory at face value, there are several problems with applying it to China. First, as Fareed Zakaria has noted, the theory really applies only to liberal democracies on the Western model, ones with restraints on government action and guarantees of minority rights. Democratization in China could just as conceivably turn in an illiberal direction, on the model of post-Tito Yugoslavia, Iran or other unpleasant examples of violent activism.

Second, the democratic peace theory does not apply clearly to civil war. Democracies must recognize each other as democracies for the theory to apply.[vii] They also have to view each other as legitimate, independent and sovereign states. No matter how many Americans and Taiwanese believe that Taiwan is or should be a sovereign state, this view is widely rejected on the mainland (and is not a premise of past or current U.S. policy).

Third, while liberal democracy is pacific, the process of becoming a democracy can be violent and destabilizing. This is particularly true of democratizing states that lack developed civil societies, independent news media, healthy outlets for popular grievances, and a marketplace for ideas where countervailing views can be debated. This gives elites incentives to manipulate populist or nationalist themes and to adopt tough international policies as an electoral strategy.[viii]

The Chinese Communist Party has behaved like many authoritarian regimes, but with much more success. It has systematically prevented the rise of both an independent press and a civil society. Although the foreign press has penetrated China, domestic political publications are still strictly circumscribed by the state. As the recent crackdown on the Falun Gong demonstrates, the Party is afraid of any group that organizes for any purpose without state sanction, regardless of how apolitical it appears to be.

The Chinese government's concerns about its legitimacy are not mere expressions of paranoia. The intensity of criticism of the leadership that one hears privately in places ranging from taxi cabs to government offices is astonishing. Awareness of its unpopularity gives the government in Beijing incentives to use nationalism as a replacement for the now hollow shell of communist ideology. But the Party is also aware that nationalism is not an inert tool to be pulled out of a kit and manipulated at the whim of the government. It is double-edged. Volatile and potentially uncontrollable, especially on emotional issues such as relations with Japan and Taiwan, nationalism is powerful enough to prop up a communist party in a capitalist society, but it could also severely damage the party if it were turned against the state. Officials in Beijing are aware that nationalism was a major force in the Communist Party's overthrow of the Kuomintang, as it was in the 1911–12 revolution that overthrew the Qing dynasty. This is probably why, during the row with Japan over the Senkaku Islands in the summer of 1996, the Party actively prevented students and workers from marching in protest to the Japanese embassy.

According to one prominent Chinese foreign affairs expert, since the May 1999 NATO bombing of the embassy in Belgrade, the authorities in Beijing have been very concerned about an increasing trend in public opinion that views the leaders as soft in responding to international humiliations, and sees them even as "traitors" (*maiguo zei*) interested only in business prospects. He and others argue that the protests outside the American embassy in Beijing were not so much instigated by the Communist Party, as many in the West assumed, but rather were managed, controlled and ultimately suppressed by the Party. One retired Chinese military officer touched on a similar theme during the 1996 Senkaku crisis. He maintained that, if the Party allowed the people to protest unhindered, the first day they would be protesting against Japan, the next day against the lack of response by the government, and on the third day against the government itself.

In the early phases of democratization, China should be ripe for jingoism. Hypernationalism could be exploited to mobilize popular support and to deflect criticism of the state, especially given the existence of irredentist claims, and the danger of ethnic and regional "splittism" on the mainland and in Taiwan. If democratization were to occur in the current context of weak institutions, political leaders and opposition parties would have incentives to appeal to nationalism in ways that could destabilize the region. In fact, this is a favorite, though perhaps cynical, argument offered to foreigners by communist opponents of multiparty democracy.

There are, however, plausible scenarios in which Chinese democratization might reduce international conflict. Democratization could make the mainland more imaginative with regard to the frameworks for unification offered to Taiwan, thus making meaningful cross-strait political dialogue more likely. Political liberalization might also make the prospect of eventual accommodation with the mainland more palatable to Taiwan and discourage the island's diplomatic adventurism. But that possibility is not necessarily more likely than its opposite: a renewed belief by Taiwan that the island has its own national identity, that unification with the mainland under any circumstances is unacceptable, and that democratization on the mainland is a threat to Taiwanese goals. Taiwan may see a closing window of opportunity, with the hopes of gaining true independence reduced as the West's sympathy for Taiwan's opposition to unification hardens.

If Americans view mainland democratization as genuine, such fears on Taiwan are well placed. Would the United States risk war to prevent a democratic Taiwan from becoming part of a larger democratic China? The main reasons a president could currently use to mobilize Americans around action in defense of Taiwan's democracy would simply disappear. Many observers view democracy as Taiwan's biggest security asset, because it increases U.S. support. They are right. But it is not just democracy that provides Taiwan's security; it is the current contrast between Taiwan's democracy and the mainland's authoritarianism.

Can the Mainland Conquer Taiwan?

The possibility of war with China over Taiwan is arguably the most dangerous threat that U.S. security policy faces in the coming decade. No other flashpoint is more likely to bring the United States into combat with a major power, and no other contingency compels Washington to respond with such ambiguous commitment. U.S. policy regarding the defense of Taiwan is uncertain, and thus so is the understanding in Beijing and Taipei—and in Washington—over how strongly the United States might react in different circumstances. Because Taiwan is more independent than either Washington or Beijing might prefer, neither great power can fully control developments that might ignite a crisis. This is a classic recipe for surprise, miscalculation and uncontrolled escalation.

Traditional questions about Chinese intentions and capabilities miss the mark in analyzing the likelihood of war and the probable course war would take. A PRC attack on a Taiwan following the pursuit of formal independence from the Chinese nation would be viewed (quite sincerely) in Beijing as purely defensive, to preserve generally recognized territorial sovereignty. Many outside China would view the attack as a sign of belligerence. But military activity against an independence-minded Taiwan might have little relevance to Beijing's behavior on other issues, even for other sovereignty disputes such as those over the Senkaku or Spratly Islands.

The niceties of balance of power calculations could prove relatively unimportant in determining whether China would use force over Taiwan and whether it would do so effectively. U.S. efforts to create a stable balance across the Taiwan Strait might deter the use of force under certain circumstances, but certainly not all. Moreover, such efforts would miss the major point of cross-strait strategic interaction. China's military strategy in a conflict over Taiwan would likely be to punish and coerce rather than to control, tasks for which its military may be able to use force to great effect. The PLA's ability to mount a Normandy-style assault on the island is not the toughest question. Geography (the water barrier), together with U.S. supplies, would provide powerful means to Taiwan for blocking such an invasion, even without direct U.S. combat involvement.

A greater challenge would be a blockade by the PRC, which has a large number of submarines and mines. Taiwan's proximity to the mainland and its dependence on international trade and investment enhance the potential effect of blockades—or coercive campaigns involving ballistic and cruise missiles—even if the military impact would be modest. The PRC might thus be able to damage severely the island's economy regardless of the number of F-16s, AWACs aircraft and theater missile defense batteries the island can bring to bear. Moreover, to break a blockade by sweeping the seas would likely require a direct attack on Chinese vessels. If Chinese forces had not already targeted U.S. ships by that point, it would be up to Washington to decide to fire the first shots against a nuclear-armed country that was attempting to regain limited control of what it believes is its own territory.

Some think that the United States should give Taiwan military assistance or defend it directly even in the extreme case that it openly declares legal independence. Many assume that the United States could deter an attack from the mainland and that, if worse came to worst, the United States would prevail in a war should deterrence fail. These assumptions, unfortunately, are suspect. Before being deterred, Beijing would have to weigh the costs of inaction against action. The perceived cost of inaction against Taiwanese independence is very high. No leader can count on survival if labeled the next Li Hongzhang, the diplomat who ceded Taiwan to Japan in the 1895 Treaty of Shimonoseki.

Many in Beijing believe that the United States lacks the national will to pursue a war against China to save Taiwan. If the prospect of casualties did not deter the United States from intervening, the reasoning goes, even low levels of casualties would frighten it into early withdrawal. Following this logic, China need not defeat the U.S. military in wartime or close the gap in military power in peacetime. Rather, the strategic requirement is much lower: to put a number of American soldiers, sailors and airmen at risk.

It is dangerous that so many Chinese seem to subscribe to this "Somalia analogy." Washington would probably not be deterred by fears of casualties if it decided that Taiwan was being bullied without serious provocation, any more than it was deterred from attacking Iraq in 1991 by high pre-war casualty estimates. Nor is it likely that, once the United States had made the momentous decision to gear up for combat against a power like China, it would quit easily after suffering a small number of casualties.

Thinking over the long term, however, it is hard to imagine how the United States could "win" a war to preserve Taiwan's independence against a resolute China. Too many analyses inside the Beltway stop at the operational level of analysis, assuming that tactical victories answer the strategic question. Sinking the Chinese navy and defeating an invasion attempt against the island would not be the end of the story. Unless the U.S. Air Force were to mount a massive and sustained assault against mainland targets, the PRC would maintain the capability to disrupt commerce, squeeze Taiwan, and keep U.S. personnel at risk. As one American naval officer put it, as a nation much larger than Iraq or Yugoslavia, "China is a cruise missile sponge." This will be doubly true once China builds more road-mobile, solid-fuel missiles and learns better ways to hide its military assets.

Moreover, strikes against the mainland would involve huge risks. Recall that for three years, while Chinese forces were killing U.S. soldiers in Korea, the Truman administration refrained from carrying combat to the mainland for fear of a wider war—and this at a time when China had no nuclear weapons and its Soviet allies had fewer than China now has. China maintains the capacity to strike the U.S. homeland with nuclear missiles, and to strike U.S. bases in the region with both conventional and nuclear missiles. China has or is feverishly obtaining increasingly sophisticated systems, including Russian SA-10 air defense batteries, stealth detection technologies, anti-ship missiles, land attack cruise missiles, accurate ballistic missiles, and new submarines. Any of these could give the United States and its regional allies pause before widening a campaign against the Chinese mainland.

And if the issue is a PRC blockade of Taiwan, who will bear the onus of starting a war between China and the United States? If a conventional engagement leaves U.S. naval forces in control of the Taiwan Strait, can anyone be confident that Beijing would not dream of using a nuclear weapon against the Seventh Fleet? And then what? Such a scenario of nuclear escalation seems fancifully alarmist to many in the post-Cold War era. But is it any more so than such concerns ever were when defense planning focused on crises with the Soviet Union? Is this an experiment a U.S. commander-in-chief should run?

Even if we dismiss entirely any nuclear danger, there are still considerable problems for the United States. If Chinese conventional capabilities do not deter American escalation, and if Chinese forces prove relatively ineffective against U.S. weaponry, a broader question remains: How long would the United States be willing to continue a war of attrition against a country of more than a billion people? How long would it be willing even to camp multiple aircraft carrier battle groups and minesweepers off the Chinese coast? What would American allies such as Japan—where crucial U.S. bases are located—do? Taiwan will always be just 100 miles from mainland China, and Chinese nationalism is extremely unlikely to wither under American bombardment. Indeed, it would probably harden. What, then, is the endgame? A negotiated deal that rejected Taiwanese independence but protected de facto autonomy would be tempting in this situation. In this limited but very real sense, the effort to defend an independent Taiwan would have failed and China would be victorious, since occupation and direct control of Taiwan is not Beijing's stated strategic goal.

The point here is not that a U.S. commitment to defend Taiwan is meaningless. It could be a major factor in deterring more activist impulses in Beijing among those who might want to do more than just prevent a declaration of independence, or those who view current trends in cross-strait relations with much more pessimism than their colleagues. But we should not overestimate the U.S. ability to deter and defeat China in all circumstances.

Reasons for Pessimism

Optimists on the China challenge are often guilty of contradictory arguments. On the one hand, they argue that China will only become a dangerous enemy if the United States treats it like one. At the same time, they attempt to demonstrate why China will not be able to develop the military capacity to pose any appreciable threat to us for a very long time. How can China be both hopelessly weak and potentially dangerous?

There are ways to square this circle by asking the right questions. China can pose security challenges to the United States even if it is unlikely to narrow the gap in military power. This is true because of geography; because of America's reliance on alliances to project power; and because of China's capacity to harm U.S. forces, U.S. regional allies, and the American homeland, even while losing a war in the technical, military sense.

Optimists are correct to focus on Chinese intentions and the potentially pacifying influences that the United States and other international actors can have on China. But they often assume too much about the positive effects of globalization, interdependence and political liberalization, because they underestimate the role of nationalist emotion and the possibility of misperceptions and inadvertence in war. They also forget that interdependence is a two-way street that restrains not only the Chinese, but China's potential adversaries as well.

In addressing the China challenge, the United States needs to think hard about three related questions: first, how to avoid crises and war through prudent, coercive diplomacy; second, how to manage crises and fight a war if the avoidance effort fails; third, how to end crises and terminate war at costs acceptable to the United States and its allies.

In terms of coercive diplomacy, the United States needs to balance deterrence and reassurance, recognizing that, on the one hand, deterrence is complicated by the increasing capabilities of the PLA, and that, on the other hand, if certain core interests of China are disregarded by the United States, even a relatively weak China might resort to force. The essence of deterrence and war planning lies in considering military responses—including crisis management and diplomacy—to a Chinese attack. It might be advantageous to have the capacity to sink a Chinese destroyer preemptively before it launched its missiles, but an American admiral might never receive authorization to do so in a real crisis. Similarly, it might be beneficial to have the capacity to strike theater missile sites preemptively, but such action might cause unwanted escalation and alienate needed allies. This is one reason that effective local missile defenses are a good idea, even though they may be much less effective and much more expensive than "shooting the archer."

The United States also needs to consider for how long and at what cost it is willing to fight for certain goals. For how long would the United States be willing to fight to keep Taipei from an agreement with Beijing in which Taipei maintains a very high degree of military and political autonomy, but is nonetheless, in terms of abstract sovereignty, part of China? (In answering this question, remember that the United States made similar concessions to Belgrade regarding Kosovo after defeating Yugoslavia militarily.) It is better to ask such questions about the end of a war before the unpredictable forces of emotion regarding sunk costs and reputation take hold after a war breaks out.

China's growing power causes so many headaches largely because its strategic implications are not fully clear. But before one laments the rise of Chinese power, one should consider an even more uncertain alternative: Chinese weakness and collapse. Nothing ordains that China's march to great power status cannot be derailed. Severe economic dislocation and political fragmentation could throw the country into disorder, and the central government could prove too crippled to use external adventures to rally support and maintain unity. Hard-bitten realists should hesitate before hoping for such developments, however. The last time China was weak and disunified—in the era of warlordism and revolution in the first half of the twentieth century—it was a disaster, not only for China, but also for international peace and stability.

NOTES

[i] Michael Pillsbury, ed., *Chinese Views of Future Warfare* (Washington, dc: National Defense University Press, 1997), part 4.

[ii] See James Lilley and Carl Ford, "China's Military: A Second Opinion", *The National Interest* (Fall 1999).

[iii] Quoted in *China, Nuclear Weapons, and Arms Control* (New York: Council on Foreign Relations, 2000), p. 31n.

[iv] This point would come between 2013 and 2040, depending on whether purchasing power parity or official exchange rates were used to estimate. William C. Wohlforth, "The Stability of a Unipolar World", *International Security* (Summer 1999), p. 33n.

[v] See David Zweig, "Undemocratic Capitalism: China and the Limits of Economism", *The National Interest* (Summer 1999).

[vi] Richard Rosecrance, *The Rise of the Trading State* (New York: Basic Books, 1986), pp. 146-7.

[vii] John M. Owen IV, *Liberal Peace, Liberal War: American Politics and International Security* (Ithaca, NY: Cornell University Press, 1997).

[viii] Edward D. Mansfield and Jack L. Snyder, "Democratization and the Danger of War", *International Security* (Summer 1995).

7

The World Shakes China

*Bruce Cumings**

One might trace the history of the limits, of those obscure actions, necessarily forgotten as soon as they are performed, whereby a civilization casts aside something it regards as alien. Throughout its history, this moat which it digs around itself, this no man's land by which it preserves its isolation, is just as characteristic as its positive values.

—Michel Foucault

In the recent Italian film *Il Postino*, the Chilean poet Pablo Neruda teaches an uneducated mailman first the word and then the art of *metaforé*. The mailman is a quick study, and soon he is asking Neruda an intriguing question: "Is the world perhaps a metaphor for something else?" Neruda pauses and then says that he will have to think about this question. But he never gives the postman his answer.

China has not been a nation for Americans, but a metaphor. To say "China" is instantly to call up a string of metaphors giving us the history of Sino-American relations, and fifty years of "China watching" by our politicians, pundits, and academics: unchanging China, cyclical China, the inscrutable Forbidden City, boxes within boxes, the open door, sick man of Asia, *The Good Earth*, agrarian reformers, China shakes the world, who lost China, containment or liberation, brainwashing, Quemoy and Matsu, the *Little Red Book*, Ping-Pong diplomacy, the week that changed the world, the China card, the "Gang of Four", the four

---

* Bruce Cumings is Norman and Edna Freehling Professor of History at the University of Chicago.

This essay first appeared in *The National Interest*, No. 43 (Spring 1996).

86

modernizations, China as insatiable market, Tiananmen, butchers of Beijing, China shakes the world (again), cycles of rise and decline (again), unchanging China (yet again).[i] Beyond all that, our pundits and experts remain captured by a master metaphor: that of China's unfathomable-in-a-lifetime vastness, its historical depth and profundity, and (therefore) its overriding importance to the world we live in.[ii]

The accompaniment to this operatic "China" din is a cacophony of expert opinion offering "scenarios" for where China is going, and what we must (by all means) do about it. Pick up almost any journal or magazine of expert opinion and you will read that China is disintegrating, or that it is united and stable; that Sino-American relations are frayed to the breaking point, or that they are just over yet another nettlesome hump; that fearsome China must be "contained", or that outward-opening China must be "engaged"; that its military is growing ominously, or that it is underfunded and fitted out with obsolescent weaponry; that its commerce is drastically overheated and facing crisis, or that it is in great shape; that China may attack Taiwan, or that Taiwan may soon be China's biggest foreign investor; that China may take over the Spratly Islands, or that it will not because it cannot; that China will subjugate Hong Kong after it is no longer a British colony in 1997, or that Hong Kong has been colonizing China for years; that a budding civil society was crushed at Tiananmen, or that the protesters themselves did not know what they were doing, or wanted; that post-Deng China will dissolve into chaos, or that a new leadership will pluralize China's politics.[iii] Atavistic China seems to be lying in wait for the next trough in history's recurring cycle—or not, as the case may be.

Contrast all this with George F. Kennan's sober remark back in the 1940s, around the time that Mao mounted the Gate of Heavenly Peace (i.e., Tiananmen) to found the People's Republic: "China doesn't matter very much. It's not very important. It's never going to be powerful."[iv] China had no integrated industrial base, which Kennan thought basic to any serious capacity for warfare, merely an industrial fringe stitched along its coasts by the imperial powers; thus China should not be included in the containment strategy. Japan did have such a base, and was therefore the key to postwar American policy in East Asia.

Such clear-eyed thinking, informed by a shrewd realpolitik, is a better place to start than with the chorus of alarms and diversions always surrounding the China issue. If we can think realistically about where China has been, maybe we can make better judgments about where it is going. That begins with recognition that China has yet to shake the world; its external influence has been comparatively inconsequential since the industrial revolution. Instead, it is the world that has shaken China.

Castle and Moat

Foucault's metaphor gives us culture as a feudal castle protected by a moat of ingrained practices, habitual choices, and unconscious rejections through which the heterodox and the alien are kept at bay or subdued. It might be taken as a restatement of the reigning metaphor for Chinese civilization: dignified, aloof, self-contained, content with itself, always ready to reject the barbarian—or, if it must succumb temporarily, to dissolve the foreigner in the absorbent sea of Chinese custom and practice. For centuries this fate awaited the Mongols, the Manchus, and according to many accounts, the Westerners.

The Chinese "castle", however, was an empire encompassing for its occupants the known universe, and its "moat" delimited civilization itself. Two hundred years ago King George III of England sent a mission to the Chinese court, asking for the opening of trade relations. Emperor Qianlong replied:

> Swaying the four seas, I have but one goal, which is to establish perfect governance; strange jewels and precious objects do not interest me . . . the virtue and prestige of the celestial dynasty have spread far and wide, the kings of the myriad nations come by land and sea with all sorts of precious things. Consequently there is nothing we lack. . . .

Alas, there was all too much that China "lacked." Modern history began for China when the British banged on its door and when, in C.P. Fitzgerald's perfect metaphor, "to the amazement of all, within and without, the great structure . . . suddenly collapsed, leaving the surprised Europeans still holding the door handle."

A structure that could hold together the entirety of China was not put together again until the country had experienced a century and a half of debilitation, rebellion, central collapse, and disintegration, followed by false starts, blind alleys, civil and international wars, and an immense social revolution. When Mao announced atop Tiananmen in 1949 that "China has stood up", he stirred the hearts of Chinese everywhere, for at least China was again unitary, the humiliation had stopped, and the foreigner had been expelled. But, that done, China again pulled up the ramparts and closed itself off against the Western challenge, only to fall behind once more. It adopted the modern world's only significant alternative to industrial capitalism, namely communism, and imagined that in so doing it was leaping ahead of the decadent West—only to fall behind. In the 1960s it closed itself off from both the Soviets and the West in the name of "self-reliance", and fell even further behind. The only untried strategy was to join up with the West, as Japan had done after 1868; which meant falling in well behind Japan, a former tributary.

In the 1980s Chinese intellectuals were able for the first time in decades to travel to the West and to appreciate the wealth, power, and civic order of societies long caricatured as capitalist nightmares; meanwhile the very leaders who had penned the caricatures were now looking to the West for a way out of China's developmental impasse. Thus even the one remaining achievement of the Chinese revolution, the re-establishment of national dignity and pride, seemed a mere illusion. "No foreigner can understand the depth of our pain", a respected intellectual told a visiting American.[v]

In all these encounters, spanning two centuries, we can appreciate the alpha and the omega of China's relationship to the modern world. Standing at the center of the only world it knew, supremely self-confident of the inherent superiority of its own civilization, China has still not overcome the humiliation of encountering a West that prevailed against all Chinese stratagems. It was not for want of trying.

Three Strategies

The 1950s produced some classic metaphors for Sino-American relations but no contact, other than the bloody Korean War, which made mutual accommodation impossible for a generation. Before that war, Harry Truman's secretary of state, Dean Acheson, attempted to construct a different policy, one that Richard Nixon—Acheson's antagonist in the 1950s—was to fulfill only in the 1970s.

That policy was to recognize communist China, as a means of weaning it away from Moscow and bringing it into the world economy, thus rendering it dependent on the West. Acheson, like George Kennan, thought that Moscow could not really do much to rehabilitate and industrialize China; sooner or later it would have to turn to the West for help. An Anglophile and an internationalist, Acheson wanted to work with Britain to keep China open, in the hope that this would divide Beijing and Moscow, and ultimately scatter China's insurgent impulses in the solvent of free trade. The way to do that was to try to stay on the good side of Chinese anti-imperial nationalism, and hope to enmesh China in the world economy. The direct confrontation of the United States and China in the Korean War killed that hope for two decades. It also committed the United States to maintaining the separation of Taiwan from the mainland, a separation that continues to this day.

This early 1950s history shaped China's development strategy profoundly. In essence, three broad conceptions of political economy, each with a foreign policy corollary, have animated post-1949 China. All have had the goal on which all Chinese nationalists could agree: to foster China's wealth and power. All have had the stunning and unnerving aspect of requiring thorough change abruptly initiated from the top, first by Mao and then by Deng. And all have sought to contend with the same circumstance that the Qianlong Emperor faced: a vibrant world economy, led first by England and then by America.

Orthodox Stalinist industrial policy defined the first phase in the 1950s, something that was perhaps inevitable but that was deeply reinforced by mutual U.S.-Chinese hostility and American blockade: extensive, heavy industrial development, taking steel as "the key link", with the foreign policy corollary that China "leaned to one side" in the bipolar Cold War conflict. Mao emphasized China's relative backwardness and its "late" industrialization in world time. Buoyed by China's strong growth in the mid-1950s, he launched the Great Leap Forward to catch up with England in fifteen years. Instead he caught up with a profound economic crisis, compounded by the deaths through famine of millions of peasants. The foreign policy corollary of the 1950s program also collapsed, as the Sino-Soviet split deepened and China found itself under threat by both Washington and Moscow. But as a book widely circulated in China last year pointed out, Mao's agrarian policies and institutions also worked to root China's vast peasantry to the soil for thirty years. Rather than being allowed to flood the into the cities, as they were doing in most Third World countries (and as they now do in today's China), they were kept in place and indoctrinated to believe they were "making revolution."[vi]

No statement captures the reasoning behind China's next dramatic departure better than Mao's judgment, made in 1961, on Nikita Khrushchev's doctrine of peaceful coexistence and competition with capitalism: "This is changing two de facto world markets into two economic systems inside a unified world market." That is, while China's lean-to-one-side policy had been predicated on withdrawal from the capitalist market system and the building of an alternative socialist system—one in conflict with and seeking to replace the capitalist one—Soviet revisionism was now effectively giving up this struggle. What little was left of Stalin's alternative system, moreover, was corrupt, fostered dependency, and had lost its original raison d'être. And, of course, a unified world market, led by the United States, remained as strong as ever.

If this critique of Moscow's revisionism was valid, China was now faced with a choice: It could either go it alone through a self-reliant strategy, or join the world market on the best terms it could get. Broadly speaking, China was to choose the first course in the mid and late 1960s, and the second course from the late 1970s up to the present. Both choices assumed a single world economy, but the first spelled withdrawal from it while the second implied enmeshment.

The self-reliant strategy of the 1960s was pre-eminently and uniquely a Maoist political economy—drawing upon mass mobilization, moral or ideological incentives, with "class struggle" as the key link. Its domestic expression was the Cultural Revolution, and its foreign policy corollary was solidarity with the Third World. Class struggle turned out to mean intense political infighting at the top, and growing chaos, violence, and alienation everywhere else. A certain nadir was reached in 1971 when Mao's "chosen successor", Lin Biao, sought to flee to Russia after a failed coup attempt, only to be shot down. After that, few Chinese could believe anything the central regime said, and the dictatorial elite did not know what it was doing.

In that same year that Lin Biao was killed, Nixon and Kissinger opened relations with China, seeking to reinforce Sino-Soviet differences and thus to use communism to contain communism. It was a grand diplomatic success, and soon Sino-American relations warmed to the brink of strategic alliance. In December 1975 Deng Xiaoping welcomed Gerald and Betty Ford to a sumptuous dinner in the Great Hall of the People. With maotai glasses held high, they heard Deng offer this toast to the presidential party:

> There is great disorder under heaven and the situation is excellent. . . . The factors for war and revolution are increasing. Countries want independence, nations want liberation, and people want revolution. . . . The wind in the bell tower heralds a storm in the mountains.

But what Deng might really have wanted to say was this:

> There is great disorder under heaven and the situation is terrible. The factors for war are decreasing and those for revolution, nonexistent. Countries want interdependence, nations want wealth, and people hate revolution. The wind in the bell tower heralds a catastrophe in China.

The Man Who Loved Croissants

Within ten months of President Ford's visit Mao would die and his mandate would end, events that were appropriately accompanied by China's most destructive earthquake of the century. Slowly, gradually, all the metaphors with which we had come to understand the Chinese revolution were now reversed: Mao, it turned out, had not been the titan who brought revolution, national unity, and egalitarian prosperity to "the sick man of Asia", but a murderous despot to be ranked with Hitler and Stalin—except that he also liked to molest little girls. China's intellectuals were not the effete scholar-officials who had delivered their nation to nineteenth-century imperialism—let alone the "stinking ninth category" abused by Mao's wife, Jiang Qing—but the new hope for an incipient civil society, the green shoots emerging after a revolutionary nightmare. And Deng was not the "capitalist-roader" renegade who had notoriously said it didn't matter if a cat was yellow or black as long as it caught the rat, but a bridge-playing, soccer-loving family man who had developed a taste for croissants when he lived for five years in France as a youth (having, by one account, been shown by a certain Ho Chi Minh where to find the best ones). Time magazine's "Man of the Year" twice (in 1978 and 1985), Deng was the folksy reformer and would-be democrat who in 1979 toured a Houston rodeo waving a ten-gallon hat. His economic reforms, helped along by a supportive United States, had finally opened the path to the wealth and power all of China's reformers had long sought.

Then came the massacre of young people at Tiananmen on June 4, 1989, and all the West's metaphors for China reversed yet again. But while the effect of Tiananmen on Western attitudes was profound, its effect on Deng's economic policy was minimal. No change has been deeper, or more systematically sustained, than China's reform strategy since 1978. There has not been a single lurch or tortuous passage since then that is comparable to the pre-1978 period; instead there has been a comparatively steady tendency, almost a textbook example of how to introduce a developing country into the world economy. Hu Yaobang, general secretary of the Communist Party in the 1980s, later claimed that the Third Plenum of the Eleventh Central Committee in December 1978—which marked the birth of the new policy—was a turning point in party history comparable only to the changes of 1927 and 1936.

By the beginning of 1980 a new political leadership, led by Deng Xiaoping, had established firm control over the Chinese state. Always thorough when embarking on major new programs, the Chinese leadership made the requisite revisions in basic theory and assumptions. In place of the Maoist emphasis on class struggle and the relations of production, Deng Xiaoping pushed the "theory of productive forces" and the epistemological doctrine of "seeking truth from facts." The motive force in history was not class conflict, it turned out, but an all-round development of human and material forces of production. Deng deemed science and technology to be politically neutral, thus contradicting Jiang Qing who had declared that a socialist train running late was better than a capitalist train on time. China's economists began studying Keynes and Friedman, preferring the former since he blessed a central role for the state in the economy. More subtly, the determinist "productive forces" theory nudged communist China toward learning from capitalist Japan, which had always emphasized the acquisition of advanced technologies in its march to economic prowess.

In 1981 the new premier, Zhao Ziyang, said, "We must abandon once and for all the idea of self-sufficiency . . . all ideas and actions based on keeping our door closed to the outside world and sticking to conventions are wrong." He continued, "Greater exports are the key . . . we should boldly enter the world market." Zhao cited China's vast labor pool as its key advantage in the world economy, and was not above waving the fabled potentialities of the China market in the face of Western businessmen. By that time China had joined the IMF and the World Bank, and had most-favored nation status with the European Community. The broader logic, of course, was that there was but one world—not three as Mao had said—the world of global capitalism, Acheson's world.

Slowly the staggering nature of China's "reform" became apparent. Agriculture was virtually privatized in a massive decollectivization, prices were decontrolled, the currency floated against the dollar, central planning moved in the direction of Keynesian macroeconomic regulation, and the massive state sector began to cut free of the government's subsidies and umbilical cord. It would take an unreconstructed determinist to have predicted, however, that the same treaty ports that fueled China's economy in the imperial era would now be touted as models to emulate. Yet in April 1981, the State Council called on everyone to "learn from Shanghai, the coastal provinces, and the advanced"—not the Shanghai that was a radical bastion in the Cultural Revolution, but the Shanghai that provides about 15 percent of China's total exports and 70 percent of its textile and light-industrial exports (bicycles, clothes, sewing machines). Soon high communist leaders were referring to "China's gold coast", while others, hardliners, drew the analogy with the old treaty ports and foreign concessions. Today China's treaty-port region is becoming another country, a rapidly growing, vast market that both fuels and benefits from the export program.

Those experts who project Chinese disintegration have no trouble locating several Chinas already: the inland provinces where the peasant majority lives, with a per capita GNP of around three hundred dollars; coastal provinces with perhaps twice as much wealth per capita; and selected enterprise zones and big cities (especially Shanghai and Canton) where huge fortunes are being made, and where average wealth is at least fifty percent higher again than in the non-urban coastal provinces.

But that is a limited perspective, for there are still other Chinas. The proximity of Taiwan, Hong Kong, and overseas Chinese in Southeast Asia, all now making enormous investments in China, suggests that ever-increasing involvement with the several countries of "greater China" is a far more likely outcome than domestic disintegration. Counting Taiwan, Hong Kong, Singapore, and the southeast Asian Chinese diaspora (particularly active in Malaysia and Indonesia), a Chinese population of nearly fifty million beyond China's mainland borders deploys a per capita GNP averaging about fifteen thousand dollars. Here is the advance guard—or the yeast—for the ongoing transformation of the livelihoods of perhaps five hundred million Chinese in the coastal provinces. This is why Hong Kong will remain as a capitalist *entrepôt*, the centerpiece of an enormously productive sphere of Chinese capitalism. It will be the nodal point at which the world economy will continue to shake China.

Many China watchers seem to think that something is amiss because so much of the "exporting" from the new zones has been to China's interior. Yet this merely recapitulates within China the triangular nature of China's trade in the world economy: generally speaking, it buys from the core and sells in the periphery, and inner China is still very much peripheral in the world system. In 1985 the World Bank found that the industrial market economies took 32 percent of China's manufactured exports, the developing economies 63 percent; its imports were overwhelmingly from the former. This trend has only deepened in the last decade. Furthermore, a potentially huge domestic market gives China a great advantage over most other newly-industrializing countries, which, with low purchasing power in their home markets, run into trouble when protectionism limits their access to the American or Japanese market. The five hundred million people of the coastal zones alone represent ten times as many potential consumers as South Korea, twenty-five times as many as Taiwan.

There are, of course, many opponents of reform, now called "conservatives" in the literature. The debacle at Tiananmen in 1989 energized many aging Stalinists and Maoists, who counterattacked with the battle cry of communist orthodoxy, claiming that Tiananmen proved that the noxious, polluting influences of capitalism could not be prevented while importing Western technologies and ideas "for use." Jiang Zemin, by now Deng's designated successor, said this about Tiananmen:

> Hostile forces at home and abroad created this turmoil to overthrow the leadership of the Party, subvert the socialist system, and turn China into a bourgeois republic and into an appendage of big Western capitalist powers once again. The victory and nature of this struggle represent an acute opposition between the Four Cardinal Principles and bourgeois liberalization, and it is a political struggle bearing on the life and death of our party, state, and nation. It is also a serious class struggle.

The "four upholds", as these principles were known, constituted "the foundation of the nation", according to Jiang, "whereas reform and opening to the outside world are means of strengthening the nation."

It was a restatement of the century-old *ti-yong* formula of Chinese experience and philosophy as the "base" and Western learning and technique "for use"—except that the "four principles" seemed to have been fabricated by a madman. As China deepened its export-led developmental program, bringing bankers and businessmen running from all corners of the globe, it was also to uphold "Marxism-Leninism-Mao Tse-tung thought, socialism, the dictatorship of the proletariat, and the supremacy of Party leadership." These four principles might have been appropriate for a communist country like North Korea, which remained closed (and constantly harped on similar themes), but they merely became the butt of after-dinner jokes in 1990s China—when, that is, they were not occasions for despair. The one constant candidate for such a principled center since 1949 has been China's zealous and absolute concept of national sovereignty, about which it has been a good deal more sensitive than the Western powers that introduced the idea to China in the first place. But then, it is the only principle China now has left.

"A China That Doesn't Smell"

The economic imperative, together with Chinese jealousy over sovereign prerogatives, provide perhaps the best starting point for speculations about China's future. Prognostication about China is no easy task, as is demonstrated by the well nigh infinite collection of bad predictions that Americans of every political persuasion have made over the years. Whether it was the Right arguing for "unleashing" Chiang Kai-shek against the mainland when he had just contrived to lose a nation there, or the Left claiming that Mao had invented a new form of democracy, or Richard Nixon saying all things about China over the course of his long career, the record is abysmal.

Almost all thinking about China today, whether by trained expert or grazing pundit, remains colored by the events of June 1989. In a game that might be called "What's my atavism?" we have heard everything, from Henry Kissinger lamenting the 1989 events "with the pain of a spectator watching the disintegration of a family to whom one has a special attachment", to China expert W.J.F. Jenner's judgment that "the experience of medieval Europe" should be our guide to "Chinese futures."

Last year, Deng, now reconverted from the croissant-loving man in the ten-gallon hat to the "butcher of Beijing", took perhaps his last stroll through one of his "open cities", the marvelous Sino-European treaty port of Qingdao. Here is what he said then:

> The policy of taking economic construction as the key link must never be changed; the reform and open-door policy must never be altered. The party's basic line must not be shaken for 100 years. . . . We must properly draw the lesson from the former Soviet Union. . . . The Chinese Communist Party's status as the ruling party must never be challenged. China cannot adopt a multi-party system.[vii]

There you have it: economic perestroika and glasnost, but political counterparts of neither. Our newest capitalist "miracle" just happens to be run by communists. Deng's persistent hypothesis has been that if China's living standards keep rising, his party can rule forever. He is probably wrong about his party, but right about the equation between prosperity and political legitimacy. Since 1978 the economy has grown at an average rate of 9 percent, quadrupling China's GNP. While the growth is stunning, his vision makes him no visionary; Deng is really nothing more than the Park Chung Hee of China.

This comparison is not made lightly: anyone who knows South Korea's history from 1965 to the present should know that all manner of political disorder can proceed without disrupting economic growth or dislodging the ruling groups.[viii] Park declared martial law and promulgated a frankly authoritarian constitution in 1972, ran thousands of dissidents off to military boot camp, jail, or the torture chamber, bivouacked his army on the campuses—and at the same time pushed a state-dominant, radical heavy industry strategy against all the best advice of our economists. Always his theory was that economic growth would buy political legitimacy. His own security chief blew Park's brains out in 1979, his protégé Chun Doo Hwan took over the security agencies and then (probably) provoked an uprising in the southwestern city of Kwangju in May 1980 that can be compared in precise detail to what happened in June 1989 in Beijing, complete with regular military units exterminating students (the Kwangju death toll was if anything higher). Seven years later Chun was overthrown in massive street protests by students, workers, and ordinary middle class citizens. Meanwhile through the entire period, Korea's growth rates were usually the highest in the world, and Park still sits atop Korean public opinion polls as the most respected former president. Similarly, the economic transformation of Taiwan, Korea's rival in growth rates, went on under a full martial law regime, enforced from 1949 to 1987.

China is quite frankly pursuing the latest version of the developmental state theory, one our economists cannot understand but that makes complete sense to Asians as diverse as former Japanese Prime Minister Kishi Nobusuke, Chiang Kai-shek, Park Chung Hee, Lee Kwan Yew, and Deng Xiaoping. The Economist notes that consumption patterns in China today mimic those of Taiwan around 1970. And Chinese analysts point to Harvard political scientist Samuel Huntington's theory that while political instability can be expected as per capita GNP moves from three hundred to four thousand dollars, it will end after that, and therefore so will Communist Party rule (or so it is hoped).[ix]

Korea and Taiwan each had a huge state economic sector that owned the banks and most large industries, courtesy of a half-century of Japanese colonialism; the state sector produced 57 percent of Taiwan's industrial production in 1952, 40 percent in 1964, and 15 percent in 1975. Rapid growth rates in Taiwan and Korea occurred in spite of this state sector, with private firms often expanding by nearly 20 percent per year. Now in the China of the 1990s, we find a state sector that is a drag on the economy (though a huge employer of its people). This sector retards a private sector growth rate of as much as 20 percent, but is slowly giving way. By the year 2000, the state sector is expected to account for 30 percent of industrial production, and by 2010, for 18 percent or less.

The current leadership's model of preference is not Korea or Taiwan but Singapore, and indeed several newly-emerging cities (designed to absorb huge rivers of peasants leaving the villages) are laid out on the fastidious and totally managed Singapore pattern, in search of what Chairman Jiang describes as "a China that doesn't smell." When we move from the half-country of South Korea to the island of Taiwan to the city-state of Singapore, we see that China is not another "Asian tiger" but a ten thousand-pound elephant proposing to clean up its act while squatting in the middle of the world economy. It is difficult to imagine what that will ultimately mean, but perhaps our economists can explain how 1.2 billion smart people pursuing their "comparative advantage" will avoid trampling on all the rest of us. (Shades of "China shakes the world"; could Beijing's fiendish goal be to use capitalism to break capitalism?)

At any rate, this is the unarguable and inevitable direction of contemporary China. Beijing's vintage "conservative" central planner, Chen Yun, is about as smart as our economists: he illustrated his worldview by likening state planning to a cage and the market to a bird flying around inside it; rarely has an analogy so confirmed an utter misunderstanding of the world market's inexorable logic, which is "to batter down all Chinese Walls" (in Marx's 1848 metaphor). In this sense the Colonel Sanders dummy, standing in front of the Kentucky Fried

Chicken outlet at Tiananmen Square, knows more than all the leaders who have stood atop the Gate of Heavenly Peace, scratching around for another way to wall in their people.

This ten thousand-pound Chinese elephant will not be a liberal. When television's window opened on the terrible events of Tiananmen, Western experts and pundits called the deposed premier Zhao Ziyang a "soft-liner", a "moderate", and a "liberal." This same Zhao personally sponsored the 1980s campaign for "the new authoritarianism", as did economic reformer Zhu Rongji, the leader incessantly fingered as a "moderate" successor to Deng. This campaign also explicitly took Korea and Taiwan as models, arguing that both examples showed how an echelon of technocrats under strong state guidance could transform a backward economy through financial subsidies, cheap state credits, and successive multi-year economic plans. As Zhao put it, "The major point of the theory is that the modernization of backward countries inevitably passes through a phase . . . centered on strong, authoritarian leaders who serve as the motivating force for change." Deng was typically shrewder, telling Zhao that the theory wasn't bad but the name wouldn't make for good politics.

Thus China today uses the full panoply of authoritarian measures, pioneered by Park in the early 1970s, to keep people's noses to the economic grindstone and out of politics: ubiquitous surveillance by enormous security agencies, prompt deployment of riot police, expulsions from elite universities, blacklists of forbidden books, absence of habeus corpus, and the torture of recalcitrant dissidents. Meanwhile under Deng's "863 Plan", put into effect in 1986, China's technocrats (who constitute around 25 percent of new Party members since 1980) figure out how to move into "high technology" industries like semiconductors, genetic engineering, and materials science.

As well as the repression, there is much else that is ugly. Recently China was judged by businessmen to be second only to Nigeria as the most corrupt major economy in the world. Informed Americans lament the millions of peasants flooding into China's cities, cluttering the train stations and sleeping on the streets (Beijing is now said to have a "floating population" of about three million). Public manners have degenerated into shoving old ladies and breaking queue lines for buses and taxis; vast clouds of black pollutants spew from overcrowded buses chugging down the streets; a spirit of pettiness and money-grubbing seems to affect everybody. The only refuge is down the back alleys, where the worst thing one might encounter is an open sewer or an old man brushing his teeth. If this is Beijing today, these are also one's indelible memories of Seoul in 1967. In brief, to figure out where China will be in the next couple of decades, one should look at where Korea and Taiwan have been since about 1970.

China and the Tigers: Who, Whom?

These days no country suffers the slings and arrows of human rights activists more than China, but from Beijing's point of view all the criticism is the sheerest hypocrisy. Where, after all, were those activists when Korean troops ravaged Kwangju, only to find General Chun rewarded with a quick state visit to Washington? Beijing argues that the British never allowed anything resembling democracy in their Hong Kong colony until it became apparent that it was going back to China (true), and that Taiwan only rescinded the "Period of Mobilization for the Suppression of Communist Rebellion" in 1991, four years after it ended Taiwan's martial law regime (also true). But that was then and this is now: The developmental states of East Asia have moved toward direct elections and basic political freedoms, even if their model is Japan's long-lasting system of single party democracy. Therefore China can look forward to a never-ending conflict between advocates of human rights and democracy, on the one hand, and economic growth on the other, as long as it fails to decompress its political system.

More significant for China's future, however, will be the strong economic undertow that Taiwan and Hong Kong will exercise on China's open cities and "golden necklace" for many years to come. China's export zones were not placed by accident: Zhuhai is opposite Macao, Shenzhen is across from Hong Kong, and Shantou and Xiamen face the Taiwan Straits. They are export entrepôts and pivots for China's involvement in the world economy: China's exports rose an astonishing 62 percent in the first quarter of 1995, with fully 40 percent of the value coming from Guangdong Province, opposite Hong Kong.

The top two foreign investors in China are Hong Kong and Taiwan, followed by the United States, with Hong Kong and Macao accounting for 63 percent of all foreign investment by the end of 1994. Will this strong counter-influence provoke China forcibly to shut down Hong Kong's politics? More likely Hong Kong's posthaste democracy will begin to colonize China's near reaches, as its economy has done. Will China continue to fire its Dongfeng (East Wind) medium-range missiles across the bow of General MacArthur's "unsinkable aircraft carrier" (as it did in July 1995), or will it deepen the twenty billion dollars worth of trade it now does with Taiwan, a trade heavily in China's favor? The growing exchange across the Taiwan straits is the dominant tendency, reinforced by the surprising strength of a party favoring reunification with the mainland in Taiwan's recent elections. This burgeoning exchange has already reduced Taiwan's "three no's" policy (no contact, no negotiation, no compromise) to merely the last one: no compromise. But that, admittedly, is a big "no."

Roosevelt and Churchill decided to give Taiwan back to Chiang Kai-shek at the Cairo Conference in 1943. They did so more to punish Japan than to reward China. Until recently, the nationalists did much worse than the Japanese at winning the hearts and minds of the natives. Taiwan was never more than a remote province to the last Manchu dynasty, and when Japan colonized it in 1895 there was next to no resistance. As late as 1970 a political scientist sojourning in Taiwan found nostalgia for the Japanese colonial era at every turn. But a deal is a deal, and the Cairo agreement was deeply reinforced by the decisions of two presidents, Nixon in 1972 and Carter in 1978, to trade away the independence of the island for a new relationship with China. China is completely within its international rights when it says, as it often does, that any sovereign state "is entitled to use any means it deems necessary, including military ones, to uphold its sovereignty and territorial integrity." This is a sacred principle to China, precisely because, again, it has so few principles left. Thus China clings to the formula that in the final instance it is willing to use force if the people of Taiwan declare their independence.

Deng Xiaoping's foreign policy has echoed the pragmatism of his reform program, however, just as China's foreign policy under Mao was always cautious and calculating, despite its bluster. Deng's "one China, two systems" formula is meant to imply long-term autonomy for Taiwan. He stated in 1984 that China needs peace for the next two decades to develop itself, and proceeded to slash spending for the People's Liberation Army. The share of the state budget going for defense was halved from 1977 to 1986, dropping to 9.3 percent; it rose by an average of about 12 percent annually from that point to the present, with the figures skewed by early-1990s spending increases to placate and assure the loyalty of the military, and to assuage the military's shock at the effectiveness of American weaponry in the Gulf War. Deng has moved to ensure control of the military: nineteen full generals were promoted in June 1994, and the key appointees were Deng loyalists rather than career soldiers. Much of China's recent saber-rattling over Taiwan and the Spratlys has been done by military figures hoping for more funds, or by civilians hoping to placate the military with tough rhetoric.

Hardliners have threatened Taiwan time and again in recent months, culminating in military exercises involving one hundred and fifty thousand infantry, air force, and naval personnel conducted just opposite the island in March 1996, and designed to intimidate voters in the presidential elections that Taiwan will hold on March 23, 1996. Hotheads in Beijing have also provoked nasty editorials in the United States by suggesting that Americans care much more for Los Angeles than they do for Taiwan, and would not dare intervene if China attacked the island. The top leaders like premier Li Peng, however, give priority to the reversion of Hong Kong in 1997 and Macao in 1999, and say that a Taiwan settlement must at minimum await those events; clearly any fighting over Taiwan in the near future would demolish the reversion of all three. Besides, China's capacity to defeat Taiwan is questionable.

Today the People's Liberation Army spends little more than South Korea and Taiwan combined on defense, and imports far less weaponry that Taiwan. Beijing's recent two billion-dollar deal to import seventy-two Russian SU-27 fighter planes, for example, does not begin to compare to Taiwan's purchase of one hundred and fifty F-16 A/BS (a superior U.S. fighter) and many more French Mirage 2000-5ES. Indeed, Taiwan is the second largest buyer of U.S. weaponry in the world, spending 7.8 billion dollars from 1990 to 1993.[x] Beijing mostly has Soviet equipment similar to that which the United States devastated in the Gulf War, and lacks the amphibious and air cover capability to take over Taiwan.[xi] Still, the question of democracy will bedevil China's growing economic relationship with Taiwan as long as it bedevils China itself. It is inconceivable that the Taiwanese majority, finally able to disabuse itself of the mainlanders who imposed their rule at the point of a gun in the late 1940s, would succumb to the straitjacket of Beijing's authoritarian politics in the 1990s. Therefore a reunification without bloodshed will only be possible when some successor to Deng begins to democratize Chinese politics.

Letting Well Enough Alone

Charles Krauthammer has argued in *Time* (July 31, 1995) that "we must contain China"—a China led by a "ruthless dictatorship" that seeks "relentlessly to expand its reach." Moreover, "containment of such a bully must begin early in its career", that is, now. Other prominent observers, like Karen Elliott House writing in the *Wall Street Journal* (July 1995), have argued that the United States and China "are on a collision course." Whereas other East Asian countries "have pursued the U.S. model of economic and political development" and value the U.S. presence in the region, House maintains that China's political economy is deeply insecure, causing it to pursue "a foreign policy that is part petulance and part paranoia."

Going directly against George Kennan's conviction concerning China's relatively modest weight in global politics, the United States fought two Asian wars with the goal of containing the Chinese revolution. Rough peasant armies, Chinese and North Korean, fought our troops to a standstill in Korea; another rough peasant army, led by the man who advised Deng Xiaoping about croissants, did even better. The two wars left about 110,000 Americans dead. Now we are advised to try once again to contain a China, this time an allegedly paranoid China armed with nuclear-tipped ICBMs that can reach the American heartland. But there is another way to think about such problems, and we have a recent example to make the point. From 1990 to 1994 the Pentagon thought seriously about fighting North Korea again, this time over its nuclear program, egged on constantly by many commentators. But instead a policy of engaging North Korea diplomatically was followed. The policy has worked successfully, against nearly all the advice of our pundits.

Some Americans cannot recognize a victory when they see one. In two decades of peace since 1975, Vietnam has made substantial progress toward becoming the country we always wanted it to be: pro-American, opening to the world market, a buyer of American goods. China has moved in the same direction, to an extent inconceivable in 1975, and even North Korea, that moat-builder par excellence, now wants entry to the only game in town. They all just happen to be led by men who still prefer to call themselves communists, though what meaning that term now carries is unclear. That said, it should also be underlined that not a single East Asian country pursues "the U.S. model." They all follow Japan.

Imagine what it must have been like for Chinese and Koreans to watch Japan, the country that ravaged their nations and their souls, get rich after World War II, while they fought bloody wars and suffered agrarian misery beyond American comprehension. But Kennan was right: Japan is the active factor in East Asia, still today the sole comprehensively industrialized Asian nation operating at a technologically advanced level, and thus the only real rival to the Western powers. As Chalmers Johnson has pointed out in these pages, we have been busily if surreptitiously containing Japan since 1945, and if anything our concern in this respect has deepened in the 1990s, as the Pentagon's main object of containment, the USSR, disappeared.

How—and why—should we now attempt to contain China, which wants to contain Japan? A rough balance of power now obtains in East Asia and will for many years, with Japanese economic might offset by China's military might, and with formidable conventional armies in both Koreas, Taiwan, and Vietnam also working to prevent dominance by any single power. Why not let well enough alone?

A principle reason why we find it difficult to do that is because, for us, China is still a metaphor. It is a metaphor for an enormously expensive Pentagon that has lost its bearings and that requires a formidable "renegade state" to define its mission (Islam is rather vague, and Iran lacks necessary weight). China is a metaphor for some conservatives who no longer have a Left worthy of serious attack. It is a metaphor for American idealists in search of themselves, who see it as their defining mission to bring democratic perfection to a flawed and ignorant world. And it is a metaphor for an American polity that imagines itself coterminous with mankind, and is therefore incapable of understanding true difference.[xii] China has had many vices, true, but one virtuous difference through history has been its benign neglect of its neighbors. As a civilization widely perceived to have given much more than it took away—especially in contrast to Japan—China assumed that a great nation leads by example (Kennan has often said the same), that all who wish to come to the Middle Kingdom will do so, and that all the rest can stay put. This generality excludes China's subordination of Tibet since 1949, of course, but it helps to explain the long-term orientation toward the Middle Kingdom of several tributary states.

For a great scholar, C.P. Fitzgerald, the first pillar of Chinese civilization was the empire—long the fused Greece and Rome of East Asia. Settled agriculture and the "good earth" were the second pillar, placing an implicit limit on the reach of that empire. The third was Confucian orthodoxy. The peasant cultivated the soil and the scholar-official the classics, thus to satisfy the body and soul of all under heaven and maintain the moat of self-sufficiency. No emperor could have his mandate without the support of both classes. Whatever else one may say about him, Mao matched the old emperors on all fronts: He unified a China expanded to its historical full breadth with the conquest of Tibet and the intervention in Korea; he formulated and deployed a distinctively Chinese version of communist orthodoxy that was very quickly at odds with Moscow's orthodoxy; he had a policy for the peasantry that, however disastrous in economic terms, kept them on the land; above all he built the necessary moat that enabled China to remain isolated for another generation.

Thus it is not a matter of small concern that China today has neither empire nor orthodoxy, earns the contempt of the scholars, and projects for its vast peasantry a daily disappearance of both the soil and the ancient livelihood that it sustained. Orville Schell recently lamented that "there is almost nothing that is fixed or certain" in today's China; imagine how the Chinese must feel about that. At the end of this century the ancient pillars crumble and none but the expediency of "getting rich" remains. Still, China does have the officials, long accustomed to the delivery of goods and services whether under Confucianism or communism. The central state is now transforming itself along the lines of Japan's model; it will try to ride the capitalist tiger in the interest of a China that is both rich and powerful. Like its near neighbors, it will reach unforeseen limits placed upon it by the world economy, and will have to join rather than dominate the hierarchy of advanced industrial states. Then we will see if China has established a principle allowing it to be modern and Chinese at the same time.

China's contemporary leaders desperately want a moat, any moat, to establish distance between China and the world economy, but to have one they must have a principle of Chinese difference to enforce, and there is none at hand. Predictably, China fragments into imperialists who want to use China's military power to forge a new suzerainty, intellectuals who want their internal island of freedom, bureaucrats who harp about "bourgeois liberalism", reactionaries nostalgic for peasant China, and leaders who want to repress heterodoxy in the name of a lost orthodoxy. None of these programs can win a decisive victory; they can all cause endless trouble. But if the economy continues to grow rapidly in the context of greater China, these groups will merely be troublesome; none will shake the world. The domestic race will go to the bureaucrats and the corporate leaders, who will complete the circle of capitalism with an East Asian difference. The world will once again have shaken China.

Various "realists" deploying the "logic of power" have been quick to argue that China's growing capabilities will soon yield an assertive China intent on dominating East and Southeast Asia, or even the world; powerful China will want its place in the sun. The burden of this essay is that China is different: its history has been singular, confining its expansion to its near reaches and constraining its choice of means. When China has used force since 1949, it has done so only within its historic region, and, more often than not, judiciously and effectively.

Chinese leaders may still proclaim the inherent superiority of their culture, but that heritage can teach them the ultimate weakness of a power that only expresses itself militarily. Nor can military force solve China's deepest problem, which is the continuing predominance of the West. The answer to that challenge is civilizational, not military.

China is a country whose central leaders have swayed it this way and that for two centuries in search of a principle for involvement with the modern West. Certainly no foreigner can suggest what that principle might be. For us, the route to understanding China is through self-knowledge. A wise American policy will begin with the contemplation of China's long-term humiliation at the hands of the West, and therefore with Western humility: We have shaken China enough as it is. We should do what little we can to encourage a less dominant central government, the rule of law, and basic political rights for China's citizens—but without illusions that we will make much of a difference.

The main theme in our relations with China should be to nurture a long period of economism. Do we want a China shooting missiles across Taiwan's bow, or a China that in November 1995 reduced tariffs by an average rate of 30 percent to polish its application to the World Trade Organization? This is not a hard choice, and the fact that it can be posed illustrates how far China has come in two decades. Probably it will all end with China being captured by the gravity of the world market. But it might also end with both peoples, Chinese and Americans, rediscovering the core of their own, different, civilizations. A wealthy China again capable of asserting the weight and richness of its civilization would give much to the world, and would allow both peoples to discover a new relationship. Then "China" will finally become, for Americans, not a metaphor but simply China. And then perhaps, finally, China will have shaken the world.

NOTES

[i] Napoleon is alleged to have said that "When China wakes up, it will shake the world." Jack Belden used that title for his classic account of the Chinese revolution, but two new books on China by our best experts open with Napoleon yet again: Nicholas Kristof and Sheryl WuDunn use this aphorism for their title in *China Wakes: The Struggle for the Soul of a Rising Power* (New York: Times Books, 1994); also Kenneth Lieberthal, *Governing China: From Revolution Through Reform* (New York: W.W. Norton, 1995), p. xv. Harry Harding frames his useful account of Sino-American relations with cyclical metaphors in *A Fragile Relationship: The United States and China Since 1972* (Washington, DC: The Brookings Institution, 1992), as does Suzanne Ogden in *China's Unresolved Issues: Politics, Development and Culture* (Englewood Cliffs, NJ: Prentice-Hall, 1995), p. 6. W.J.F. Jenner, who by his own account once sympathized with the Chinese revolution, argued that Tiananmen proved that China was still captured by its ancient, unchanging, and probably irremediable tendency toward tyranny. See Jenner's *The Tyranny of History: The Roots of China's Crisis* (New York: Penguin Books, 1994), pp. 1-11.

[ii] Vaclav Smil begins his important study of China's environmental calamities this way: "For knowing China—really knowing this continent-like country of diverse environments, ancient habits, contradictory leanings, and unpredicted challenges—even a lifetime is not enough." One is tempted to say, well, a lifetime will still have to do. See Smil's *China's Environmental Crisis: An Inquiry into the Limits of National Development* (Armonk, NY: M.E. Sharpe, 1993), p. vii.

[iii] Nearly all the alarmist images are present in a recent book by one of Hong Kong's foremost China watchers, Willy Wo-Lap Lam, in his *China After Deng Xiaoping* (New York: John Wiley & Sons, 1995), pp. 383-430.

[iv] Quoted in Bruce Cumings, *The Origins of the Korean War, II: The Roaring of the Cataract, 1947-1950* (Princeton: Princeton University Press, 1990), p. 55.

[v] Richard Madsen, *China and the American Dream: A Moral Inquiry* (Berkeley: University of California Press, 1995), p. 185.

[vi] Anonymous, *Looking at China With a Third Eye* (Taiyuan: Shansi People's Press, 1994). Lam, in *China After Deng Xiaoping*, calls it "the hottest book in China in 1994."

[vii] Quoted in Lam, p. 386.

[viii] Chinese economists who write in China's premier economic journal, *Jingji yanjiu* (Economic Studies), have been frank about their borrowings from Korea. For a recently translated sampling of their views on East Asian development in Korea, Taiwan, and elsewhere, see the special issue of Chinese Economic Studies (July/August 1994).

[ix] For Japan the pioneering work on the developmental state was done by Chalmers Johnson, *MITI and the Japanese Miracle* (Berkeley: University of California Press, 1983); for the same in regard to South Korea, see Jung-en Woo, *Race to the Swift* (New York: Columbia University Press, 1991). For China see Chen Yizhi, "The Developmental Model for Establishing a 'Hard Government and Soft Economy'", a 1988 article cited in Ruan Ming, Deng Xiaoping: *Chronicle of an Empire* (Boulder: Westview Press, 1994). Huntington's theory used different figures, see *Political Order in Changing Societies* (New Haven: Yale University Press, 1968); Chen seems to be thinking of the income trajectory and subsequent democratic opening of Taiwan and Korea.

[x] *Time*, December 12, 1994; *Far Eastern Economic Review*, January 19, 1995; *New York Times* February 7, 1996.

[xi] Michael C. Gallagher, "China's Illusory Threat to the South China Sea", *International Security* (Summer 1994), pp. 169-93.

[xii] See Madsen, op. cit., where these themes are explored with great sensitivity.

8

The Revolution Reversed:
China's Islamist Problem

*Charles Horner**

A generation ago, men of divergent personal appearance, political experience, and cultural inheritance ascended to political leadership in the Third World and decided to embrace a transcendent secular radicalism. Whatever their inherited differences, they hoped to construct a united front against the First World and all its evil works, and thereby gain standing for themselves and power for their countries. This was an ambitious project, for as partisans of a broadly-conceived Third World they would need to submerge intramural rivalries of religion, race, culture and conquest into a vocabulary of left-wing solidarity that had been devised by and intended for Europeans.

China invested heavily in this undertaking, for there seemed to be good possibilities in it. The old China—that is to say, mere Imperial or Republican China—could not have imagined the extension of its influence into so much of this world. The ambitions of Imperial China had certainly been great and its confidence in its own universalism highly developed. It was also long-accustomed to being the richest and most powerful country in the world. Even more, Confucianism, China's homegrown ideology, was integral to the growth and consolidation of China's influence in Korea, Japan and Vietnam. But the New

* Charles Horner is a senior fellow at the Hudson Institute. During the administrations of Presidents Reagan and George H.W. Bush, he served in the Department of State and the U.S. Information Agency.

This essay first appeared in *The National Interest*, No. 67 (Spring 2002).

Thinking of New China—Communist and Maoist China—carried even grander ambitions to make China a force in places where it had never before been well-established. Among those were the core countries of that other great non-European center of culture and power, the Islamic world. This was an improbable development, perhaps, but one made at least conceivable by the Cold War's admixture of geopolitics and ideology.

In at least this one respect, China's day-to-day encounters with the Islamic parts of the post-colonial world resembled our own. The representatives of the "new emerging forces" (the term is owed to Sukarno of Indonesia, then and now the most populous Muslim nation in the world) convened conferences, held summit meetings, issued declarations, and established worldwide personal reputations. Their comings, goings and pronouncements were closely scrutinized. A new kind of Great Game was being played in all these regions, and it required the contestants with real power to pretend that their local interlocutors were something more than buffoons.

But there was another part of the play that was neither flamboyant nor ridiculous, but deadly—murderous internal violence and protracted cross-border warfare. To stay for a moment with Indonesia—a prominent case study of the day—one can cite the events of 1965, when secular radicalism informed both Chinese strategic ambitions in Southeast Asia and Indonesia's own internal political vocabulary. The Communist Party of Indonesia, made up mostly of local Chinese, attempted a coup d'état that, had it succeeded, might have solidified a much-feared Beijing-Jakarta axis. Instead, what we remember about "the year of living dangerously"—aside from the classic motion picture made about it—is that it laid the foundation for decades of anti-Chinese authoritarian government in Indonesia, beginning with the murder of hundreds of thousands of ethnic Chinese Indonesian nationals.

Our worries today, of course, focus on other sources of political energy. The most dangerous plotting in Indonesia now is based in extremist Muslim madrassas, not in Maoist cells. ("Mr. Abu Bakar, 63, is the leader of Jemaah Islamiah, a regional terrorist organization whose goal is to create Daulah Islamiah, an Islamic state that would include Indonesia, Malaysia, and the southern Philippines. Under pressure from its neighbors, Indonesia has agreed to summon him for police questioning." So begins one account.) If we imagine a successful Islamist coup d'état, one that does not miscarry as did the Communist one, we do not see Beijing at the other end of the axis but rather some "Islamic" power or person—and with local Chinese again on the receiving end of great brutality in the bargain. Even Indonesia's separatist movements have lost their secular "internationalist" character; the oil-rich enclave of Aceh on Sumatra wants greater independence from Jakarta to give greater sway to local Islamic intensity and to hold on to more of its money. If it succeeds, it will become another statelet too rich for its own good, a financier for Islamic violence and terror, and perhaps a pivot in some kind of international Islamic archipelago in Southeast Asia.

It is a similar story in other countries nearby, where "Islam" is understood to have replaced "Third World Solidarity" as the wellspring of political energy. In Malaya during the 1950s—even before there was a Malaysia—Communist China had bet on an insurgency based on local ethnic Chinese to produce a pro-Chinese regime. In the Philippines, China had comparable hopes for the Huks' "national liberation movement." Today, these episodes are remembered in footnotes, if at all. Now, it is Muslim, not Maoist, malcontents who have achieved worldwide celebrity and, were they to prevail, it would not be a strategic gain for Beijing but an enormous setback. This, then, is one measure of the changing situation on the Islamic side of the Sino-Islamic frontier in Southeast Asia and the South China Sea. It is as though China's situation vis-à-vis the Islamic world has been turned upside down in the course of a mere quarter century.

There have also been changes on the Chinese side. Twenty-five years ago, China stopped looking to Mao Zedong Thought and its slogans to inspire socialist construction at home or to gain standing in the world. The Chinese know that Mao's grand world design failed as utterly as did his domestic one. The World Countryside did not surround the World City after all. Relieved by China's abandonment of blood-curdling rhetoric and massive subversion, the outside world decided to help this change along. But neither China nor its associates in America, Europe or East Asia thought very much about an Islamist challenge to China as these changes worked their way along. Now we must. Of course, whenever we imagine the Chinese pondering their place in the scheme of things, it is our conceit that they are somehow deeper, more introspective, and subtler than we are, that they go about it more incisively and more profoundly. But whatever their level of sophistication, it is clear that the Chinese are thinking about "Islam" today, and that their thought process is colored by history.

China's Islamic Narrative

"Orientalism" is a disdainful term used by some contemporary intellectuals to describe the Western interest in things Islamic (usually in the Near East, but easily extended to Southeast Asia or Inner Asia, too), which actually masks the West's pursuit of imperial grandeur and economic domination. It is said to be a phenomenon of both cultural study and social science, so that even an eccentric's naive infatuation with the exotic becomes, somehow, part of an expansionist design.

A gimlet-eyed Muslim scholar of China's age-old interest in far-flung Islamic places—someone, that is, interested in defending the far corners of the Islamic world against Western and Chinese encroachment—might allege the same combination of insouciance and cynicism in China. He might connect the ebb and flow of Chinese political and economic influence in Islamic places, whether in the South Seas or in Central Asia, to a comparable Chinese "orientalist" outlook. Armed with the West's formidable intellectual weapon of "post-colonial studies", and warned by it not to trust the professed friendship of any non-believer, such an engagé scholar might find an abundance of confirming evidence in a vast Chinese literature.

The rise of Islam is itself closely coincidental to the flourishing of China's great Tang dynasty (618–907), a dynasty renowned through the ages for its many splendors. There are Chinese accounts of Arab traders in Canton offering a dazzling array of goods. There are records of intrepid Chinese pilgrims like Xuanzang, the 7th-century monk who traveled the Silk Road westward. There are Chinese versions of the travels of Hungarian-British archaeologist Aurel Stein (1862–1943; Stein, for good measure, died in Kabul) and the Swedish explorer Sven Hedin (1865–1952), famed travelers in Central Asia once well known to European schoolboys as well as to their Chinese contemporaries. There have also been modern Western political travelers, most of them apologists for the expansion of Communist Chinese influence into historically Islamic domains. Lately, some contemporary Chinese literary travelers have been recovering an older Chinese sense of the "journey to the west" (to Inner Asia, that is) as a route to personal self-discovery and introspective escapism.

China has also produced its own version of a Chinoiserie mania in the form of a venerable interest in natural and man-made artifacts from far-off Islamic lands. A generation ago, the aspiring student of Tang-era China learned how the country created part of its sense of wealth, worldliness and conspicuous consumption by reading Edward Schafer's canonical catalogue of wonders, *The Golden Peaches of Samarkand* (1963). In earlier centuries, of course, the cultivated Chinese mandarin had himself come to the topic through books based on this sensibility, "pre-political" in a way, yet celebratory of the great Islamic emirates that provided the Chinese empire and those who ran it with useful and beautiful things from all over the world.

The contemplation of such vaguely-defined and exotic realms far away was, for a very long time, just a pleasure and not a problem for Chinese. But, eventually, it did become a problem when the Empire and its Republican successor concluded that vast tracts and large populations of peoples who were palpably not Chinese—including many millions of Muslims of Central Asian origin—nonetheless belonged inside "China." Over time, it became an accepted axiom of Chinese statecraft that these people simply had to stay in China.

It remains an axiom still, but the foundation beneath it has shifted over time, and continues to shift today. The Chinese understanding of what "China" is, and why some places belong in it and others do not, is found in many sources: in the writings of scholars and literati across the centuries who romanticized distant realms; in the records of political debate since the mid-18th century about the Empire's ideal boundaries (China's narrative about "imperial overstretch"); in notions of geopolitics and grand strategy (such as "control of the heartland" or "the influence of sea power") that entered China in the 19th and early 20th centuries; in the mantra of "nation" and "race" and "ethnicity" and "culture" that are mid-20th century inventions; in secular radical ideas like "proletarian internationalism" or "solidarity among the peoples"; and, now, in early 21st-century "threat assessment."

These concerns can lead to a kind of meandering. Just as we in the United States shift focus in the war against terrorism from Afghanistan to the Philippines and then to the Near East, so too have the Chinese shifted focus from Southeast Asia to the South Seas to the heart of Asia. At the moment, for example, Beijing's most important preoccupation is drawing the Sino-Islamic boundary in Xinjiang ("New Territories" in Chinese, or Chinese Turkestan or East Turkestan in our gazetteer), a 600,000 square-mile chunk of land that accounts for about 20 percent of the territory of the "People's Republic of China." Perhaps twenty million people live there, of which about 13 million are Muslim. Of those, 9 million are Uighurs, and 4 million are a mix of Kazaks, Uzbeks, Tajiks and others.

The region's Muslim presence alone gives the place its heightened relevance right now, though its exotic past is more than enough for some. Even more than the majestic mountain ranges, like the Pamirs or the Tianshan, which virtually surround the territory, Xinjiang's defining topographical feature is the great Taklamakan desert—"a true wilderness . . . intimidating, beautiful, dangerous, that preys on the mind and enslaves the senses."[i] That describes the forbidding spirit of this inland ocean of silicon—50 degrees below zero (centigrade) in the winter, blinding sandstorms in the summer—well-captured by Christopher Tyler, who visited there in 1996 wanting to retrace the route of Sven Hedin, the first European to go to the heart of the great desert a hundred years before. The place is no less harrowing a century later.

But it is not so much what the Taklamakan is as where it is. Settlements strung out along its northern and southern rims were way stations on the ancient Silk Road. Centuries later, the larger region as a whole, finding itself situated between expanding Romanov and Manchu empires, became a place of rivalry—and this well before anyone had internalized the significance of large oil deposits in Xinjiang's Tarim Basin. Before then, it was only rare jade and fine gold that mesmerized outsiders. As for matters strategic, Owen Lattimore once tagged Xinjiang the "pivot of Asia", the "heartland" view of things at its highest.[ii]

One can recite, then, reasons for the region's importance to China, but this will not of itself tell us how Chinese came to think of Xinjiang as China. To understand that, we need know that in the mid-18th century, Qianlong (1736–96), the greatest of the Manchu emperors, brought Qing imperial rule there. James Millward of Georgetown University has reconstructed for us the debate over this great enterprise and has especially recapitulated the opposition of the Manchu emperor's Han Chinese counselors of state.[iii] These men saw no point in wasting the empire's resources on the conquest of barbaric wastelands. The Emperor argued back that the incorporation of the New Territories would prove an economical way of defending the core of the empire in China proper over the longer run. The Emperor's real justification for the huge expeditions, however, lay in his personal understanding of the meaning of the great empire he was creating. Qianlong conceived his subjects in their sameness, all equal on account of their loyalty to him, rather than as inferiors or superiors to anyone or anything else. Hence, a place might be a wasteland, but that did not necessarily make it barbaric as long as its inhabitants honored his rule.

As it happened, the decay of the Qing dynasty's power resulted in the loss of Xinjiang to local "rebels" in the mid-19th century. The Manchu rulers were certainly not pleased by this turn of events, but seemed resigned to it, the better to focus on the seaborne threats of the Western maritime powers. Now, however, it was members of the Chinese mandarinate who began to argue for the re-establishment of imperial power in the region, seeing the problems there as the result of prior misunderstandings of how to govern the place. In this view, a re-conquered Xinjiang properly run—that is, run along traditional Chinese, not Manchu, lines—would contribute to the solution of the country's difficulties, not exacerbate them; it would somehow make the country stronger in the face of the seaborne threats, not weaker. The 18th-century approach would thus have to change. These men were advocates, as Millward puts it, of "nothing less than the political, demographic, economic, and even ecological remaking of the Western Regions in China's image."[iv] Central to the Manchu view of things was the notion that "China" and "Xinjiang" were separate places, joined only at the head, not at the hip—and certainly not in the heart. But once originally indifferent to this distinction, many high-ranking Chinese officials came to conclude that the two needed to become one and the same.

To be sure, this conclusion was easier to establish in the Chinese mind than on the non-Chinese ground. Over time, it became relatively easy for political figures in the far northwest to exploit imperial weakness and international rivalries to free themselves from Beijing's de facto control. Yet, as one might perversely expect, the more this became the reality in Xinjiang, the stronger became the psychological, philosophical and ideological denial of it in Beijing. When the dynasty was strong, sinicization had not been the preferred policy of the empire. But the weaker the central government became and the less able it was to enforce its writ, the more committed to sinicization it became. Indeed, a traveler in Xinjiang today will be told by local Chinese that "Taklamakan" means "you go in, but you don't come out." The quip aptly expresses what they think about Xinjiang's entry into China more than 200 years ago.

Meanwhile, the ancient connections and affinities of Islamic Central Asia overall have been constantly affected by the ebb and flow of politics elsewhere. The Manchu dynasty ended in 1912, the Romanov in 1917. The other empires based in Western Europe either disappeared or were debilitated after World War I. But Xinjiang and its neighbors were too far from Wilsonian influence to be shaped by it. They were to experience instead the effects of the Leninist alternatives to it. First, Russian influence returned in the form of the Soviet Union and its Stalinist mode of governance. East Turkestan thus had good reason to cherish its separateness from its Sovietized neighbors in the adjacent "stans." On the other hand, though the new Chinese Republic may have held legal title to the place in the opinion of international lawyers, the struggles among the warlords and the Nationalists and the Communists were tantamount to a Xinjiang independence movement by default. In fact, between 1944 and 1949, there was even a formally-proclaimed East Turkestan Republic. It was soon brutally crushed by the new People's Republic of China, even as Beijing was enthusiastically offering support to decolonization movements elsewhere. In this convoluted way, the re-conquest once envisioned by Chinese strategists in the Manchu court of the 19th century was finally brought about.

In the early 1950s, the regimes in both Stalin's USSR and Mao's PRC were sufficiently synchronized in their debased brutality that a Turkic person on one side of the line had no particular reason to envy his brother on the other. They also shared a roughly similar radioactive peril: while the Soviets were busily contaminating Kazakstan, the Chinese were establishing their nuclear testing site at Lop Nor, in Xinjiang. But with the death of Stalin, the inhabitants of East Turkestan could sense a certain moderating of conditions to the west, contrasting all the more with their own experiences of Maoist madness during the Great Leap Forward and then the Cultural Revolution. In the 1970s and 1980s, the advantage moved again to the east, for the post-Mao reforms could be contrasted favorably to the last-gasp effort to shore up the Soviet Union. But with the end of the USSR, the Turkic peoples of Xinjiang could only envy their brethren who had not only gained independence but, in an astonishing feat of bureaucratic legerdemain, had even become a part of Europe—as members of the Organization for Security and Cooperation, and with their "desks" in the Bureau of European Affairs in our own Department of State.

Xinjiang as Imperial Atavism

The situation in Xinjiang today is anomalous. It is the last place of its kind that is still part of someone else's multi-national empire, in this case, the Chinese one. Contemporary Chinese rule is modern enough in name; Xinjiang is a "self-governing autonomous region of the People's Republic of China." But Beijing is not modern-minded in tolerating "diversity." Like some empires in the 19th century, it promotes a total transformation, a total sameness of "Xinjiang" and "China." Moreover, Xinjiang has no international standing. It has no "decolonization" cachet (unlike, say, tiny East Timor, whose independence advocates received the Nobel Peace Prize.) And because the population of Xinjiang is thought to consist of "militant Muslims", not "gentle Buddhists", it has no pop-culture cachet either (unlike, say, Tibet, whose leader-in-exile has quite a following in Hollywood).

In another sense, though, Xinjiang is thoroughly up-to-date—in the Islamic Internationalist character of its politics. The phenomenon is almost instantly recognizable in its form, content and worldwide connections. The war in Afghanistan in the 1980s is the archetype—local fighters backed by Muslims of every stripe, including Islamic governments such as Iran and Saudi Arabia, who otherwise may be bitter enemies. Whereas a "liberation struggle" of the 1970s had as its objective the creation of a "democratic republic" of Leninoid cast, an "Islamic struggle" has as its objective another kind of regime entirely. Similarly, while one combats a 1970s-type "liberation movement" with a political-cum-security program broadly understood, those who wage jihad announce in advance that they are incorrigible, so that the only way to deal with them is to kill them.

As this is a novel problem in the modern world, it is also a novel problem for China. A droll PLA general might describe it as confronting a "People's War with Islamic characteristics." This struggle in Xinjiang has been going on for a number of years now, and the Chinese report to us about it from time to time. Executions are announced and successes against local separatist and terrorist cells are publicized. The "splittists" will occasionally assassinate pro-Beijing collaborators, murder local officials, and set off bombs, not only in Xinjiang but in China proper. Sometimes there are reports of ethnic conflict and communal rioting. People outside the country who support their Xinjiang kinsmen report on Chinese repression beyond that which Beijing itself publicizes, so that Beijing admits to "hundreds" of arrests, while others say "thousands." Beijing admits to "dozens" of executions, while others say "hundreds." We also know that Beijing has deployed to the territory ever-larger numbers of regular PLA forces as well as so-called People's Armed Police.[v] Reminiscent, too, of that older notion of turning "Xinjiang" into "China" are the government-sponsored migrations of Han Chinese into the area and the promotion of large-scale investment (also intended to help narrow a growing and politically dangerous income gap between the country's hinterland and its far more prosperous coastal areas.)

Thus far, Beijing seems satisfied by its success in quarantining Xinjiang from well-meaning liberal internationalism, or soft-headed trendy internationalism, or "concerned" busybodies generally. Indeed, Beijing's contempt for "world opinion" and the "international community" is empirically well-justified. But "Islamic opinion" and the "community of the faithful" are different. Beijing's insistence on repression in Xinjiang creates a need to disentangle Xinjiang from the Islamic world, and as the repression grows, so does the effort at disentanglement.

But the brutal pursuit of an anachronistic Chinese imperialism at home has as its mirror image abroad a supine Chinese diplomacy in the Islamic world; it is little more than appeasement and payoff on a grand scale. That the policy is undignified should not cause us to be dismissive of it, however, for it has not yet failed—and it may even succeed.

Since China fears, for example, that Iran and Saudi Arabia might stir up and subsidize discontent among Turkic Muslims in Xinjiang as they once did among the Afghans, the Chinese response is to cool proliferation concerns and supply arms and "problem technologies" to them—at generous prices. Since China fears that the now-independent "stans" will harbor sympathizers and supporters of independence for East Turkestan, it subsidizes their trade, overpays for their mineral rights, gives them weapons, and, most of all, provides great ceremonies for their leaders. (In this respect, the theatricality of it resembles the lavish attention paid to Third World leaders of the last generation. It is a fine art in China, honed across the centuries—the host's exquisite politeness as a way of showing contempt for his guest.)

To be sure, these efforts have a history. Long before the world worried about Islamic extremism, China was hard at work building back doors through the Islamic world to the world beyond as, for example, the fabled Karakoram Highway chiseled into forbidding mountains, ultimately designed to connect China's far west to the Pakistani port of Karachi. There is also the need for oil; China is now a major importer and, therefore, a competitor for access to energy in the Persian Gulf, the Caspian Sea, the Indonesian archipelago, and the waters adjacent. Obviously, these projects are advanced by the co-optation and isolation of extremist Islam, not only by China, but also by others.

In the end, though, China's experience of Islam at home and abroad has likely created a kind of cognitive dissonance in the Chinese political mind. Everywhere it encounters Islam it appears at best opaque, more often as irrational and dangerous to China and Chinese. Yet there seems to be an unalterable commitment within the Chinese government to keep millions of such bloody-minded people under Chinese control, with the risk of turning Xinjiang into a Chinese Chechnya. Indeed, it is not only kindred Islamist states who may have an interest in doing this. The United States itself, committed though it is to the struggle against international terrorism, may come to see a distinction between "terrorism with a global reach" on the one hand, and a "struggle for human rights among an oppressed Turkic minority" on the other. After all, Beijing cannot but notice that U.S. efforts against terrorist influence in Malaysia, Indonesia and the Philippines also manage to strengthen the American position against China in the contentious South China Sea. The civil and military presence of the United States and its NATO allies in Afghanistan and the other "stans" is comparably ominous from Beijing's perspective. No wonder, then, that the Chinese government has complained bitterly to Pakistani President Pervez Musharraf about his having granted the United States exclusive access to airfields at Jacobabad and Pasni, and to his allegedly having allowed U.S. intelligence agencies to set up listening posts in the north opposite Xinjiang and Tibet.[vi]

The late Chairman Mao liked to describe the policies of China's opponents as ultimately self-defeating: "like lifting a rock only to drop it on their own feet", he used to say. Early in 2002, China may have, perhaps unwittingly, reminded us that the rock of its policy in Xinjiang may have become a little heavier to carry. The regime issued an official paper linking heightened disorders in Xinjiang to Osama bin Laden saying, among other things, that "bin Laden has schemed with the heads of Central and West Asian terrorist organizations many times to help the East Turkestan forces in Xinjiang launch a holy war with the aim of setting up a theocratic Islamic state in Xinjiang."[vii] The intent of saying such a thing, of course, was to gain international sympathy and acquiescence—a truce, if you like, in the international human rights wars against China—so that China can go about its business in Xinjiang, not only for its own benefit but, presumptively, for ours, too. Yet in so doing, Beijing has underscored the depths of its difficulties, its lack of success thus far, and its potential vulnerabilities in the future.

China's problems in Xinjiang cannot but become a temptation for the United States if a future deterioration in Sino-American relations focuses attention on China's most deeply-seated structural weaknesses. It is of course a dangerous temptation; we will succumb to it only if China itself transforms Muslim militants in and around Ürümqi into our friends—just as the Soviet Union once did to their cousins in and around Kabul. Then, Beijing's great modernization project, however well-launched and energetically consolidated, will fall victim to China's anachronistic imperial pretensions.

NOTES

[i] Tyler, "Life Stripped to its Essentials in the Desert", *Financial Times*, May 18/19, 1996.
[ii] Susan Whitfield of the British Library captures these enthusiasms in her book, *Life Along the Silk Road* (Berkeley, CA: University of California Press, 1999).
[iii] Millward, *Beyond the Pass: Economy, Ethnicity, and Empire in Qing Central Asia, 1759–1864* (Stanford, CA: Stanford University Press, 1998). The larger movement from discovery to exploration to intellectual absorption to imperial annexation has been addressed by Laura Hostetler in her *Qing Colonial Enterprise: Ethnography and Cartography in Early Modern China* (Chicago: University of Chicago Press, 2001).
[iv] Millward, p. 245.
[v] The national government deploys substantial military forces in the region. In addition to regular PLA formations, there are People's Armed Police, military construction units, and specialized border guards. Since the war in Afghanistan began in October 2001, more forces have been added. The overall total now is certainly well into the hundreds of thousands; dissident sources claim it is far larger.
[vi] *Pakistan Today*, January 11, 2002.
[vii] Quoted in the *South China Morning Post*, January 22, 2002.

9

Small Mercies:
China and America after 9/11

*David M. Lampton**

"This changes everything" was Senator Chuck Hagel's verdict as he surveyed the transmogrified landscape of international and domestic politics in the immediate wake of the "911" attacks. Others, such as retiring senator and China nemesis Jesse Helms, asserted that nothing fundamental has changed in U.S.-China relations, and that nothing should change. As for Taiwan, it hopes Helms is right but fears Hagel may be. It worries that Washington may seek to win Beijing's help in the struggle against global terrorism at its expense; as the China Post in Taipei put it: "Communism . . . is no longer considered a serious threat but rather a helping hand in the new war against terrorism."[i]

The unsurprising but useful truth is that some things have changed and others have not. The trick is to figure out which is which. What has not changed is the careful calculation of national interest that guides Beijing's decision-making process. What has changed is that the United States is now more focused and disciplined in defining its interests with respect to China. In dealing with Beijing, Washington has learned quickly to pursue a less cluttered agenda, with sharper

* David M. Lampton is George and Sadie Hyman professor and director of China Studies at Johns Hopkins-SAIS and director of Chinese Studies at The Nixon Center. He is the author of *Same Bed, Different Dreams: Managing U.S.-China Relations, 1989–2000* (University of California Press, 2001) and the editor of *The Making of Chinese Foreign and Security Policy in the Era of Reform* (Stanford University Press, 2001).

This essay first appeared in *The National Interest*, No. 66 (Winter 2001/02).

priorities filtered through the lens of national security. This is imposing a discipline on the U.S. political system that has not existed since the Tiananmen bloodshed of 1989. As for Beijing, its elite sees an opportunity to improve relations to an extent that it has not perceived possible for over a decade.

The principal feature of U.S.-China relations for the foreseeable future will be that two realist decision-making elites will be dealing with each other within the constraints of their respective domestic political circumstances and the uncertainties inherent in wartime. But while the two governments have stumbled into a new framework for limited security cooperation, other realms of policy will be affected minimally—unless the common threat to both nations rises further, making more intimate cooperation both necessary and politically feasible.

Security cooperation will be limited because important constituencies in each nation remain skeptical of the other's long-term intentions. Both sides are uncertain about which forms of cooperation would serve its interests. For example, in October as Washington sought Chinese support for the struggle against terrorism, and tried to create a positive atmosphere for President Bush's meeting with President Jiang Zemin in Shanghai, the Bush Administration found itself internally divided over whether to waive a Tiananmen-era sanction against supplying the Chinese with spare parts for previously sold Black Hawk helicopters. The administration demurred. In short, while there is a new context that fosters some cooperation, old problems ranging from Taiwan to proliferation to human rights have not disappeared.

Amid this mixed circumstance, four questions beg further examination. First, how do Beijing and Washington define their strategic circumstances, and how do those circumstances differ from the 1971–72 era when Richard Nixon and Henry Kissinger went to China? Second, what domestic constraints may make intimate cooperation difficult for both Beijing and Washington? Third, what can Washington expect in terms of Chinese cooperation, and will it be significant enough to overcome deeply embedded problems in the bilateral relationship? In turn, what steps might the American side take to facilitate more meaningful cooperation with Beijing?

A New Basis for Cooperation?

When President Richard Nixon and Chairman Mao Zedong set U.S.-China relations on a new trajectory in Beijing on February 21, 1972, the U.S. President said, "What brings us together is a recognition of a new situation in the world and a recognition on our part that what is important is not a nation's internal political philosophy. What is important is its policy toward the rest of the world and toward us."[ii] The shared perception of threat from Moscow was so powerful that Beijing and Washington subordinated their many disagreements about territory (Taiwan) and ideology (human rights and democracy) to the exigencies of security cooperation. Thereafter, the United States and China engaged in parallel opposition to Soviet proxy wars in Africa, and Washington sought to deter Moscow from using armed force against China in the late 1960s and the late 1970s. The two governments cooperated in monitoring Soviet missile tests from western China. And most intimately, the two cooperated in opposing the Soviet invasion of Afghanistan by supporting the Afghan *mujaheddin*.

The comparatively long period of Sino-American security cooperation was brought to an end by a series of developments, the principal ones being that China's national power grew much more rapidly than had been anticipated in the 1980s and early 1990s, and the sharp reaction of Americans to the 1989 Tiananmen bloodshed. The coup de grâce to strategic cooperation was delivered when the Warsaw Pact crumbled and the Soviet Union imploded in 1991. With security concerns no longer a trump card to discipline potentially dissenting voices in Congress and deter other claimants on America's China policy (such as economic and human rights organizations), interest group politics in America filled the void.

The new disciplining effect of renewed security cooperation in the wake of September 11, however, will be considerably weaker now than it was in the 1970s and 1980s—again, unless the perceived common threat to China and America rises further. Security cooperation in the war against terrorism is likely to be limited and ambivalent because constituencies in both countries are deeply divided over how much of a long-term threat each society poses to the other, because Beijing is so focused on its domestic problems, and because China does not feel as threatened as America. As a senior Chinese scholar put it to an American group in October 2001, the events of September 11 are "still regarded as an American misfortune, still very far away. So, how much political risk will Chinese leaders take?" Consequently, in both Washington and Beijing, defining a common security agenda has become much more complex than it was for Nixon and Mao.

The ambivalences created by the tension between the need for short-term security cooperation in the war against terror and long-term strategic distrust is nowhere so well illustrated as in the Quadrennial Defense Review (QDR), issued by the U.S. Department of Defense almost three weeks after September 11, 2001. While some hasty revisions were made in the QDR after "911", neither the U.S. effort to build a global coalition nor President Jiang's almost immediate personal pledge to President Bush on September 12—that "China is ready to strengthen dialogue and cooperation with the United States and the international community in combating all manner of terrorist violence"[iii]—prevented the following from appearing in the QDR: "The possibility exists that a military competitor with a formidable resource base will emerge in the region [East Asia and the East Asian littoral]."[iv]

To Beijing these words mean that Washington sees China as a potential security challenge and that the United States is building future capabilities with that in mind. This posture clearly weakens the elite and popular basis for Chinese cooperation with the United States, but it does not remove it altogether. Beijing will still provide meaningful assistance to the struggle against terrorism because it, too, fears Central Asian and Middle Eastern terrorism (particularly with the 2008 Olympics coming up in China), and because it wants to protect its economic interests with the United States. In addition, America and China now share an obvious interest in a stable Pakistan, and Beijing does not want to be isolated regionally or globally. The point of departure for Chinese strategic thinking is the need to maintain a set of external relationships and conditions that permit internal development to proceed with minimum feasible difficulty. Among external players, the United States has the greatest impact on that environment and hence on China's prospects for development.

Nonetheless, as China's leaders survey their country's periphery they see one major trend and from it they sense one major fear. The trend is that most of the major states around China are aligning with the U.S.-led coalition against terrorism to various degrees and for undefined durations. Russia has veered considerably closer to the West by allowing U.S. military overflights destined for the Afghan theater; making it clear that Russia has no objection to former Soviet Central Asian republics being used as staging grounds for U.S. military and intelligence operations in Afghanistan; indicating that it will consider modifications to the ABM Treaty; and suggesting a desire for closer relations with even a further expanded NATO. Washington's relations with a nervous New Delhi have improved, as have U.S. ties with Pakistan, Beijing's long-time ally on the subcontinent. Japan has taken the opportunity (some Chinese call it a "pretext") of the coalition against terrorism to be more helpful than it was in the Gulf War, and has broadened its security role in the rear-area support dimension, a sensitive issue throughout Asia. Even Iran, by indicating a willingness to assist with downed American aircraft, may be setting the stage for improved relations with Washington. That the United States could emerge from the present conflict with a stronger diplomatic position in the region—and perhaps a larger military presence as well—is a concern to Beijing.

This trend around its periphery feeds into China's millennia-old fear: encirclement. One Hong Kong analyst admirably summed up the perspective of at least some in Beijing: "To China, it means that the United States fills the last gap in the northeast of its ring of encirclement. . . . China will feel prickles down its back."[v]

Other factors will also affect the level and tone of U.S.-China cooperation. One is China's relative propinquity to the action. If one conceives of the coalition against terrorism as a series of concentric rings, where countries closer to the core cooperate more extensively with Washington than those toward the periphery, China lies at some intermediate point moving toward the outer rings. NATO will be close to the center, with Pakistan, selected Central Asian and Arab states, Japan, and India occupying progressively more distant rings. President Bush, through his telephone calls and other communication with President Jiang, as well as his compressed trip to the APEC leaders' meeting in Shanghai on October

19–21, has promoted cooperation with Beijing, but there are constraints on how far he can, will or should go. His discussions with President Jiang in Shanghai and their joint press conference there on October 19 made clear that China is not at the core of the coalition.[vi] President Jiang did not explicitly endorse the use of force against Afghanistan and raised the Taiwan question. President Bush noted issues of proliferation and human rights, saying, "The war on terrorism must never be an excuse to persecute minorities", a reference to initial Chinese attempts to link "separatist" tendencies in China's west to terrorism.

Not only can the coalition against terrorism be visualized as a set of concentric rings, but the actual and potential targets of U.S. action can be thus arrayed as well. The Taliban and Al-Qaeda are the core targets, and every critical government has agreed initially with that. Building a broad coalition to deal with those targets, to include China, has been comparatively easy. But if the military phase of the campaign spreads beyond Afghanistan, then Washington must anticipate increasing misgivings and perhaps resistance from Beijing, among others. Moving toward the next ring of target states (Iraq springs immediately to mind) would be very difficult for Beijing to support, unless such a state were shown unambiguously to have been actively complicit in terrorist attacks on the United States—or, in the future, on other coalition members. As Walter McDougall put it in a broader context, Beijing may be "in for a dime, but not necessarily for a dollar."[vii]

More immediate considerations also preoccupy Beijing. With roughly 19 million Muslims in China, Beijing is anxious not to be seen as participating in a clash of civilizations. This internal security fear is mirrored externally, with so many Muslim states to its vast, sparsely populated and vulnerable west. China is also becoming increasingly dependent upon oil supplies from abroad (30.1 percent dependent in 2000, and an anticipated dependence of 60 percent in 2020). The Middle East is particularly important, accounting for 60 to 70 percent of China's crude oil imports, and so, quite predictably, Beijing is reluctant to alienate the major oil supplying countries or see the price of crude jump because of instability.

Domestic Limits to Cooperation

Beyond the strategic and security inhibitions noted above lies the critical realm of domestic politics in both America and China. Domestic constraints in the United States inhibit Washington from taking certain steps that Beijing's leaders could use to justify positive steps of their own toward America. Similarly, domestic constraints in China make it hard for Beijing to take certain steps that might lead to change in Washington. The modesty of the cooperation that is likely before us makes it hard to justify a transformation of the overall relationship in either capital—though both President Bush and President Jiang probably desire such an outcome. For example, Chinese leaders must ask themselves, "If the Americans won't even sell us spare parts for grounded Black Hawk helicopters that they sold us more than a decade ago, what will our cooperation achieve?" The American response is that these helicopters can be (or have been) used in theaters such as Tibet and the Taiwan Strait where Washington does not want them employed.

Looking more deeply into domestic constraints in both societies, when George W. Bush came into office, his administration was divided over China policy, and the schism deepened with the April 2001 incident involving the collision between a Chinese jet fighter and a U.S. EP-3 reconnaissance plane. The contours of this ongoing division are complex, but the principal protagonists are Secretary of State Colin Powell, who is in the broad "engagement school" of the preceding six U.S. administrations, and Secretary of Defense Donald Rumsfeld, who is more impressed by China's suspected and documented proliferation activities and Beijing's muscular posture toward Taiwan. The President seemed positioned mid-way between his two subordinates. He has pointed continuously to the importance of economic and cultural engagement and "productive relations" [viii] with China (by supporting Beijing's entry into the World Trade Organization, extension of normal trade relations to China, not opposing the selection of Beijing as the site for the 2008 Olympic Games, and by traveling to Shanghai for the APEC meeting as anthrax attacks were unfolding in the United States). But by saying on April 25, 2001 that he would do "whatever it takes" to resist an attack on Taiwan by the PRC, he sought to deter possible Chinese adventurism; and in early September 2001 the President imposed sanctions on a Chinese arms manufacturer for allegedly proliferating missile technology to Pakistan.

The result of these twin impulses within the administration—and seemingly within the President—was that by the time of the September 11 attack, the President and his colleagues had slid from campaign formulations of China as a "strategic competitor", through interim formulations of "We view China as a partner on some issues and a competitor on others" and "China is a competitor and potential regional rival, but also a trading partner willing to cooperate in areas such as Korea, where our strategic interests overlap", to simply dropping the "competitor" formulation altogether. As Secretary Powell put it in July 2001, indicating that he wished to dampen the differences within the administration, "The relationship is so complex, with so many different elements to it, that it's probably wiser not to capture it with a single word or single term or cliché." [ix] In Shanghai, on October 19, 2001 Bush simply said, "America wants a constructive relationship with China."

Another constraint on U.S. action is public opinion. Public attitudes are not immutable, and they are subject to the influence of strong leadership. Nonetheless, public opinion toward China has not improved in the dozen years since the violence at Tiananmen. [x] While lukewarm public opinion does not make improved bilateral relations impossible, neither does it create any pressure on the President to act. A pre-September 11 survey reported that, "Most [Americans] see China as at least a serious problem, but only one-in-five call it an adversary." Further,

"Overall, a 46 percent plurality believe that Bush is taking the right approach with China, while 34 percent say he has been too soft."[xi] In short, with the administration divided, Chinese cooperation in the struggle against terrorism limited (but positive), and public opinion ambivalent about improved relations, something dramatic is needed to overcome the inertia. Thus far, Beijing has not provided anything dramatically positive.

Single-issue interest groups and the mass media invariably move into any significant vacuum created by bureaucratic division and popular skepticism. Shortly after September 11, pro-Taiwan interests began to argue that the island should not be "sold out" to win Beijing's cooperation; Chinese domestic and exiled pro-democracy forces urged that their cause not be forsaken for geostrategic reasons; Western human rights organizations argued that their issues should be pushed harder with Beijing; and anti-proliferation and conservative security organizations asserted that China is part of the problem, not the solution. Once again, these pressures could be overridden by American statesmen, but those who would do so must plausibly show both that Beijing's cooperation is essential to core U.S. security interests and that it is attainable.

President Jiang faces his own constraints. Beyond the suspicions that Chinese security, intelligence and military officials have of the United States, China's civilian leaders judge almost every policy issue from the perspective of how it will affect prospects for domestic economic growth and socio-political stability. They face serious problems. China's financial system is in an advanced state of disrepair. The rate of its export growth is sagging due to the global economic slowdown. Unemployment is already high and is likely to increase dramatically with China's entry into the WTO. Rural dissatisfaction with mounting inequalities and slow rural income growth is spilling over into confrontation and violence as income-starved local governments impose arbitrary fees on increasingly estranged peasants. Within this combustible domestic setting, China confronts independence tendencies in both Tibet and the western region of Xinjiang. Beijing fears that if China becomes too closely aligned with Washington in the struggle against terrorism, it could dangerously energize some parts of its own Muslim population, particularly the Uighurs in Xinjiang, a small number of whom China alleges have ties to Osama bin Laden.

Beyond all this, President Jiang is widely perceived in China to have been too accommodating to U.S. pressure in the past, whether in his having accepted minimum compensation and expressions of regret for the 1999 Chinese Embassy bombing in Belgrade and the April 2001 reconnaissance plane incident, or for having accepted very stringent terms for Chinese accession to the WTO. This charge of "soft" on the Americans comes against the backdrop of a popular undercurrent of anti-Americanism, an undercurrent to which the regime has contributed in the past when it seemed expedient to do so. With the rough Chinese equivalent of general elections coming up in the fall of 2002 (the Sixteenth Party Congress), and President Jiang desirous of either holding onto some significant position himself or, at a minimum, having trusted protégés succeed him, he must not allow himself to be seen as putty in American hands. In short, he needs something significant from Washington before he can be as forward leaning as he otherwise might wish to be. Thus far, however, he has not even been able to get Washington to lift some sanctions imposed as long as twelve years ago.

Modest Prospects

Beijing and Washington will both seek to avoid any appearance of deteriorating relations during the war against terrorism, and modest progress will likely be made in trade and leadership exchanges. Bilateral discussions about contentious issues such as human rights and proliferation will continue, but results will probably not be dramatic. With respect to Taiwan, China will continue to employ a mixed strategy of coercive diplomacy (e.g., missile deployments, force modernization and international isolation) to deter Taipei from moving toward independence, while simultaneously seeking to integrate Taiwan's economy ever more closely with that of the mainland and building a "united front" with all Taiwanese political forces opposed to the government of President Chen Shui-bian. As long as Beijing continues to believe that a Taiwanese declaration of independence is unlikely, and that current policy makes eventual reunification at least plausible, China's current leaders are unlikely to use force against the island. That said, the outcome of Taiwan's December 2001 legislative elections, and the character of future U.S. weapons sales to the island, could change the dominant assessment in Beijing.

With respect to the global struggle against terrorism, Beijing has its own reasons to cooperate in the intelligence sharing and money laundering areas, as it already has done. In the United Nations, we can expect Beijing to support General Assembly and Security Council actions that give the United States considerable practical latitude, but which do not formally endorse specific forceful U.S. actions in specific places. Beyond the visible spectrum of cooperation, China may provide further help "behind the curtain" (*muhou*). Some policy analysts and low-level Chinese officials have suggested to me that U.S. aircraft forced down in China would now receive a much friendlier welcome than did the crew of the U.S. EP-3 in April 2001. Were wounded Americans to need treatment in China, that too is possible. These are small mercies.

Even within this context, each capital could take modest steps that would provide the other with reasons to enhance cooperation. For instance, the Pentagon is still stuck in neutral on military-to-military exchanges with China's People's Liberation Army. Renewing contact with forces that one may wish to cooperate with in the struggle against terrorism seems elementary. Likewise, with Beijing entering the WTO, the world economy slowing, and U.S. firms still investing heavily in China, the longstanding prohibition against Overseas Private Investment Corporation activity in China is, at best, silly. For its part, Beijing needs to stop doing counterproductive things, most notably its attempt to use dangerous weapons and technology transfers as leverage against U.S. weapons sales to Taiwan. Moreover, China could publicly support the movement of humanitarian relief to Afghanistan through its territory. Many things are possible, but until Americans see real cooperation from the Chinese side, the gridlock will continue in Washington.

When all is said and done, unless the perceived common threat to both nations rises sharply, driving both political leaderships to further subordinate domestic divisions to security cooperation, Sino-American cooperation will remain limited and ambivalent. This adds up to a good prospect for marginal improvement in U.S.-China relations, but not for anything resembling strategic transformation. Yes, then, the world has changed; in this regard, however, it has not changed much.

NOTES

[i] "Anti-Terrorism Helps Mainland China Rise, But...", *China Post*, October 16, 2001.

[ii] Nixon quoted in William Burr, ed., *The Kissinger Transcripts: The Secret Talks with Beijing & Moscow* (New York: The New Press, 1998), p. 64.

[iii] Jiang Zemin quoted in *Reuters World Report*, September 13, 2001.

[iv] *Quadrennial Defense Review* (Washington, DC: Department of Defense, September 30, 2001), pp. 2, 4. The East Asian littoral is defined "as the region stretching from south of Japan through Australia and into the Bay of Bengal."

[v] Ba Ren, "The United States Meddles with Afghanistan to Kill Three Birds with One Stone", *Ta Kung Pao* (Hong Kong Internet version in Chinese), September 24, 2001.

[vi] Office of the Press Secretary, October 19, 2001, "Remarks by President Bush and President Jiang Zemin in Press Availability", Western Suburb Guest House, Shanghai, People's Republic of China.

[vii] Walter A. McDougall, "Cold War II", *Orbis* (Winter 2001).

[viii] "Bush on China: 'Different Values, Common Interests'", *New York Times*, April 13, 2001.

[ix] Powell quoted in "China is 'Strategic Competitor' No More", *Agence France Presse*, July 30, 2001.

[x] See my *Same Bed, Different Dreams: Managing U.S.-China Relations, 1989–2000* (Berkeley: University of California Press, 2001), p. 385.

[xi] The Pew Research Center for the People & the Press, "Public Behind Bush on Key Foreign Issues: Modest Support for Missile Defense, No Panic on China", http://www.people-press.org/china01rpt.

Part 2

Political Economy

10

The Short March:
China's Road to Democracy

*Henry S. Rowen**

When will China become a democracy? The answer is around the year 2015. Some might think such a prediction foolhardy but it is based on developments on several fronts, ones inadequately reported in the American media. There are, indeed, unmistakable signs of important positive changes in China. These changes are undoubtedly related to China's steady and impressive economic growth, which in turn fits the pattern of the way in which freedom has grown in Asia and elsewhere in the world.

Bad, But Getting Better

According to the latest survey of political rights and civil liberties by Freedom House, China's freedom rating is, in effect, zero.[i] At first glance it is easy to see why. The country remains a one-party state under the rule of the Communist Party; the Justice Ministry admits to having 2,700 "counter-revolutionaries" in prison (many of them actually political dissidents and labor and human rights activists); officials admit to over 2,000 summary executions in 1994; people are often detained for long periods without trial; and many people, especially peasants, are ill-treated by local authorities.

On the other hand, things have improved. China has come far since the disastrous Great Leap Forward of the 1950s, and the lunatic Cultural Revolution in the 1960s and early 1970s. Higher incomes have given people more personal

---

* Henry S. Rowen is director of the Asia/Pacific Research Center, and a senior fellow at the Hoover Institution.

This essay first appeared in *The National Interest*, No. 45 (Fall 1996).

space, agents of the state have less control over citizens' lives, and the typical Chinese is freer to move about the country. The coercive one-child policy is being flouted in the countryside, causing authorities to adopt economic incentives in an effort to gain compliance.

The progress that has been made, and the prospect for more of the same, can be considered under three headings: the growth of grassroots democracy; the struggle toward a rule of law; and the liberalizing of the mass media.

Grassroots Democracy

Reforms in village elections came out of the disasters of collectivized agriculture. Faced with starvation in the late 1970s, peasants in Anhui province disbanded local communes and returned to family plots. Thus began a process of de-collectivization and transition to a market economy, which is now far advanced.[ii]

The dissolution of the commune system left in place no institution capable of addressing infrastructure needs, schooling, or any of the other functions of local government. In Guangxi province, villagers responded by organizing committees to maintain social order, mediate disputes, and manage public utilities and welfare. The political vacuum created by de-collectivization led to the amendment of the Chinese constitution in 1982 to provide for village government. A crucial decision concerned the role of the Communist Party in the new arrangement. Was the Party to appoint village officials? Were provincial and town officials to appoint them? Instead of adopting either of these arrangements, in 1987 the central government decided that they would be chosen by elections, and these began in 1988. The political crackdown after the Tiananmen massacre immediately raised questions about the future of this institution, but it has survived.

Village government now consists of a Village Committee functioning as the executive, and a Representative Assembly as a form of legislature. By the early 1990s, 90 percent of village committees had been elected, but the process has been ragged. Elections were unfamiliar phenomena and procedures were understandably irregular. Many people did not take them seriously, as past elections had been only a formality. At first most presumed that upper levels of the government and Party would rig the outcomes, and in fact local Party cadres have continued to resist relinquishing their privileges, and non-Party members have often been subjected to various forms of discrimination. Some representative assemblies dominated by members of the old establishment still hold that Party membership is the main qualification for candidacy. Foreign observers have witnessed instances of probable ballot fraud, and it is safe to assume that in elections without such observers the incidence of fraud is higher. Although the law provides for a secret ballot, provisions for privacy in voting are inadequate.

Despite all these drawbacks, substantial progress has been made. Fujian province is perhaps the most advanced in this process, with four rounds of elections behind it. (It has the advantage of being on the coast and benefits from contact with the Taiwanese.) In 1993, the Fujian People's Congress passed an election law, the first provincial legislature to do so. Among other things it changed the basis of voting from one vote per household to one vote per person. In the 1991 elections, 49 percent of the winners were non-Party members; however, in 1995, the Washington Post reported that although 40 percent of the candidates who won were not members of the Communist Party, half of them joined later.

Observers of the 1994 elections in Fujian reported, not surprisingly, that Party members were worried about their diminishing control of the various village economies, and expressed these concerns through active lobbying efforts. But these were not always successful in preventing competition. It is up to local officials to decide if an election will be competitive, as distinct from voters facing a "choice" of only one candidate. When there is no competition the only recourse for those who object is abstention. If a significant number do abstain the election is perceived as a failure, and this constitutes a form of pressure for future competition.

In Nanping City in Fujian province, more than thirty peasants from Tiantou village wrote an open letter to election organizers claiming that, "In the past few years, the work style and morality of the village officials have become intolerable and the situation is really serious." They proposed the election of one Chen Jinman and four other lesser local luminaries to the village committee. When the five nominees posted a three-year work plan at the gate of the village committee office, some officials complained that this was going too fast toward democracy. Nonetheless, the nominees' management plan was advertised, a competitive election was held, and the five were elected.

For all the defects of the electoral process, the principle of selecting village leaders by competitive election rather than appointment from above is established, as is the principle of fixed terms of office. Local government is becoming more transparent, and information on village affairs, including finances and officials' salaries, is being posted in public. More elections are being contested. "Class struggle" is no longer employed in dealing with political and social conflicts, nor are those who stand against Party members automatically denounced as "enemies of the people."

It is likely that this process will continue, with election procedures steadily becoming more comprehensive, standardized, and transparent. Growing numbers of peasants are learning about legal procedures, and may be expected to use the law to protect their rights. The Communist Party will face more competition from businessmen, clan organizations, and others expressing a variety of interests. What was begun at the grassroots has already started to influence behavior higher up in the system, too. Recently, several provincial deputy governors who were not on the official slate have been appointed, and they have been accepted by Beijing; and some prominent members of the Party, scheduled for election to the National People's Congress, have lost.

A Rule of Law

The rule of law was never established in modern China, and under Communist rule law has been until recently a political and administrative instrument of the Party dictatorship.[iii]

As late as 1980 there were only three thousand lawyers in a country of over one billion people. Since then there has been more than a twentyfold increase in the number of legal professionals, and Chinese courts now hear over three million cases a year. But this is still seen to be inadequate: In June 1992 President Jiang Zemin said that China needs 300,000 lawyers, and the current goal is to have 150,000 by the year 2000. That about equals the combined number of lawyers in Germany, France, Benelux, and Denmark—though China has nine times as many people.

This expansion comes in response to a growing demand for the rule of law. Specifically, the Chinese people are demanding that the government observe its own stated rules. Values consistent with Western ideals of equality, justice, and legality—as well as with ancient Chinese ideals—are being expressed at all levels of society, and are finding their way into legislation.

Chinese officials are explicit in acknowledging that China needs a more developed legal system, because a market economy must be governed by law. Foreign firms in particular require consistency and transparency in the laws to which they must adhere, and these are often lacking. In Shanghai, a principal center of foreign business activity,

> There is no distinction between official policy and officials' references. . . . Lawyers report that when they contact the tax bureau to ask about changes in the law . . . they are advised to consult the bureau's consulting company (for a substantial fee). . . . In the absence of laws, there are rules and then clarifications. And because these often appear contradictory to confused foreign businessmen, it seems that there are no rules at all, just the arbitrary interpretation or whim of the official asked.[iv]

There is good reason to question China's ability to sustain rapid growth in the absence of stable and fairly enforced rules that foreign investors find acceptable. (This applies less, however, to overseas Chinese, who have a comparative advantage in a game without formal rules, because of their contacts and skill in personal dealings.)

The growing weakness of the state also elicits demands for law and order. This is evident in the general frustration with massive corruption at all levels: illegal businesses run by government agencies, the theft of government assets, and evasion of price controls and taxes. At the same time, the weakening power of the state makes it more difficult to achieve an effective judicial system.

Among the many shortcomings of the legal system, Anthony Dicks asserts that the most fundamental is the fact that "the Communist Party is outside the jurisdiction of the ordinary courts", despite a 1982 constitution that says that "the political parties . . . must abide by the Constitution and the law", and that "no organization or individual is privileged to be beyond the Constitution or the law."

There are several other serious problems, including slack enforcement of decisions in civil proceedings. In practice, enterprises run by the military are not penalized and large and medium sized state owned enterprises are often protected by local officials, which amounts to being outside the law. Nor are courts themselves exempt from the endemic corruption; lawyers bribe judges, who often make it known to those appearing before them that they are interested in stepping down soon from the bench to enter private practice.

The criminal process is the least reformed of all, and it still serves functions established by a totalitarian regime. Pre-trial detention often exceeds the statutory three months, and arbitrary arrest, detention, and torture continue. Police can impose low-level punishments for minor offenses and may also sentence offenders to "labor re-education" of up to three years for offenses that are defined loosely and in moralistic language.

However, in Beijing, the National People's Congress is rewriting the criminal laws to state that defendants shall not be presumed guilty, that they shall have lawyers, and that the police shall no longer be able to hold them without charge. Doubtless, for some time to come these new laws will often be observed in the breach, but their passage is an indicator of the growing demand for democratic procedures.

The level of competency and professionalism of lawyers in China is low. According to Alford and Lubman, few lawyers (and even fewer members of the judiciary) have university law degrees, and many of those who do studied law for a centrally planned economy, much of which has been superseded. They are better suited to be state legal workers than autonomous lawyers. There is not yet a widely shared understanding of the distinction between public and private interests, or of how these are to be reconciled. Tripling the number of lawyers by the year 2000 will not by itself solve these problems.

For all these many shortcomings, notes Alford, Chinese lawyers in some instances "are now able to represent in an unprecedentedly vigorous manner clients whose interests may not be wholly synonymous with the state's." Arguably, the Supreme People's Court has begun to make law through its interpretations and decisions, a role that is contrary to communist dogma, which allows no place for an independent institution. This process seems likely to continue.

Among academics, and increasingly in the public security bureaucracy, there are calls for change—at least for rationalization, if not for liberalization. According to Lubman, "as institutions of the Party-state erode, legal rules and institutions, however incomplete and tentative by Western standards, may grow more able to exercise the functions of Western private law in the emerging sectors of the economy outside the economic plan."

Another indication of a shift from an ad hoc to a rule-based system is a recent change in China's tax system. In 1994, separate national and local taxes and tax services were established. Such a separation, it is important to note, is an essential feature of a federal system of government—fiscal federalism—as distinct from one that is merely administratively decentralized.[v] While the latter can be easily reversed, fiscal federalism is more likely to endure, becoming de facto constitutional. Within the American constitutional structure, fiscal federalism has been the source of enormous economic and political benefits. It is, of course, far too early to predict similar benefits for China from an initiative that is still in its infancy, but it is another bit of evidence for the emergence of a system based on rules.

The demands of a market economy require such rules, as well as transparency and fairness—all attributes directly at odds with a Leninist ruling party. A choice must be made and it is evident that, slowly and irregularly, the market path is being chosen.

Media Self-Liberalization

As described by Minxin Pei, the liberalization of the Chinese economy after 1979 had the unintended, and to the regime unwelcome, effect of leading to the self-liberalization of the mass media.[vi] This came about through the combined effects of market forces, foreign influences, and changes in technology. Together with a more active and critical Chinese intelligentsia, these factors have produced a remarkable increase in freedom of information. The process was led by book publishing and was followed by journals and newspapers. The electronic media lagged, evincing little liberalization in the 1980s, but it too is following the general trend in the 1990s. The net effect of all this has been significant. For example, a history of the Cultural Revolution was published despite government efforts to ban it; a book attacking the Chinese character (The Ugly Chinese) became a bestseller; stories about official corruption began appearing; and works opposing the Three Gorges Dam and favoring deeper respect for the rule of law were published.

The shift to the market was the major cause of this Chinese glasnost. The market increased the channels of production and distribution of materials because there was money to be made by entrepreneurs; at the same time, the government was losing money in its many state-owned publications and outlets. As it cut back on state subsidies for publication, many journals and newspapers were forced into the market. In 1984 the government permitted collective private publishing houses (in effect partnerships) to function. This soon led entrepreneurs to adopt many of the functions of the former state publishing houses: finding authors, translators, paper, and printers. In Xinhua's bookstores in 1979, the huge state media empire held 95 percent of the market; by 1988, its share had shrunk to one-third. In Beijing in 1992 there were about two thousand kiosks, and for many of them, profits came largely from the sale of illicit publications.

The newspaper business has evinced a similar trend: non-Party papers have gained market share at the expense of Party publications. According to Pei, 1,008 newspapers were founded between 1980 and 1985, only 103 of which were Party controlled.[vii] As Party papers lost market share they reduced their propaganda content in order to compete. Nonetheless, hampered as they still were by censorship, circulation and advertising decreased.

Initially, the government was better able to manage the electronic and film media. This was partly because the costs of entry were much higher than for print media. But the market eventually made its power known. The government's censored materials were unpopular and falling demand led to mounting losses. Unprofitable government operations were spun off to private operators. Government stations such as Dongfang TV in Shanghai introduced live coverage of breaking stories, talk shows, call-in programs, 24-hour broadcasting, and celebrity interviews of liberal intellectuals whom the hardliners had silenced after 1989. Callers complained about the quality of government services, putting pressure on them to improve. Taken together, these developments have made censorship increasingly impractical. Hence something very basic has changed: The state is losing control of information.

The film business went through a similar evolution. Dreary and unpopular state productions resulted in revenue losses. Already in the 1980s, the government allowed foreign films and TV programs to enter China and in 1992 it ended the state monopoly on film distribution. The result: more private activity, leading to greater competition, which in turn has led to greater variety and higher quality.

The Chinese government's decision to seek foreign investment in order to acquire advanced technology and expertise reinforced these domestic changes. This meant admitting many more foreign businessmen, sponsoring more technological and business exchanges, and creating more electronic links to the rest of the world. Western newspapers found their way to major tourist hotels (and beyond) and access to CNN was approved in the mid-1980s.

Both were cut off after the Tiananmen massacre and restrictions on foreign investment in media were imposed—all to little effect on the flow of information. Working against the regime's efforts to maintain control were growing incomes combined with advances in technology. Televisions, radios, cassette players, and VCRs proliferated widely. In 1985, the government allowed local TV stations and educational and research institutions to set up their own satellite ground stations; by 1990 more than sixteen thousand had been established, creating a system too large for the authorities to monitor effectively. In the 1990s Chinese manufacturers began to make home satellite dishes. The national authorities decreed prohibition but failed to enforce it; by the early 1990s an estimated 4.5 million were operational. Broadcasts from Hong Kong greatly increased their penetration of the market in south China, to the discomfiture of the censors in Beijing. Also, by 1991 more than eighty thousand firms, institutions, and government units were equipped with fax machines, with a projected market increase of ten thousand a year through the decade.

The Chinese government has not pursued a consistent policy line on freedom of information. Between 1978 and 1993 there were waves of liberalization with intervening periods of repression. These oscillations have resulted from shifts among factions in Beijing, developments in the market, and in response to some unpleasant events. Even the crackdown after the Tiananmen massacre did not prevent further liberalization in late 1992, after Deng's visit to south China. The message is clear: Once a totalitarian regime ventures down the path of market reforms, it loses control of its information organs. In China this process was hastened by the gradual loss of control over many other aspects of political life.

Clearly, there is a widening zone of tolerance within which journalists and editors operate. Because those in the media have a financial stake in not being shut down, they stay clear of the (ill-defined) far edge of the zone; in short, there is a good deal of self-censorship and government monitoring. Unsurprisingly, too, a great deal of what is published freely is commercial in character—instructions on how to get rich, for example—and politically unthreatening. What Ramon Myers of the Hoover Institution calls the "ideological marketplace" of politics is still outside the zone of tolerance. Dissidents who oppose the government do not have access to the media because they are considered by editors to be too hot to handle, and they must resort to distributing leaflets and to hunger strikes. But with the exception of some journalists accused of selling state secrets to Hong Kong, there have been no criminal proceedings against journalists for several years.

There will continue to be waves of progress and regression, no doubt, but the underlying tide is raising the overall level of freedom of information. This, taken together with the strengthened rule of law and democracy at the grassroots, shows clearly that the long march away from the totalitarian character of the Communist Party is well underway.[viii]

China is No Different

These changes at the grassroots in China are similar to those that took place in Taiwan at a comparable stage of development. China's per capita GDP is now about $2,500. When Taiwan reached that level in the early 1970s, the Kuomintang Party (KMT) was firmly in charge but changing its ways, much as the Chinese Communist Party is today. Local elections had been held every three years after 1950; over time local bosses had become more responsive to the popular mood, and non-KMT individuals had become active in local politics. In 1973, Taiwan's Freedom House democracy score was 25 (on a scale of 0 to 100). Then its political liberalization began to increase significantly (as is happening in China today)—although at first no organized opposition was allowed (again, as in

China). The first open, free election for parliament occurred in 1992, and in March of this year Taiwan held its first presidential election—also deemed free and fair.

The path of political liberalization in South Korea was different but the end point was similar. After the coup that brought Park Chung Hee to power in 1961, elections were held but results were determined by the ruling party. The country's 1974 freedom rating was 33. Political change came rapidly during the mid-1980s and by 1995 its rating had jumped to 84. South Korea was becoming increasingly wealthy as these changes were taking place.

The political evolution of Taiwan and South Korea are but two examples of a wider phenomenon. The worldwide norm, first clearly established by Seymour Martin Lipset, is "the richer the country the freer" (the exception being those enriched through oil, such as Saudi Arabia and Brunei).[ix] The curve marked Worldwide Freedom-Income Regression in the figure below shows the relationship between per capita income and Freedom House's 1995 ratings for all countries, indicating an average. The correlation is not perfect in East Asia or anywhere else; Singapore, for example, has a low freedom rating for its income level and the Philippines a high one. But the overall fit is good and it shows that the wealth-democracy connection is not a European artifact. This bears on the assertion by various Asian authorities and intellectuals, mostly in Singapore and Malaysia, that Asian democracy is different from its Western cousin. Perhaps it is in some ways, but the reality is that, although the East Asian income-freedom pattern shown in the figure is a bit lower than the worldwide average, this region is like others in that the wealthier a country, the more (Western-style) freedoms its people enjoy.

The prospects for Chinese liberalization thus rest, above all, on continued rapid economic progress. Since 1979, China has grown annually at over 5 percent per capita (at international prices).[x] If it continues on this trajectory—by no means a certainty—China's per capita GDP will be between $7,000 and $8,000 (in 1995 dollars) by the year 2015. This figure is very significant. Several scholars have suggested that the transition to stable democracy correlates with mean incomes between $5,000 and $6,000, and becomes impregnable at the $7,000 level.[xi] There is a compelling logic behind the statistical relationship. Growing wealth is accompanied by increased education, the building of business and government institutions with some autonomy, and the formation of attitudes that enable democratic governments to survive when they have a chance at power. Spain, Portugal, Chile, and Argentina, in addition to Taiwan and South Korea, all made the transition to democracy while they were within this income range.

No one can know precisely how democracy in China will evolve, but its record over the past fifteen years and the experience of other countries in East Asia suggest more competition in local and provincial politics, ultimately reaching the National Congress—although organized political opposition on the national level might be banned for a long time. Freedom of information will expand further and the rule of law will become ever stronger. This process is unlikely to be smooth and there may well be setbacks, as in the regime's reaction to the 1989 Tiananmen demonstrations. To the extent that China's current leaders anticipate a political evolution, as they must if they are realistic, they probably prefer the Singapore model, although Taiwan's seems more in keeping with the Chinese character—and the political history of Taiwan is well known to elites across the strait.

What could go wrong? Although there is a consensus on Deng Xiaoping's dictum, "To get rich is glorious", sustained rapid growth is not assured. Lagging growth in the poor interior provinces might impede political evolution of the country, and an ongoing conflict with Taiwan could become an obstacle. Or, after all, China might just be different—but in light of the evidence reported above, that is not the way to bet.

This is the Deal

The key inference for everyone is patience: Only twenty-odd years separate us from 2015, and the advent of Chinese democracy promises abatement of several current problems. For the people of Taiwan, to be a province of a prospering China—or perhaps a member of a Chinese confederation—in which governments on both sides of the Taiwan Strait are popularly elected and the rights of their citizens are protected by law, should be a far more attractive prospect than joining today's China. But the period between now and 2015 (or whatever the precise year) will be volatile, because Beijing will not give up on the goal of unification. And it will become militarily more powerful as time passes. Taiwan needs to keep its powder dry and behave prudently.

For the United States there are two main implications. The first is that it is a good thing that the Chinese become rich, for it will benefit the American economy in the process. The second, and more important, reason is that a richer China will become more democratic. This will not necessarily make it easier to deal with, but experience has shown that democracies are less dangerous interlocutors for other democracies than are dictatorships. Washington should therefore stop holding trade relations hostage to an array of current political disputes. The United States should instead make most-favored nation status for China permanent, and impose no extra obstacles to its admission to the World Trade Organization. Our economic interests need to be pressed on the many trade issues in contention, but it is much better to address them in the WTO forum than in the current, highly politicized bilateral tit-for-tat manner in which we have been engaged in recent years.

If trade sanctions are ruled out-of-bounds in dealing with non-trade matters, how are we to dissuade China from exporting weapons and delivery systems capable of mass destruction? This is a question the Clinton administration has failed adequately to address, and it is a failure that is likely to encourage similar transfers in the future. One answer lies in our taking actions in the security domain rather than in economics. There is much in the way of arms for defense that we have not provided to Taiwan or to other countries in the region that worry about China that we might supply.

The second main policy implication for us is to defend strongly Taiwan's de facto independence. We have an interest in a peaceful East Asia, and we share more values with a democratic Taiwan today than we did with the authoritarian one of days gone by. If Beijing resumes military pressures against the island, we should not only supply more advanced arms to Taiwan but make it clear to China that it will confront American military power if it crosses our red line. We need also to make it clear to Taipei that a condition of our support is that it abjure *de jure* independence, for that would escalate the confrontation with Beijing, something that we and the Taiwanese should both want to avoid. This merely restates long-standing American policy that there is only one China but that we resist any attempt to unify by force. The difference now is that political evolution in China can be expected to ease the problem.

It follows from this analysis that we should not assume that China will inevitably become a threat to U.S. interests. We have a common interest with China in seeing its people prosper, in peace, in dealing with environmental problems, and in coping with the dangers associated with the spread of weapons capable of mass destruction. This common agenda would be better advanced if China were a member of the various organizations that make the rules on such matters. Nonetheless, American criticism of China's human rights violations should and will continue, but it should not be linked to trade issues. Our criticisms will have increasing resonance inside a China with a better educated and informed population that has access to greatly improved telecommunications, one that is growing freer year by year.

Put another way, the deal—better left tacit than made explicit—is this: Beijing bets on the many benefits of getting rich, including military power and peaceful reconciliation with Taipei. Taipei bets that a democratic China will emerge and holds off declaring itself independent. Washington bets that a rich China will become democratic and that the Taiwan issue will be peacefully settled in the context of a moderated Chinese foreign policy.

Americans sustained the Cold War with the Soviet Union for forty-five years until victory came. The prospect of a twenty-year (more or less) effort to help the Chinese people to become free—while helping Taiwan to retain its freedoms—is a much less daunting prospect. There may be trouble with China during its passage to democracy—or even after—but the odds should go down as it becomes more prosperous. We should do nothing to interfere with that process.

NOTES

[i] *Freedom in the World: The Annual Survey of Political Rights and Civil Liberties, 1995-6* (New York: Freedom House, 1996).

[ii] Material in this section draws on the "Study on the Election of Villagers' Committees in Rural China" (December 1, 1993) and the "Report on Villagers' Representative Assemblies in China" (December 1994), both by the China Rural Villagers Self-Government Research Group, China Research Society of Basic Level Government; on the "Election Observation Report of the People's Republic of China" by the International Republican Institute (a private U.S. nonprofit organization dedicated to promoting democratic institutions), May 1995; and on *Far East Economic Review*, June 23, 1994.

[iii] This section is based on "China's Legal Reforms", in a special issue of *The China Quarterly* (March 1995). In particular, the contributions of Stanley Lubman, "Introduction: The Future of Chinese Law"; William Alford, "Tasseled Loafers for Barefoot Lawyers: Transformation and Tension in the World of Chinese Legal Workers"; Pittman B. Potter, "Foreign Investment Law in the People's Republic of China: Dilemmas of State Control"; Donald Clarke and James Feinerman, "Antagonistic Contradictions: Criminal Law and Human Rights in China"; Donald Clarke, "The Execution of Civil Judgments in China"; and Anthony R. Dicks, "Compartmentalized Law and Judicial Restraint: An Inductive View of Some Jurisdictional Barriers to Reform."

[iv] *Far East Economic Review*, June 23, 1994, p. 55; quoted by Potter.

[v] Yingyi Qian and Barry Weingast, "China's Transition to Markets: Market-Preserving Federalism, Chinese Style", Hoover Institution, 1995.

[vi] Minxin Pei, *From Reform to Revolution: The Demise of Communism in China and the Soviet Union* (Cambridge: Harvard University Press, 1994).

[vii] Pei, p. 161.

[viii] A Lexis/Nexis search of coverage on these topics—and of human rights abuses—in five major U.S. publications (the *New York Times*, *Wall Street Journal*, *Washington Post*, *Time*, and *Newsweek*) for the period January 1991 through June 1996 shows, on the one hand, 356 stories on abuses of various kinds, and, on the other, three on local elections, sixteen on efforts to introduce a rule of law, and ten on the liberalizing of the mass media; in short, an overall ratio of twelve to one. How can one explain such scant coverage of such important developments? Aside from the propensity of the press to print bad news, one explanation is that the Tiananmen Square massacre imprinted on the minds of American editors that Beijing is unrelentingly repressive.

[ix] Seymour Martin Lipset, *Political Man: The Social Bases of Politics* (Baltimore: Johns Hopkins University Press, 1981).

[x] In using international prices, all goods and services produced in a country are valued in the same currency, usually dollars, and not in local currencies.

[xi] Samuel P. Huntington, *The Third Wave: Democratization in the Late Twentieth Century* (Norman, ok: University of Oklahoma Press, 1991), and Adam Przeworski, Michael Alvarez, Jose Antonio Cheibub, and Fernando Limongi, "What Makes Democracies Endure?" *Journal of Democracy* (January 1996).

11

China's Democratic Prospects
A Dissenting View

*George T. Crane**

China today is roiling with turbulent economic and social change. As a result, Chinese politics is transforming as well. The Communist Party (CCP) struggles to maintain its authority in the countryside, where peasants have given up on corrupt officials and seek community in clan organizations and new religions. In the cities, persistent nationwide efforts to establish a formal opposition party have left communist leaders scrambling to shore up their control. Information, once easily monopolized by the state, now flows through cell phones and computer networks, enabling communication and organization among those disaffected with failed Leninism. The territorial integrity of the state is being challenged by the separatist aspirations of Uighurs and Tibetans. At no time in its fifty years of power has the CCP faced such a wide array of potentially disastrous problems.

How the People's Republic of China manages these various perils, and in what condition the country emerges, is a matter of great moment for the world at large. If growing domestic frustration is deflected into a more aggressively nationalistic foreign policy by a desperate CCP, a catalogue of international issues could be adversely affected, from Taiwan to trade balances to thermonuclear weapons. Conversely, the long-standing U.S. policy of engagement looks forward to a gradual transition to capitalism and a subsequent democratization that is expected to moderate Chinese diplomacy. It would seem that, for American

* George T. Crane is associate professor of political science at Williams College.

This essay first appeared in *The National Interest*, No. 57 (Fall 1999).

policymakers, nationalism is the enemy and capitalism the hero of China's tumultuous reformation.

Two articles that also appear in this volume challenge both of these formulations. John Fitzgerald argues that the discourse on dignity inherent in any nationalist narrative may lay the conceptual groundwork for democratization in China. And David Zweig demonstrates that Chinese economic reform may work against the more optimistic hopes of engagement supporters. Is nationalism, then, really the hero and capitalism the enemy of Chinese democratization? Not quite. Each of these respected authors is only partially correct in his analysis. Indeed, the ineluctable logic of nationalism and economic reform may turn out to be less a determinant of China's future than the simple will of Chinese democrats and their oppressors.

Nationalism

John Fitzgerald, an accomplished historian of Republican-era China (1911-49), makes a convincing argument that national identity is rooted in a struggle for human dignity. Politics, he says, cannot simply be reduced to a calculated clash of material interests; it is driven by seemingly "irrational" aspirations and desires. People yearn for recognition and dignity, which are often found in the "imagined community" of the nation, and they will kill and die for the sense of solidarity that nationality imparts.

But what happens, Fitzgerald asks, when the state, in the name of the nation, tramples upon personal dignity? In China, momentous political disasters such as the Cultural Revolution, institutionalized corruption and official repression have robbed many individuals of their self-respect. When instructed by state leaders in the glories of the nation and the need to sacrifice for the collective, disillusioned individuals hesitate to identify with the common cause. The subsequent resentment produces the belief that national dignity must be built upon the personal dignity of the members of the nation. And here, Fitzgerald argues, is an opening for a move toward liberal democracy. In emphasizing communal dignity, nationalist rhetoric indirectly supports the ideal of individual dignity, the starting point for the defense of individual rights and the institutions that protect them. In his own words: "The politics of individual dignity, far from being antithetical, appears to be parasitical on the idea of national dignity."

Nationalism, by this reckoning, is a prerequisite for democracy. Indeed, Fitzgerald is willing to suggest that even chauvinistic arguments, such as those expounded by the authors of the various China Can Say No books, may inadvertently contribute to democratization. Although they blame foreigners for China's economic and political troubles, the resentment of the Say No nationalists also reflects their shame for a regime that denies its citizens their personal dignity. Their desire to invigorate China's national greatness will, therefore, set them on a path that "leads inevitably to challenging head-on existing constraints on thought, speech and assembly." Ironically, some of the most pointed Chinese nationalist critics of the 1989 democracy movement implicitly share the goals of that movement.

But there is a problem here. Nationalism is an obstacle to democracy—at least to liberal democracy. While Fitzgerald may be right in pointing out that the discourse of national dignity can enliven an appreciation of personal dignity, it is also true that state managers and jingoistic commentators regularly and powerfully assert a need to sacrifice individuals to protect the nation. This is especially true of nationalisms that are not explicitly built upon individualistic-libertarian ideals, which is to say most nationalisms. Liah Greenfeld points to the authoritarian tendencies of various European nationalisms:

> Originally nationalism developed as democracy. . . . But as nationalism spread in different countries and the emphasis in the idea of the nation moved from the sovereign character to the uniqueness of the people, the original equivalence between it and democratic principles was lost.[i]

The problem is seen most clearly in the resurgence of ethnic nationalisms, collective identities that emphasize the cultural or racial "uniqueness of the people." The exclusionary possibilities are obvious: if the state is said to serve the nation, those who are not of the unique national community will not have a legitimate claim to be afforded full rights before the state. Koreans in Japan, Russians in the Baltic states, Turks in Germany all experience this kind of discrimination. In more extreme cases—Kosovo, Rwanda, Indonesia—ethnic outsiders are slaughtered and driven out to preserve an imagined ethno-national purity. Nationalism, in all of these cases, is quite actively used against democracy.

Chinese nationalism, in its official rendition, is not ethnically based; it is political and civic. But its anti-democratic tendencies are prominent. People of various ethnic backgrounds are recognized as members of the Chinese nation, so long as they accept the legitimacy of the regime. A common political life, defined by the state apparatus and ideology, is central to the definition of the nation. Socialist China promises equal status for all who faithfully adhere to the "Four Cardinal Principles" (Marxism, Socialism, the Dictatorship of the Proletariat, the hegemony of the CCP), and equal opportunity for all who assiduously pursue the "Four Modernizations" (Industry, Agriculture, Science, Defense). If a person works against the state, however, he is not just politically suspect; he is, in the Maoist formulation, an "enemy of the people."

The problem of Chinese nationalism, then, is the failure of its civic promise. For the common political life is seen by many millions not as a glorious socialist fraternity, but as a corrupt and repressive ordeal. The subsequent resentment has, as Fitzgerald suggests, led some to a fervent belief in democracy. It has also led to other reconstructions of Chinese national identity centering on geopolitical power or neo-traditional greatness, neither of which supports a more democratic politics.

Military ideologues promote the idea of China taking its "rightful place" among the world's Great Powers and castigate anyone, particularly the United States, they see as thwarting China's rise. National reunification and territorial integrity are central to this project, producing a belligerent approach to the issues of Taiwan and Tibet. In this image of the Chinese nation, democracy is quite clearly subordinated to the drive for power and unity. Similarly, the CCP has worked hard since the massive legitimation crisis of 1989 to revive traditional cultural symbols and practices. As a part of an ongoing patriotic education campaign, Standing Committee member Li Ruihan undertook the most un-communist of acts when he laid a wreath at the tomb of the Yellow Emperor, the legendary progenitor of the Chinese people. Such actions are designed to link the CCP with China's past, a heritage that is used not to bring forth Confucian humanism, but to justify hierarchy, obedience and autocracy.

In these instances, nationalism is no friend to democracy. Indeed, for democratization to proceed, collectivist-authoritarian national narratives must be explicitly rejected in favor of individualistic-libertarian identities. Nationalism's democratic connotation must be clearly and completely articulated.

Capitalism

A more widely held view is that democratization will emerge from economic reform. Faced with daunting inefficiencies and all too aware of the fate of the Soviet Union, Chinese leaders have gradually reduced the role of the central state bureaucracy in the economy. For twenty years they have improvised their way from one problem to another, from inflation to unemployment to international crisis, but they have, by and large, succeeded in creating a dynamic economy. Although CCP ideologues insist that they are building "socialism with Chinese characteristics", it looks more like a fitful transition to capitalism. Might this change, then, bring with it a new regime of property rights and an expanding bourgeoisie interested in protecting its hard-won wealth by means of democratic restraints on state power?

Probably not, argues David Zweig, a shrewd analyst of China's political economy. His case makes three key points: In China, markets are not free, workers cannot find work, and the world economy is not as significant as some may think.

China's economic reform, Zweig contends, involves not a decisive move to free markets but merely a shift of the locus of economic power. While central government bureaucrats in Beijing have given up a good portion of their previous authority, the beneficiaries of this change have not been private entrepreneurs. Instead, lower level public officials have seized strategic economic positions. Their corrupt rent-seeking behavior limits the rise of an independent bourgeoisie, and their vested interests sway them against private property and democracy. Why should they encourage change that might endanger the institutional basis of their wealth?

Beyond this powerful anti-democratic constituency,   Zweig points to a mind-boggling unemployment level that brings threats of rising crime and social instability. Violence has erupted, confirming for CCP patriarchs their suspicion that democratization is a recipe for disaster.

A third impediment to democracy, Zweig maintains, is the institutional sclerosis that has characterized China's opening to the world economy. In theory, integration into world markets should spark competitive pressures to deregulate and privatize the domestic economy. The PRC, however, has resisted the liberalizing effects of global capital. "Opening China to the world, therefore", writes Zweig, "does not necessarily translate into opening China within itself."

Zweig thus makes a formidable case against the democratizing potential of Chinese economic reform and the more naive expectations surrounding U.S. engagement with China. While generally supportive of engagement, he cautions against placing too much faith in an "inevitable, rapid and smooth democratic transformation." This counsel is wise, but Zweig may be overly pessimistic.

Specifically, three recent policy initiatives suggest that an influential sector of the Chinese leadership is working hard to overcome the problems Zweig outlines. First, in July 1998 the CCP leadership announced that military, police and judicial units would have to divest themselves of their business interests. Hu Jintao, a member of the Standing Committee of the Politburo and a close political ally of President Jiang Zemin, was quite clear about the intent of this measure:

Facts show that the practice of engaging in business activities by these organizations not only seriously interferes with their performance of duties and affects their impartial enforcement of laws, but it could also breed corrupt and unhealthy practices, such as influence-peddling and 'putting money above all else.'

Actually implementing this ban will be difficult, as wily officers find ways to protect their spoils. But it is apparent that anti-corruption crusaders at the very top of the Party hierarchy take their missions seriously. Senior military officers, for example, forcefully championed the business closure campaign at the most recent session of the national parliament in March 1999.

Second, and at that same parliamentary conclave, an amendment to the state constitution was passed that enhances the formal recognition of private enterprise. The amendment defines private companies as "important components of the country's socialist market economy", and pledges that the state will "protect legitimate rights and interests of the private economy." Although hardly an adequate legal protection of private property, this measure is designed to promote, in the words of one parliamentary delegate, "a rule-based market that guarantees equal competition for state-run and private companies." And there are signs that more concrete actions are in the works to support private business: for example, the governor of China's central bank, Dai Xianglong, announced plans to increase commercial credit for private enterprises.

Third, in the run-up to Prime Minister Zhu Rongji's trip to the United States this year, Chinese representatives showed remarkable flexibility in World Trade Organization (WTO) negotiations with the United States. By one account, China offered "huge openings of its markets—in telecommunications, banking, insurance and agriculture—in return for getting the country into the WTO."[ii] Only political considerations on the American side kept the deal from being closed during Zhu's visit. The Chinese initiative highlights the reform strategy of an important part of the PRC elite, for the WTO will be powerful leverage against domestic protectionists.

Taken together, these three policies do not signal an imminent outbreak of free-market capitalism in China. They do not disprove Zweig, but they suggest another side to the story. Economic reform in China continues to move, however imperfectly, toward liberalization and privatization. Although Jiang Zemin and Zhu Rongji believe in the "superiority of socialism", they are pragmatic enough to recognize that the crushing economic problems they face, especially the specter of mass unemployment, can only be addressed by enlivening private enterprise and attracting global capital. In twenty years, Zweig's "quasi-private managerial class" may well be challenged by a rising bourgeoisie. While such a development would reinforce liberalization, it would not guarantee democracy, for bourgeoisies are, in general, politically ambivalent. If a repressive regime promises reliable profits, they may willingly accept limitations on political rights and activities (as they have, for instance, in Singapore). Moreover, the exigencies of capitalism may foreclose democratically determined political choices: tax rates can increase and regulations constrain only so much before global capital quickly seeks a safer haven. Capitalism can work for democratization up to a point; but, in China as elsewhere, a more meaningful democratic outcome depends upon particular political struggles.

Democracy

Democracy cannot be reduced to either nationalism or capitalism. Nationalist rhetoric may convey democratic ideals, but unless these ideals are institutionalized they can be overwhelmed by the authoritarian command to subordinate individuals to the fatherland. As for economic reform, a 1997 comparative study by Adam Przeworski and Fernando Limogi in *World Politics* argues for a more voluntaristic view of democratization, one that avoids deterministic emphasis on conditions, whether socioeconomic or rhetorical, and focuses on the strategies and actions of the protagonists and antagonists of democratic struggles: "Democracy is or is not established by political actors pursuing their goals, and it can be initiated at any level of development."

Elsewhere, in a rigorous little book, Przeworski outlines the political logic of liberalization and democratization.[iii] A crucial prerequisite for a significant move away from dictatorship, he insists, is a reform group within the regime willing and able to act. Popular struggle alone rarely breaks authoritarianism.

A crisis of some sort, Przeworski suggests, may forge such a reform group and stir it to press against regime hardliners. A defeat in war, as with the Argentine loss in the Falkland Islands, might push a junta toward democratization; an international diplomatic crisis, such as Taiwan faced when the United States withdrew its recognition, might convince a Leninist party to accept real opposition; or widespread public demonstrations, which helped propel change in South Korea and East Germany, might present officials with a stark choice between heightening repression or compromising. None of these crises, in and of itself, automatically translates into liberalization, but any one may influence the political calculations of rulers in need of legitimation beyond sheer coercion.

Reformers, however, need partners in society, groups with whom they can compromise. Here, a moderate faction of opposition activists is required, people who are pressing for change but willing to accept some sort of accommodation with those in power. Moderates have to be able to control radical dissidents suspicious of outcomes short of immediate and complete democracy. If moderates can do this, they might be able to attract regime reformers away from hardliners and develop a strategy for liberalization. Such has been the pattern, Przeworski demonstrates, in many transitions to democracy.

In China, the political elements for liberalization are taking shape. Within the regime a reform group emerged in the 1980s, centering around Party Secretary Hu Yaobang. After the 1989 Tiananmen demonstrations, during which reformers momentarily outmaneuvered hardliners, the liberalizing project was weakened but not destroyed. In November 1997 Fang Jue, a former government official, circulated a report that was said to reflect the thinking of the "Democratic Faction", a group of "mid-level and high-level" CCP members frustrated with the repression of the 1989 democracy movement and the lack of meaningful political change.[iv] Although Fang himself is not a member of the Party, he is apparently close to some very important people, possibly Central Committee members, and his statement has been recognized by veteran dissidents Wei Jingsheng and Liu Qing as an "exciting first signal" that supporters of democracy are emerging within the CCP itself.

Fang and his fellow-travelers have called for competitive elections for all levels of legislative assemblies: local, provincial and national. The Democratic Faction supports the creation of formal political parties, to stand in opposition to the CCP, and informal non-political associations, a sort of Tocquevillian civil society. In the economic realm, it advocates further expansion of market forces and greater openness to global capital. It is also in favor of self-determination for Tibetans and the elimination of "all forms of armed threats and plans for armed solutions" in China's relations with Taiwan. The overarching theme is a comprehensive and consistent liberalism.

Fang has been jailed for advocating these ideas. The key point, however, is that political liberalization continues to be a contested issue within the Chinese power structure. Reformers are present and pressing for change. Indeed, some of China's highest ranking political leaders may be willing to contemplate political change, even if they would not go as far as the Democratic Faction's full agenda.

Li Peng, now chairman of the national parliament, is reliably hardline, and can be counted on to resist liberalization. Prime Minister Zhu Rongji, however, has revealed reformist sympathies. In his keynote address to the national parliament in March, he stated that the government should avoid "brutal measures" when confronted with popular dissatisfaction. He is more open to opposition to certain high-profile state projects, such as the Three Gorges Dam, and he has recognized the democratic aspirations of the 1989 Tiananmen demonstrations.[v]

President Jiang Zemin sends more mixed signals. He was tacitly supportive of the relaxation of political speech from late 1997 to mid-1998, during which authorities allowed, even encouraged, discussion of a wide range of political topics.[vi] On the other hand, he has endorsed the call by Li Peng against any sort of "Western democracy" for China, and he has accepted the recent crackdown against dissidents attempting to create a formal opposition party.

If some top political leaders, in concert with the broader Democratic Faction of the Party, were to opt for modest political change, they would find a variety of potential allies in society. The activists involved in the Chinese Democratic Party, a formal opposition party founded in the summer of 1998 and still clinging to political life in spite of persistent government repression, have demonstrated a certain moderation in their strategy. They have attempted to work within the existing constitutional structure to maximize possibilities for political association and speech. They do not call for a wholesale transformation of the political order. Although their leaders are currently languishing in jail with harsh prison sentences, they could prove to be useful partners for regime reformers in any effort to stem more radical opposition demands. In addition, the families of victims of the 1989 Beijing massacre continue their campaign to "reverse the verdict" of that terrible tragedy. They, too, are not looking to overthrow the state, but simply for recognition that their fallen sons and daughters were not traitors.

A choice on the part of party-state reformers to accommodate any one of these groups would be a liberalizing move for the regime, not a sudden breakthrough to democracy but a fragile first step toward a less authoritarian political order. But such a choice is unlikely without some kind of pressure on the regime, a crisis that would embolden reformers and unbalance hardliners.

Not just any crisis will do. The costs of a cataclysmic meltdown of central authority might overwhelm any liberalizing tendencies. War is too dangerous and uncertain: the Clausewitzian fog might clear to reveal an even more repressive regime. A diplomatic crisis could be tricky as well. If such a situation was fomented from without, it could play into the hands of hardline military chauvinists eager to blame China's troubles on nefarious foreign forces. It would be utter folly and hubris, therefore, for U.S. policymakers to believe that they can engineer the emergency that pushes the CCP toward democracy. A dramatic reversal of U.S. engagement and a determined isolation of China would simply fulfill the prophecies of the Say No nationalists and strangle moderate political dissidents.

Perhaps the best prospect is an upsurge of domestic turbulence born of economic reform. If the hard-pressed working class, threatened by rising unemployment, organizes and gets out on the streets, what would—what could—the regime do? Call out the "People's Army" to again fire upon the people? A Solidarity-like trade union movement, generated from within China itself, might push regime reformers away from repressive political alternatives. Or what if the student movement were to regenerate and rally the millions of city dwellers exasperated with ever increasing official corruption? Or if a peasant-based, millennial religious movement were to challenge the state from below? Would the CCP leadership, some of whom have publicly rejected "brutal measures", be willing to take extreme action to prevail? While there is no guarantee that the choice for liberalization would be taken, power holders would at least have to contemplate seriously the merits of a political opening as against brutal suppression.

Is this far-fetched? Not really. Remember, a little over a decade ago, just before that remarkable Autumn of 1989, many of us were fairly convinced that totalitarianism was firmly entrenched in the Soviet Union and Eastern Europe. East German apparatchiks would never let the Berlin Wall crumble. Ceausescu was unmovable in Romania. Soviet militarists would never allow the Party to fall. How quickly things changed.

NOTES

[i] Greenfeld, *Nationalism: Five Roads to Modernity* (Cambridge, MA: Harvard University Press, 1992), p. 10.

[ii] David E. Sanger, "How U.S. and China Failed to Close Trade Deal", *New York Times*, April 10, 1999.

[iii] Przeworski, *Democracy and the Market: Political and Economic Reforms in Eastern Europe and Latin America* (New York: Cambridge University Press, 1991), chap. 2.

[iv] Fang, "A Program for Democratic Reform", *Journal of Democracy* (October 1998).

[v] Daniel Kwan, "Students Wanted Democracy, Says Zhu", *South China Morning Post*, April 15, 1999.

[vi] Willy Wo-Lap Lam, "The Wait for the Promised Mainland", *South China Morning Post*, April 22, 1998; Susan Lawrence, "Agent of Change", *Far Eastern Economic Review*, July 23, 1998.

12

Undemocratic Capitalism:
China and the Limits of Economism

David Zweig[*]

The Clinton administration's China policy has come under attack from many quarters for being too conciliatory, too optimistic and too compromised by a nexus of money and insider politics. But the President and his aides deflect each jab by contending that, despite episodic problems and pratfalls, a policy of engaging China on a broad range of issues has the best chance of maximizing American influence and impelling China toward positive change. The key dynamic is assumed to be rapid economic growth, which, it is tenaciously held, will result ultimately in political liberalization. That, in turn, would not solve all problems between the United States and China, but it would conventionalize those problems and, presumably, make them easier to manage.

In this line of assumptions the administration has many scholarly allies. Henry Rowen, Minxin Pei and many others have argued that one of the few hard conclusions of comparative politics—that rising income levels are conducive to political democratization—applies to China no less than it has applied to Europe and Latin America.[i] In this view, increased wealth, information and trade will create and mobilize a new middle class whose interests and social power will ultimately undermine the Communist Party's monopoly on political power, leading in due course to some form of democratic politics. According to this view, too, elections in rural China, advances toward the rule of law, the strengthening of

---

[*] David Zweig is associate professor, division of social science, at the Hong Kong University of Science and Technology.

This essay first appeared in *The National Interest*, No. 56 (Summer 1999).

the National People's Congress (NPC) and media liberalization exemplify political change already afoot in China as a result of economic marketization and growth.

While continued growth cannot be guaranteed, China's leaders have demonstrated an impressive ability to manage the economic difficulties foisted on China by the post-July 1997 Asian crisis. More important, they have demonstrated seriousness and flexibility in pursuing continued economic reform. President Jiang Zemin's policy proposals at the 15th Party Congress, held in September 1997, were bold. Promising to reform moribund state-owned enterprises (SOEs), Jiang reinterpreted the Marxist concept of state ownership of the means of production to include publicly held stocks (by both individuals and other firms). Bankruptcy law, takeovers, mergers and acquisitions—all features of a capitalist economy—received the Party's official blessing. Since then, China has demonstrated a further commitment to reform by reducing housing subsidies and the volume of public employment generally—efforts quite likely spurred on by revelations of structural deficiencies in the "Asian model" that have triggered the region's continuing economic crisis.

It is likely, therefore, that China's economy will grow enough over time to keep the basic question relevant: Will economic growth produce political liberalization? The answer is unclear. For economic growth to produce democratic politics—or at least more liberal politics—a middle class of private property owners who want to get the state off their backs must emerge. To generate such a class, China needs the growth and expansion of market forces, an effective system of property rights protected by the rule of law, and a much reduced role for bureaucratic authority in the economy. Ultimately, too, it needs enough political stability to allow this middle class to emerge, and it will require new political institutions to manage the demands of that class in a way that will not push Party leaders to co-opt it or even crush it before it achieves greater liberalization.

Many signs point to these positive trends, but strong counter-trends are also working against political liberalization despite—and in some cases because of—the rapid economic growth of recent decades. To sort out the evidence, three questions need especially careful examination. First, who will check the enormous power of China's bureaucrats whose authority and personal economic interests depend upon their ability to manipulate market forces? Second, if labor unrest stemming from the current reform of the SOEs threatens social stability and business profits, will managers advocate a more open political system? Third, will China "open" more to the outside world in terms of trade, and what would the social and political consequences of such an opening be?

In my view the answers to these questions do not support current assertions that China is rapidly liberalizing but suggest that the process of change will be slower. Let us take them in turn.

A Rent-Seeking Culture

Many observers assert that powerful political and economic forces are pushing for a continued transition to market capitalism in China. As their argument goes, the decentralizing of economic decision-making authority from the center to the localities, combined with a shift from planned allocation of goods to market allocation, is leading to greater decision-making freedom for individuals and firms. This means, in turn, expanded market activity and, ultimately, a transition to free-market capitalism.

There is a logic to this projection. As enterprise managers pursue greater efficiency, economies of scale and lower transaction costs—i.e., the cost of doing business—they advance liberalization. Firms with comparative advantage in particular products are helping to dismantle regional barriers so that they can expand their markets. When foreign-funded enterprises expand their market share, domestic firms become more competitive and more responsive to market forces—or else they do not survive. Popular hostility toward pervasive corruption is also impelling Chinese leaders to further embrace the market economy. Much of the dual price system has disappeared as more and more goods are exchanged on the open market. As early as the end of 1992, only 5.9 percent of retail sales, 12.5 percent of agricultural sales, and 18.7 percent of the sale of capital goods came from products priced by the state.[ii] The decisions of the 15th Party Congress are likely to accelerate these trends. In particular, with less pressure on banks to prop up inefficient SOEs, markets are likely to play a greater role in the allocation of domestic capital. So there is, indeed, plenty of hopeful news.

But rapid growth alone does not ordain a liberalized economy. How exchanges occur, limits on interregional flows of goods and services, the scope of bureaucratic interference, the scale of transaction costs, and the ability of local state agencies to intervene in economic decision making are all important indicators of where China's economy really rests, and of where it is headed. These indicators suggest that a mixed economy, where decentralization empowers non-democratic forces, is equally likely. China's property rights regime and the ferment of economic development may not be creating a large middle class of private property owners who will seek autonomy from the state. Instead, economic growth without privatization, in a society that has experienced little democracy, could create a semi-private managerial class that does not support democracy. Add to this a strong ethos in China favoring collective interests, and the likelihood of a corporatist China seems far greater than a democratic one.

This likelihood is increased by the cultural reality that economic power in China already rests largely with bureaucrats, as it has for a very long time. The deep involvement of administrators in the economy makes China, above all, a rent-seeking society. "Rent" in this context is defined as the difference between free-market prices and higher prices that exist because regulations limit competitors from entering the market. Regulation acts to limit supply, yielding above-market prices. Rents nourish corruption, as bureaucrats find themselves in a position to charge fees both for services and for selectively ignoring the regulations that they and their colleagues create. The payoffs can be substantial. Higher tariff barriers—another form of rent—insure higher profits than would occur in a non-tariff economy for those who smuggle goods into China. The Customs Service itself and the People's Liberation Army (PLA) are two actors that benefit handsomely from the rents arising from tariff barriers.

According to Wu Jinglian, a leading Chinese economist, rents created by the difference between free-market and planned commodity prices, between the official value of foreign exchange and its free-market value, and between low official interest rates and the real cost of money, accounted for 20-25 percent of gnp in 1981-89—a higher rate than in India or Turkey in the 1960s, both of which are considered classic rent-seeking societies. Little wonder, argued Wu, that government-connected Chinese businessmen "try by every means to maintain the existing rent system and establish a new rent system to expand the scope of rents."[iii]

Also, in the current transitional economy, managers of corporatist economic structures, army officers, semi-public companies, and mayors of towns, cities, development zones, and former people's communes (now called townships), and even Party secretaries in villages control and manage key sectors in China's developing economy. They are all rent-seekers in one way or another.

Hence, despite assertions that a growing private sector is creating a strong middle class, one actually finds severe limits on the role of the private sector in China's cities. No doubt, the validation of the private economy as "an important part"—not just a "complementary" sector—of the national economy at this year's National People's Congress will create an upsurge in the private sector's role in China. Many private firms who have worn a collective hat to protect themselves may, over time, be more willing to admit the private nature of their property rights. However, private entrepreneurs build government networks as protection from rapacious bureaucrats who would otherwise plunder their profits and extort funds for their local coffers. Such norms of high government interference are, needless to say, not conducive to the ethic of the free market as we know it in the West.

Nor is it the intention of the present reformist government to build such an ethic. While Jiang Zemin has called for increasing the diversity of investors in SOEs in order to separate "administrative functions from enterprise management and change the way enterprises operate", he has also called for continued state management of China's core enterprises. That means insuring that bureaucrats will continue to dominate the commanding heights of the economy. That, in turn, means that managers of the 500-1,000 key state enterprises will remain beholden to state bureaucrats for cheap capital and technology inputs. Jiang also echoed pre-Congress commands to managers to rely on their factory's Party committees before deciding on layoffs, prices and production levels when he said that enterprises must "give play to the role of the Party organizations" in the plants "as political nuclei."

China's top leaders still reject genuine privatization even in principle, preferring that shares be sold to workers or to other companies. One key reason, at least according to researchers at the Chinese Academy of Social Science in Beijing, is precisely their deep fear of the emergence of a real, autonomous middle class. As a result, the stripping of state assets and the sale of land and equipment to other companies need not, and probably will not, create a large private ownership class. Bureaucrats will retain a significant hand in making key decisions; a distorted market will persist; and close relations between captains of industry and the state will continue.

This means, too, that despite a shift of decision-making authority from the center to the localities, many key economic decisions remain under the purview of local governments. What is emerging is a form of local economic corporatism, replete with regional monopolies, rent-seeking opportunities and "relational contracting"—a characteristic of early capitalism (as well as socialist transitional economies) where firms carry out business transactions based on long-term, personalized trading relations and trust, not on maximizing profits and market efficiency.

This system of local protectionism is a phenomenon already a decade in the making. In the mid-1980s China reformed its fiscal code, creating a tax farming system under which all levels of government were given tax quotas to pass up to the next level of government. Some or all enterprise profits and taxes above the quota were retained by local governments. Further, as the state withdrew tax subsidies, many local governments suddenly had to swim on their own. These conditions gave local governments powerful incentives to maximize local output, sales, profits and taxes. It also provided incentive to establish barriers to trans-regional trade in order to keep products from other regions out. Thus, for example, taxi companies in Shanghai can buy only Santana vehicles produced by the city's joint venture with Volkswagen. The prospect of discontented unemployed workers laid off by bankrupt SOEs under Jiang's new reform initiative could increase pressures on cities to protect their remaining SOEs from regional competitors.

Most businessmen avoid inter-regional trade for other reasons as well. Shortages of quality goods, weak market signals and information, and widespread corruption create great uncertainty for enterprises in China's emerging semi-market economy. There is little sense of the sanctity of contracts, and the legal system favors local firms. When money alone cannot insure supply, firms resort to relational contracting. Thus in the 1980s Wuhan's department stores bought most of their stock from factories with whom they had long-term relationships. Similarly, officials in the First Machinery Factory in a large urban center used close government ties to secure loans at rates significantly below those available to their competitors. The result is a far less than perfect market, significant waste, limited inter-regional competition and high transaction costs as firms invest excessive time and money maximizing business-bureaucracy relationships as the major mechanism for making profits.

Finally, Chinese firms, awash in a sea of rent-seeking, accept payoffs to bureaucrats as part of doing business. Many of these companies resulted from "downsizing with Chinese characteristics", a process in which governments lay off bureaucrats from their official payrolls only to help them establish new semi-public firms. Situated strategically between the government and genuine enterprises, these firms earn income by charging a handling fee for transferring goods and resources. Like barnacles on ships, they draw their sustenance from their parastatal relationships with the ministries from which they were spun off.

Labor Unrest as a Liberalization Brake

Jiang and Zhu's plans for restructuring the SOEs suggest their commitment to greater liberalization of China's transnational economic relations and their understanding that there is a close link between international competition and domestic reform. As China continues to lower its barriers to the outside world and takes steps to accede to U.S. demands for World Trade Organization accession, most of its SOEs will face economic extinction. In the face of such threats, China's leaders know, too, that they can no longer afford to throw good money at bad firms. Unprofitable SOEs will fend for themselves, while the state will choose and help "winners."

But the social stresses liable to be generated by the winnowing out of China's SOE sector are staggering. China's approximately 350,000 SOEs employ over 70 million workers, pay benefits to another 20 million retirees, and in total support about another 200 million dependents. With as many as 45 percent of them in the red, China's SOEs have a combined debt of 620 billion Renminbi (RMB), or $75 billion. The past decade's policy of paying laid off SOE workers their "basic" salary—usually comprising 40 percent of current wages and excluding all subsidies and bonuses—worked much like unemployment insurance schemes in the West. But that strategy has now left China with a welfare problem of catastrophic proportions.

Even in a very imperfectly competitive market, ending subsidies will expose many SOEs to the pressures of competition. But if closing down large numbers of SOEs, without an effective unemployment insurance scheme to cushion the impact, promises to put 10-12 million workers on the streets, regional and local governments may strongly resist such a policy. Recent eyewitness reports from Sichuan Province tell that threats of worker violence have so frightened managers that they hesitate to fire workers until they have been retrained and helped to find a new job. In fact, these pressures forced the Politburo in June 1998 to decide to stop laying off urban workers in order to avoid an urban explosion. Instead, many unprofitable firms may be merged with stronger firms that may be pressured to keep on more workers. Already powerful conglomerates (*jituan*) are buying up the assets of weaker firms. A more oligopolistic economy could emerge in which a few large firms dominate different sectors. This would not promote increased marketization in China any more than a roughly similar situation has promoted broad marketization in Russia.

The reform of SOEs also directly affects the liberalization of China's financial system, which needs to become more market-oriented. Chinese banks have loaned money according to national or local policy, not at its real cost. In 1996 alone China's banks loaned out over 4 trillion RMB, of which 75 percent went to support SOEs.[iv] Many of those loans are non-performing. Clearly it will take years to sort out these problems. Even if widespread selling of bank shares occurs, the banks will still be under enormous political pressures to make loans based on personal and political, rather than market, factors, until the day that the central and local banks really do become independent of the political system. But that day is far off.

The politics of regional disparities will further limit genuine economic reform. Under Deng, China deregulated the economies in coastal provinces, granting them preferential treatment that helped their economies boom. Inland areas remained apart from global markets, even as the state suppressed the prices of the natural resources that are the heart of their economies. Consequently, the coast flourished while inland areas languished. Based on my own calculations, while 60.8 percent of China's gross value of industrial output (GVIO) was produced in coastal cities in 1984, a decade later those same cities produced 70 percent. Although inland areas might prefer an end to policy favoritism and an even playing field, they are also home to some of the most inefficient SOEs, whose closing will only exacerbate their economic plight. Under the current regime their interests lie in supporting central bureaucrats who believe that the state—not the free market—must redistribute resources and resolve regional inequalities.

It is likely, then, that looming instability will undermine any impulse toward political liberalization. The current middle strata of corporate directors and local government leaders—those locked into the existing property rights regime of state or publicly owned industries—will surely prefer corporatism and soft authoritarianism to democratic change. If social unrest stemming from SOE reform challenges their managerial rights and threatens them with recrimination for their side payments to bureaucrats, they will even support hard authoritarianism if it is necessary to protect "public order." They are likely to interpret democracy under such circumstances as tantamount to chaos.

In the countryside, too, where most private firms exist, there is little support for democratization among the rural business elite.[v] As of 1992, only 0.5 percent of the millions of rural enterprises at or below the county level had trade unions, and there is little reason to believe that the number of union shops has increased since then. And even as China's leaders let farmers elect villager committees in order to stabilize the countryside, weaken oppressive cadres, and persuade farmers to invest in public works projects, elections remain restricted to the lowest levels of rural society. Top Party leaders are likely to prevent these elections from sparking a nationwide democracy movement. The key test will be whether similarly open elections as those taking place in China's villages will take place at the next level up in the rural bureaucracy—the township level. As for the more economically advanced coastal areas, rural people there seem too busy making money to care about political liberalization, and so long as limited economic reform allows them to do so they are unlikely to become a source of democratic advocacy.

China's Opening to the World

The role of the bureaucracy is also critical when it comes to foreign trade. Opening China to the outside is, according to the optimists, a key dynamic in China's eventual marketization and eventual political liberalization. But it hasn't worked out that way so far. China's official foreign trade, which has grown from $30 billion in the late 1970s to $290 billion in 1996, at an average annual rate of 16-17 percent, has surpassed all expectations. Few predicted that such a large country could become so trade dependent, with some estimates suggesting that over 40 percent of GNP is now derived from international trade. Indeed, the level of foreign direct investment—by 1997 totaling $250 billion—which allows foreigners to be directly involved in managing Chinese enterprises, suggests that China's economy in recent years has been more open than those of Japan and South Korea, which have relied more heavily on, respectively, foreign purchases in equity markets and foreign loans.

China's comparative advantage in foreign trade has created thousands of relatively small, labor-intensive, export-oriented firms in the countryside that want to expand their export opportunities. Both they and SOEs want to import resources duty free and circumvent state-run foreign trade companies so they can deal directly with foreign markets. The result is a "joint venture fever" that undermines state controls over China's boundaries. That seems good, if greater economic integration between China and the rest of the world is the end to be sought.

But rent-seeking of a different sort propels the search for joint venture partners, and it is not of a sort likely to advance marketization. In protected sectors, where high tariffs prevent imports of competitively priced foreign goods, joint ventures help Chinese partners create products that are highly competitive within the domestic market. Even if their prices are a little high and their quality a little low, Chinese firms and their joint venture allies can nevertheless earn large profits since their goods face no serious competition. Therefore, those apparent advocates of increased internationalization have strong interests in limiting that process as well. The profits are rent in that they flow from a non-competitive market arrangement. Real competition would make such ventures less attractive, not more.

Indeed, due to its highly regulated nature, the foreign trade sector remains rife with opportunities for corruption. China's bureaucrats know that excessive restrictions and fewer foreign transactions mean fewer rents, so they favor more trade and investment—but only under their administrative purview. For them the choice is clear: no flow, no dough! The result, however, is de facto, not de jure, trade liberalization, for much trade ensues through smuggling and corruption. According to the World Bank, goods smuggled from Hong Kong to China equal 15 percent of all legal trade between the two economies. According to the *South China Morning Post*, the scale of smuggling actually forced China's television manufacturers to cut domestic prices by 10 percent.

Other data broaden the picture. While the World Bank reported that China's nominal tariff rate in 1995 averaged 32 percent, the effective rate that was collected was only 6 percent. While half of that seepage was due to special policy privileges given to foreign invested enterprises, the other half was the result of bureaucrats who waived regulations in return for payoffs. Today, for infrastructure projects in Hong Kong, for example, large foreign companies reportedly must give large equity shares to mainland brokers who provide no value-added except to certify that the project can go forward. One American firm working in east China froze its power project because it refused to donate an equity share to a company run by a top leader's son.

Such high-placed Chinese intermediaries have no interest in a transparent trade system. Thus while China has carried out the easy part of trade liberalization, or what the World Bank calls "shallow integration"—reforming its import regime and limiting controls on foreign exchange transactions—China has balked at "deep integration", including greater market access, regulatory transparency, non-tariff barriers and wage policies. China's trade liberalization essentially plateaued in 1994 and has not moved forward since.[vi]

At the bottom of such problems is the plain fact that China has never wanted an open trade regime. Since 1978 it has erected a transnational sector—Special Economic Zones, Export Processing Zones, joint ventures, swap markets for foreign currency conversion—to cordon off the domestic economy from external influences. These special deregulated spaces and organizations receive what the Chinese call "preferable policies" that exempt them from tax, trade and investment rules governing non-open territories. This has created a dual economic system of open, favored localities, and more closed, highly regulated regions. According to Chinese economist Hu Angang, the inequalities generated by this system create "all sorts of special and independent economic and political interest cliques within the state apparatus", who "although they are communists, regard it as their goals to maximize the interests of their own cliques, and to seek monopolies and privileges through their economic and political pursuits."[vii]

In light of these interests, one must marvel at the audacity of Zhu Rongji's wto offer, which, if accepted and fully implemented, will severely limit bureaucratic rent-seeking and management of foreign trade. But the deal is not completed, and China remains a mercantilist state where the majority of leaders, bureaucrats, industrial managers and regional officials support state involvement in China's foreign trade. Their view is that China's trade should grow but in directions set by official definitions of China's interests, rather than by domestic or global market forces. Chinese leaders still advocate an East Asian style "developmental state", with an industrial policy geared at competitive export industries. As was the case in South Korea and Japan, China wants to "create" comparative advantage where it does not now exist. In particular, Chinese industrial policy is meant to protect sunrise industries, which bureaucrats see as the source of future trade competitiveness. It has targeted the electronics, telecommunications, transportation, pharmaceutical and other high-tech export industries as key sectors that will drive its economy in the next century. Similarly, insurers and banks that have yet to adapt to global competition would get swamped should China open these sectors up. It is worth remembering that China is hesitating to open to the WTO too quickly in order to protect and develop its own future global Fortune 500 companies; otherwise, these sunrise companies would get swallowed by the global giants. Still, protection leaves these firms with little incentive to become fully market-oriented.

The same applies to government ministries. China's bureaucrats benefit far more from regulated trade than from anything approaching real free trade. As China opened up in this constrained and selective manner, ministries were empowered to establish monitoring agencies that control threats to their own industries posed by trade liberalization and global competition. The Ministry of Machine Building established an Equipment Approval Division to monitor and approve all imports of equipment, including equipment for joint ventures. In 1995, as China opened the construction industry to foreign direct investment, strict guidelines were introduced and new foreign-funded enterprises needed approval from the Ministry of Foreign Trade and Economic Cooperation as well as the Ministry of Construction, which owns and operates its major competitors. According to the U.S. Trade Representative, one of the strongest advocates of continued protection is the vulnerable pharmaceutical industry, whose State Pharmaceutical Administration issues quality certificates for pharmaceutical products.

In sum, despite the conventional wisdom that increased global transactions will liberalize China's trade regime, forcing it from autarky into global interdependence, strong forces will limit China's movement along such a trajectory. Also, the involvement of foreigners in China's economy does not necessarily support the emergence of a market-oriented middle strata. Foreign direct investment throughout China is partnered with local governments or the PLA at all levels of the system. Even Hong Kong's investment partners in wild and woolly Guangdong Province are mostly local township officials, not private entrepreneurs. Rather than undermine government authority, foreign direct investment strengthens its legitimacy by increasing economic growth and helping local governments meet social welfare obligations. Opening China to the world, therefore, does not necessarily translate into opening China within itself.

China as a Democracy?

It appears, then, that while there are social and economic trends in China pressing for greater marketization, strong counter-trends seem to limit it. There are some impulses toward greater political liberalization, but again strong counter-impulses that would stymie it as well. As for the picture as a whole, there is no evidence of a necessary or automatic lockstep relationship between economic development and market liberalization, broadly defined, and the political liberalization that many pundits and politicians have predicted.

The truth is, no one really knows what will happen in the political domain in China. On the one hand, the confluence of corruption, inflation and economic recession could again trigger massive protests. In 1989, 30 percent annual inflation dropped real incomes for Beijingers even as a nouveau riche or "princeling" class composed of the children of high-ranking cadres emerged. If a substantial sell-off of state enterprises in 1999 brings large profits to managers even as it puts millions of unemployed workers on the streets, new protests could bring the regime to its knees. On the other hand, without alternative political parties in readiness, such a collapse would be far more likely to lead to a military dictatorship than to a democratic regime.

And there is little reason to anticipate the emergence of competitive political parties or an institutionalized movement for democracy. As in Hungary, where factions in the communist elite in the 1980s turned into competitive parties, stark differences over development strategies among Chinese factions made a similar scenario seem plausible in the China of the 1980s. But today is different. Jiang Zemin's struggle to maintain legitimacy as the "core" of the leadership makes concessions and institutionalized division of authority or separation of powers difficult. The core of any factional opposition, Qiao Shi, was removed from office in 1997, and such a party structure simply cannot arise outside mainstream influences under current circumstances.

Tiananmen sent a message to the Chinese people that public protest will be met with violent counterforce. Since then—and despite some signs of division at the top—most urban Chinese have accepted the government's offer to pursue private interest through business; to seek personal freedom through amassing wealth; and to maintain economic growth through political passivity. Chinese also compare the chaos in the former USSR to their own country's economic vigor and say the equivalent of "there but for the grace of God go we." As far as political models are concerned, the specter of Russia more than outweighs the lure of Hong Kong to most Chinese who have political power.

American Choices

This reality poses hard choices for U.S. policy. The widespread belief in an evolutionary process in which economic liberalization drives political democratization in China is narcotic in its policy impact. Through it one can excuse nearly any short-term accommodation, using the rationale that buying time makes sense because time is on the side of all that is benign. But what if this is wrong? China may change more slowly than anticipated; it may become corporatist rather than democratic; or it may even implode violently.

All three developments would be problematic in one way or another for the United States. But all three, and particularly the first two, are more likely than the comforting thesis of inevitable, rapid and smooth democratic transformation. While marketization is forcing economic institutions to liberalize somewhat, political liberalization, in terms of the emergence of real competitive politics, appears nowhere on the national agenda. Powerful vested interests would be threatened by a free press and public disclosure of the activities of China's middle and upper strata, particularly as they seek to profit from SOE restructuring. Moreover, the social unrest likely to emerge from massive layoffs simply cannot be accommodated by a system undergoing political liberalization. A reality check on China today tells us that—pace Henry Rowen—China is very unlikely to be a democracy by the year 2015.

So what should the U.S. government do? It must accept that while a major swing in economic reform and global market liberalization appears to be looming, those changes will face severe domestic opposition that could in the end push China in a decidedly illiberal direction. In the mid-term, it might be that encouraging China to liberalize—by holding out the prospect of WTO membership, for example—would instead trigger a system collapse. Corruption could easily accelerate under the current SOE reform strategy, and the sell-off of state firms might be more vigorously pursued if China attained WTO membership. According to various reports, as much as $10 billion worth of state assets have been stripped by private and public interests in the name of economic reform. The sale of shares in public firms could exacerbate this problem: factory managers and bureaucrats could borrow bank funds to buy up large amounts of shares in public companies, and then sell off the companies to other firms who lay off redundant employees. The result would be windfall profits for bureaucrats while workers are dumped on the streets. Could such a state of affairs persist for a long time without an explosion? Perhaps, but it would not be a sound bet.

Would a collapse in China be a good thing for American interests? A collapsed Soviet Union is widely interpreted as having been a favorable development—although the hobbled Russia that emerged from it has won decidedly mixed reviews. If the Chinese political system today is in fact unreformable, as the Soviet system proved to be, could people really still prefer that the system collapse? The negative global repercussions would be enormous.

Who knows what would arise in place of the semi-reformist Chinese government we have now? While there is little doubt that a democratic China would be a better partner than an authoritarian one, China's long march from authoritarianism to democracy must traverse many dangerous passes, where a simple misstep could lead to disaster. Does the United States want to push China onto a path that could undermine the first extended period of economic growth and development experienced by the Chinese people in over a century and a half? Would that make for long-term stable relations? American policymakers need to address these questions, rather than operate on the flawed assumption that economic reform will produce political liberalization without radical political discontinuity in the bargain.

What is needed, then, is a continued policy of engagement that helps China move down the road of liberalization, but that does not justify that policy on short-term predictions of dramatic political change. The United States must engage China because of China's rising power and influence, because of its market, and because greater American involvement in China increases the likelihood of more positive, long-term developments. But the administration must not win supporters for its China policy based on promises it cannot keep and on developments in China that it can neither predict nor control. China will change at its own pace, taking into consideration the need for social stability, the power and interests of its now frightened bureaucrats, and the real limits that exist on the power of the top leaders. Only then will Sino-American relations be established on a stable footing that will weather the difficult times that lie ahead as China continues its dangerous, but nonetheless remarkable, reform program.

NOTES

[i] Henry S. Rowen, "The Short March: China's Road to Democracy", *The National Interest* (Fall 1996); and Minxin Pei, "Is China Democratizing?" *Foreign Affairs* (January/February 1998).
[ii] Lin Yimin, *The Competitive Advantage of Firms After Communism: State and Market in Post-Mao China* (Cambridge University Press, forthcoming).
[iii] Interview with Wu Jinglian, *Jingji ribao* (Economic Daily), April 6, 1993.
[iv] Nicholas R. Lardy, *China's Unfinished Economic Revolution* (Washington, dc: Brookings Institution Press, 1998).
[v] David Zweig, *Freeing China's Farmers: Rural Restructuring in the Reform Era* (Armonk, NY: M.E. Sharpe, 1997).
[vi] See Margaret Pearson, "China's Integration into the International Trade and Investment Regime", in *China Joins the World: Progress and Prospects*, ed. Elizabeth Economy and Michel Oksenberg (New York: Council on Foreign Relations Press, 1999).
[vii] Hu Angang, "Why I am for No Preferential Treatment for Special Economic Zones", *Ming bao*, August 23, 1995, in FBIS-CHI-95-188, September 28, 1995.

13

Unsettled Succession:
China's Critical Moment

Bruce J. Dickson[*]

Who will be the next leader of China? This question has been a perpetual preoccupation of scholars and journalists for decades, and the reason is clear: In one form or another, the succession issue has been the central drama of Chinese politics almost since the beginning of the People's Republic in 1949. The absence of institutionalized procedures for selecting China's top leader led to the most serious political conflicts of the Maoist era: the Gao Gang-Rao Shushi episode of 1954, resulting in the "suicide" of one and the disappearance of another of two leading figures; the Cultural Revolution and its attack on Mao's supposed successor Liu Shaoqi; the Lin Biao affair, culminating in deadly plane crash of another of Mao's designated successors; and the arrest of the "Gang of Four" a month after Mao's death.

The Deng Xiaoping era has also seen its share of political intrigue as succession arrangements unraveled: first when Hua Guofeng and other Cultural Revolution beneficiaries were outmaneuvered by reformers in the early 1980s; later when Hu Yaobang lost Deng's favor and was forced into retirement in 1987; and most recently when Zhao Ziyang similarly lost Deng's confidence and was

[*] Bruce J. Dickson is associate professor of political science and international affairs at the Elliott School of International Affairs, The George Washington University. He is the associate editor of *Problems of Post-Communism*, and the author of *Democratization in China and Taiwan: The Adaptability of Leninist Parties* (Oxford University Press, 1997).

This essay first appeared in *The National Interest*, No. 49 (Fall 1997).

removed from his posts in the wake of the pro-democracy movement of 1989. Reports of infighting and jockeying for power among the five or six likely successors to Deng continued thereafter, fueling the perception that the succession issue was among the most—if not the most—serious problems of Chinese politics.

And then, finally, on February 19, 1997, Deng died—and nothing happened. Mourners did not march on Tiananmen Square, turning the death of a leader into a protest against remaining leaders, as occurred after the deaths of Zhou Enlai in 1976 and Hu Yaobang in 1989. Nor did one faction of leaders arrest its opponents, as happened after Mao died in 1976. There was no massive public grieving or disruption of everyday life. And to date there have been no significant shifts in Chinese policies, foreign or domestic.

Was the importance of leadership succession in China, then, simply overrated? Not entirely. China's leaders were aware that the death of a prominent leader could be taken as an unspoken signal initiating spontaneous protests and they took steps to pre-empt any hint of unrest. Additional plain-clothes and uniformed police were dispatched to likely trouble spots, such as college campuses and Tiananmen Square. Those few citizens who tried to bring flowers to Tiananmen were deflected, detained, and then ushered away in police cars. Foreign dignitaries and media were barred from Deng's funeral, denying potential protesters a sympathetic audience. If Deng's death was anti-climactic, it was partly because great care was taken to make it so.

Still, while succession is not an insignificant issue, it is easily oversold. The absence of formal procedures for selecting a new leader, the infrequency of such events, and the tendency of Chinese elites to struggle against each other for political power combine to give the problem of leadership succession its persistent fascination for China-watchers. But the potential for political crisis at times of transition should not obscure the fundamental truth that no communist government has ever collapsed as the direct result of leadership succession. When a leader dies in office, his survivors have always been able to reach a consensus around a new standard bearer in short order. Not all such leaders were inspired choices (Hua Guofeng and, in the case of the Soviet Union, Konstantin Chernenko come quickly to mind), and not all remained in their new posts for very long. But in all cases the normal operations of state continued with little disruption at the time of succession.

Succession remains a serious issue, however, because so much is at stake in the longer run. In China's case, the succession to Deng, once it plays out, may determine whether the policies of *gaige* and *kaifang* (reform and opening to the outside world) are continued and perhaps deepened, or abandoned. It may rearrange significantly the relative power of the current constellation of leaders and influence the degree of political order in China. If intra-elite strife were to ensue, political instability would likely follow. If, as a consequence, China's leaders were to lose control over society, and over the many thousands of local officials who run China on a daily basis, the survival of the regime itself could be at stake.

Such apocalyptic consequences are unlikely, however, for at least three reasons. First, there was no power vacuum when Deng died because he held no formal posts. Remembering the havoc wreaked by the succession issue during and immediately after Mao's tenure, Deng took the trouble to work out his own succession far in advance. His status as China's paramount leader was not undermined by having more junior officials formally fill the top posts in the Chinese Communist Party (CCP) and government. Like Mao, however, Deng lost confidence in his initially designated successors (Hu Yaobang and Zhao Ziyang), pushed them out of office, and replaced them with new heirs apparent, the last being Jiang Zemin. When Deng died, the top leadership positions—general secretary of the CCP, prime minister, president, and chairman of the Military Affairs Commission—were all filled.[1] Few outside observers believe that the current ranking of leaders will remain fixed beyond the next few years, but the fact that the primary contenders already hold formal positions at least postpones the problem. The real shape of the post-Deng era will therefore take time to clarify.

A second reason for expecting scant policy discontinuity in the near term is that there is little dispute among current leaders concerning policy preferences. As was not the case during the Mao succession period, all the potential competitors hold positions relatively close together on the policy spectrum, exemplified by a general consensus on *gaige* and *kaifang*. Despite occasional shifts in the direction and pace of reforms, none of China's front-line leaders is calling for a return to a centrally planned, heavy-industry based economy. Any attempt to recentralize power, especially over the economy, would be resisted by local leaders, the main beneficiaries of market-oriented reforms during the Deng era. Indeed, already in the early 1990s resistance by several provincial governors forced Prime Minister Li Peng to abandon his attempt to recentralize control over financial and investment matters. Nor is anyone calling for an immediate transition to a full market economy, or putting political reform back on the agenda. All Politburo proponents of political liberalization were replaced in the summer of 1989.

There are undercurrents favoring political reform in China, but they are not strong enough by themselves to break the surface. Some of those who were demoted for their support of reform have subsequently returned to political life in less prominent positions (e.g., Hu Qili as minister of electronics and Yan Mingfu as vice minister of civil affairs). They may still privately favor political reform and may still have extensive networks of supporters. In 1995, there were rumors that Jiang Zemin had reached out to Hu Qili and Yan Mingfu to solicit their support, but was rebuffed; Hu, Yan, and other proponents of political reform have little reason to support Jiang, whom they see as an opportunistic and mediocre leader. Perhaps, too, they were waiting for the post-Deng succession to reassert themselves, but their marginal posts make such a reassertion difficult.

There may be other closet supporters of political reform as well. Qiao Shi, for instance, has often been portrayed as a potential Yuri Andropov—a former spy chief transformed into a symbol of political reform. While there is little in the public record to lend credence to such speculation, Qiao has been active in invigorating the National People's Congress (NPC), China's nominal parliament, as an important political institution. No longer a mere rubber-stamp body under the absolute domination of the CCP, the NPC now has permanent committees and permanent staff to review and in some cases revise laws drafted by the CCP. Larger numbers of NPC delegates are now willing to oppose party initiatives, such as the Three Gorges Dam project or Jiang's nomination of one of his Politburo allies for the post of vice premier. In the March meeting of the NPC, the first after Deng's death, an unprecedented 40 percent of delegates refused to approve the government's work report on crime and corruption, criticizing the effectiveness of the efforts to fight crime. The CCP has still never lost a vote in the NPC, but the Congress can now force the postponement of a vote on controversial matters or the revision of pending legislation.

A former president of the NPC, Wan Li, is also seen as sympathetic toward political reform. He is generally credited with initiating the move toward private farming in the late 1970s, and he also has contributed to institutionalizing the NPC's role in the policy process. During the 1989 pro-democracy demonstrations, he cut short a foreign trip to convene a meeting of the NPC's Standing Committee to consider the legality of imposing martial law. Rumors that he was placed under house arrest upon his return to China appear to be unfounded. Moreover, his continued presence on the Politburo until the 14th Party Congress in 1992 indicates that he made his peace with other leaders, regardless of his position on the student movement. At 82, he is too old to be appointed to a front-line post, but he could remain an influential supporter of reform behind the scenes.

In short, while Qiao Shi and Wan Li have strengthened the NPC as a forum for monitoring party decisions, they have not yet opposed a party initiative. The NPC may further strengthen its role as a safety check on party decisions, but it is unlikely to directly challenge the CCP's authority from below.

The third reason for doubting the imminence of a regime crisis is a consequence of the first two: Since there was no power vacuum when Deng died, and since all potential successors espouse similar policy positions, societal interests will not be aroused by the outcome of this succession, as was the case at the time of Mao's death. One main consequence of the post-Mao reforms has been the depoliticization of everyday life in China, meaning that the party/state is less intrusive, and therefore less important, in the daily lives of most Chinese. Although there is still immense interest in the elite's jockeying for power, most Chinese will not be much affected by which technocrat comes out on top. Moreover, Chinese citizens have no direct say in how their national leaders are chosen. When considering the main problems facing China, the political prospects of half a dozen elderly men matter far less to most than the economic, social, and environmental problems facing the country.

Crisis = Dangers + Opportunities

The Chinese word for crisis, *weiji*, is a combination of the words for danger and opportunity, and this is indeed the best way to see the current succession "crisis." From the perspective of China's leaders, there is the ever present danger of elite conflict and the loss of power by one group or another. This inherent uncertainty makes a period of protracted succession struggles particularly worrisome. But there is also opportunity at hand for policy innovation and consolidation.

A divided leadership is especially dangerous if one leader or group of leaders reaches out to society for support against his opponents, real or imagined. This was a favorite tactic of Mao's, and it was also used successfully by Deng during the Democracy Wall movement in late 1978. Zhao Ziyang tried a similar tack in 1989, when, after losing the support of Deng and other party elders, he sided with the student demonstrators. Zhao's public statements of sympathy for the goals and methods of the protesters (combined with private communications between political reformers within the party and student leaders) signaled a split within the leadership, emboldening some protesters to press their demands, confident that at least some party leaders would support them. In a perhaps apocryphal but nevertheless telling exchange between Deng and Zhao during this struggle, Deng boasted that he had the support of three million soldiers, and Zhao replied he had the support of one billion Chinese. Deng then answered, "You have nothing"—and of course Deng was right. Amorphous popular support is no match for political organization and live ammunition.

Nevertheless, despite Deng's early support for an immediate crackdown, and despite his high prestige and network of supporters in the party, government, and military, the student movement continued for over a month before its tragic dénouement. Much of Deng's political capital among his colleagues, within Chinese society, and in the international community was spent imposing martial law. In Deng's absence, elite consensus on behalf of such severe measures will be even harder to achieve. With political dissatisfaction running high in society, populist appeals will be that much more threatening to party leaders against whom they are directed, and that much more tempting to party leaders who can rally popular support for their cause.

Periods of succession are also rare opportunities for policy innovation. The opacity of top-level policymaking in China makes it difficult to predict what form any innovation may take, but Chinese leaders, as well as those in the former communist countries of Eastern Europe and the Soviet Union, have often used succession as an opportunity to embark on sudden and unanticipated reforms.

For the past several years, Deng was too weak physically to have much direct involvement in the policy process, but his political influence remained strong. Hence, while he no longer initiated change, his presence blocked others who might have done so for fear of exposing themselves to charges of disloyalty and factionalism. Now such constraints are removed. Leaders are free to promote their own agendas, and to garner support for further advancement they will need to distinguish themselves from Deng's old line. Thus, policy innovation becomes not only a possibility but a necessity for the ambitious. Previous leadership successions, in China as well as in other communist countries, have led to populist-minded reforms that improved standards of living and eased political restrictions.[ii]   The succession to Deng may be an occasion for similar liberalizations.

There were hints this past summer that China's leaders are considering a resumption of political reform.[iii]   One possibility is the extension of direct elections of local leaders from the village up to the county level. Reformers confront the dilemma of how to initiate even the discussion of political change without raising expectations, which can lead to instability when those expectations are not met. Frustration over the slow pace of political reform resulted in student-led demonstrations in the winter of 1986-87 and spring of 1989. Will China's next generation of leaders be able to balance their desire for political reform with the general preference for social stability any better than the previous generation?

We will soon have an opportunity to assess the prospects for such changes. Attention has now turned from the death of Deng to the 15th Party Congress, scheduled for late October 1997. Party Congresses typically approve leaders for top posts and issue programmatic statements outlining the party's agenda for the next several years. During the run-up to the Congress, behind-the-scenes jockeying for power and positions on the CCP's Politburo and Central Committee has intensified. Deng's death has aided those who wish to depart from his policy combination of economic dynamism and political stasis, but straying too far from his line might appear unseemly so soon after his death. The roster of party leaders and the Congress' programmatic statement will be scrutinized carefully for indications of whether the current leadership is prepared to innovate in either the economic or the political sphere.

Present circumstances in China entail dangers and opportunities for society as well as for elites, and for similar reasons. The alternative possibilities of political stalemate and disunity both could increase anxieties about the future. Worse, there is some small chance that new leaders will roll back recent reforms, limiting economic opportunities within China and reducing access to the outside world. Recent efforts to restrict access to the Internet and the closing of computer bulletin boards are dismaying reminders that not all of China's leaders welcome the free exchange of ideas.[iv]

Just as periods of succession are rare opportunities for policy innovation by elites, so are they rare opportunities for mass-mobilized political protest. In political systems where organizing collective action is extremely difficult, the death of a leader can trigger bandwagoning behavior—as occurred in 1976 after the death of Zhou Enlai and again in 1989 after the death of Hu Yaobang. In 1991, China's leaders were so worried about the potential for mass protest following the suicide of Jiang Qing, Mao's widow, that they delayed announcing it for three weeks. The prospect of mass protest could increase significantly if a potential leader or group of leaders were to reach out to society for popular support against intra-party rivals. Despite the 1989 crackdown, there was clear evidence that many party leaders at the time supported the popular movement, and political activists may be waiting for an opportunity to try again. For those who have concluded that the current regime is beyond hope, and that the only possibility for political change lies not in reform but revolution—a conclusion that many East European activists had come to long before the revolutions of 1989—the succession period may be seen as a window of opportunity. Indeed, if a crisis does arise, it is most likely to involve an explosive combination of divided elites and mobilized masses that could lead China abruptly away from the fragile order upon which Deng insisted, and toward a ferocious turbulence he and others feared deeply.

Alternative Futures

Contemplating the years ahead, four scenarios are worth considering. They are ranked here in ascending order of their potential for producing political instability.

First, there could be a smooth though protracted process of leadership succession, with the policy status quo essentially preserved. In the immediate future—say, the next three or four years—this is the most likely course of events. If it comes to pass, Jiang Zemin will remain in his posts atop the party, military, and state, not least because he has succeeded in recent years in bringing cronies from Shanghai to central party and government posts, and in building bridges with key PLA leaders. But Jiang will find it difficult to be an autonomous or decisive leader. Aside from his own limitations, he will be constrained by a collective leadership wary of letting him accumulate the power to match his posts. Qiao Shi, Li Peng, Zhu Rongji, and others may not covet the job of paramount leader, but they have a common interest in checking the expansion of Jiang's power. Power may continue to reside in individuals more than institutions, but increasingly China's leaders are institutionalizing political authority, both to rationalize the political system and to limit the potential for personal aggrandizement.

A second scenario is a future marked by growing regionalism. Economic decentralization in the post-Mao era has led some to envision a return to the warlord-style of Chinese politics that existed during the early twentieth century, and with it a return to political instability, regional rivalry, and perhaps civil war.[v] Others draw a different conclusion from the same trends: an emerging federalism, with economic development decisions in the hands of local government. One consequence of such a federalism would be to enhance prospects for the survival of market-oriented reforms for the simple reason that many local governments benefit from them. As their tangible benefits are demonstrated, such reforms are more likely to be adopted by an increasing number of local governments.[vi] The declining power of the central government over the economy, and the competition by localities for access to foreign trade and foreign investment, are fully compatible with the federalism scenario and need not presuppose the collapse of the central government.

In any event, it is extremely unlikely that growing regionalism will result in the disintegration of China, as it did in the former Soviet Union and Yugoslavia. Unlike those two countries, China is not an artificially manufactured multinational state. Several non-Han nationalities live in China, but roughly 95 percent of the population belongs to the Han nationality. Except for the strategically important—but economically marginal and sparsely populated—areas of Tibet and Xinjiang, there is no tradition of non-Han national independence elsewhere within the present borders of China, and—again with those exceptions—the deeply rooted traditional norm of a unified China will prevent regions from declaring independence. (Taiwan, of course, is an entirely different matter.) Regional leaders may contend with one another for de facto autonomy and the power that goes with it, all the time declaring their allegiance to national unity. But with nationalism on the rise in recent years, literal secession is not an option for local leaders.

Third, there could be a retreat from reforms and an increase in authoritarian controls. This scenario is especially likely if political activists, party reformers, or an alliance of the two try but fail to promote democratization. While Deng himself was blind to it, most of China's leaders recognize the trade-off between the goals of economic growth and political stability, and many are willing to slow the pace of economic growth and roll back reforms if it proves necessary to restore or maintain political order. Indeed, conservative leaders were able to bottle up the economic reforms and slow economic growth until Deng's "southern tour" of 1992, when his visits to and approval of economic hot spots kick-started the double-digit growth that China has experienced since. In the post-Deng era, conservatives may again try to roll back reforms. The increasingly decentralized nature of China's economy steeply raises the cost of such an attempt, but conservative leaders will be willing to pay it if their fears of instability begin to mount.

In the fourth and last scenario, there could be revolutionary change in Chinese politics, sponsored either by current leaders or through social revolution, or by a combination of the two. The explosive mix of elite mobilization and popular participation clearly represents the biggest threat to political stability in China in the years ahead. In the past, the regime has gone to great lengths to demobilize society after popular upsurges, and the norm of democratic centralism was a powerful constraint on populist appeals by leaders. But during a protracted succession struggle, some leaders might decide that linking up with social protest movements is their last best hope to promote their own candidacy, the political reform agenda, or both.

Several events could trigger the sort of social upsurge that ambitious politicians could seize for their own purposes. Rumors have circulated for years that some party leaders are ready to reassess the official verdict on the 1989 Tiananmen demonstrations as a "counter-revolutionary rebellion." Reversing the verdict would be popular, but would require repudiating Deng's assessment that the demonstrations were both a planned conspiracy and a dangerous turmoil. Moreover, it would legitimize the demonstrations themselves and could encourage their revival, just as the reversal of the verdict on the 1976 Tiananmen demonstrations to honor Zhou Enlai fueled the Democracy Wall movement of 1978-79. Similarly, a reappraisal of Hu Yaobang may be in the offing. In 1987, Hu was forced to resign his post as the CCP's general secretary for being too supportive of political reform, and his death in 1989 triggered demonstrations. Hu and many of his accusers are now dead, so a reappraisal would have little practical significance, but as a political symbol it would legitimize demands for the kind of political change with which he is still identified. Similarly, restoring Zhao Ziyang to an official post would vindicate his support for the demonstrators of 1989. Any of these steps would signal the ccp's willingness to depart from Deng's line and to consider radical and wide-ranging political reform, along with the risk of instability that would inevitably accompany it.

Recent evidence suggests that mobilizing popular support on behalf of political change would be rather easy.[vii] Organizing and controlling it, however, would be a much greater challenge. In China, as in other Leninist systems, the ruling party maintains a monopoly on political organization. Those organizations that do exist (the Communist Youth League, Women's Federation, Writers' Guild, Federation of Trade Unions, Student Federation, and so forth) are controlled by the party, and are therefore very ill-equipped to channel popular sentiments upward. Indeed, one of the key demands of the 1989 demonstrations was for the state to recognize the legitimacy of autonomous unions for students and workers, but this was rejected as being incompatible with CCP rule. China lacks the autonomous organizations needed to express and pursue collective action without creating political chaos. Extra-governmental collective action in China is by definition rebellion; they are acts targeted against state policy without authorized organization, planning, or leadership. Similarly, the outcome of rebellion is often framed in zero-sum terms: either the state suppresses the rebellion or its own survival is jeopardized. That was the calculation of conservative leaders in 1989, and the same calculation may hold in the post-Deng succession.

Many of China's leaders recognize that the imbalance between economic and political freedoms is not sustainable over the long run, but remain deeply divided over how best to correct it—by pulling back on economic reform or by opening the political system. Even those who would prefer more political reform do not know how to implement it without jeopardizing the CCP's power. The experience of former communist countries in Eastern Europe and the Soviet Union that tried to reform, but collapsed in the process, is a chilling reminder to China's leaders of the dangers of attempted adaptation.

Even if revolutionary change were to come to China, democracy would by no means be the inevitable outcome. Given the array of severe political, economic, social, and environmental problems confronting China—and given its huge population's lack of experience in representative government—it is by no means certain that a democracy could effectively deal with such challenges. Hence, democracy might not be consolidated even if attempted. While the historical record suggests that failed democracies of the past often lay the foundation for successful democracies in the future, it is also true, as Samuel Huntington has observed, that failure can delegitimize democracy as a plausible alternative in the near term.[viii] The country's size and level of economic and social development being as it is, an old-fashioned authoritarian regime similar to the current one, but stripped of all ideological pretension and perhaps dominated by the military, could arise instead—either directly or from the ashes of a failed democracy.

One last but important point on this matter: Under any of these four scenarios, Chinese nationalism is likely to become more assertive than it already is. Under those scenarios that suggest the possibility of increased authoritarianism, nationalism could and undoubtedly would be used to mask, or justify, heightened repression within and aggressiveness without.

Throughout the post-1949 period, the CCP has been unwilling to accommodate popular demands for political change. The experience of other communist parties suggests that it may be unable to do so. Indeed, the historical record suggests that communist governments do not evolve, but collapse. So while it would be foolish to predict when major political change will come to China, it is possible to say how it will come: suddenly and dramatically, not gradually and incrementally. In 1989, Chinese students and East European intellectuals had no inkling of the events about to unfold, or any sense that a window of opportunity was about to open before them. But once the opportunity appeared, a rapid social momentum developed, sometimes from unexpected sources, to drive events forward. A peaceful, incremental, elite-sponsored transformation from Leninism to pluralist democracy is as remote a possibility in China as it always was in the Soviet Union, and it has been made all the more remote by the historical baggage accumulated by the CCP during past episodes of popular protest. Clearly, for democracy to ever come about in China, the incumbent regime must be replaced.

Many of China's intellectuals know this, and many political activists are undoubtedly looking for the next window of opportunity to resume political protest. Political leaders, wary of this possibility, are anxiously alert for the same type of signal. The succession to Deng may or may not lead to upheaval or revolution, but it is a "critical" moment, full of dangers and opportunities for all concerned. With the stakes so high and the outcome so uncertain, the next few years may well determine the political future of China for many decades to come.

NOTES

[i] The Military Affairs Commission is the CCP's body for setting military policy and maintaining civilian control over the military. Its chairman is generally seen as China's paramount leader. Past chairmen have been Mao Tse-tung, Hua Guofeng, and Deng Xiaoping; the current chairman is Jiang Zemin.

[ii] See Joseph W. Esherick and Elizabeth J. Perry, "Leadership Succession in the PRC: 'Crisis' or Opportunity?", *Studies in Comparative Communism* (Autumn 1983); and Valerie Bunce, *Do New Leaders Make a Difference? Executive Succession and Public Policy under Capitalism and Socialism* (Princeton: Princeton University Press, 1981).

[iii] See Steven Mufson, "China Tolerates Talk of Reform", *Washington Post*, August 10, 1997.

[iv] See "china.com?" by Diane Wolff, *The National Interest*, No. 49 (Fall 1997), for details on the Internet in China.

[v] See Jack A. Goldstone, "The Coming Chinese Collapse", and Yasheng Huang, "Why China Will Not Collapse", *Foreign Policy* (Summer 1995).

[vi] See Gabriella Montinola, Yingyi Qian, and Barry Weingast, "Federalism, Chinese Style: The Political Basis for Economic Success in China", *World Politics* (October 1995).

[vii] Public opinion surveys reveal consistent dissatisfaction with the current political system. See, for instance, Wenfang Tang and William Parish, "Social Reaction to Reform in Urban China", *Problems of Post-Communism* (November/December 1996).

[viii] Samuel Huntington, *The Third Wave: Democratization in the Late Twentieth Century* (Norman, OK: University of Oklahoma Press, 1991).

Part 3

Culture and Society

14

Two Cheers for "Asian Values"

*Nathan Glazer**

Questions about "Asian values"—whether they justify authoritarianism, or have contributed to the remarkable economic ascent of East Asia, or to the region's subsequent and almost equally startling descent—have been the subject of wide and controversial discussion over recent years. But there is another question that has not been as widely considered: Will Asian values—can they—survive the homogenizing effects of globalization?

"Globalization" is a protean word, capable of taking on many meanings. I shall use it here to mean the worldwide spread of Western-dominated information and entertainment media, with their presumed effects on values in the places they reach. Václav Havel has offered the image of "a Bedouin mounted on a camel and clad in traditional robes under which he is wearing jeans, with a transistor radio in his hands and an ad for Coca-Cola on the camel's back." Perhaps the jeans and the Coca-Cola are, so to speak, only skin-deep; but the transistor radio, the television set and Hollywood movies: do they not undermine Bedouin values, whatever those may be?

The issue of the future of Asian values is rather more serious than that of the survival of Bedouin ones. For it is in East Asia that we find together the fullest developed version of a cultural or civilizational ethos that successfully nurtures rapid economic growth, and that in some key respects (or so it is generally believed and widely asserted) contrasts with what we find in "the West."

---

* Nathan Glazer is professor emeritus of education and sociology at Harvard University and co-editor of *The Public Interest*.

This essay first appeared in *The National Interest*, No. 57 (Fall 1999).

The most dynamic branch of Western civilization is that rooted in Western Europe, the United States and a few overseas societies of British origin. When we think of the "globalization of culture", what we have in mind is the influence of this branch of Western civilization, and in particular of America, on the other civilizations of the world. Will this influence lead to the homogenization of world culture as societies, cultures and civilizations seek economic development and material advancement? Or will deep cultural features, very different from those of the West, shape the impact of modernization and industrialization and ultimately survive these forces? Does the spread of the common technology-based economy, to which all societies and cultures seem to aspire, mean that their underlying distinctive cultural differences are destined to disappear?

Early Days

The key area for the consideration of this problem is East Asia. It is there, in Japan, that a non-Western country first became a major and independent industrial-economic power, fully equivalent in its economic capacities to Western Europe and the United States. Clearly, the industrial, technical and organizational features of Western civilization that took root in Japan were initially borrowed from the West. But to what extent are the culture and values that accompanied these technical and organizational features so organically bound up with them that borrowing the latter also means adopting the former?

In the Seventies and Eighties we were surprised to see other East Asian countries—the "four little dragons" of Taiwan, South Korea, Hong Kong and Singapore—join Japan in taking the path to successful industrialization and competition with the industrialized countries of the West, and as they did so, the same questions assumed a wider significance. And then, when mainland China, Thailand, Malaysia and Indonesia also joined the procession, the questions became urgent.

This series of developments can be interpreted in purely economic terms, and that is for the most part the way we have understood it. But why did we see this economic development first in poor East Asia, and not elsewhere? In the 1940s, according to *The Economist*, India and Ghana were expected to do better in economic performance than Japan and South Korea. In 1955 Simon Kuznets, later to win the Nobel Prize in economics, along with two distinguished collaborators, Wilbert E. Moore and Joseph J. Spengler, published a book entitled *Economic Growth: Brazil, India, Japan*. The grouping of these three countries together suggests that leading economists and social scientists at the time saw some equivalence in their economic situation, a notion that now seems outlandish.

The remarkable rise of Japan and its rapid postwar recovery and economic expansion led early on to consideration of whether a distinctive ethic or set of values played a key role in this then-unique case of non-Western industrialization. As long ago as 1957, Robert Bellah, in his *Tokugawa Religion*, sought an equivalent to the Protestant ethic, which in Max Weber's enormously influential interpretation played a key role in the rise of Western capitalism. In 1970 Herman Kahn, in his remarkably prophetic book, *The Emerging Japanese Superstate: Challenge and Response*, pointed to Japanese values, and perhaps Confucian values, to help explain the economic ascent of Japan, which he expected would in a few decades reach and surpass the United States in per capita GDP (which indeed it did, according to some ways of measuring). In the early 1970s, Henry Rosovsky and Hugh Patrick launched a project at the Brookings Institution to explain Japan's remarkable postwar economic growth (it eventually became a book edited by them, *Asia's New Giant: How the Japanese Economy Works*, 1976), and I considered for this project the role of "social and cultural" features in Japan's economic growth. Indeed, one could not but be deeply impressed by the distinctive values and effectiveness evident in Japanese education and the Japanese workplace.

In 1980 Roderick McFarquhar published a much-discussed article in *The Economist* on the role of Asian values in the economic explosion of the "little dragons." (Only ten years before, Herman Kahn had expected that the role of countries like South Korea and Hong Kong would be restricted to providing cheap raw materials and labor for the emerging Japanese superstate. Even his prophetic powers did not extend to foreseeing how rapidly they would emerge from that subsidiary economic status.) Another relatively early speculator on the role of Confucian values in the economic success of the little dragons was Peter Berger, who in 1985 organized a conference with Hsin-Huang Michael Hsiao, which led to an interesting volume, *In Search of an East Asian Development Model* (1988).

By the 1980s the role of Confucian values in the rise of East Asia had become a growth industry, and nowhere more so than in Singapore, which was then exploring the possibility of introducing them into its school curricula. Tu Wei-Ming of Harvard became one of Singapore's chief consultants, and a fascinating book, *Confucian Ethics Today: The Singapore Challenge* (1984), records his consultations with Singapore educators on this enterprise. He later edited *The Triadic Chord: Confucian Ethics, Industrial East Asia, and Max Weber* (1991). The American Academy of Arts launched a seminar on the issue, one product of which was another volume edited by Tu Wei-Ming, *Confucian Traditions in East Asian Modernity* (1996).

In the Eighties and Nineties the challenge of identifying a link between Asian values and economic growth became more complicated as other East and South Asian countries with very little or no connection to Confucianism—Malaysia, Thailand, Indonesia—began showing remarkably high rates of economic growth. In an effort to redeem the Confucian hypothesis, its proponents emphasized the central role that populations of Chinese origin played in these economies. And, of course, the economic boom was most marked in mainland China itself.

The People's Republic, however, had purportedly cut off all ties with its Confucian past with the communist victory in 1949. Indeed, Confucianism had been denounced as the source of China's backwardness long before by Sun Yat-sen and other Chinese intellectuals and reformers. Were they wrong? Could we still see surviving fragments of the Confucian ethic in China after half a century of totalitarian communism? And would we need to take into account a Buddhist ethic and an Islamic ethic as well as a presumed Confucian ethic in order to accommodate the success of Malaysia, Thailand and Indonesia? Or perhaps a relabeling with the vaguer term "Asian values", to accommodate the countries without a Confucian past, would do the trick.

While the dominant reason for the investigation of a distinctive East Asian set of values has been the need to explain the dramatic economic success of the area, there is another equally important question concerning them: regardless of what role they play in explaining the economic rise of East Asian countries, can the distinctiveness of East Asian values survive that rise? We call the kind of change we have seen in East Asia "modernization", which encompasses not only the economic aspect of development—factories, money and credit, banks, commercial relations, cities and skyscrapers, a consumer economy—but also the social and value changes that seem inevitably to accompany that economic aspect. Indeed, we so take for granted that economic and cultural changes occur in tandem, as they did in the West, that we sometimes call the larger change "Westernization." But this may be a misnomer: for so far in East Asia, economic change has in fact not been accompanied to the same extent by the social and value transformations that characterized modernization in the West—that is, secularism, the nuclear family, individualism, hedonism and the like.

We have then in East Asia the unique case in which (1) a distinctive non-Western value tradition existed, and still appears to exist, and (2) there has been a successful establishment and spread of a modern industrial culture. But if Asian values survive and even flourish, the expectation of the homogenization of culture through globalization is belied, and globalization may therefore be compatible with different values and cultures. Economic growth may lead to the extinction of species of flora and fauna, but the varieties of human culture may survive, perhaps even flourish, as a result of it.

Second Guessing

The economic collapse of Thailand, Indonesia, Malaysia and South Korea, the collapse of the speculative boom in Hong Kong, and the prolonged economic depression in Japan have prompted a gleeful response in the West, which we might describe as "good-bye—and good riddance—to Asian values." Either the presence of those values was an illusion, it is now claimed, or they did not possess the virtues ascribed to them by observers, Western and Eastern, who were blinded by Confucian homilies. With the stress now on cronyism and corruption, perhaps Asian values were always quite the opposite of what we had thought they were.

A process of second-guessing quickly got under way. *The Economist*, which had done so much to advance the Asian values thesis over the years, now checked in with "Asian Values Revisited: What Would Confucius Say Now?", asserting that, "Asian values did not explain the tigers' astonishing economic success, and they do not explain their astonishing economic failures." The *New York Times Magazine* ran an article by Walter Russell Mead, "Asia Devalued: The financial crisis has exposed the 'Asian Values' of hard work, thrift, and family for what they always were: bunk." In the *Wall Street Journal*, a review of Christopher Patton's *East and West* by William McGurn informed us: "If there is a theme that unites the chapters it is a liberal democratic contempt for 'Asian values', which Mr. Patton describes as 'shorthand for the justification of authoritarianism, bossiness, and closed collusion.'"

This dumping on Asian values deserves four comments. First, not all East Asian countries followed Thailand, Malaysia and Indonesia into an economic abyss. Japan, despite its difficulties, remains an economic powerhouse, with great exporting power, low unemployment by international standards, and a populace that seems not much affected by the economic downturn. Mainland China, Taiwan and Singapore have escaped the troubles of the badly afflicted countries, and South Korea and Hong Kong are recovering from their economic difficulties sooner than Thailand, Malaysia and Indonesia.

Second, note that the countries that are least affected by the East Asian economic collapse and that are most likely to recover soon are those located within the presumed zone of influence of Chinese and Confucian culture. Perhaps, then, so-called Asian values, if we limit them to the Chinese-Confucian sphere, are working at least to moderate the economic downslide.

Third, it is worth noting that the setback experienced by the region in 1997-98 was of a kind and dimension that had occurred repeatedly in the West in earlier years. But no one then drew the conclusion that Western values were thus proved to be incompatible with, or irrelevant to, the West's economic development, and there seems to be no reason for drawing such a conclusion about Asian values.

Finally, glee over the Asian economic collapse has tended to concentrate on only one aspect of Asian values—namely, the aspect promoted by the rulers of Malaysia and Singapore to defend the authoritarianism of their regimes. But when we come to what most people have understood by Asian values—not necessarily the versions promoted by the prime ministers of Malaysia and Singapore—I think this general dismissal is facile and overstated. As the reviewer of Christopher Patton's book goes on to say:

> Clearly many of those in power did equate Asian values with authoritarianism. Yet readership surveys by the Far Eastern Economic Review suggest that Asians themselves

thought of Asian values as having to do more with strong families, education and hard work than with autocratic government.

Asian or Confucian values have generally been presented to us as a single package, in which the virtues of hierarchy and discipline and the obligations of obedience form a single ladder, reaching from the ruler down to the humblest. Hence the obedience of the son to the father, the wife to the husband, the younger to the elder brother is mirrored in the submission of all to the state. The promotion of this single package of relationships, binding families together and to the state, is naturally in the interests of ruling elites. But in fact, we find today no distinctive conception of the state as respected teacher and father in the countries of former Confucian culture. That aspect of Confucianism is quite dead, notwithstanding the efforts of the prime ministers of Malaysia and Singapore. Instead, we find riots in South Korea, governments voted out of power in Japan, electoral competition in Taiwan, and grumbling at authoritarian government in communist China and in Singapore.

We also find in various countries of the Confucian sphere the immoral cronyism and self-aggrandizement that have been so sharply evident in the economic setbacks of a number of Asian countries. (Singapore, rated by businessmen as among the cleanest of societies, being the exception.) In none of these countries, though, do we find a pronounced ethos of subservience to the state. True, the state may be powerful and may sustain itself through force and brutal means, but that is different from a distinctive value orientation: anyone is prone to submit to threat and force.

At the family level, and in the commitment to education and work motivated by the interests of the family, we *do* find a distinctive pattern that is clearly not based on any external force. Anyone reading through the research on Asian values is likely to be astonished by the evidence of strong family connections and of the commitment to education and work. A few scattered items from this research make the point: in Korea, the divorce rate was reported to be 1.16 percent in 1980. While it had indeed increased four times since 1965 from a mere 0.28 percent, the tide of Westernization still seemed remote. Divorce figures from other East Asian societies may be slightly larger, but compared with Western societies they are minuscule. So are rates of illegitimacy. Again from Korea: a 1967 survey asked, "If you had sufficient economic means to live on for the rest of your life, what would you do?" An overwhelming 97.7 percent of respondents said they would continue working. An item from Taiwan: "The majority of Taiwanese parents are living with at least one of the married sons."

The research by Harold Stevenson and his colleagues comparing schools in Japan and Taiwan with those in the United States finds that classes in Japan and Taiwan are larger, expenditure is less, achievement is greater, and the obligation of children to perform well for the sake of their families is overwhelming. Failure to do well is routinely attributed by parents not to the school, the teacher, the curriculum or the genes, but to insufficient effort by their children.[i] We find the same in Korea, Hong Kong, Singapore and mainland China. "The most outstanding feature of the learning environment in Hong Kong", one report asserts, "is the pressure put on the student, both by parents and teachers, to study for examinations." American teachers regularly see these characteristics in the children of Asian immigrants.

The Survival Question

We could multiply such items. But the question remains: Do such features—can they—survive under the impact of industrialization, urbanization, the new consumer society, the new means of communication, the universal appeal of *Titanic* and McDonald's, the "globalization" of culture?

Two of the major enterprises that attempt to trace the changing values of a range of contemporary societies argue that they do not and cannot. This is the position of Alex Inkeles, in his studies of modernization across nations[ii], and of Ronald Inglehart, in his extensive inquiries into the rise of post-materialist values. For our purposes, one serious problem with relying on these studies is that they include very few Asian countries. Inkeles, in his original research on modernization, includes India but no East Asian country. Inglehart, among his forty-three societies, includes from Asia only Japan and South Korea, and on many survey items he has no reports from the latter (*Modernization and Postmodernization: Cultural, Economic, and Political Change in 43 Societies*, 1997).

But even in this research, whose main thrust is to support the globalization thesis, we find some revealing items that run counter to it. In Inglehart's *Modernization and Postmodernization*, for example, we note some interesting East Asian variations. On the item, "A woman has to have children in order to be fulfilled", we find a very low level of agreement from the usual Western advanced countries but high positive response from Japan and South Korea (along with such unlikely company as Argentina, South Africa and Hungary). On whether one approves of a woman having a child as a single person, Japan comes out lowest. On whether one has a duty to love and respect one's parents, regardless of their faults, Korea scores at the very top.

Then, too, Inkeles reports in a roundup of recent research: "Between 1963 and 1991, the proportion of Taiwanese who claimed to have attended an ancestor worship ceremony increased from 39 percent to 75 percent." For Japan we have one of the longest series of values studies anywhere available, national surveys that have been conducted every five years since 1953. Preference for filial piety has been rising: 61 percent in 1963, rising to 73 percent in 1983. Inkeles reports that despite forty years of communist rule in Shanghai, in a 1990 survey the value of "diligence and frugality" scored first. And 72 percent "considered that failure in life was due to 'not working hard enough'", which is similar to the attitudes of

Japanese and Taiwanese parents in judging their children's academic performance. In Baoding, on the mainland, 95 percent of elders and their children stress the importance of filial piety, while in Hong Kong, "a strikingly large proportion of 88 percent agreed with the idea that 'government should punish the unfilial.'"

And yet, of course, there is change. Inkeles reports that on the important tradition of maintaining the family line through a son, the proportion in Taiwan considering this "very important" dropped from 70 percent in 1963 to 32 percent in 1991. Arranged marriage in Taiwan has fallen sharply. And in the Japanese surveys, support for some traditional values has fallen.

The Family is Universal

Tu Wei-Ming, in *Confucian Ethics Today*, tells the story of a plaque that Taipei sent as a gift to its sister city, Houston, bearing the Confucian sentiment, "Men have their careers, women have their families." Houston's feminists protested, the matter was put to a vote, and eventually a modified translation was accepted. Ko Byong-Ik, a Korean sociologist, writing in Tu Wei-Ming's *Confucian Traditions*, tells us that most Koreans continue to adhere to Confucian beliefs and Confucian practices, despite their adherence to other religions. "Statistically, 90 percent of Korean Catholics and 76.4 percent of Korean Protestants . . . can be said to be Confucian according to their convictions and practices." And he concludes, "All men are Confucian."

Are we speaking, then, of Confucianism, or post-Confucianism, or vulgar Confucianism, or popular Confucianism—all terms which have been used in discussions of Asian values—when we report such findings? In none of these countries is there an official Confucianism, either in government or in education. Are we speaking of anything more than a strong family ethic, not very different from that which prevailed in the United States until recent decades (and that still prevails among many recent immigrants)? How different are Asian values, as revealed in this research, from the family ethic that has been the almost uniform brick and mortar of all traditional societies before the outset of Westernization, modernization, industrialization, mass communication and their corrosive influences?

When we speak of Asian values, it seems to me that we have something in mind that extends beyond the specific tradition of Confucianism, something that needed no great tradition, great books or classic philosophers to codify. This is the role that family, extended or nuclear, plays in almost all societies that have not reached the level of industrialization, urbanization and state welfare provisions typical of the economically developed nations of Western Europe and North America. In other words, when we say "Asian values", are we not really thinking of—one must excuse the banality of the expression—what American politicians have in mind when they extol "family values" and mourn their demise?

The family is universal. Some particular degree of closeness and responsibility and trust binding family members is also near universal. Mothers are expected to rear children, and do. Fathers are expected to help. Brothers and sisters have certain relationships and responsibilities they are expected to maintain. Heads of families deserve respect and deference from children, and get it. And so on. Admittedly the definition of who is to be included in the family may differ—in one society, the father's relatives but not the mother's, in another, more or less of the relatives outside the nuclear family are included. But the nuclear family remains the basis of society. Its scope and significance become markedly reduced in advanced modern society, where various functions are taken over by extra-familial institutions. While we still count on the family, for the most part, to raise, socialize and educate children, advanced Western societies have also developed substitutes for the family. Day-care centers, schools and old-age pensions gradually became essential, owing to the weakening of the family under the strains of industrialization and urbanization. Perhaps the existence of these family-replacing functions weakens the family structure further. That is, of course, a subject of permanent dispute between liberals and conservatives.

Clearly these family bonds are important for economic effectiveness. Children are spurred to work harder in school and to achieve, not only for the honor of the family but because they are expected in time to support aged parents. Businesses often find their most trustworthy employees among family or quasi-family members, their most dependable subordinates and successors in children and nephews. Superiors demand and expect respect and deference the way fathers do, and inferiors give it. This is the way the world has run for millennia. And this is what social scientists find in the East Asian countries.

But, helpful as it may be, this cannot be the sole or key ingredient in economic success and achievement. For if it were, we would be at a loss to explain why the Indian subcontinent lags behind. India, after all, has no family values problem. Indians viewing American films often ask, where is the family? In Indian films the hero has a family, the heroine has a family, even the villain has a family—fathers and mothers, brothers and sisters, aunts and uncles, with duties, demands and obligations, populate these films, as they do Indian reality.

The question of, why some familism contributes to economic success (as in the East Asian countries), and some fails to (as in India and Africa) should lead us to contemplate the differences in conceptions of family ties among societies and cultures. It is commonly reported that in Africa a family connection means not that family members will assist the entrepreneur by providing willing and loyal employees, which seems to be a key function in East Asia, but that they will use up his resources by moving in and insisting they have a right to be supported. Family connection and closeness can also mean inefficient nepotism.

Not Starting, But Spurring

The values that we now think support economic development were once thought to restrain it, and the economist John Wong of Singapore, in his contribution to Tu Wei-Ming's *Confucian Traditions*, is still skeptical about the economic benefits of Confucian values:

> It is not enough to argue in general terms that the Confucian ethos is conducive to increased personal savings and hence higher capital formation. It must also be demonstrated forcefully and specifically whether such savings have been productively invested in business or industry or have been squandered in noneconomic spending, such as the fulfillment of social obligations, which is also a part of the Confucian social system. It must also be shown how Confucian values have actually resulted in effective manpower development in terms of promoting the upgrading of skills and not in encouraging merely intellectual self-cultivation or self-serving literary pursuits. A typical Confucian gentleman in the past would have shown open disdain for menial labor.

One concludes that the family features described by social scientists as a central part of the great tradition of Confucianism can serve a variety of ends. In East Asia, in combination with effective economic policies, they seem to have served to strengthen economic development, despite earlier expectations that they would only hamper it. Perhaps, as the quotation from John Wong suggests, it was only after Confucianism was sharply reduced, stripped of its ceremonial elements, and restricted to the realm of the family that it could facilitate and speed economic growth.

In resorting to the concept of Asian values, we seem to be referring to features we find in *all* traditional societies. The East Asian experience suggests to us that these values may not help to *initiate* rapid economic development, but can be extremely helpful—in combination with other key factors such as political stability and the right economic policies—in *spurring on* economic development once it gets started. Then the family loyalties, the commitment to aid family members, the commitment to education, the saving for family advancement all come into play. It is precisely these features that we fear are undermined by economic development in the West, where we have been alerted by Joseph Schumpeter to the destructive effects of capitalism on bourgeois values, and have been taught about "the cultural contradictions of capitalism" by Daniel Bell.

With rapid economic development well under way, we see rising concern in the countries of East Asia that the traditional values they took for granted before economic development are now being undermined. It is at this point that "Confucian values" come into their own and leaders, such as those in Singapore, typically begin to worry about how long they can shore them up. None of the leaders of East Asia thought Asian—or Confucian, or traditional—values would be helpful in getting their countries started on the road to economic development. Those same leaders now worry about the threat to these values from

Westernization—because, in retrospect, those values seem to have been important in spurring their surprising take-offs.

But by Western standards, Asian values are still surprisingly firm. It is this continuing firmness that has not been taken into account in the recent trashing of their significance. Globalization undoubtedly affects social and cultural features, and, yes, undermines them. But the rate of undermining is surprisingly slow, and the difference in the rates of change in these key social and cultural characteristics between East and West still gives the East an advantage.

In the early 1970s, my economist colleagues in the Brookings study of the causes of Japan's economic success seemed convinced that we would see a slowdown there because of the huge increase in the price of oil, as Japan possessed no oil and had no alternative energy sources. It stood to reason, but it didn't happen. Again, with the economic troubles of the late 1990s in East Asia, we see the widespread assumption that the Asian economic surge has passed its peak. I am skeptical, as I was about the expectations of the American economists in 1973. The main reason for my skepticism is that values do undergird economic growth, and the values in East Asia that serve to maintain family stability, a commitment to education and high savings rates still show a surprising steadiness compared to developments in the West. Tradition maintains itself even in the face of so many aspects of globalization. It is much too early to count out Asian values.

NOTES

[1] Harold W. Stevenson and James W. Stigler, *The Learning Gap* (New York: Summit Books, 1992).
[2] Alex Inkeles and David H. Smith, *Becoming Modern* (Cambridge, MA: Harvard University Press, 1974); Inkeles, "Continuity and Change in Popular Values on the Pacific Rim", in *Values in Education*, ed. John D. Montgomery (Hollis, NH: Hollis Publishing Co., 1997); Inkeles, *One World Emerging: Convergence and Divergence in Industrial Societies* (Boulder, CO: Westview Press, 1998).

15

Another Way to Skin a Cat:
The Spirit of Capitalism and the Confucian Ethic

*Grace Goodell**

One morning when I was last in Hong Kong I asked my friend Miss Lim, who always cleans my room at the University's guest house, what she did with the money she earned as a Hong Kong chambermaid. "Have you ever been to Petra?" she replied. Having arrived in the colony penniless twenty-three years ago, she had just returned from a tour of the Nabatean, Roman, and Greek ruins of the eastern Mediterranean.

In 1960 Hong Kong was just above Malta in per capita GNP; today it has overtaken Israel, and is soon expected to surpass the United Kingdom. At the close of the Korean War, 75 percent of Korea's adults were illiterate; now a teenager there has a greater chance of going to university than his counterpart in Japan.

A 1960 World Bank study proclaimed Singapore "unviable" as a country, should it separate from Malaysia. Thereupon the city-state began a period in which it sustained for over three decades the fastest growth rate the world has ever seen. This former "opium den" and "basket case" now has the world's busiest container port, the third largest oil refining facility, and the second highest per capita GNP in Asia, second only to Japan.

Thirty years ago Brazil's per capita GNP was double that of Taiwan; today Taiwan's is six times Brazil's. Indeed, the combined merchandise exports of East Asia's four Little Dragons—South Korea, Taiwan, Hong Kong, and

* Grace Goodell is Professor of International Development at Johns Hopkins' School of Advanced International Studies. She has lived and traveled extensively in East and Southeast Asia.

This essay first appeared in *The National Interest*, No. 42 (Winter 1995/96).

Singapore—are twice the total of the entire Latin American continent, which has six times their population and sits on the doorstep of the world's richest and most open market. Astonishingly too, in transforming themselves at this astounding rate, all four dragons have avoided a severe income gap between rich citizens and poor.

In 1988 I began to examine the non-economic factors that have contributed to the Little Dragons' remarkable achievements. Of the many journalistic pieces done on their success, few have been written by cultural anthropologists and virtually none has considered all four side by side. I have focused mainly on businessmen, government officials, and factory workers who were active players during the decisive years from the early 1950s, up to 1980. Prominent public figures such as Lee Kuan Yew and Dr. Goh Keng Swee in Singapore, and K.T. Lee in Taiwan, were among the eight hundred who participated in the research, as were the CEOs of various large East Asian firms and of Japanese and Western multinationals' regional headquarters. Contrary to the warnings I received from U.S. businessmen, most of their Little Dragon counterparts seemed delighted to discuss the questions that interested me: What is the meaning of life? Where are the ancestors? Can you explain the concept of "China" or "Korea" to me? Who should rule? Many of them considered such questions more pertinent to their societies' economic success than those usually posed by Western interviewers concerning production and sales statistics, export figures, labor costs, and the like.

One evening I was sitting with one of Korea's industrial magnates in a restaurant overlooking Seoul's $800 million Lotte shopping mall, a structure larger than the Houston Astrodome. The complex houses several athletic clubs, eight wedding halls, several hundred boutiques, as well as an Old Cornish Tea Room, a Wild West bar, a North African casbah, a medieval French castle, and a roller coaster along a facsimile Great Wall of China. My host brought me to the window and pointed to the mall's glittering entrance:

> I grew up right there. . . in a bamboo hut, no electricity, no toilet, no road. This vast commercial world you look down upon was built by the boys who tended oxen in that swampland. And who is spending all that money? Their chums who sloshed around in the paddy mud with me, collecting half a bucket of snails for family dinner. Our kids now come here to eat steaks from Omaha and Haagen Dazs ice cream.

So, how *did* the Little Dragons pull off—in less than one generation—the transformation that Europe, the United States, and Japan required one hundred and fifty years to achieve? One thing is certain: They did it their way.

While many aspects of these societies superficially look like our own, beneath the surface the Dragons defy virtually all the basic Western theories about how capitalist development takes place, and what its requirements are. Indeed, my research indicates that an integral set of cultural factors—ones that Max Weber, perhaps our leading theorist of capitalist development, pinpointed as *preventing* capitalism from taking root—in fact substantially accounts for its rapid burgeoning in the Little Dragons.

Even at first glance these societies present our theories of development with difficulties. Two of them—Hong Kong and Singapore—are not even countries, and both are so poor in resources that they have to import their water. Nor could development spring from natural resources in any of the four, for such resources were, and are, few. Again, contrary to the 1994 Cairo Population Conference claims, these, the only four societies to launch themselves from poverty to affluence since World War II, are among the most densely populated places on earth. Like many poor countries and regions in the world—Honduras during the Sandinista regime in Nicaragua, Rwanda's neighbors now, and in some respects, southern California—several of the Dragons were the "victims" of enormous influxes of unskilled refugees: between mid-1945 and late 1949 tiny Hong Kong had to absorb seven thousand refugees per month, and throughout the following decade, over one hundred thousand per year. Somehow they saw human beings as wealth, not burden, turning these "dregs", such as my chambermaid, into productive and prosperous citizens.

The Dragons pose difficulties for political scientists, too. During the period of their most spectacular growth none supported the theory that capitalism needs a free press, democracy, and the substantive rule of law to curb the arbitrary powers of a dictator. At least two of the four—South Korea and Taiwan—have had highly intrusive governments that challenge the free market model. Korea, Taiwan, and Singapore have had scores of state-owned companies, and in Hong Kong the government controls the entire land market—the colony's scarcest factor of production. Even today the notion of a self-conscious civil society remains a foreign concept in these modern cultures. There has been no Magna Carta here to lay the foundations of an "open" or transparent social order, and none is to be expected anytime soon.

Culturally, these four societies reverse many basic tenets of the common traditional Western understanding of capitalism. These include the following: that individuals defined in terms of a single functional role and economic resources considered apart from their social context constitute modern society's primary units of interaction and exchange; that the value of all assets, inputs, and outputs of economic production and even of government administration—including all workers and managers—can be expressed in monetary terms, thereby made mutually fungible; that since rational management is linear it cannot deal with factors (including goals and values) that have equal weighting, and hence it must formulate all organization and all choices in terms of ranked priorities; that business and government transactions have to be open to all legitimate players, whether they know one another or are total strangers (indeed, their being strangers makes them more objective); and that mathematics and formal laws provide the model for how society should organize its public life according to impersonal logic, purified of all subjective or social elements. In short, they refute our insistence that "predictability" requires transactions that are formally rational and publicly visible, leaving no room for discretion or ambiguity.

The Little Dragons are characterized by cultural combinations that Western theory finds irreconcilable. Thus, colorful rags-to-riches entrepreneurs at every level of society—whose eccentric individualism constitutes the essence of the Dragon self-image—attribute their own successes to group bonding on a high moral plane, which to our mind precludes individual identity and initiative. Again, cut-throat competition and exuberant materialism thrive in the Dragons through self-sacrifice. Or again: While the Dragons wholeheartedly embrace modern technology, speed, the constant turnover of markets and new products, and the incessant drive to streamline production, their organizational efficiency is based on ritual and a deep respect for traditional authority.

Let us examine in greater detail five of the Little Dragons' challenges to the Western paradigm of capitalist development. First, the classical paradigm maintains that in capitalism businessmen and government officials must deal with each other *impersonally*. Capitalism and bureaucratic efficiency require standardization; in official transactions individuals should only convey the facts, and all resources should be reducible more or less to monetary terms. Any trace of sentimental or subjective interchange obfuscates efficiency.

The Little Dragons turn this fundamental principle on its head. In them a prerequisite for long-term business or business/government dealings is personal bonding, usually in a very primal sense, with each individual exposing his "raw person" to the other. For Koreans, this usually involves getting drunk together; for the Chinese, perhaps drinking but certainly lavish meals. Conversation on these occasions should range over non-utilitarian topics such as hobbies and family. The point of getting drunk is not, as suspicious Westerners believe, to get the other person to reveal important business information, but rather to lay bare each one's real character and to experience trust in an intensely physical or mutually precarious situation. Would-be business partners need to establish an intricately textured personal context prior to any serious dealings: the greater the risk, the thicker the interpersonal meshing required.

The West's utilitarian strictures are expressed in office decor, the environment that the businessman or government official creates for carrying out his work. Consistent with the strictly functional criteria of the market and of Western law, the office furniture of Westerners whom I interviewed manifested little variation from what one would find in their company offices worldwide: simple, straight-lined desks and chairs suitably designed for work but uniform and boring. Windows look out onto the skyline, demanding an extroverted and objective mental orientation. Views of the city and its streets establish that what will happen in the office belongs to the public world accessible to all comers, whomever they are. After a handshake, one gets right down to business.

While some of the Little Dragon CEO offices also gave onto skylines, many were parsimonious with windows or had curtains that closed off the view, so that attention turned inward to the personal interaction at hand. Upon entering, one is always offered tea, dissipating the strictly utilitarian atmosphere and replacing it with the moral relation of host and guest. Instead of functional reminders setting the tone, the East Asian CEO almost always used office decor to present himself visually, welcoming the visitor into his personal world. Religious images or portraits of ancestors had a place in more than 60 percent of the offices (several had pictures of Jesus!). Holy icons stared down on meetings, as silent participants. In sharp contrast, a Western businessman keeps only small desk photos of the family, meant to be noticed by him alone. Enormous golf trophies, oil paintings the CEO had done himself, tiger pelts, or a highly idiosyncratic collection of Chinese porcelain disclose what the Asian executive is like as a whole person. I came home with dozens of books the Little Dragon businessmen and officials had written on Confucian philosophy, Chinese linguistics, the history of advertising since the fourteenth century in Asia, and the like. The head of one of the most successful fast-food franchises in East Asia discoursed for half an hour on Jacques Maritain's aesthetics. A Korean tycoon gave me a tape of himself singing Verdi arias. In the Far East, how a gentleman spends his leisure time is key to sizing up his character, which is more essential than law for securing reliable business relations.

Such details announce at the outset that, though enormously successful financially, a businessman or official is not exclusively interested in economic or administrative efficiency, but rather is ready to treat the other person with social and moral sensitivity. While Westerners in the workplace tend to standardize themselves and their contexts, their Little Dragon counterparts particularize people and setting—always blurring the boundary between work and the rest of one's life. They consider that nothing standardized can be permanent or predictable.

Waiting for my appointment in the reception area, in a Western firm I would find a few photos of the company's factories, or of the CEO handing out employee awards for top performance or long service. *Functional* criteria again. In contrast, as you enter a Little Dragon firm you are apt to see pictures of the CEO at employees' weddings and birth celebrations, or of executives and workers at a party in a park surrounded by nature. In more than one Chinese firm, the wife of the company founder holds a party for all employees—not on society-wide holidays but on the highly personalized occasion of the boss' return from a trip abroad, as though to welcome Dad home.

A second tenet of classical Western theory about the cultural requirements of capitalism that the Little Dragons dispute is our insistence on universalism. Capitalist investment is said to require that all factors of production—land, labor, and capital, as well as information—be able to move wherever they can most efficiently be put to use. Our economic system opposes any social or political obstacle to a totally free-market allocation of resources—what economists call "segmentation." In the personal recruitment process common to business management, as well as in the administration of public bureaucracies, this Western requirement takes the form of "meritocracy."

Such an understanding of how capitalism works and what defines market efficiency is foreign to the Little Dragons and to their extraordinary success. There, virtually all markets are segmented—one might say "privatized"—and inaccessible to the public at large. One executive said to me, "We don't have a yellow pages economy." Employment positions, even of the lowest level workers, are not usually filled through newspaper advertisements but through personal networks. Nor does capital flow mainly through public channels: 45 percent of the business loans made in Taiwan in 1993 were transacted in the informal (interpersonal) sector, mainly among family members. Within the past decade, when Thailand was trying to attract investment from Little Dragon Chinese, it invited delegations of businessmen, not according to their industry or even according to their country, but according to their clan. From Taiwan or Hong Kong, all prominent members of a particular family line who traced their ancestry to a particular village or valley in China were invited to Bangkok as a group (there to meet their "cousins" as it were, presumably to make business partnerships). According to some estimates, over 85 percent of all overseas investment in China's southern provinces is allocated through such personal networks.

The insider/outsider distinction dominates all Little Dragon government and business transactions—indeed, it dominates all Little Dragon social organization. There is no universal free market in which every business is open to all comers and anyone can bid on any deal. All political and economic transactions, and thus the system of business ethics, are structured around this same insider/outsider distinction. I often probed those whom I interviewed for their attitudes about the most internationally publicized cases of Little Dragon fraud. One of Hong Kong's most brilliant tycoons, a graduate of a prestigious U.S. college, summarized each of four recent scandals in the same fashion: "George Tan didn't do anything wrong. The only people he ripped off were Westerners, Indonesians, and the like, almost no one from our community. . . .Well, one Hong Kong banker has lost a lot, but he's a British lackey." Little Dragon morality is localized or segmented, not universalist. It distinguishes between many degrees of social—and hence ethical—closeness and distance. That does not make Little Dragon businessmen less ethical; to the contrary, they impose stronger moral sanctions on themselves than most Westerners seem to do, albeit sanctions that are applied with refined differentiation.

The third common Western assumption about capitalism from which the Little Dragons deviate is that the mindset of a scientific culture must permeate a capitalist society, because economic efficiency and the government that promotes it require a high degree of rationality. Indeed, in our view of our own history the development of capitalism's efficient allocation of resources was inseparable from the scientific revolution. Science-based instruments, industrial technology's domination of the workplace, and scientific management principles are simply incompatible with superstition and religious fanaticism.

But here again Little Dragon culture challenges what seems to us to be irrefutable logic. South Korea, the world's seventeenth largest industrial power, annually imports over four thousand pounds of male tiger bones and eight metric tons of deer velvet for aphrodisiacs—at prices that suggest a highly educated, executive clientele. In Hong Kong, those same billionaires who so successfully built up the capitalist economy pay hundreds of thousands of dollars for an automobile license plate number with a particularly auspicious numerical combination. Two-thirds of all Chinese executives and officials I interviewed in Hong Kong consult geomancers for critical business or professional decisions. And as for religious fanaticism, within the past decade we have seen more than a handful of Korean university students, normally among the best in the class, immolate themselves in protest against some government policy about which they felt passionately. (During the heyday of Japanese economic prowess in the 1970s and 1980s, various leading Japanese ceos committed ritual suicide because of the guilt they bore, for such things as the mechanical malfunctioning in a company airplane that resulted in deaths, or industrial accidents with which they had not the remotest personal contact.)

The fourth way in which the Little Dragons spell out their distinctive conditions for capitalism pertains to the radically different way they perceive the role of law in economic development. Flying directly in the face of our insistence that capitalism requires "transparency" and "the rule of law", Little Dragon businessmen and officials almost unanimously consider formal law the downfall of Western society, certainly the downfall of Western morality. Contrary to the Western lawyers' ideal of very precisely crafted laws that leave no room for the bureaucrats' personal interpretation, in all four Little Dragons—including British Hong Kong—laws are considered best written and most useful when they are vague. They should state purposes but not details and conditions, so that as much as possible is left to the discretion of individuals in each particular situation and case. In Korea, senior officials in important finance and trade-related ministries stressed that the ministry itself should make regulations or new directives, then get them firmly in place, understood, and habitually used by all the technocrats before proposing them as laws to Parliament for its approval. "We know what is best and what will work", they explained. "The purpose of law is to ritualize the correct procedures."

As for contract, so sacred to Western theories of the free market's foundations, nothing seems more counterproductive to Little Dragon businessmen than our slavish adherence to written agreements. One of East Asia's large ship-owners said to me, "If you and I are discussing a point of disagreement, the moment I pull out a contract that we drew up—as proof that I am right—and show you what you signed, then at that moment all moral obligation between us terminates. We can probably never do business with each other again."

Whatever we Americans think of the importance of law, it cannot be disputed that the Little Dragons—and Japan—have industrialized with exceptional flexibility and unprecedented speed in large part because of their implacable mistrust of formal law. I often inquired, citing some particularly notorious crook, how the local business or government community punished wrongdoers, if recourse to formal law is to be avoided. Typical of my host's response would be something along these lines: "See that man sitting alone? [say in a posh luncheon club]. He was one of our crowd. Now we will greet him, even converse with him, but our wives no longer socialize with his, and he has to read the newspaper to know what's going on. We call him a street-sweeper—all he has is public information." In such a culture, ostracism is far more painful than the sanctions of law. "Hwang there has lost his social context. Without that, no business", the head of a prominent Hong Kong bank commented. "He'd give anything to trade that punishment for a lawsuit." The president of one of the Hyundai firms explained to me, "You can't imagine the pain of loneliness out there."

Finally, what about our fondest piece of Weberian folk theory: that capitalist development springs from the Puritan ethic? The Dragons have among the highest domestic savings rates in the world and are renowned for their hard work. On some counts their societies do share some of the values of our Puritan forefathers. But then the question arises, which "Puritan" values? America's Jewish, Irish, Italian, and more recently Salvadoran and Mexican immigrants have all been committed to hard work and savings, as well as to strong, patriarchally-governed families. Puritans had no monopoly on these cultural traits.

Several years ago, Korea had its own Watergate, which found former President Chun Doo Hwan guilty of serious corruption. The high tribunal sentenced him not to jail, but to years of penitential rigor in a monastery deep within a mountain fastness. Not exactly the Puritan way of handling things, but rather in the same spirit. Imagine the U.S. Congress sending Richard Nixon to repent of his deeds in a Trappist monastery!

But then what would the Puritans have made of the vibrant animal energies that pervade the Little Dragons' culture? The flood of Taiwan's morning-commuter motorcycles that turns Taipei's sidewalks into superhighways. Business lunches and dinners that barely fall short of Roman gluttony. The inveterate Chinese passion for gambling in every form conceivable to man. As for women, Hong Kong and Taiwanese housewives, secretaries, and even executive assistants abandon their work responsibilities to play the stock market like roulette, day after day. What would Cotton Mather have made of the correlation between sexual license and economic prosperity in these cultures, the successful businessmen's incurable love for their concubines? Or, indeed, of government corruption, rampant at various times even among the British administration in Hong Kong—particularly in the police force and in the highest judicial tribunals?

In short, the more we learn about these fabulously plucky societies, the more we appreciate the diversity of capitalism and how it may thrive in a variety of cultural contexts. The more questions we raise about ourselves and our own history—how we got to where we are now—the more humble should we become about the correspondence between our theories and the way the world really works. Human society is wonderfully variable. As Confucius so wisely said, "There is more than one way to skin a cat."

16

China and the Quest for Dignity

*John Fitzgerald**

That the people is without shame means that the state is without shame.
—Kang Youwei, c.1900

Marxism has completed its historical tour of duty. Thus although the relationship between Marxism and nationalism has hardly been exhausted as a subject of theoretical inquiry, it barely seems to matter any longer in contemporary China. What does beg analysis now is the relationship between *liberalism* and nationalism in contemporary public life.

In recent years, the respective—and, to both participants and most Western observers, conflicting—claims of individual human rights and collective national rights have been thrown into relief by the publication of Wei Jingsheng's *Letters From Prison[i]* alongside a series of books that have appeared in China under variations on the title *China Can Say No*. In his letters, Wei recounts his struggle for individual dignity over almost two decades of internment and intermittent political activism. His message is that the state should recognize the inherent dignity of individuals. The authors of the *Say No* books, on the other hand, have no time for "individualism" or for "American-style human rights." Instead, they rise to defend China's dignity as a nation, and brand local human rights activists as foolish if not treacherous for conspiring with foreign governments to obstruct the

* John Fitzgerald is professor of Asian studies at La Trobe University in Melbourne, Australia. His book, *Awakening China: Politics, Culture and Class in the Nationalist Revolution* (Stanford University Press, 1996) was awarded the 1998 Joseph Levenson Prize by the Association for Asian Studies.

This essay first appeared in *The National Interest*, No. 55 (Spring 1999).

country's rise to great power status. For all their differences, both are concerned with the same issue: that of dignity.

This, however, does not mean that the differences between liberal and nationalist discourses in contemporary China can be reduced to a simple conflict between individual and national dignity. For both sides share a concern for the national dignity of China. Wei wrote his first articles on democracy precisely to show that the Chinese were not "a bunch of spineless weaklings", and that when individual citizens learned to straighten their spines China would stand tall in the world. Similarly, there is no lack of concern for individual dignity in the writings of his nationalist opponents. The resentment that surfaces in the *Say No* literature is grounded in deeply etched personal experiences of national humiliation.

Liah Greenfeld has argued that the politics of indignation, or *ressentiment*, drives nationalism.[ii] I shall argue that *ressentiment*, grounded in personal indignation, also drives the struggle for individual dignity and human rights. The motive we commonly ascribe to China's drive for economic development and its citizens' struggle for civil rights is the rational pursuit of self-interest—variously described as the self-interest of a party seeking to maintain its legitimacy in an ideological vacuum, or of a government intent on maximizing revenues and authority, or of citizens hoping to multiply options for the pursuit of life, liberty and personal happiness. We make too little allowance for the possibility that China pursues wealth and power for the sake of asserting national dignity, and that citizens demand rights, not in pursuit of liberty or happiness, but out of concern to preserve personal dignity. If this is indeed the case, then personal resentment and nationalist *ressentiment* appear to be fused in a complex and explosive mixture.

The most volatile element in this mixture is what Francis Fukuyama has termed the struggle for "recognition." In *The End of History and the Last Man*, Fukuyama identifies the passion that drives people to make war against one another with the longing that drives them to fight for democracy. This he terms (after Plato) *thymos*, or the "desire for recognition." *Thymos* accounts for a "propensity to feel self-esteem":

> It is like an innate human sense of justice. People believe that they have a certain worth, and when other people treat them as though they are worth less than that, they experience the emotion of anger. Conversely, when people fail to live up to their own sense of worth, they feel shame, and when they are evaluated correctly in proportion to their worth, they feel pride.[iii]

In the field of China studies, the idea of recognition has been tainted by association with a discredited nineteenth-century ethnography of "face." As Fukuyama defines it, however, *thymos* is not a particular cultural trait but a universal characteristic of human societies, and he appeals to it in order to answer one of the critical political questions of our time: Is there a necessary connection between the pursuit of national wealth and power, on the one hand, and the attainment of liberal democracy and human rights on the other?

Some have argued for a mechanical, functional connection between the two, on the assumption that democracy alone is capable of mediating the tangled web of conflicting interests created in the course of developing a complex modern economy. Fukuyama disagrees. Others have argued for a managerial relationship, suggesting that as autocratic regimes degenerate over time, elites responsible for managing the state come to assume a leading role in liberalizing it as well. Again Fukuyama disagrees. Another well-known line of argument is that democracy arises when successful industrialization produces an ascending middle class that develops an interest in defending its class position by institutionalizing its rights. Yet again Fukuyama disagrees. Democracy, he argues, has no simple economic rationale. "The choice of democracy is an autonomous one, undertaken for the sake of recognition and not for the sake of [material] desire."[iv]

Fukuyama's emphasis on *thymos* presents a serious challenge to the analysis of national development and international politics, for it undermines the rational, empiricist assumptions of Anglo-American political philosophy, while celebrating the triumph of its political achievements. Basically, Fukuyama—and Isaiah Berlin, too[v]—argues that the impetus for both national economic development and liberal democracy is best explained by reference to "irrational" forces arising from the struggle for recognition, not as an outcome of the rational pursuit of self-interest. The drive for economic self-improvement is not the engine of political development; both are by-products of an even deeper impulse.

This hypothesis presents a particular challenge to students of modern China. Fukuyama presses us to identify with precision the processes whereby rising prosperity may lead to political pluralism. Of itself, the economistic argument that economic development leads to democracy is abstract and dehistoricized. "It papers over the interval until the calm of wealth prevails", Eric Jones has observed, "a time that in reality has to be *struggled through*" [emphasis added].[vi] We need to consider the forms such struggles may assume in different historical instances—in particular, the forms assumed by thymotic desire for national and personal dignity in China today.

National dignity clearly held a prior claim over individual dignity in public life when the Chinese people "stood up" in 1949. The two were momentarily congruent: when the state was without shame, the people who made up the nation were without shame as well. After the Cultural Revolution petered out in the 1970s, space emerged in public life for people to challenge such congruence. Jonathan Spence caught this moment in his foreword to a translated collection of Chinese short stories published in 1983:

> There is extraordinary agreement among these writers about the loss of dignity that afflicts all Chinese denied privacy, in housing as in thought, forced forever to jostle and bargain and plead until the shouts become cries and the cries blows.[vii]

For many people, the loss of private dignity casts the achievement of national dignity into doubt. What is the good of a whole people "standing up" in the world if they cannot "stand up" as individuals in their own homes? This question has left its traces in biography, essays, wall-posters and letters produced in China over the past decade. In this essay I select a sample of recent literature touching on the subject of dignity—Li Zhisui's memoirs, *The Private Life of Chairman Mao*[viii], examples of the *China Can Say No* genre, and selected writings of Wei Jingsheng—to highlight the incongruence between a China that "stood up" in 1949 and the felt experience of a people reduced to jostling, crying and trading blows at home. The same body of literature hints at the potential for reconciling the claims of individual and national rights around the idea of dignity itself.

Are there grounds for hope for China in this respect? I shall argue that a common ideal of dignity lies at the heart of nationalist discourse and liberal democratic theory alike. I shall argue, too, that, inadequately, Chinese nationalism has inadvertently incubated an ideal of individual rights and individual self-determination within its discourse on national rights. For almost half a century, official nationalism has developed a popular language of exploitation, oppression, dehumanization and humiliation through which people could explain and resolve affronts to China's dignity. Today, they can appeal to an identical language to press their claims for individual rights before the state. The politics of individual dignity, far from being antithetical, appears to be parasitical on the idea of national dignity. Paradoxically, then, resurgent nationalism does offer ground for hope that China's wheel is turning, slowly but surely, to recognizing the inherent dignity of the individual.

Standing Up: The Rhetoric of National Dignity

Li Zhisui's *The Private Life of Chairman Mao* is infamous within China for divulging intimate court secrets about the founder of the People's Republic. In passing, however, Dr. Li also discloses the personal ruminations of an educated Chinese doctor from a comfortable family background who happened to be traveling abroad before becoming Chairman Mao's physician. Dr. Li was in Sydney, Australia, in January 1949 when news came through that the People's Liberation Army had occupied Beijing. He was elated that "China could finally assume her rightful place in the world" and within six months had resolved to return home to devote his life to his people and his country.

Over the course of his travels in China and abroad, Dr. Li had grown acutely aware of China's decline as an imperial power, a decline, he says, that was captured poignantly by "the famous sign at the entrance to the riverside park along the Shanghai Bund—'Chinese and dogs not allowed.'" He encountered further evidence of China's national humiliation in Sydney:

> As a Chinese, I could live there temporarily, practice medicine, and make good money, but I could never become a citizen. My pride and self-respect cried out against this racist policy. Still, I stayed in Sydney, in a small boardinghouse, surrounded by Australians who thought China was hopeless. I became increasingly depressed.

Dr. Li cured his depression in Beijing, to which he returned in time to witness the triumphal founding ceremony of the People's Republic at Tiananmen on October 1, 1949. He recalled Mao Zedong's role in the event:

> Mao's voice was soft, almost lilting, and the effect of his speech was riveting. 'The Chinese People have stood up', he proclaimed, and the crowd went wild, thundering in applause, shouting over and over, 'Long Live the People's Republic of China!' 'Long live the Communist Party of China!' I was so full of joy my heart nearly burst out of my throat, and tears swelled up on my eyes. I was so proud of China, so full of hope, so happy that the exploitation and suffering, the aggression from foreigners, would be gone forever.

After some time back home, Dr. Li learned to attribute to impersonal historical forces all of the personal humiliation that he had suffered. He also learned to attribute to the communist battle with these impersonal forces all of the pride and joy that he felt in Tiananmen in October 1949. Once the Communist Party had been installed in power, Dr. Li recalls people learned to attribute their shame and their pride to China's battle with "the foreign powers . . . what we later called imperialism." His personal struggle against racism was now subsumed into the greater struggle against that malign force. Hence when the "People" stood up, so did Li Zhisui.

As they unfold, however, Dr. Li's memoirs highlight a mismatch between his personal sense of grievance and pride, and the formulaic prescriptions of communist official ideology. The basic Maoist idea—that foreign capital had allied with domestic feudalism to bring China to its knees—only partly explained the humiliation and indignation people felt as the old empire collapsed about them and the new Republic failed to deliver on its promises. While for the moment that explanation sufficed for Dr. Li, in the nature of things it would never be able to explain the humiliation and suffering forced upon the people of China by Mao himself, after the founding of the People's Republic.

Virtually all popular Chinese memoirs published since the Cultural Revolution have been, in one sense or another, chronicles of disappointed expectation. *The Private Life of Chairman Mao* is no exception. Li Zhisui traces a downward spiral of frustration over two decades of service at the inner court of Mao Zedong. He is exceptional, however, in the privileged vantage point from which he observes the personal as political. By focusing on the sexual behavior of Mao Zedong, in particular, he exposes a striking incongruence between the depersonalized Maoist language of national pride and longing that first drew him into the service of the Chairman, and the intimately personal experience of shame and humiliation that the Chinese people endured under Mao. As a Chinese abroad,

Dr. Li knew from personal experience how it felt to be despised by foreigners. From his time at court, he discovered as a professional functionary among ideologues how it felt to be despised by Marxist-Leninists. It felt much the same.

In searching for an alternative idiom in which to recount his personal experience, Dr. Li resorts to two widely shared memories of national shame and pride: one of the sign in a Shanghai park, barring "Chinese and dogs", and the other of Mao Zedong announcing that "the Chinese People have stood up." The resilience of these two motifs is all the more remarkable for their having virtually no basis in fact. There never was a sign by the entrance to a park in Shanghai that proclaimed "Chinese and dogs not allowed" (or any similar form of words), nor did Mao say that "the Chinese People have stood up" (or any similar form of words) when he declared the founding of the People's Republic.[ix] Nevertheless Dr. Li, along with many others in China in recent years, chose to locate his life story between these two historical boundary markers, one of national humiliation and the other of recovered national dignity.

The tenacity of these two literally incorrect, yet psychologically authentic, memories of China's triumph over national humiliation demonstrates the persistence of *thymos* in cultural memory. Beneath the authorized Maoist rhetoric of "imperialism" and "feudalism" is another language that has lain submerged these four or five decades past. This alternative language revolves around issues of humiliation, recognition and dignity, in contrast to the official language of oppression and liberation. Hence in the remembered history of national dignity, "dogs" and "standing up" are misrepresented *together*: the motif of a dog that gets around on four legs is redeemed by the motif of a state that stands up on two.

The idea of China "standing up" in 1949 has many different discursive roots in Chinese literature and ritual practice. The most important source is probably the one that gave us the legendary sign in the park in Shanghai. Basically, when China "stood up" in 1949 it signaled to the world that the country had straightened its back and would no longer tolerate humiliation at the hands of foreigners. In a style characteristic of British municipal administration the world over, there appears to have been a sign listing a number of regulations governing use of the park in the Shanghai International Settlement, including one concerning the entry of dogs, and another dealing with the admission of local Chinese (but permitting entry by Chinese servants of Europeans). The intervening regulations needed to be elided by an editorial stroke of the nationalist imagination to arrive at the condensed statement that dogs and Chinese were forbidden.

It took time before the sign could reveal itself with such elegant simplicity, for the residents of Shanghai had first to learn that their daily routines and personal habits were linked to the welfare of the nation.[x] But once the municipal noticeboard was read as a sign of racial subjection, it stimulated the people of China to get up on their hind legs, or "stand up." Lao She's novel, *Ma and Son* (1929), offers an explicit example of this rhetorical connection:

> In the twentieth century attitudes towards 'people' and 'country' are alike. Citizens of a strong country are people, but citizens of a weak nation? Dogs! China is a weak country, and the Chinese? Right! People of China! You must open your eyes and look around. The time for opening your eyes has come! You must straighten your backs. The time for straightening your backs has come unless you are willing to be regarded as dogs forever!

Lao She concedes the comparison between Chinese and dogs only to turn it back on his countrymen as an injunction to stand up. This connection goes a long way toward explaining the persistence of the mythical Shanghai sign as an historical signpost marking one of the boundaries of modern Chinese political life. It also summons into existence another sign announcing that China has recovered its dignity.

The second of these signs, Mao's famous statement that "the Chinese People have stood up", shows similar evidence of historical tampering. In this case, the tampering serves the added purpose of encoding the personal experience of individual shame and racial humiliation in the language of Marxism-Leninism.

What did Mao actually say at Tiananmen in October 1949? After Lin Boqu, newly appointed secretary of the Council of the People's Government, introduced the Chairman of the People's Republic to the crowd assembled on the square, Mao ascended the podium to announce, "The Central People's Government of the People's Republic of China has this day been established" (*Zhonghua renmin gongheguo zhongyang renmin zhengfu yi yu benri chenglile*). He stepped aside while the flag of the People's Republic was raised over Tianan Gate, and then read aloud from a prepared statement on the formal arrangements of government, on key personnel who would take up leading positions in government and military agencies, and on the status of the new government as the sole legitimate government of China for the purpose of diplomatic recognition. Next came the swearing in of numerous state functionaries before the proceedings continued with an impressive military parade. As the ceremony drew to a close, members of the crowd cried out, "Long live the People's Republic of China!" and "Long live Chairman Mao!" Mao responded by raising his hand in acknowledgment and calling back, "Long live Comrades!"

The significance of the event today is far better captured by Dr. Li's capricious recollection than by an accurate record of what was actually said, and he is in good company in misremembering the event. On October 1, 1984, Deng Xiaoping drew a similar connection. "Thirty-five years ago", Deng recalled at an anniversary ceremony in Tiananmen, "Chairman Mao Zedong . . . solemnly proclaimed here the founding of the People's Republic of China. He declared that the Chinese people had finally stood up."[xi] Western memories are no more reliable. Harrison Salisbury repeats the same story in *The New Emperors*[xii], and Western video and film records of Mao's speech from the podium at Tiananmen invariably carry an English voice-over statement along the lines of "the Chinese People have stood up", over the top of Mao's statement on the establishment of the Central People's Government. Regardless of what Mao in fact said on that day, that is how it has been remembered.

In fact the expression "the Chinese People have stood up" (*Zhongguo renmin zhan qilai le*) dates from the title ascribed to a talk that Mao had delivered a week earlier, to an assembly of old warlords, former bureaucrats, aging literati, "democratic elements", overseas Chinese and delegates drawn from all regions of China, all of whom had gathered to convene the opening session of the Chinese People's Political Consultative Conference (CPPCC) on September 21, 1949. Mao's speech on this occasion bore little relation to anything uttered at Tiananmen. Its tone was not faithfully captured by the formal title either. Mao appealed for the unity of the Chinese nation, made a number of gestures to evoke China's heroic and glorious past, and paid due reference to Sun Yatsen's contribution to the national revolution. While he repeated the phrase "stood up" several times in the course of the talk, he refrained from using the Leninist term "people" (*renmin*) in favor of the particularistic "we" (*women*), "nation" or "race" (*minzu*), and "Chinese" (*zhongguoren*). His first reference reads, "The Chinese, who occupy one quarter of humankind, have now stood up." The second refers pointedly to the humiliation of the Chinese at the hands of other nations: "Our nation", Mao assured his audience, "will never again be a nation despised by others. We have stood up." I stress the point because the universal term "people" does not quite catch the sense of racial or national pride conveyed in Mao's address.

This should not perhaps surprise us, given that the speech was targeted not at the "people" but at an aging audience of Republican functionaries, who were long accustomed to mulling over China's lost imperial dignity and recent history of national humiliation. At the same time, Mao's failure to mention these humiliations when he stood before the "people" a week later at Tiananmen was an omission in need of correction. The compound memory of these events, as they are recorded in Mao's collected works, is a curious blend of primordial racial pride and instrumental Leninist reasoning, mixed by an imaginative editor whose contribution to history has passed largely unacknowledged. This contribution involved yoking an earlier language of thymotic racial pride to a new, depersonalized, Marxist language of imperialist oppression and national liberation.

Dr. Li was not alone in imagining that these two languages came together when Mao spoke at Tiananmen. In the years that followed, he was not alone in attributing to "imperialism" the personal humiliation that had been etched on his soul as a youth. Nor was he alone, later still, when he abandoned this official language in favor of a cruder idiom of national humiliation and personal betrayal to portray the private life of Chairman Mao.

Saying No: The Rhetoric of Indignation

Thymos, Fukuyama reminds us, compels us not just to "stand up" and be recognized but also to "say no" to others. The muse of thymotic resentment has been busy in China in recent years. The books that have appeared under variations on the title *China Can Say No*—for example, *China Is Still Capable of Saying No, The China That Can Say No, Why Does China Say No?*—point consistently to the humiliation of the Chinese people at the hands of foreigners. It is only in terms of those humiliations, write the authors of the sequel to *China Can Say No*, that "we can understand why China's writers have been crying out to the heavens for a hundred years now: 'When will China become great and powerful?'" And the answer to that question, it seems, is only when the country finds the courage to stand firm and "say no."

One notable feature of the genre is the casual displacement of Marxism-Leninism-Mao Zedong thought by unadorned *ressentiment*. While many of these works refer to Mao's reported statement that "the Chinese People have stood up", they draw little further inspiration from his voluminous speeches and writings. They waste no effort, for example, reiterating the old Maoist explanation for China's historical condition that would attribute blame to international capital or feudal forces of reaction. They offer instead a simple catalogue of grievances set against a crude inventory of recent economic achievements. On the whole, the authors resent the fact that China is not treated with the dignity that they believe it deserves in light of its size, its history and its present rate of economic development.

All the same, Qin Xiaoying reminds us in his foreword to *China Is Still Capable of Saying No* (1996) that Mao's place in history is assured. Many foreigners appear to believe that economic reforms and the opening to the outside world initiated in 1978 marked a clean break with Mao's New China, he continues, but in this they are mistaken. China is simply accelerating its quest for status. Hence the economic reforms of Deng Xiaoping are read as enabling China to rise in the twenty-first century as firmly as it stood up in the middle of the present one:

> As our chief architect, Deng Xiaoping, once pointed out: 'When did the Chinese people stand up in the world? It was in 1949. In years to come, once we have achieved modernization, the Chinese people won't be merely standing up. We'll be flying up!'

In the literature of national humiliation, then, Deng emerges as Mao's equal, because he helped China to straighten its wings and "fly up."

The achievements of Deng's economic reforms are valued for enhancing national self-esteem. "There is no dignity to be had in poverty", complain the authors of one of these books, "no matter what country you come from." If it came to a choice, they would have the country raise its standing in the world before it raised its GDP another percentage point. We tend to assume that the legitimacy of the present regime rests largely on its capacity to deliver the good life to China's citizens. But little respect is shown in China's literature of complaint for a government that would deliver prosperity at the price of national dignity. Its tone confirms one of Fukuyama's stronger statements: "The nationalist is primarily preoccupied not with economic gain, but with recognition and dignity."[xiii]

The favored metaphor for economic growth—that of stretching one's wings and flying up—is now framed in the idiom of "national self-respect." It is not the "people" who fly up but the Chinese nation. Qin Xiaoying, for example, records that Deng once remarked at a meeting with Richard Nixon that "a country lacking in national self respect [_minzu de zizunxin_] and failing to cherish its own national independence, can never straighten itself up [_li bu qilai_]." Like Li Zhisui's memoirs, the _China Can Say No_ books remind us that the anti-imperialist, anti-feudal model of Maoist nationalism overlies an earlier form of nationalism, one grounded in personal experience of racial or national humiliation, rather than general and anodyne recollections of political and economic oppression. Again, like Li Zhisui, the authors inadvertently acknowledge that their loss of dignity has been institutionalized in perpetuity by the Communist Party state.

Neither the party nor the regime is presented with any appreciable sympathy in this literature of complaint. While its "no" is directed explicitly against foreigners, the present government is held implicitly to account for yielding too readily to foreign political and commercial demands, and for surrendering China's national dignity in the process. Even more pertinently, the texts shed light on a parallel struggle for personal dignity within China itself. They demonstrate a significant loss of self-regard among people within China, and reluctantly acknowledge that this loss lies exposed for all the world to see.

Basically, the "say no" authors appear to resent the twist of fate that delivered them into the world as citizens of a state that cannot afford the liberties that citizens of other states take for granted. None concedes that the time is ripe for democracy in China. None questions the wisdom of the armed suppression of democracy activists in 1989. Yet none can draw comfort, either, from the knowledge that they belong to a state that refuses to acknowledge their dignity as individual citizens. By abandoning hope for civil liberties, China's nationalists have discovered _shame_. This appears to be the indirect source for much of the resentment driving the _China Can Say No_ phenomenon. It is sired by the anger of a nation not taken at its worth, and the shame of a people who tried to stand up before their own state and discovered that it could not be done.

Life Itself Plays the Master

In Fukuyama's terms, the popular protests of 1989 were staged to achieve "universal recognition"—that is, to assert the value of the individual citizen before that of the state. Since 1989, state repression has had the effect of redirecting this quest back onto the old and more familiar track of national recognition. This redirection has been effected partly through brute force, partly through censorship and misinformation, but chiefly through the state playing upon a feeling of the inevitability of things that seems to be widely shared by people in China today. The idealism of 1989 has yielded to "realism" today. "Unrealistic hopes of 'universalism' [*tianxia zhuyi*] are no more than wishful thinking", writes the team headed by Song Qiang. The day for cosmopolitanism might dawn in a hundred years, although by Song Qiang's reckoning this, too, may be unduly sanguine. Mao's timetable was more like one thousand years. The Chinese people have a long wait ahead of them before they can realistically expect to enjoy the freedoms that are theirs by right.

Impotence in the face of history means, in Fukuyama's words, that people cannot live up to their own sense of worth. China's nay-sayers seem simultaneously resigned to their fate and frustrated by the circumstances that compel their acquiescence. One way or another, the outcome is a feeling of shame. But nay-sayers are compelled to acquiesce to the "realistic" conditions governing life in their own sovereign state. The Chinese *nation* may have stood up long ago, we are told, but the Chinese *people* remain slaves to this day. They have become "slaves of life", inescapably tied to their families and their children, and bound to their country for want of a passport. Much as they might like to "mount political resistance in Hyde Park" (an indirect reference to Tiananmen), or join the Greens and "save the whales", China's people are for the moment prevented from becoming "citizens of the world." Their servile condition has not been forced on them by the state, nor can it be attributed to foreigners. In this particular master-slave relationship, life itself plays the master. There is no escaping it.

Such admissions hint at the shame of growing up in a society and a state that offer no hope of realizing the simple aspirations of the common citizen. Worse, they hold out no hope of liberation. For "slaves of life", bondage is a condition of existence and not a consequence of the particular arrangements or policies of a given regime.[xiv] The rhetoric of shame and indignation running through the *Say No* literature suggests that the quest for individual dignity on the part of ordinary citizens is still far from reconciled with the quest for national dignity. What little respect people can muster is found by "saying no" to foreigners, in the belief that foreign critics fail to appreciate and make little allowance for the particular conditions that apply in China.

But the claims of national dignity and individual dignity cannot be reconciled by saying no to foreigners alone. National liberation offers no way out for "slaves of life." The path to liberation entails challenging the conditions that threaten personal dignity. This path leads inevitably to challenging head-on existing constraints on thought, speech and assembly.

The "Irrationality" of Wei Jingsheng

Fukuyama identifies the passion that drives a people to "stand up" in the world with the longing that drives them to "stand up" for civil rights and democracy. This longing is the desire for recognition, and it is not a rational longing in the standard instrumental or utilitarian sense of the term. In pursuit of recognition, people set aside their better judgment and risk their lives and livelihoods to fight for a nation, for a creed or for the right to be counted the equals of their masters. Developments in the economy and society may enable these sacrifices and struggles to take place, but in the absence of human desire and human agency there is no struggle at all. It takes irrational nationalists to make nations, and irrational democrats to make democracies.

Wei Jingsheng is a democrat in Fukuyama's mold, a "thymotic man", a "man of anger who is jealous of his own dignity and the dignity of his fellow citizens."[xv] Wei's critics in China and abroad (and he has many) complain that he is out of touch with the mood of his country. They are right. His routine insistence on maintaining personal dignity before his political leaders, his jailers and his family presents a model of behavior not widely practiced in China today. What is more, he refuses to share the feeling of political impotence that afflicts many of his compatriots, and has avoided the shame that comes of failing to live up to his own expectations.

Fukuyama insists that "there is no democracy without democrats." The case of Wei Jingsheng asks us to carry Fukuyama's line of reasoning a little further, to ask whether there can be *nationalism* without democrats in China today. Is it possible for the people of China to recover national self-regard without first recovering their individual self-esteem through recognition of their universal rights? In other words, is it possible for the Chinese people really to take pride in their nation while they still remain ashamed of themselves?

Wei is proud of his country because he can look himself in the eye. One source of his self-esteem is his refusal to concede a point on which his critics have long yielded: that the people of China deserve less than others. His critics generally concede that democracy is a universal aspiration of people in all societies, including China's, yet for now they place democracy beyond realistic expectations. Democracy is not something to struggle for, his critics assume, but something history delivers to the door when the order is ready. Again, Wei demurs: "Which country has acquired democracy, freedom, and human rights without hard struggle, without shedding sweat and blood? You could not possibly wait for someone to present you with democracy."[xvi]

Wei Jingsheng is just one of many Chinese citizens who have spent time in jail for speaking their minds. Some have endured considerably longer terms in jail; some have held equally fast to their views. He stands out in this company, however, not simply on account of his international status, but because he has attempted to reconcile the claims of national and universal recognition in an old and familiar language that was forged in the country's struggle for national recognition. He is the first to acknowledge the power of national dignity in the armory of his enemies. Indeed, national dignity is a source of inspiration for him as well. He wrote and posted his major essay on democracy, "The Fifth

Modernization", to demonstrate to his fellow countrymen that not all Chinese were spineless weaklings. His subject was democracy; his muse was thymotic nationalism.

By his own account, Wei had thought long and hard about the condition of his country and people for many years before the advent of the Democracy Wall Movement. Still, he had no intention of posting anything on these subjects until he overheard bystanders complain that Democracy Wall activists would probably pack up their pens and go home once Deng Xiaoping had issued a veiled warning, which he did on November 27, 1978. Wei took this complaint as a slight on his country and his people, and it stirred him to action:

> As soon as [Deng's] notice was posted, citizens all over Beijing were critical: 'The Chinese are simply inept, and spineless. Look at it, having the freedom only for a couple of days, being able to speak out, now with a little directive from someone, they want to retreat. A bunch of spineless weaklings. (Sigh) There is no hope for China.'
> After I heard such commentaries, I was particularly saddened. I felt that not all Chinese were spineless. Certainly my thoughts and my ideas, with years of deliberation, had long been stored in my mind. I decided to utter them, do something, with the primary motivation to prove to everyone that not all Chinese were spineless. So I posted 'The Fifth Modernization' there. It was written one night, and posted there the next day.[xvii]

Wei thrilled to see people queuing ten deep to read his new poster, and felt reassured when they nodded in agreement. What moved him most was public acknowledgment that the people of China could stand up for their rights. He alludes to this nationalist motive in the opening paragraph of the second section of "The Fifth Modernization", which was pasted up shortly after another writer had urged Wei to stop criticizing the regime. "Our young men are not the 'sick men of the East'", Wei began. "They have sufficient courage to put up and to read posters, and to discuss different views even though some of them are taboo."[xviii] Everyone, he later recalled, could now acknowledge that "the Chinese were brave and fearless people after all."[xix] The language through which he has conveyed this conviction is the same language employed by Mao Zedong in his speech to the CPPCC, when he proclaimed, "Our nation will never again be a nation despised by others. We have stood up." Now, however, the nation was asked to stiffen its spine *against* Mao's Communist Party itself.

These few references to national dignity stand out in a body of work otherwise devoted to the dignity of the individual. In "The Fifth Modernization", Wei mounted his argument for democracy around the implicitly Hegelian framework of the master-slave relationship. People everywhere wanted democracy in order to become "masters of their own destiny", Wei asserted. In China, however, "it may be more correct to call them slaves." A people that could not maintain its autonomy was forced into servitude.

Wei scorned apologists who argued that the regime had fed and clothed the Chinese people. First, they were plainly wrong: Mao had systematically starved the people in his Great Leap Forward. Impoverished and ill-fed people had every reason to feel angry when they saw their masters gorging on fluffy white rice. What caused gravest offense in Wei's eyes, however, was the servitude that their hunger revealed in their relations with their masters, who denied them the simple right "to lead a normal life." Bowls of white rice represented more than the promise of a full stomach. They whetted the appetite for equality between slave and master. The heroes of the centuries-old epic *Water Margin* rarely went hungry, Wei observed, but they fought and struggled with their masters all the same. So they should. Their struggle was identical to his own: "exactly the kind of struggle aimed at winning equality of rights for man as a human being." The bravery and bravado of the *Water Margin* heroes has served as a model for many different kinds of rebellion in China's modern history, not all by any means undertaken in pursuit of human rights. For Wei, however, these heroic tales signified the historical continuity of the political struggle of the Chinese people's desire for recognition.[xx]

In his letters from prison, Wei refuses to concede the shameful inevitability of being born into a state that will not grant him recognition as an autonomous human being. Even after it takes away his freedom, he refuses to kneel. The simple audacity of this refusal can be measured by the scale across which Wei pitches his complaints from prison, ranging from self-confident letters to Deng Xiaoping through to the studied naivety of brief notes to his jailers complaining about the fittings and facilities of his prison cell.

To some, such behavior suggests madness, and in fact Wei feigns madness. In his childhood, he recalls, Wei and his sister used to play the roles of legendary "mad geniuses" of folklore, to flaunt local customs and criticize national political figures with impunity. He learned at an early age that the mad enjoy a degree of licence that is denied sane people. He hints at another source of his irrational behavior in one of his asides on the people of China: "The people have great reserves of self-confidence, self-respect, and self-consciousness stored away." The source of both his madness and his confidence is Wei's self-respect.

Individual self-respect is a sturdy foundation on which to claim national respect. This is not, however, how the relationship between democracy and nationalism is generally understood in China today. As Edward Friedman has recently observed, "Recent events have fostered a feeling among many educated Chinese that promoting democracy is virtually synonymous with treason, with splintering China and blocking its rise and return to greatness."[xxi] It is worth recalling that Wei Jingsheng was initially jailed for selling state secrets, not for democratic activism. Since his release from prison in November 1997, he has again been branded a national traitor for speaking out against continuing civil rights abuses in China. Far from constituting treason, Wei's behavior demonstrates that the fight for individual dignity is a powerful antidote to the shame and self-loathing that converts national pride into parochial chauvinism in China today.

Others among Wei's critics are prepared to concede the inevitability of democracy, although on economistic grounds rather than thymotic ones. There is no place for dignity or democrats in their divinations. Democracy will simply arrive, under its own steam, once the elite responsible for the ship of state finally acknowledge its practical advantages. Wei places little faith in any newly emerging bureaucratic "bourgeoisie." The major beneficiary of market-driven economic reforms, he says, has been a new bureaucratic class "cultivated intentionally and systematically by the Communist Party", one that has no interest in democratic reform. Ordinary people will fight and die for democracy, he maintains, not because they are growing rich but because they no longer wish to be treated as slaves. It follows that democracy can only come to China through an economically irrational and politically naive choice on the part of aggrieved citizens who want the state to recognize their dignity as ordinary human beings.

So the *ressentiment* that pushed China to "stand up" in 1949 now drives the struggle for liberal democracy. Nationalist *ressentiment* is of course still alive and well—the ideal of national dignity drives the literature of *Saying No*. Yet the nay-sayers themselves highlight a growing incongruence between national pride and personal indignation when they boast of China's long and glorious history in an angry and grumpy tone. The incongruence arises in part because the problem lies closer to home than many will concede. Hence, the more indignant they become, the more China's "say no" nationalists are likely to inflame the desire to restore some balance, or symmetry, between individual and national dignity. More importantly, the incongruence arises because personal indignation can no longer be mollified by China "standing up" in the same old fashion. The solution also lies closer to home.

People in China increasingly acknowledge that the world has become reluctant to recognize states that treat their citizens with derision—and there is no dignity without recognition. As Hegel observed, it takes two subjects to turn a slave into a master: one to stand up, and the other to witness and acknowledge the standing up. Even if China manages to "fly up" in the twenty-first century, as the nay-sayers predict, the world is unlikely to extend it full recognition until the Chinese citizen is allowed to stand up as well.

When all is said and done, however, the world is a relatively minor witness to China's predicament. An old and familiar vocabulary of national rights, national self-determination and national equality continues to supply a framework for personal reflection by Chinese themselves on individual rights, individual self-determination and equality before the law—all grounded in the pursuit of recognition. People who can say no to foreigners can, of course, eventually learn to say no to anyone they choose. True, when they resort to thymotic resistance to the state or try to appeal to their formal rights before the state, they risk landing themselves in jail. "Sensible", rational people do not expose themselves to such risks. Unless they do, however, they run the greater risk of surrendering their dignity. Many people in China are acutely aware of this dilemma.

Wei Jingsheng has pressed on, regardless of the risks, because he places dignity first. The fight for democracy is not a fight for comfort, or for happiness, or for profit, as Wei understands it, but a struggle to retain one's sense of self-worth. Asked recently how he managed to survive his seventeen years in prison, he answered, "For your own dignity, you have to endure. . . . For people like us, death was not the outcome we feared most. What we feared most of all was the possibility of developing a mental disorder, of losing our dignity—that would have been the worst outcome."

NOTES

[i] Wei Jingsheng, *The Courage to Stand Alone: Letters from Prison and Other Writings*, ed. and trans. Kristina M. Torgeson (New York: Viking, 1997).

[ii] Greenfeld, *Nationalism: Five Roads to Modernity* (Cambridge: Harvard University Press, 1992).

[iii] Fukuyama, *The End of History and the Last Man* (New York: Free Press, 1992), p. xv.

[iv] Ibid., pp. 117, 205-6.

[v] Well before Fukuyama, the place of dignity in history was eloquently conveyed by Isaiah Berlin in a lecture delivered in New Delhi in 1961. In it, Berlin maintained that what drove nationalism was "a wounded or outraged sense of human dignity, the desire for recognition." See Berlin, "Rabindranath Tagore and the Consciousness of Nationality", in *The Sense of Reality: Studies in Ideas and Their History*, ed. Henry Hardy (New York: Farrar, Straus & Giroux, 1997).

[vi] Jones, "Kegs of Powder, Barrels of Oil", *Quadrant* (November 1996), pp. 80-1.

[vii] Spence, foreword to *Mao's Harvest: Voices from China's New Generation*, ed. Helen Siu and Zelda Stern (New York: Oxford University Press, 1983).

[viii] Li Zhisui, *The Private Life of Chairman Mao: The Inside Story of the Man Who Made Modern China* (New York: Random House, 1994).

[ix] See Robert Bickers and Jeffrey Wasserstorm, "Shanghai's 'Dogs and Chinese not Permitted' Sign: Legend, History and Contemporary Symbol", *The China Quarterly* (June 1995).

[x] See my *Awakening China: Politics, Culture and Class in the Nationalist Revolution* (Stanford: Stanford University Press, 1996), chapter 3.

[xi] Cited in Richard Evans, *Deng Xiaoping and the Making of Modern China* (New York: Viking, 1994), p. 273.

[xii] Salisbury, *The New Emperors: China in the Era of Mao and Deng* (Boston: Little, Brown & Co., 1992), p. 187.

[xiii] Fukuyama, p. 201.

[xiv] Geremie R. Barme, "To screw foreigners is patriotic: China's avante-garde nationalists", in *Chinese Nationalism*, ed. Jonathan Unger (Armonk, NY: M.E. Sharpe, 1996), pp. 183-208.

[xv] Fukuyama comments on China: "It is only thymotic man, the man of anger who is jealous of his own dignity and the dignity of his fellow citizens . . . who is willing to walk in front of a tank or confront a line of soldiers", p. 180.

[xvi] Interview with Wei Jingsheng, *China News Digest*, January 1998.

[xvii] Interview with Wei Jingsheng, *China News Digest*, February 15, 1998.

[xviii] Wei Jingsheng, "The Fifth Modernization", in *The Fifth Modernization: China's Human Rights Movement, 1978-1979*, ed. James D. Seymour (Stanfordville, NY: Human Rights Publishing Group, 1980), pp. 47-70, 56.

[xix] Interview of February 15, 1998.

[xx] The *Water Margin* epic is the *locus classicus* of China's many tales of popular rebellion found in the democratic literary canon. Only a few years before Wei's poster was mounted on Democracy Wall, in 1975 and 1976, *Water Margin* had been the focus of an orchestrated political campaign. See my "Continuity within discontinuity: The case of *Water Margin* mythology", *Modern China* (July 1986).

[xxi] Friedman, "Thoughts on Wei Jingsheng", H-ASIA, January 24, 1998.

17

The New Mandarins

*Robert M. Pease**

A prim twenty-one year-old with a perpetual smile, Yumi is quick-witted, energetic, and thus, one would think, eminently employable. But the Japanese job market, tough for a young woman in the best of times, has been downright forbidding in the past few years of economic slow-down. So Yumi has ventured to multilingual Singapore to improve her job prospects, betting that foreign language skills will raise her chances.

There are many young Japanese women with similar intentions at Yumi's language school. There are also students—teenage, college-age, and middle-aged—from around the world. A thirty-something husband and wife from Korea; a pair of middle-aged sisters from the Philippines; academic exchange participants from the United States, Australia, Europe, and even Russia. But when these foreign students pass in the hallways it isn't with the typical English greetings *hello* or *what's up* but rather the Mandarin Chinese *ni hao* (are you good?) or *zenmeyang* (how's it going?). For these individuals, like thousands of others in university and commercial classes throughout Asia, are betting that Mandarin Chinese will be the next business language of the Pacific Rim.

Will the economic transformation of China spread the use of Chinese language throughout the Asian region, as these students expect? Could the increasing utility of Mandarin erode English as the second language of choice in

---

* Robert M. Pease, a director of the Compass East-West Group, was a Fulbright scholar in Singapore during 1993-94.

This essay first appeared in *The National Interest*, No. 46 (Winter 1996/97).

Asia? And now that the sushi, sumu, and karaoke crazes have subsided, is the world turning not Japanese but Chinese after all?

Despite the growth of Mandarin language instruction in Asia and elsewhere, these questions may still seem farfetched from an Anglo-American point of view. We have become so accustomed to English as *the* global language of commerce, science, and entertainment that no alternative seems practicable. English can be heard, read, and spoken from Buenos Aires to Brussels to Beijing, and it is commonplace to overhear a Thai and German, or Indonesian and Japanese executive conversing in English within the lobbies and lounges of Asia.

But commonplace is not always commonsensical. The initial momentum toward English as a global language was provided by two conditions no longer evident: the British Empire and U.S. postwar economic predominance. The language itself is a frustrating one to master through study. Compared to most languages, English uses an enormously large vocabulary. It has numerous phonetic and grammatical inconsistencies. As one Chinese professor in Beijing confesses, "I have been studying English for fifty years, and still I'm afraid of your prepositions."

Chinese is no picnic either. Spoken Mandarin may have relatively simple grammar and an economical use of words. But the reading and writing of 2,500 to 3,500 essential characters or ideographs is a daunting task even for native speakers. In any post office in China one can hear appeals for help: Hey, how do you write Harbin (a northern provincial capital)? Which is the Shan of Shantou (a southern coastal city)?

In many respects, however, computerization of Chinese will facilitate commercial functions, and the race is already on, among start-up firms and corporate giants alike, to produce the software of choice for the Chinese language market.

The English term "Mandarin" refers to the northeastern Chinese dialect that China's rulers have long promoted as a unifying language. Within China this dialect is referred to as "standard speech" (*putonghua*); outside China, it may be called "country language" (*guoyu*) or simply "Chinese" (*huayu*). Most Taiwanese speak fluent Mandarin, as do most educated mainlanders. Large numbers of Hong Kongers, who traditionally speak Cantonese dialect, are brushing up their Mandarin for post-1997 PRC rule. Similarly, business and cultural ties with China and Taiwan are reinvigorating Mandarin usage among the twenty to twenty-five million ethnic Chinese throughout Southeast Asia.

Mandarin has always been the language of high culture among the Chinese within China and abroad. It is now becoming the language of pop culture as well. Taiwanese and Hong Kong movies, television shows, and music formerly produced in dialects, like Cantonese or Hokkien, are increasingly made for distribution to the wider Mandarin market. The international success of Chinese artists such as filmmakers Chen Kaige (*Farewell My Concubine*) and Zhang

Yimou (*Raise the Red Lantern*; *To Live*) adds to the allure of Mandarin among the young.

Until recently the designation of Mandarin as the world's most spoken language was mainly due to the size of the population of China itself (1.2 billion and climbing). But now Mandarin may be poised to spread beyond the Chinese world as a language of commerce and influence among the elite and professional classes of Asia. The economic impetus is clear: Trade within the region is expanding twice as fast as Asia's trade with other regions. And if reformist policies are sustained, the growing China market stands near the center of those trade flows. China could also become Asia's largest source of tourist revenue. In 1995 PRC citizens represented the third largest group of Asian tourists, a relatively new and growing phenomenon.

The potential for Mandarin as an Asia-wide language rests on historical as well as economic foundations. Japan, after all, was the major source of finance and tourist revenue in the region for two decades until its recent recession. Yet the Japanese language never did catch on. The legacy of the Second World War threw up some obstacles, as did the peculiarities of the language itself. More fundamentally, however, Japanese language offered other Asians access only to Japan, not the wider region. Japan is a unique cultural entity centered on itself; by contrast, Chinese influence has long circulated throughout East and Southeast Asia. Classical Chinese characters provide the foundation for written Japanese and, to a lesser extent, Korean languages. The Korean President Kim Young Sam has called for efforts to standardize Chinese character usage in East Asia, thus facilitating document translation and second language study. While Chinese characters no longer occur in written Vietnamese, spoken Vietnamese still contains a large percentage of Chinese loan words from the many centuries (111 B.C. - 939 A.D.) of Vietnamese tributary status. This means that native speakers of Korean, Japanese, and Vietnamese may find the study of Mandarin easier and more stimulating than that of English.

In Singapore, where 78 percent of the population is ethnic Chinese, the government's "Speak Mandarin" campaign has been in force for seventeen years. Originally intended to unify the many Chinese dialect groups in Singapore, both culturally and politically, the campaign now touts Mandarin as the key to business success in Asia. Not surprisingly, a growing number of minority citizens in Singapore (Malays, Indians, Eurasians) are petitioning to have their children admitted to Mandarin courses.

The potential for Mandarin elsewhere in Southeast Asia is still problematic and yet is progressing. Chinese minorities have long been viewed with suspicion by the dominant ethnic groups for their cliquishness and business acumen. Indeed, suspicions have intermittently erupted into hostility, as with the post-coup chaos of mid-1960s Indonesia. However, this has not prevented Southeast Asia from having two national leaders of partial Chinese ancestry in recent years—former President Corazon Aquino of the Philippines and former Prime Minister Chuan Leekpai of

Thailand. Similarly, while private Chinese language schools were barely tolerated in Southeast Asia three decades ago, now they are prospering. Commercial Mandarin study is on the rise in Thailand and the Philippines among students of both indigenous and ethnic Chinese backgrounds. The Malaysian government is expanding the study of Mandarin as a third language (after Malay and English) in government schools. Even in Indonesia, where resentment of Chinese commercial influence runs deepest, there has been a relaxation of long-standing Chinese language prohibitions. Two Indonesian universities now have Chinese language departments, and a wider circulation of Chinese newspapers and tourist brochures has been permitted to stimulate commerce and tourism.

The mates down under are also in on the trend. The Australian government has launched an Asian language campaign as part of an ambitious effort to integrate Australia with the Asian economies. Their target is for 60 percent of all secondary school graduates to be functional in one of four Asian languages (Mandarin, Japanese, Bahasa Indonesia, or Korean) by the year 2006. The Australian military has also announced that it will use Asian language fluency as a promotion criteria.

The question of whether more Mandarin in Asia will mean less English is a complex one. Many societies pursue successful bilingual education programs, but trilingual communities are rare. A remarkable number of EU citizens do speak three or four languages with virtual fluency, yet these languages have basic similarities. Some Hong Kongers and Singaporeans function effectively in three languages, but many more fail in the attempt.

English will clearly remain the predominant global language, even as Mandarin usage spreads in the Asian region. There is too much momentum behind English for it to be easily displaced. Yet a growing number of aspiring young Asian professionals, like Yumi and her classmates, will be weighing the relative advantages of English against Chinese as they chart their careers. "Can I master both English and Chinese?" they will ask themselves. And for those who cannot there will be a further question: Which is more useful, appealing, and easier to learn?

At the same time, Asian government officials and educators will be pondering different questions around the same issue. And their assessments will be affected by geopolitical and macroeconomic trends. Is China becoming a more or less responsible actor in the region? A more or less coherent economy? Are the United States and other English speaking economies integrating more or less closely with Asia? And, last but not least, which language is least upsetting to the existing political and social order? The answers to both sets of questions, in English and/or Mandarin, will be heard in the hotels, airports, and classrooms of Asia for decades to come.

18

Asia Tomorrow, Gray and Male

*Nicholas Eberstadt**

Certain kinds of developments, though rife with consequence for economics, politics, and strategy, are intrinsically difficult to anticipate. Wars, revolutions, and economic panics are typical cases in point. Yet there are also important sorts of developments that are less subject to historical caprice or political calculation, more likely to unfold in a regular manner over a relatively long time, and thus inherently easier to envision in advance. Population change is one of these.

Barring the contingency of utter catastrophe, we can already estimate, often in surprising detail, what lies in store for East Asia in demographic terms over the next fifteen to twenty years.[i] Such projections point to a number of new and unfamiliar conditions for the region—each of which could have sweeping ramifications. One involves the ratio of young to elderly in a population, a factor that necessarily influences pension burdens, savings rates, and hence general economic conditions. Another concerns manpower availability, which also affects economic potential and thus, ultimately, national power. A third—imbalanced sex ratios—can portend social tension and, possibly, political trouble. While the social and economic implications of demographic facts are harder to discern than the facts themselves, some conclusions may be reached with a reasonably high level of confidence. Taken together, these implications in turn form a significant element of the context in which political and strategic dynamics will play out.

---

* Nicholas Eberstadt holds the Henry Wendt Chair in Political Economy at the American Enterprise Institute and is a visiting fellow at the Harvard Center for Population and Development Studies.

This essay first appeared in *The National Interest*, No. 53 (Fall 1998).

Knowing the Numbers

East Asia's population today stands at roughly 2 billion people, accounting for about a third of the world's population. Approximately 1.5 billion of those 2 billion reside in Northeast Asia (that is, mainland China, Taiwan, Japan, and Korea), the other half billion in Southeast Asia (that is, the countries between Burma to the west and Vietnam and the Philippines to the east). East Asia also contains three of the eight most populous states in the world today—China, number one with about 1.25 billion inhabitants; Indonesia, number four with about 200 million; and Japan, number eight with about 125 million—as well as five other states with over 40 million people.

To a considerable degree, East Asia's population profile between now and the year 2015 has been set already by past mortality and fertility trends. Despite a series of regional paroxysms that claimed millions of lives in the post-World War II era—the Korean and Vietnam Wars, China's Great Leap Forward, Indonesia's post-Sukarno convulsions, and Cambodia's Khmer Rouge period, among others—average life expectancy at birth for East Asia as a whole is believed to have jumped from a bit over 40 to almost 70 between the early 1950s and the late 1990s. In both Northeast and Southeast Asia, the tempo of mortality decline has exceeded the world average for almost half a century. Only in Burma, Cambodia, East Timor, and Laos do life expectancies rank below the mean for contemporary developing regions as a whole.

Like mortality, fertility has also fallen dramatically. In the late 1950s, only Japan reported a total fertility rate (births per woman per lifetime) that, if maintained, would have resulted in long-term population stabilization. Elsewhere in East Asia, the average woman was typically bearing five to seven children. By the late 1990s, however, fertility levels appear to have dropped roughly to the replacement level for East Asia as a whole, a breathtaking transformation of childbearing patterns in just four decades. Apart from Mongolia and possibly the still-mysterious Democratic People's Republic of Korea (DPRK), sub-replacement fertility is today characteristic of every Northeast Asian locale—including China, where fertility rates are lower than those in the United States. In Southeast Asia, too, fertility levels have dropped by over half since the late 1950s, with most of the decline having taken place in the past twenty years. In Singapore and Thailand, fertility levels are well below replacement; in Indonesia and Vietnam levels are rapidly falling toward replacement.

East Asia's population trends between now and the year 2015 will also be shaped by the intervening trajectories for mortality and fertility (migration plays only a marginal role in the region's current population dynamics). Those trajectories, of course, remain a matter of conjecture—although usually fertility rates are harder to guess at than mortality rates, depending as they do upon such unknowable, and possibly fickle, qualities as future parental preferences. Yet those imponderables notwithstanding, the various fertility estimates now contemplated for East Asia do not substantially alter the region's demographic profile for the year 2015. If the UN Population Division's current "medium" scenario proves accurate, for example, East Asia's population will rise to about 2.25 billion in 2015—roughly a 13 percent increase.[ii] The high variant implies about 18 percent growth, the low variant about 8 percent—but in the great scheme of things, these are not dramatic differences. More to the point, virtually everyone who will be in the East Asian labor force, marriage pool, or retirement population in the year 2015 *is already alive today*—and demographic techniques permit us to estimate their numbers two decades hence with fair precision. We can therefore talk today with reasonable confidence about East Asia's coming demographic situation, and its coming demographic problems.

The End of "Unprecedented Growth"

In the generation just past, demographic specialists and informed non-specialists alike spoke of the "unprecedented growth" in human numbers in East Asia. To many observers, East Asia's population explosion evoked images of a host of Malthusian dangers: unending food shortages, mounting poverty, labor markets and cities overburdened by new, discontented job-seekers, and increasingly fragile governments confronted by ever deeper domestic problems.

As we now know, this grim presentiment was far off the mark. Despite rapid population growth, East Asian economies grew robustly, and regional political stability gradually increased rather than diminished. Population growth will continue in East Asia in the decades immediately ahead, but at far slower rates. For East Asia as a whole, the UN Population Division's "medium variant" projections contemplate average annual increases of about 0.8 percent between 1995 and 2015. (That compares with an estimated 1.6 percent annual rate of natural increase in 1975-95, and 2.1 percent a year in the 1955-75 period.) In absolute terms, this would mean an increase of 350 million in the 1995-2015 period—a large number, to be sure, but distinctly less than the estimated 490 million increment of 1975-95 or the 480 million increase of 1955-75. In Southeast Asia, current "high variant" projections would make for absolute population increases slightly greater than those recorded in the 1980s and 1990s. Even those high variant projections, however, imply a slower growth rate than any recorded for the area since 1945. For East Asia, all projections point to smaller annual absolute additions to the area's population after 2010 than those experienced in the 1960s; some variants indicate smaller increments than those of the early 1950s.

The dramatic slowdown in anticipated demographic growth is the direct consequence of the broad movement toward replacement or sub-replacement fertility rates in the region's major population centers. Prolonged sub-replacement fertility could in fact bring some East Asian countries to the point of zero population growth, or even population decline, by the year 2015. *All* projections, for example, suggest that Japan's population will shrink after the year 2010. Under the low set of fertility assumptions, too, population growth would virtually cease by 2015 in both Thailand and the Republic of Korea. Under comparable assumptions, population decline for Northeast Asia as a whole would commence around 2020.

East Asian radical fertility declines beg the question of causation. Demographers, unfortunately, are able to offer precious few explanations that are neither trivial nor riddled with important exceptions. To be sure: mass education, rapid urbanization, income growth, and anti-natal population programs are among the many factors often mentioned in fertility decline for East Asia and elsewhere. But for now it is impossible to offer any reliable quantitative estimates of the impact on fertility decline of these diverse possible influences. Lacking a workable general theory for fertility change, demography is also consequently unable to predict fertility trends with any accuracy over the long run.

We do know, however, that future population issues in Asia will differ from those of the Cold War era in fundamental respects. For the region as a whole, accommodating burgeoning human numbers will no longer be the pressing concern. But a host of new demographic concerns loom on East Asia's horizon. Three of the most important are rapid population aging, declining manpower availability, and unnaturally imbalanced sex ratios.

The Graying of East Asia

East Asia's revolution in life expectancy, in conjunction with its transition toward replacement or even sub-replacement fertility levels, has set the stage for a dramatic process of population aging. In many countries, the aging of populations will proceed very swiftly, demographically speaking. The "graying" of East Asia is sure to have major social and economic ramifications; it may have political repercussions as well.

As recently as the early 1980s, nearly all of East Asia's populations were young: the median age for both Northeast and Southeast Asia stood in the low twenties or high teens. At that time, persons 65 years and older accounted for just over 5 percent of the total population. As recently as 1985, children under 15 outnumbered persons 65 and older by five to one in Northeast Asia, and by over ten to one in Southeast Asia.

Things will be very different in 2015. By then, for example, the median age in Northeast Asia will be about 37—several years older than the current American level, and similar to levels in today's "gray" northern Europe. Though population growth rates throughout East Asia will be slowing over the next two decades, the pace of growth for each country's elderly age groups will be accelerating. Thus, the share of the older groups will increase, and the ratio of children to older persons will fall. In 2015, Southeast Asia will have not ten children under the age of 15 for every person 65 or older—as is now the case—but only four; and Northeast Asia will have fewer than two.

Regional averages, however, obscure the disparate impact that aging will have on local populations. Some East Asian countries will remain youthful: for example, in 2015 the median age in the Philippines will be about 26, and in Cambodia under 25. Estimated median ages in Thailand (about 35) and China (36) will be comparable to those in today's graying OECD countries. Other East Asian locales, however, will contain populations *grayer than any yet witnessed in human history*. Barring radically changed migration trends, for example, Singapore's median age in 2015 will be about 41, Hong Kong's 44, and Japan's nearly 45. The United Nations defines an aging society as one in which 7 percent or more of the population is 65 or older. In 2015, that age grouping is likely to account for about 8-9 percent of the population in Thailand and China, about 10 percent in South Korea, over 11 percent in Taiwan, around 15 percent in Hong Kong, and an amazing 24 percent in Japan.

Due to the magnitude of their sudden longevity explosions and the precipitous nature of their fertility declines, many parts of East Asia will also experience a much more rapid process of population aging in the decades ahead than was recorded in developed regions in the recent past. It took forty years (1955-95) for the median age of the world's predominantly European "more developed regions" to rise from 28 to 36; Northeast Asia will make the same transition in less than twenty years (1995-2015), and some of its countries will grow old even more rapidly. And although Southeast Asia will stay relatively youthful in 2015, given an anticipated median age of about 28, that median age will jump nearly five years between the turn of the coming century and 2015; in those fifteen years, Southeast Asia will age as much, in absolute terms, as the more developed regions did in thirty (1955-85). East Asian societies and governments thus have less time than their industrial European predecessors to prepare for the challenges that aging will inevitably pose.

What challenges? Rapid population aging will have profound social and economic consequences. From Singapore to Northeast Asia, for example, the neo-Confucian social order will be tested by a proliferation of the elderly and, presumably, a vast concomitant increase in the number of infirm and aged dependents.

For thousands of years an East Asian tradition that venerates age and emphasizes the hierarchical obligations of children to their parents was reinforced by prevailing demographic trends—that is to say, very old people were rare and children were plentiful. By 2015, however, in Japan, Hong Kong, and possibly Singapore, grandparents will outnumber their grandchildren. In many other places (China, Taiwan, Thailand, Korea), that momentous generational reversal will be fast approaching.

In a high-tech twenty-first century, furthermore, the ancient Confucian presumption that the elderly should be honored for the special knowledge and wisdom they possess will surely look distinctly less self-evident than in earlier days. And peoples long inculcated in the virtues of filial piety may have an especially difficult time coping with the prospect of huge inter-generational resource transfers, as parents and other older relatives emerge as pervasive, and possibly major, financial burdens upon the able-bodied.

In particular, rapid population aging heralds the advent of truly imposing pension obligations. The most extreme squeeze will be felt in Japan. By 2015, for every Japanese 65 or older there will only be 2.5 people of "working age" (15-64)—and not all of those will actually be working. The budgetary implications of such a metamorphosis are arresting. In the United States, the unfunded liabilities of the social security system are enormous; yet Japan's relative liabilities are already over three times greater, amounting today to an estimated 70 percent of current GDP.[iii] On this budgetary path, Japan's net public debt burden would rise from the 11 percent of GDP recorded in 1995—one of the OECD's lowest—to a projected 102 percent of GDP in 2015—which would be very nearly the OECD's projected highest. (By way of comparison, America's level of net public debt, widely regarded as disturbingly high, will amount to a bit under 50 percent of GDP in the year 2000.) If Japan's elderly are to enjoy in 2015 the paid retirement they are promised today, the nation will have to manage a much higher burden of debt and taxes than it copes with now. Indeed, to maintain solvency on its current outlay path, the Japanese national pension system would have to raise pension taxes on basic wages from an already high 17.4 percent level to a staggering 34 percent by 2025.[iv] And none of these pension calculations takes into account the implications of financing health or home care for a more aged citizenry. Contemplating this prospect, one is tempted to invert Churchill: never before will so few have owed so much to so many.

Yet however ominous its impending fiscal burdens may appear, Japan is already an affluent country with an established system of universal retirement benefits. Apart from Hong Kong, no other East Asian locale can be similarly described.[v] Thus, the combination of relatively low levels of per capita income, incomplete pension coverage, and rapid population aging promises to produce economic and social troubles throughout the region.

China's prospective pension problem deserves special attention. By 2015, upwards of 120 million Chinese will be 65 or older, their numbers growing by roughly 7 percent (about 9 million persons) each year. Despite recent economic advances, China remains a low-income country afflicted by widespread poverty. According to World Bank estimates, China's real purchasing-power adjusted level of per capita output is lower than Sri Lanka's, and its distribution of income is less equal. Under any plausible pace of intervening material advance, hundreds of millions of Chinese will still live in crushing poverty in the year 2015. As one Chinese writer has observed, "Whereas the now-developed countries first [got] rich and then [got] old, China will first get old."[vi]

China still lacks any comprehensive official mechanism to provide for the needs of its oldest and most impoverished senior citizens. While China does manage several separate public pension schemes, nearly all of them are actuarially unsound. Worse, they cover only a small minority of China's populace—and generally skirt the remote, rural regions that constitute the heartland of China's poverty problem.[vii] How China will deal with this huge, rapidly growing, vulnerable, and currently unprotected sub-population is a grave, and as yet unanswered, question.

Rapid aging in East Asia is not only certain to create or exacerbate domestic tensions, but may also have far-reaching international consequences. Some recent studies have suggested that East Asia's remarkable savings boom during the past generation depended in part on demographic forces: rapid fertility declines among still-youthful populations permitted massive accumulations of surplus that fueled local engines of growth (which in turn helped transform the international economy as a whole).[viii] Conversely, some OECD modeling exercises indicate that, other things being equal, aging could drive down Japan's national savings rate by 8 or 9 percentage points between the turn of the century and the year 2030.

Demographic trends, of course, are not the only influence on a phenomenon as complex as national savings behavior, but they can be a big factor. In East Asia population trends will exert downward pressure on savings levels in coming decades, and the implications could be profound. By definition, a country's volume of savings equals domestic investment plus its international current account balance. If savings fall significantly and investment does not, a country can lurch from being a net exporter of capital to a net importer (as the United States did in the 1980s). As fate would have it, East Asia's two major economies—Japan and China—are both net exporters of capital today; both will face increasingly heavy demographic pressures on their savings rates in the years immediately ahead. Crude calculations illustrate the potential magnitude of the forces at play. Against current Japanese GDP, the OECD model's hypothetical 8 percentage point drop in the Japanese savings rate would make for about a $400 billion shift in domestic investment fund availability. But Japan's current account balance averaged just over an estimated $100 billion a year between 1991-96.

Do demographic trends therefore portend an inexorable reversal in Japanese and Chinese international capital positions, and increasing demands upon world capital markets by other aging East Asian populations? Not necessarily. Slower population growth might simultaneously reduce the demand for domestic investment. Some economists believe that demographic forces will depress East Asia's investment rates faster than its savings rates, thus *freeing up* capital funds for the rest of the world.[ix] This, however, remains a point of speculation. But all observers agree on two things: that absent macroeconomic policy changes and other domestic adjustments, rapid population aging in East Asia will have a major impact on international capital markets; and that such an impact could affect global interest rates, trade openness, and hence the outlook for the entire global economy.

Declining Manpower Availability

For most of the past half century, East Asian labor policies were preoccupied with accommodating a surging growth of local manpower. But East Asia's great wave of labor market entrants has crested. Overall, manpower availability will continue to expand between now and the year 2015, but the deceleration of population growth means that a region that once seemingly defined the image of surplus labor will be forced, increasingly, to confront a labor scarcity.

East Asian manpower availability trends are easy to summarize. In East Asia as a whole, the tempo of net additions to the working-age population—defined by convention as the 15-64 year-old group—exploded between the late 1950s and the early 1980s. In the second half of the 1950s, East Asia's total 15-64 age group grew by an estimated 34 million, at an annual pace of about 1.1 percent. In the first half of the 1980s, by contrast, its numbers rose over 130 million—almost four times as much—at about 2.8 percent per year.

That momentum has now been reversed. The absolute growth of working-age manpower in East Asia for the second half of the 1990s is estimated at about 90 million, down about a third from the early 1980s. The pace of growth has dropped in half, to about 1.4 percent a year. In Southeast Asia, the absolute increment of new potential workers is still on the rise, although the rate of growth has fallen. In Northeast Asia, both measures of manpower change are down sharply. In those intervening fifteen years, the absolute growth of working-age population is estimated to have dropped by half, and the pace of growth is believed to have fallen from 2.8 percent down to 1.1 percent a year.

Between now and 2015, the growth of potential manpower will decelerate still further. Internally generated increases in working-age population, now running at about 16 million a year, will likely fall below 5 million a year twenty years hence, making for a regional growth rate of only 0.3 percent annually. Indeed in Northeast Asia, the absolute size of the working-age populace will fall: for growth in Taiwan and the Korean Peninsula will be negligible; Japan's working-age population will be shrinking; and most significantly, China's manpower growth rate will have just turned negative. Within Southeast Asia, domestic manpower growth will have all but ceased in Singapore and Thailand by 2015. Virtually all of East Asia's regional manpower growth will be accruing from just three countries: Indonesia, the Philippines, and Vietnam.

The coming slowdown or actual decline of available manpower resources within East Asia will pose several challenges. Over the past generation, the formula for rapid economic growth for much of East Asia has relied heavily upon the mobilization of inputs—labor and capital—to speed development along. [x] In the decades ahead, however, new local supplies of labor will be less plentiful.

Population aging, for its part, is likely to constrain the volume of local savings available for capital accumulation. Thus, a new formula more reliant upon improvements in efficiency and productivity will have to be devised if rapid economic growth is to resume after recovery from the current downturn.

But declining manpower availability can itself complicate the task of productivity improvement. Improved labor productivity presumably requires higher skill levels and greater educational attainment for regional labor forces. The slowdown in manpower growth, however, may reduce the pace at which education-based skills percolate up into the working-age population. In almost every East Asian country, educated youth will be replacing their less well-educated elders at a far slower pace than in the recent past. In 1975, for example, youngsters in their late teens accounted for over a fifth of South Korea's working-age population; by 2015 they will make up less than a tenth of it. Much the same will be true in Thailand, Taiwan, and China. Even in Indonesia, the share of 15 to 19 year-olds within the working-age population is projected to drop from roughly a fifth in 1975 to barely an eighth by 2015. Barring major changes in the schooling and training process, such trends presage mounting difficulties in eliciting rapid education-based improvements in labor productivity.

East Asian governments, of course, will retain other options for augmenting manpower within their national economies, but a number of these appear to offer only marginal benefit and some carry potentially high costs. Encouraging temporary or permanent immigration, for example, can ease shortages of workers or of specific skills. Some smaller East Asian countries have already successfully employed this device: in recent years, as much as 15 percent of the workforce in both Singapore and Malaysia was composed of non-citizens. Larger East Asian countries, however, seem markedly less capable of either incorporating newcomers into their economy or assimilating them into their society. Japan, in particular, appears to be conspicuously unable to cope with large inflows of immigrants. In 1995 resident foreigners accounted for a lower share of national population in Japan than in seventeen West European nations for which comparable figures are available. Throughout the 1990s, moreover, fewer foreigners were being naturalized in Japan than in tiny, reclusive Switzerland.[xi] Yet, without new inflows of immigrants, Japan's "working-age" population will shrink by ten million over the next twenty years.

Promoting higher rates of labor force participation is another way to add to the domestic workforce. Compared with the United States, labor force participation rates for women are low in Hong Kong, Japan, Singapore, South Korea, and Taiwan. In all these places, however, fertility levels are already lower than in America; enticing more women into the paid workplace would likely reduce fertility still further. Hence, today's labor shortages would be relieved only at the cost of intensifying tomorrow's.

East Asia's Impending Bride Shortage

In ordinary human populations, the sex ratio for babies exhibits a strong natural predictability: around 105-107 boys are born for every 100 girls.[xii] Since the early 1980s, however, sex ratios at birth in much of East Asia have undergone a steady and eerie rise. By 1993, South Korea was registering nearly 116 boys for every 100 girls born. In 1995, a Chinese national sample population census counted over 118 boys under the age of 5 for every 100 little girls.[xiii] Unnaturally high sex ratios for infants and toddlers were also reported in the early 1990s for Hong Kong and Taiwan.

In South Korea, Taiwan, and Hong Kong, which have virtually complete demographic registration systems, the imbalances may be taken at face value. China's birth registration system, on the other hand, remains incomplete and part of the imbalance recorded in the 1995 sample census appears to have been a statistical artifact. But most of the reported imbalance is real. Recent U.S. Census Bureau reconstructions conclude that the actual male-to-female ratio for infants and toddlers in China for 1995 lay in the vicinity of 1.16 to 1.[xiv]

What accounts for these anomalous disparities? The gender imbalance emerging in China might be tied easily enough to the state's grotesque One Child Policy. Enforced through the apparatus of the State Family Planning Commission, it is a policy associated, among other things, with a resurgence of the age-old practice of female infanticide in the Chinese countryside.[xv] But in Hong Kong, Taiwan, and South Korea—places subject neither to involuntary family planning programs nor to rural infanticide—these odd sex ratios require a different explanation. It would appear that the conjuncture of sub-replacement fertility, strong son preference, and availability of sex-selective abortion accounts for these skewed ratios. Irrespective of income level, educational attainment, or the extent of political liberties available to the population in question, the problem is now in fact general to the region.

The striking imbalance portends a mismatch between prospective husbands and brides a generation hence—or even sooner. The Republic of Korea's National Statistical Office has calculated that the sex ratio for the country's marriage age population in 2010 will be over 123 men for every 100 women. Prospective trends for China are almost as striking: between 1995 and 2020, according to recent U.S. Census Bureau projections, the number of Chinese men in their early twenties for every 100 young women from the same cohort will increase from 105 to 116.

In the Chinese and Korean traditions, virtually all men and women who are able to marry ultimately do so. But the sexual arithmetic of the future will not abide such traditions. If there are 116 young Chinese men for every 100 young Chinese women, and if 2 percent of those young women never marry, then one out of every six of these young men must find a bride from outside of this cohort—or fail to continue his family line.

In theory, this problem could be finessed by marrying outside one's age cohort—for example, by finding a younger bride. This was, in fact, a traditional solution for less extreme manifestations of the same problem, and given East Asia's historic high-fertility age structure, the solution worked because each new cohort was larger than the one before. But given today's regimen of low and sub-replacement fertility, East Asia's rising youth groups will typically be *smaller* than the cohorts born just before them. Thus, if young men in Hong Kong, Taiwan, South Korea, and China solve their problem by marrying younger women from within their own society, they will only intensify the marriage crisis for those compatriots a few years their junior.

Unless bachelorhood suddenly becomes much more socially acceptable in East Asia, both China and South Korea are poised to experience an increasingly intense, and perhaps desperate, competition among young men for their country's limited supply of brides. What forms will this competition take, and how will these societies be affected by it? In South Korea, a minister of health and welfare "quoted a scholar saying that if the sex imbalance ratio exceeded 120 males to 100 females, riots may take place over the shortage of females for marriage."[xvi] (His pronouncement, one may note, was offered before the country's statistical authorities had estimated that the imbalance would actually exceed this threshold by 2010.) As for China, an essay in the journal *Renmin Luntan*, contemplating the country's future gender imbalance, predicted that such sexual crimes as "forced marriages, girls stolen for wives, bigamy, visiting prostitutes, rape, adultery . . . homosexuality . . . and weird sexual habits appear to be unavoidable."[xvii]

Such assessments sound overly dramatic. Nevertheless, the coming bride shortages will create extraordinary social strains, especially in China. In Hong Kong and Taiwan, the "next best" available solution to the shortage is obvious: import from abroad. To "clear the market" for marriages a decade or two hence, Hong Kong and Taiwan need only secure a combined total of about twenty thousand ethnic Chinese mail-order brides each year, hardly an unmanageable proposition for prospering societies so close to an enormous, and largely impoverished, Chinese hinterland.

Such a solution, of course, would make China's problem slightly worse, and it is already liable to be bad enough. It is China where the impending bride shortage looms largest and looks most intractable. China is too poor to count on securing mail-order ethnic Chinese brides, and for purely arithmetic reasons even a wealthy China could not hope to solve its problems in that way. By 2020 the surplus of China's males in their twenties will likely exceed the entire female population of Taiwan! Thus, barring a sudden and dramatic departure from existing customs, a significant fraction of China's young men will have to be socialized to forego marriage and parenthood.

For South Korea, the problem is less forbidding but more complex. Although the ROK has become a relatively affluent society, it already contains over three-fifths of the world's stock of ethnic Koreans. Matchmaking services in

Seoul are already contracting marriages with "Yanbian brides"—ethnic Koreans from communities in northeastern China. For the generation of young men who will begin entering the marriage market around 2010, however, South Korea faces a cumulative bride deficit of roughly one million women, and there are currently less than two million ethnic Koreans in all of China.[xviii] If these prospective suitors are to find ethnic Korean mates, their only viable solution is to look to North Korea.

For today's divided Korea, such a proposition is unthinkable. But even in the context of some future détente or unification on the Korean Peninsula, the problems posed by the South's hunger for Northern women would be unprecedented and, at the very least, indelicate. For the DPRK, the duty of protecting the country's women against outside "predators" might offer a powerful, primordial rationale for regime continuation. For a unified Korea, the process of healing and reconciliation might be aided in one way by North-South intermarriages—but it could also be set back by the social resentment of those in the North who are left behind (or left unmarriable).

Auguste Comte's aphorism that demography is destiny is much overused. With intelligent policies and reasoned behavior, it is usually possible to maximize opportunities and minimize risks inherent in population trends. But East Asia's mounting gender imbalances constitute a seemingly irremediable problem. It is a problem already in place, ready to unfold in the coming century. Unless sex ratios return to a more biologically natural balance, East Asia's future will be characterized by a new form of social distortion with unpredictable, and possibly far-reaching, consequences.

NOTES

[i] "East Asia" here refers to the land mass and islands demarcated by the Indian subcontinent, the ex-Soviet Central Asian Republics, and the Russian Far East.

[ii] UN, *World Population Prospects: The 1996 Revision* (New York: UN, 1998).

[iii] OECD, *Ageing in OECD Countries: A Critical Policy Challenge* (Paris: OECD, 1996), pp. 36, 83-4. Calculations are for 1994.

[iv] Kyodo News Service, December 5, 1995 (in English); reprinted in U.S. Foreign Broadcast Information Service (FBIS) as "Japan: Government Unveils Specific Options for Pension Reform", FBIS-EAS-97-339, December 5, 1997. See also Milton Ezrati, "Japan's Aging Economics", *Foreign Affairs* (May/June 1997); and David Hale, "Is Asia's High Growth Era Over?" *The National Interest* (Spring 1997).

[v] For information on East Asian pension and old age programs, see U.S. Social Security Administration, Office of Research, Evaluation and Statistics, *Social Security Programs Throughout the World*, 1997 (Washington, DC: U.S. Government Printing Office, 1997).

[vi] Lin Ying, "The Aging of the Population: A Severe Challenge", *Guangming Ribao*, April 6, 1996; translated as "PRC: Worsening Problem of Population Aging", FBIS-CHI-96-213, April 11, 1996.

[vii] For details, see Barry Friedman et al., "How Can China Provide Income Security for its Rapidly Aging Population?", *World Bank Policy Research Working Paper no. 1674* (October 1996); and Loraine A. West, "Pension Reform in China: Preparing for the Future", *Journal of Development Studies* 35:3.

[viii] See Kenneth Kang, "Why Did Koreans Save So Little, and Why Do They Now Save So Much?", *International Economic Journal* (Winter 1994); Matthew Higgins and Jeffrey G. Williamson, "Age

Structure Dynamics in East Asia and Dependence on Foreign Capital", *Population and Development Review* (June 1997); and Andrew Mason, "Will Population Change Sustain the Asian Economic Miracle?", *Asia-Pacific Issues*, paper no. 33 (October 1997).

[ix] See Williamson, "Age Structure Dynamics in East Asia and Dependence on Foreign Capital."

[x] For an extreme formulation of the problem, see Paul Krugman's "The Myth Of Asia's Miracle", *Foreign Affairs* (November/December 1994).

[xi] OECD, *Trends in International Migration*, 1995 (Paris: OECD, 1996), pp. 60, 123. Roughly half of the registered "foreigners" in Japan are ethnic Koreans whose forebears have resided in the country for up to four generations—a fact that speaks for itself.

[xii] Ansley Coale and Judith Banister, "Five Decades of Missing Females in China", *Demography* (August 1994), p. 459.

[xiii] Monica Das Gupta, "Missing Girls In China, South Korea, And India: Causes And Policy Implications", *Harvard Center for Population and Development Studies Working Paper Series*, no. 98.03 (March 1998), p. 2.

[xiv] Unpublished worksheet, U.S. Bureau of the Census, International Programs Center, China Branch; transmitted to the author March 1997. I am grateful to Dr. Loraine A. West, chief of the Census Bureau's China Branch, for sharing this research with me.

[xv] See John S. Aird, *Slaughter of The Innocents: Coercive Birth Control In China* (Washington, DC: AEI Press, 1990).

[xvi] *Korea Times*, January 29, 1995, p. 1; reprinted as "Government Planning Review of Population Policy", FBIS-EAS-95-019, January 29, 1995.

[xvii] *Renmin Luntan*, November 8, 1997, pp. 50-1; translated as "China: Female-Male Population Discrepancy", FBIS-CHI-98-042, February 11, 1998.

[xviii] The ROK bride deficit is calculated on the basis of U.S. Census Bureau projections for the year 2010. Numbers on the Korean population in China are taken from ROK National Statistical Office, *International Statistical Yearbook* 1997, p. 85.

19

City of Bad Omens

Robert Elegant[*]

As every schoolboy would once have known, traditionally the Chinese have believed that a dynasty reigns because it has been vouchsafed divine approval—the Mandate of Heaven. According to this belief, extensive natural or man-made catastrophes demonstrate that the Mandate has been revoked, and that the reigning dynasty will soon fall. Natural catastrophes began in Hong Kong the instant the regime appointed by Beijing to succeed British rule took office in July 1997.

It rained continually for months. Landslides swept away buildings and imperiled lives. The people slipped into dejection under the seemingly endless rain pelting down day after day. The business slump had already begun and was soon to dip—and then plunge—further. But initially it was the weather, not the economy, that depressed the people of the new Special Administrative Region (SAR) of the People's Republic of China.

That was not a good start. Neither was it the end.

A few weeks later, Hong Kong was afflicted by a virulent influenza carried by a virus that could leap from its normal habitat in chickens or ducks to human beings. Naturally fearful, the government ordered millions of fowl destroyed. The mass slaughter, which all but impoverished poultry breeders and traders, was not carried out adeptly. Stray dogs and cats gnawed and clawed at black refuse sacks containing dead chickens, as well as some that were not quite dead. Highly

---

[*] Robert Elegant, who speaks and reads Mandarin, has written extensively on China in novels and nonfiction for almost five decades. He lived in Hong Kong for twenty years.

This essay first appeared in *The National Interest*, No. 53 (Fall 1998).

efficient under British control, the Hong Kong Civil Service made a mess of that essential execution under Tung Chee-hwa's aegis.

Still another natural disaster struck early in 1998. Hong Kong's inshore fishing had already been curtailed by noisome pollution and by competition from Japanese, Taiwanese, and Korean boats. Nonetheless, Hong Kong's trawlers and motorized junks were still finding good catches not too far away. Then came the "red tide", a flood of scarlet algae that poisoned innumerable fish and imperiled the industry. Within two months fifty to sixty people were struck by the virulent enterovirus called Taiwan flu.

A man-made catastrophe, however, was to all but eclipse nature's malign deeds. A new airport some twenty miles away was built at great speed to replace the dangerous and inadequate old airport at the center of the city. Costing more than $20 billion, it is, after Japan's Kansai Airport, the most expensive in the world. Originally scheduled to begin operations in mid-July, it was prematurely commissioned so that President Jiang Zemin could be the first traveler to set down—and thus mark the first anniversary of Hong Kong's acquisition by China. Opened to normal traffic on July 6, it was so spectacularly incompetent that air cargo to and from Hong Kong had to be suspended for more than a week, at a cost of around half a billion U.S. dollars. Even more gravely, given the nearly simultaneous opening of competing new airports nearby in Macao and Guangzhou, the dismal spectacle severely undermined Hong Kong's reputation for brisk efficiency.

What, then, Hong Kong's people asked, of the Mandate of Heaven? What indeed. To see ahead, let us start by looking back.

In the fifth decade of the nineteenth century, Britain took the island called Hong Kong from China at gunpoint. In the last decade of the twentieth century, China took back from Britain, by *force majeure* if not directly at gunpoint, not only Hong Kong Island but the small Kowloon Peninsula, which had been seized later, and the broad New Territories, which had been leased for ninety-nine years in 1898. In none of these exchanges was the indigenous population asked its view. Nor were its interests seriously considered. In each case, too, the transfer of sovereignty ran counter to the wishes of the majority of the inhabitants.

The few thousand part-time fishermen part-time pirates using the island in 1840 preferred the nominal rule of the Manchu Dynasty in far distant Beijing to the meddling British. In 1898 the tens of thousands in the farming villages of the New Territories were not eager to exchange ineffectual Chinese rule for British intrusiveness. In 1997 the well over six million Chinese living in the Crown Colony of Hong Kong were happy with the highly effective and low taxing British administration that had made Hong Kong prosperous even by the standards of economically buoyant Asia. They also cherished civil order based upon general consent rather than coercion, as well as a degree of intellectual freedom and expression rare in authoritarian Asia. Opinion polls, and the belated introduction of a measure of democracy by the Colony's last British governor, affirmed as much. In 1995 the people of Hong Kong elected legislators sworn to resist communist tyranny. Three years later they humiliated Beijing's candidates in the first legislative election under China's sovereignty, indeed the first free election on mainland Chinese soil since the communists established the People's Republic in 1949.

Most communist leaders would have preferred a Hong Kong that continued to serve their economic interests by providing financial services and large sums of foreign money. But, above all, they wanted a Hong Kong that would not imperil their hold on power through its constant example of a more relaxed, more free, and much happier political entity next door to the mainland they ruled so harshly. Still another imperative impelled Beijing to demand the return of all Hong Kong when the lease on the New Territories expired on June 30, 1997. The sting of the humiliation and depredation inflicted on China by foreign powers from the early nineteenth century onward could only be salved by reclaiming every inch of territory that had once been Chinese. Aside from Hong Kong, minuscule Portuguese Macau was the only other foreign enclave remaining. Since it was effectively under Chinese rule already, formal reversion was less pressing. Taiwan presented a different kind of challenge—already under Chinese rule but not Beijing's suzerainty.

Hong Kong, the very first and the most conspicuous of the territories Britain had stolen from China, *had* to be reclaimed to expunge the shame of the past. And it had to be reclaimed no later than July 1, 1997, lest it appear that Beijing was truckling to London.

A very senior and very influential British diplomat assured me years ago that Hong Kong would not suffer as a result of the disorder he correctly foresaw in China, but would remain prosperous and happy after it came under Chinese rule. He was wrong. The mood in Hong Kong is now sour and pessimistic.

Such diplomats—and many in the business community—still insist that such dejection is largely the fault of Chris Patten, the last British governor, who was not one of them but a politician. Patten, they say, aroused false expectations by introducing a measure of democracy. But, they contend, the autocratic rule of previous London-appointed governors had nurtured a populace that was contented, docile, and "not interested in politics." If Patten had not interfered, the argument continues, Hong Kong would today still be a happy land. The discontent and political demonstrations that regularly test the authority of the Beijing-appointed government of the SAR would never have arisen.

Besides, this school of thought would add, the depressed state of Hong Kong today is due not to Beijing's rule, but to the fiscal crisis that has shaken all of East Asia from South Korea to Indonesia. Hong Kong's blues are economic, nothing more. That contention, however, is only half of a half-truth.

The Hong Kong economy was depressed even before the Asian downslide. The proprietor of a shop selling linen and embroidered garments replied glumly when I asked how his business was doing, "I haven't made the smallest profit since July 1st '97. Just losses all the way—and getting worse. I can't even cover the rent." A campaign to reduce greatly inflated business rents by 40 percent has been overtaken by events. But he added, "Forty percent reduction wouldn't be enough. I'd still go broke."

The old Pedder Building houses factory outlets and other cut-rate shops. All now display signs offering even greater bargains, which literally translated from the Chinese is "Great Price Cutting." By changing one of the three words, one shop has made its come-on read "Great Bloodletting! Eighty percent off!"

For the beginning of Hong Kong's economic stagnation the fall in tourism is largely to blame. The number of visitors has fallen by more than 50 percent since July 1, 1997, a slump caused by both the change in Hong Kong's political status—as witness the many empty hotel rooms the week of the handover—and by the Asian recession, which is keeping many Asian tourists at home.

But general dejection also reflects a peculiar Hong Kong psychology. Most people still repose greater confidence in Great Britain—now a small, far away, third-rate power entangled with the European Union—than they do in their presumed motherland, a colossal resurgent power on their doorstep. A majority of Hong Kong's people are either themselves refugees from People's China or descendants of refugees. During the decades I lived in the Crown Colony I found it hard to discuss China with them. They automatically disbelieved Beijing's every statement and discounted its every achievement. Their fixed conviction: "The communists only know how to lie!"

Manifestly, and however much they look alike, the people of Hong Kong are not only different from their presumed compatriots across the border, but are alienated from China. Once, in Shanghai, I fell into conversation with two men whose features were wholly Chinese, although their clothing, their confident demeanor, their command of English, and their obvious prosperity set them apart. Both were from Hong Kong. I realized after exchanging a few sentences that they were referring to the Shanghailanders as "they" and to the three of us from Hong Kong as "we", regardless of my not being Chinese at all.

In an oddly upside-down way, I recently encountered similar scorn. The common language of Hong Kong is a Chinese dialect called Cantonese. To my shame my Cantonese is poor despite all the time I've spent in Hong Kong. I therefore spoke to a non-English speaking salesman in Mandarin, which is known as *putunghua*, the common language of all China. He retorted in Cantonese, "Don't talk that language to me. I'm not Chinese. I'm a Hong Kong man!"

The alienation, all but antagonism, between mainlanders and Hong Kong people has been aggravated rather than allayed by the Colony's transformation into an integral part of the People's Republic. Immigration policy is one reason. The border between the New Territories and Guangdong Province was for five decades closely guarded to keep out "illegal immigrants", that is, refugees from China. Yet many slipped across, in part because the heart of the largely British-officered Hong Kong Police was not really in the assignment. Today the border is more closely watched, and much less permeable. Beijing does not want an influx of mainlanders seeking a better living standard and greater freedom in Hong Kong. Above all, Beijing does not want large numbers of mainlanders visiting Hong Kong and returning to compare conditions there with those at home.

Before the transfer, tourists and businessmen from China were readily distinguishable from the locals. Their clothing was shabby and badly cut, and their complexions were rather muddy. They also tended to be uninhibited, released, albeit temporarily, from harsh discipline at home. Even in free, easy, and very rude Hong Kong, the mainlanders were notably uncouth.

They still are. Looking for a particular trinket in one of the many gold shops that line Queens Road Central, I was jostled by twenty or so men and women who—even had they not been wearing plastic tags reading *Guangdong Province Tour Group*—were obviously mainlanders by their clothes, complexions, and behavior. All could afford the small solid gold objects they were eagerly pricing—and buying. Gold does not change in value as abruptly as fundamental situations can change in unstable China.

The group was shepherded by three older men wearing dark blue, high-buttoned Mao Tse-tung tunics, which are rarely seen even in China nowadays. When I began talking with a young man, one of those shepherds gently shouldered me aside. He was clearly not worried about my learning more about conditions in China; I can go to Guangdong and talk freely with most people any day. Although the authorities there would like to stop such spontaneous conversations, they cannot do so entirely without affecting trade, investment, and tourism, all big money spinners. Rather, it appeared, the man in the Mao suit was anxious to prevent his charges from learning more about Hong Kong. Still, he could not keep them from seeing prosperity unrivaled anywhere in mainland China.

Despite recession, Hong Kong glitters with riches and throbs with commerce compared even with go-ahead Shanghai. But Hong Kong is now suffering a recession that is sliding fast toward a depression. The woes are by no means limited to the merchants and hoteliers who depend on tourist dollars. Everyone is singing the blues, and with good reason. By early August it had become clear that early predictions of economic trouble were too optimistic. Data showed that the economy had shrunk 2.8 percent in the first quarter of 1998, and was estimated to contract a full 3 percent in the second quarter. Release of that data, along with news that Hong Kong's major banks were in much worse shape than anticipated, sent stocks tumbling—which in turn completed the circle of economic gloom.

There are less transient explanations for Hong Kong's troubles as well. Little is manufactured there today. Almost all industry has migrated to China itself, lured by much lower wages and by greater latitude regarding working conditions. The chief money-maker in the SAR is money itself. Investment, insurance, banking, finance, and speculation bring in the big bucks. But employment in finance has fallen some 20 percent recently, and those who hang on to their jobs have been taking swinging salary cuts.

Rents for luxury flats have not yet dropped decisively, but they are sagging. Domestic rents are faltering, instead of rising 20 to 40 percent on each renewal of a lease, as they did only recently. Firms that happily paid $12,000 a month or more for an employee's flat are now radically reducing such benefits or cutting them off entirely. Former beneficiaries of such largesse are looking for cheaper housing on offshore islands like little Lama, which had been virtually a hippie colony—by staid Hong Kong standards at least.

Overall property values are also falling, particularly commercial property. Hong Kong's formerly buoyant economy floated on inflated property values that allowed low taxation, which in turn attracted investment and the Asian headquarters of foreign firms. Taxes have so far only increased slightly. But the pledge by Tung Chee-hwa, Beijing's appointed chief executive, to build eighty-five thousand new flats for the underprivileged in each of the next three years, however meritorious, will certainly drive down rents and will probably require tax increases.

Good for the less well off *if* it really happens, the promised expansion of housing will not be good for the economy in general. Property values are already down 30 to 40 percent from their peak, and, to repeat, overvalued property has been the foundation of Hong Kong's prosperity. In order to prevent further steep decline, all sale of government land has now been suspended until March 1999. The government is the sole landowner in Hong Kong, leasing land to companies for extended periods of time, like 99 years, at very high prices. Therefore, high land prices underwrite low taxes, while declining land prices make higher taxes necessary.

All local trade is down for firms, except of course for essentials like food and funerals. Newspaper and magazine advertising has fallen sharply. And so it goes: a long, slow, funereal drumbeat. Optimists contend that the present shakedown will make Hong Kong much more competitive when the general Asian recovery occurs. That recovery is inevitable, though none can say when it will start or how far it will go. It will, of course, help Hong Kong greatly. But it will not heal the territory's fundamental malaise, for non-economic woes beset the government of the Special Administrative Region.

The heart of government in Hong Kong is its old Civil Service. Stripped of all but a few of its British members, it is, first, encumbered with an appointed executive arm that is inexperienced, impractical, and slavishly obedient to Beijing despite the pledge that "Hong Kong people will rule Hong Kong!" Second, it is encumbered with a timid judiciary that has ruled itself out of cases presenting issues that could affront Beijing; the highest court is specifically forbidden to try any case involving politics, which can mean anything Beijing wants it to mean. Third, Hong Kong was encumbered with an appointed legislature that is hardly representative—and is now encumbered with a legislature "elected" under various circumstances that prevent true representation.

Tung Chee-hwa and his sycophants have repeatedly asserted that Hong Kong enjoys real democracy for the first time, because the chief executive is no longer a governor appointed by Britain. He might just as well say, "Hong Kong people aren't interested in politics, only in making money!" That reiterated justification long comforted those Britons who felt a twinge of guilt at the arbitrary, indeed despotic, way Britain ruled the Crown Colony for most of its 155 years. By and large, the virtually absolute British governors were benevolent, but they were still despots.

The lack of interest in politics was true—but chiefly for a small minority of the population, the well-to-do. The rich really didn't—and still don't—care who ruled Hong Kong or how it was ruled, as long as they were free to make money. They *were* left free, virtually untethered by law, for the Colony practiced almost perfect economic laissez faire—and profited greatly thereby. However, the efficient execution of the vital functions of government, which said government reserved to itself, and the impartial administration of British justice provided by independent courts, were essential to Hong Kong's growth. Within that secure framework the ingenious, hardworking, and risk-taking native Chinese population transformed that "barren rock with hardly a house on it" described by Lord Palmerston in 1840.

All the people were interested in making a good living; the mass of the people was also vitally interested in practical politics. The emerging middle class, the managers, the professionals, the shopkeepers, the artisans, and even the workers had a stake in basic fairness, stability, and lawfulness. It was precisely their vital concern with politics that in 1989 first alarmed Beijing, which in its doctrinaire ignorance had thought the people of Hong Kong little different from the people of China.

Ironically, the event that put Beijing on its guard demonstrated strong sympathy between the people of Hong Kong and the mainlanders whose interest in democratic politics Beijing sought to crush. In 1989 Hong Kong was profoundly moved by the June 4 massacre in Beijing of students and workers campaigning for democracy, and by the persecution of all dissidents, however mild, throughout China. A million men and women gathered in a candle-lit vigil in Hong Kong. Such vigils on a somewhat smaller scale have occurred every year since, including 1998. Hong Kong was until July 1, 1997 a haven for refugee dissidents and provided funds for their movement. Naturally, Beijing is determined to crush that independent spirit.

The people of the Crown Colony of Hong Kong again proved themselves vitally interested in politics in 1995, when the second legislative election in its history took place. Twenty of the sixty seats were to be filled by direct public election, twenty by the governor's direct appointment, and twenty by "functional constituencies", which meant groups demarcated by occupation. That election was a further step toward democracy, not a great leap. Governor Patten, who would have liked a far more democratic election, was constrained by the diplomats' prior agreement with Beijing that only a third of the legislators would be directly elected.

Still, some 35 percent of those eligible came to the polls—and voted overwhelmingly for the Democratic Party of barrister Martin Lee. He stood for increased democracy and for vigorous resistance to the encroachment on freedom that he foresaw when Beijing took power in July 1997. The Democrats could do nothing about the handover, of course. That was an irreversible *fait accompli*. But the elections did show Beijing that most of the people did not want Chinese rule.

That election and the legislature it produced were the centerpiece of the democratic innovations introduced by Patten. Those limited changes evoked the vehement protests of the Foreign Office clique dedicated to serene Sino-British relations at any cost. Those protests were echoed by both British and Chinese *taipans*—the big businessmen who have accumulated hundreds of millions, even billions, of dollars. Among the paradoxes of Hong Kong, the rich are for the communists, while the masses definitely are not.

Both the Foreign Office and the *taipans* are now busily chipping away at Patten's solid reputation in retaliation for his reforms, which they still contend have impeded Hong Kong's chief business—which is, of course, business. Both those groups had wanted a smooth transfer of sovereignty because they believed their own interests were best served by truckling to Beijing. Neither the diplomats nor the *taipans* could imagine that Beijing's suzerainty would signal an economic decline. They believed—or professed to believe—that the mass of Hong Kong's people would be just as well—if not better—off under Chinese rule. Yet from the very beginning the new regime was dogged by unforeseen problems that have severely impeded both general economic development and corporate profits.

The first was simply a problem of credibility. Even before the takeover, the government-to-be had declared the 1995 legislative election invalid and had appointed its own legislature in waiting. An elaborate and intricate process handpicked committees to select committees to choose committees that finally elected the legislators. That complicated mummery convinced no one that the legislature that took its seats on July 1, 1997 reflected the popular will. No more did the layers of committees that selected Tung Chee-hwa as chief executive carry conviction. Everyone knew that Tung had been chosen by President Jiang Zemin, who confirmed his choice by ostentatiously shaking hands with Tung under the television lenses long before the charade of selection by committee began. Tung was selected because he would do Beijing's bidding without question. He was, after all, indebted to Beijing. Having mismanaged his father's shipping fleet into near bankruptcy, he had survived by borrowing some $250 million through friends of the regime.

Nor did the procedure for electing a new legislature in May 1998 enhance the regime's democratic credibility. There were still sixty seats, and again only twenty were filled by popular election. Of the rest twenty were appointed directly, as under Patten's reforms, because the Sino-British agreement provided for such a procedure. Twenty were again chosen by "functional constituencies", associations of, say, gold traders, doctors, bankers, lawyers, and the like. So too had they been under Patten, because the Basic Law drafted by Beijing and the Foreign Office so provided. This echo of Benito Mussolini's corporate state was either not recognized as such or else failed to disturb the architects of the new Hong Kong, which was to be ruled by democracy Beijing style—essentially a more efficient and more invasive authoritarianism than Mussolini's fascism.

Nonetheless, the first legislative election after the handover was a stunning repudiation of Tung Chee-hwa's reign. In torrents of rain and with winds of near typhoon violence, a remarkable 53 percent of the general electorate turned out to choose the twenty legislators representing the general public. They returned fifteen candidates from Martin Lee's Democratic Party and its close allies. The remaining five came from the Democratic Alliance for the Betterment of Hong Kong, a mildly leftist, old-line labor party that does not truckle to Beijing. Although the voting pattern had been rigged to favor pro-Beijing candidates, not a single one was elected by the general public. In the functional constituencies, five more Democrats were chosen, although the number eligible to vote by occupation had been reduced from some 1.15 million to less than 150,000.

It was a smashing victory for the advocates of democracy and independence, a stinging repudiation of Tung and his puppet-masters in Beijing. In immediate practical terms it was something less. A majority of the sixty legislators will vote as Beijing directs, for the twenty appointed directly and the functional constituencies, largely the realm of big business, returned some fifteen pro-Beijing candidates. Martin Lee is now all but literally the leader of the opposition in communist China, since nowhere else in the sprawling nation is any opposition party tolerated. Of course, the SAR will continue to run as Beijing directs. But a spark of democracy will glow in Hong Kong until either Beijing stamps it out or until the Chinese capital itself changes even more radically than it is changing at the moment.

In the year 2002 a committee of eight hundred is to select the next chief executive, either Tung Chee-hwa or another equally subservient to Beijing. In 2007 the successive chief executive is supposed to be popularly elected, although Tung has already said he feels that may be too soon. He has also decried Hong Kong's excessive Westernization and restricted teaching in English, a measure originally planned by the outgoing colonial administration to facilitate the Sinicization of Hong Kong. Yet switching to Cantonese as the language of instruction is downright silly. Not only will graduates of the newly restricted schools not have mastered the international language, English, but they won't even be adept in Mandarin, China's common national language.

The press, radio, and television are already constrained, mostly the result of the fears of reporters and editors under pressure from proprietors. Such self-censorship is probably more effective that outright censorship, since it knows no bounds. Direct censorship has not been imposed, but the Chinese-language media are harassed. The frankly oppositionist *Apple Daily* has been charged with violations of employment laws and other non-journalistic offenses. The English-language press, the barometer by which most outside observers assess Hong Kong's political weather, is still reasonably free of interference. But only a few regularly read the English press and they are predominantly foreigners who are mostly transients and thus don't really matter. But Radio Television Hong Kong, an editorially autonomous public entity rather like the BBC which broadcasts in English and Cantonese, has been fiercely attacked for failing to present government policy "positively." Hong Kong's new regime really cannot see the difference between a quasi-independent broadcasting service financed by the government and a wholly government-controlled service—no more than can Beijing.

Deng Xiaoping, China's paramount leader who died a few months before the handover he had enforced, made several promises to Hong Kong to sweeten the pill. He did so in part to save British face by fostering the illusion that London had successfully negotiated modifications of Beijing's original conditions, for the benefit of the people of Hong Kong. But his chief purpose was to reassure the people so that they would, as he advised, "set their hearts at ease." Deng did not want a frightened or agitated populace that would reduce a prosperous SAR's ability to spin money for the People's Republic.

Despite Deng's reassurances, tens of thousands of the emerging middle class fled each year from 1984 onwards. More would have left had they been able. They were quite right to doubt Deng's promises.

The paramount leader had guaranteed that Hong Kong's social and economic system would not change for at least fifty years after the handover. He had encapsulated his guarantees in a simple formula: *One country, two systems*. However, Tung Chee-hwa recently declared that whenever the two principles clashed, *one country* took absolute precedence over *two systems*. The principles clashed repeatedly during the first year of Tung's term. He further assured his own followers that dissenting voices on Radio Television Hong Kong would be silenced—all in good time. So would public demonstrations protesting government actions.

Such demonstrations, reasonably free at the beginning, are now much restricted. Four men have been convicted for demonstrating, two of them for defacing the scarlet flag of the People's Republic of China. Neither defacing the Union Jack nor public protest was an offense under "oppressive colonial rule." Beyond doubt, Beijing is gradually reducing Hong Kong to authoritarian servitude under cover of apparently moderate policies. We should have expected nothing else. Hong Kong cannot be allowed to become a threat to Beijing's absolutist rule of China by its example of a happier people under a more lenient government. But absolutism will be enforced "slowly, slowly", as Tung observed of the ultimate suppression of the media, electoral rights, and all freedom of expression.

Foreign influence has slowed that inexorable process—and could slow it further. Paramount is American influence, since President Jiang Zemin needs the public approval of the Clinton administration to enhance his personal prestige. American goodwill is also vital to China's industrial progress. But such influence can only slow the process. It cannot stop the smothering of the SAR's transient freedoms and residual prosperity. It cannot stop corruption either.

Tung's administration has been further marred by a general rise in crime, as well as public and private corruption. To be fair, armed robbery and bribery were already increasing under Patten's administration. Both were fueled then, as they are now, by the virtual immunity from prosecution of Beijing-owned corporations and by the alliance between the criminal secret societies of Hong Kong—the so-called Triads—and the officers of the People's Liberation Army in the nearby city of Guangzhou (the old Canton). The military have, among other transactions, sent thugs from Canton to Hong Kong to carry out crimes the Triads wished to subcontract.

Crime with roots in China is evidently widespread. The Independent Commission Against Corruption (ICAC), founded under the British to fight corruption originally in the police force, refuses to discuss cross-border issues. But then, the commission refuses to discuss any matter regarding its crusade, preferring instead to issue self-congratulatory press releases. Nonetheless, the ICAC is now much larger than it was several decades earlier—and it is still growing. There is self-evidently a need to fight growing corruption.

The ICAC's reticence may also be due to the fear the servants of the new regime feel regarding any revelation of any sensitive matter. And many matters are now sensitive that were not so under even the most discreet British governor. It is also whispered among those in the know that the Civil Service itself has now been corrupted, encouraged by the example of totally corrupt Chinese officialdom. Yet those who talk of such bribery may only believe they are in the know. Nonetheless, the fact that they believe and repeat such rumors is in itself significant. To say the least, the Beijing-appointed regime and its servants are not well regarded.

In China itself, the absolute authority of the Communist Party center is being continually undermined by the personal economic interests and the assertiveness of both officials and entrepreneurs in the provinces amid continuing economic liberalization. And, of course, Hong Kong money and expertise are vital to China's continuing economic development. Martin Lee of the Democratic Party therefore avows long-term optimism, perhaps to counter unavoidable short-term pessimism regarding the future of Hong Kong. He believes the changes already effected on the mainland by Hong Kong's influence will grow greater and will in time make the rulers of China less tyrannical.

He could be right. No one can deny the sweeping changes occurring in China, or the daunting dilemma its rulers face. As already noted, if they are to remain in power, they must deliver the material goods. Whipped up patriotism and the artificial idealism of Marxism-Leninism-Maoism are wasting assets, and even general suppression of all freedoms and the threat of "reform through labor"—or still harsher punishment like the constant drumfire of executions for crimes that are often political—can no longer keep the masses in line. Civilian officials as well as army officers are now members, even leaders, of extra-legal secret societies, and every new measure of economic liberalization effectively undermines the authority of the central leadership. Beijing is extending such relaxation while simultaneously intensifying ideology-based civil discipline. Such a self-contradictory policy simply will not work for long.

Nonetheless, the prospect of China's changing so radically as to affect its rule of Hong Kong benignly is still far distant. Rather, and paradoxically, the need to exercise autocratic control over the SAR may well grow as Beijing tries in vain to beat out the wildfires of domestic discontent. Beside China, Hong Kong is smaller than a mouse beside an elephant. But ideas and values have proved themselves more powerful than empires in the past. Presumably a mouse could in time induce an elephant to eat cheese if it were not trampled in the interim. But how long would it take?

While we wait to find out, the Communist Party closes its hand ever tighter on the Special Administrative Region of Hong Kong. Relentlessly, albeit gradually, the people are being deprived of the opportunity, the objective education, and, above all, the dignity and freedom they once enjoyed. Such an erosion of human rights is reason enough to deplore the present trend and to fear for Hong Kong's future.

Part 4

Military-Security Issues

20

The Stability of Deterrence
in the Taiwan Strait

*Robert S. Ross**

The case can and has been made that the foreign policy of the Bush Administration differs little from that of its predecessor. Only the rhetoric has changed, it has been claimed, and even some of that is falling back into old patterns—with regard to North Korea, the Arab-Israeli conflict, and what to do about Ba'athi Iraq.[i] Remaining differences of rhetoric, it is said, mask essential continuity. The Bush Administration carries a more unilateralist tone over a range of issues—the Kyoto Protocol, the International Criminal Court, proposals to verify the 1972 Biological Weapons Treaty and control the flow of small arms—but it is not clear that the Clinton Administration was really more eager to press ahead on such matters, or that a Gore Administration would have been. Even on missile defense and the ABM treaty, the differences between Clinton and Bush may end up being quite minor when all is said and done.

One could argue the general case for the persistence of policy either way, but in one specific area there is a clear difference, and not just a rhetorical one. It concerns policy toward China.

When President Bush took office, he telephoned every major world leader but Chinese President Jiang Zemin. The Bush Administration then reportedly set

*Robert S. Ross is professor of political science at Boston College, an associate at the John King Fairbank Center for East Asian Research, Harvard University, and co-editor of *Re-examining the Cold War: U.S.-China Diplomacy, 1954–1973* (Harvard University Press. 2001).

This essay first appeared in *The National Interest*, No. 65 (Fall 2001).

about revising the SIOP (Strategic Integrated Operating Plan) to target more U.S. nuclear missiles against China. It has given serious consideration to prioritizing preparation for conventional war in East Asia against China and has promoted enhanced strategic cooperation with India and Japan. It has encouraged Japan to loosen its restraints on a more active regional military presence and it has proposed development with U.S. allies South Korea, Japan and Australia of a "regional" dialogue. It has also stressed cooperation with Russia on missile defense seemingly at the expense of China. It has defined the "no foreign-made products" stricture for the U.S. military to mean essentially no Chinese-made products and curtailed Pentagon contacts with the Chinese military. It has reversed a twenty-year U.S. policy by agreeing to sell submarines to Taiwan. It has also allowed high-profile visits to the United States by Taiwanese President Chen Shui-bian and the Dalai Lama. Withal, the administration has not appointed a specialist on China to any senior position in the government.

Such a confrontational posture toward China cannot be explained as a response to the downing of a U.S. EP-3 surveillance plane and the detention of its crew for eleven days. The trend predates the incident and, despite Secretary of State Colin Powell's constructive visit to Beijing in July, has continued since. Rather, the explanation seems to lie in the administration's sympathy for Taiwan, its dour assessment of Chinese intentions and the prospect, in its view, of heightened instability in the Taiwan Strait. There is more than just talk going on: the administration is pursuing broad coordination with Taiwan's military to enable cooperation in a possible war with China, that coordination being an objective of many Republican defense and foreign policy specialists and members of Congress since 1996.

This is a well-intended but misguided effort. Such cooperation will not make Taiwan more secure, the United States more effective militarily or the deterrence of war more assured. Should the Bush Administration nevertheless continue this policy, it will eventually elicit mainland opposition because it threatens to reverse the essence of the post-1979 U.S.-China strategic understanding on Taiwan. It is worth emphasizing the core of that understanding from the Chinese point of view, to which many American analysts have somehow become oblivious.

From the days of the Korean War until 1979, Taiwan loomed in Beijing's eyes as a kind of American "Cuba." In other words, Beijing believed that the U.S. presence on Taiwan enabled the United States to threaten China's borders directly, just as the United States believed that the Soviet presence in Cuba threatened U.S. security from the early 1960s to the end of the Cold War. Indeed, in 1954 Washington and Taipei signed the U.S.-Republic of China Mutual Defense Treaty, which led to the U.S. deployment of advanced aircraft and nuclear-capable missiles on the island. But in 1979, when Washington normalized diplomatic relations with Beijing, it agreed to terminate the 1954 treaty with Taiwan and to withdraw its military presence from the island, thus satisfying China's demand that the United States cease using Taiwan to threaten Chinese security.

If Chinese leaders believe, in their bedrock strategic realism, that the United States is out to reverse the 1979 understanding, they have a full menu of riposte at their disposal. They can engage in nerve-wracking saber-rattling in the Taiwan Strait in order to heighten regional tension and political and economic instability on Taiwan. They can reduce cooperation on the Korean peninsula and renew missile proliferation to Pakistan and the Middle East. They can also impose costly sanctions against major U.S. export industries dependent on the Chinese market, such as Boeing.

In the face of such potential trouble, the Bush Administration seems to believe that if it firmly wields U.S. power, it can command Chinese accommodation to U.S. policy initiatives. But this repeats the old mistakes of several new entrants to the White House. The Carter, Reagan and Clinton Administrations (but not the first Bush Administration) each made the same error and encountered a level of Chinese resistance that required them to move back to the policy of their predecessors. Each discovered, too, that their predecessor's policy was compatible with U.S. interests in both defending Taiwan and cooperating with China.

The Bush Administration should maintain essential policy continuity with its predecessors simply because there is no good reason for any other course. There is, in effect, a firm triangle of military deterrence and political dissuasion at work: China is deterred from the use of force against Taiwan so long as American power and interests are engaged there and Taiwan does not declare independence; Taiwan is deterred from declaring independence due to credible Chinese threats to use limited but politically significant force in the face of any such declaration; and the United States is—or ought to be—dissuaded from tampering with this situation because it enables Washington to defend Taiwan, deal with China as necessary and prudent on a range of issues, and minimize the possibility of war through miscalculation. Moreover, the effective deterrence and mutual interests in stability that are characteristic of this triangle are conditions bound to last well into the 21st century.

Why China Wants Peace with Taiwan

China has three sets of interests in Taiwan—concerning security, nationalism and domestic politics—each of which provides a powerful incentive for Chinese leaders to exercise influence over the Taiwan issue. Together, these interests ensure that the mainland would be prepared to use force to reverse seriously unwelcome trends in Taiwan's international role.

China's security interest in the Taiwan issue reflects the concern of all states for secure borders. Located eighty miles from the Chinese coast, Taiwan's enduring strategic importance to China is obvious. Should any great power establish a strategic presence on Taiwan, it could use the island to challenge Chinese coastal security. This is not just a theoretical matter as far as the Chinese leadership is concerned. Japan occupied Taiwan (then called Formosa in the English-speaking world) from 1895 until 1945. The United States was ensconced militarily on Taiwan from at least 1954 until the U.S.-China agreement to normalize diplomatic relations in January 1979.

Since 1979 the United States has continued to sell advanced weaponry to Taiwan, but this commercial relationship has not enabled the U.S. military to use the island to challenge directly Chinese security. China opposes these sales, but its key strategic interest—excluding a great power strategic presence on Taiwan—is now satisfied by the status quo, thus minimizing its strategic interest in war.

Chinese nationalism demands that both the international community and Taiwan acknowledge that Taiwan is part of China, and therefore that it not declare sovereign status in international politics. While this demand is longstanding, it has taken on added energy in recent years as the domestic political significance of Chinese nationalism has grown. Now that the Chinese Communist Party leadership no longer enjoys ideological legitimacy, is infamous for corruption, represses dissent, and cannot ensure economic stability for much of its population, it depends on its nationalist credentials for political ballast. Taiwan's declaration of independence would challenge party legitimacy, especially since it would be interpreted as U.S. "imperialist" intervention in Chinese domestic affairs.

The combination of China's strategic, nationalist and political imperatives creates the latent instability associated with the Taiwan issue. Should Taiwan declare independence, the mainland would most likely use force and possibly go to war to compel Taiwan to reverse its position. This seemed increasingly likely during the 1990s, when Lee Teng-hui, Taiwan's first democratically elected leader, moved Taiwan toward a declaration of independence. His July 1999 announcement of Taiwan's "special state-to-state" relationship with the mainland came close to crossing the line of a declaration of sovereignty, but it did not. Since then, despite the election in March 2000 of the pro-independence candidate Chen Shui-bian, Taiwan has retreated from Lee's provocative stance. In his May 20, 2000 inauguration speech, Chen declared that Taiwan would not declare independence, would not change Taiwan's constitution to incorporate the "state-to-state" formulation, would not change the name of Taiwan, and would not hold a popular referendum on Taiwan's international status. He has not reversed this policy, so that mainland interest in continued recognition by Taiwan that it is part of China is met.

China will not forsake its demand for unification, but because its foremost strategic and nationalistic objectives are met, this is no more than a demand for face. Thus, in the absence of Taiwan's declaration of independence China can be deterred from using force. Taiwan's purchase of 150 F-16s and 60 Mirage 2000 jets and its domestic production of the Chingkuo fighter nearly guarantee it air superiority over the Taiwan Strait, denying the mainland the ability to sustain offensive operations against it. The mainland still lacks the amphibious capabilities required to occupy Taiwan against the island's coastal defenses. Taiwan's assets alone could enable it to frustrate a mainland effort to occupy the island.[ii] But deterrence of a more limited but nonetheless punishing and coercive mainland use of force depends on Taiwan's longstanding strategic relationship with the United States.

The United States can inflict a rapid and punishing attack against Chinese forces while emerging from war with minimal casualties. Despite recent acquisitions of Russian military aircraft, destroyers and submarines, China's air force and navy are dominated by 1960s generation hardware. Although China has already received approximately 75 Russian Su-27 fighter jets and has agreed to purchase Su-30 ground attack aircraft, the PLA's difficulty in operating and maintaining Russian jets diminishes their role in the cross-strait balance of power. The Russian Sovremmny-class destroyer is a highly capable vessel, especially when equipped with Russian Sunburn missiles, but China cannot defend the Sovremmny, and its limited stand-off range poses only a minimal threat to U.S. forces. The Russian Kilo-class attack submarine is a very capable submarine, but it is also very complex and difficult to operate.

China's military also lacks sophisticated information technologies. It possesses minimal beyond-visual-range targeting. In December 1995 China did not discover that the U.S. aircraft carrier Nimitz was transiting the Taiwan Strait, and in March 1996 it could not locate the U.S. carrier Independence when it deployed 200 miles from China's coast. China's theater missiles lack terminal guidance systems and thus cannot hit moving targets beyond visual range, including U.S. warships. Although China has been modernizing its information technologies, in the eight years between the Gulf War and the war in Kosovo the technology gap between China and the United States widened, thus increasing China's vulnerability to U.S. forces.

Chinese officers are mindful of their military deficiencies. Their studies of the Gulf War and the war in Yugoslavia underscore the U.S. ability to use naval superiority and conventional high-technology, precision-guided weapons to deter coastal adversaries and inflict devastating damage from off-shore platforms.[iii] PLA researchers and the high command understand that in decisive information technologies China is woefully backward and that its inferiority will persist well into the 21st century. There is no false optimism in the PLA that it could survive a war with the United States.[iv]

Military defeat by the United States would not only weaken China vis-à-vis the United States but would also dramatically reverse China's position in the regional balance of power. China would lose its current advantages with regard to Russia, with implications for border security in Central Asia and Northeast Asia. Similarly, Japanese and Indian power would pose greater challenges to Chinese security in the aftermath of a U.S.-China conflict. A weakened China might also face security challenges from foreign-supported disaffected minorities on its borders and Tibetan independence activists. Indeed, Chinese territorial integrity depends on its avoiding war with the United States.

The strategic costs to China of a war with the United States are only part of the deterrence equation. China also possesses vital economic interests in stable relations with the United States. War would end China's quest for modernization by severely constraining its access to U.S. markets, capital and technology, and by requiring China to place its economy on permanent wartime footing. The resultant economic reversal would derail China's quest for "comprehensive national power" and great power status. Serious economic instability would also destabilize China's political system on account of the resulting unemployment in key sectors of the economy and the breakdown of social order. Both would probably impose insurmountable challenges to party leadership. Moreover, defeat in a war with the United States over Taiwan would impose devastating nationalist humiliation on the Chinese Communist Party. In all, the survival of the party depends on preventing a Sino-American war.

But sure knowledge of defeat in war will not deter Chinese leaders from attacking Taiwan unless they are convinced that the United States will in fact intervene. Is the United States credible? The short answer is "yes." Chinese government analysts understand that domestic politics contributes to the likelihood of U.S. intervention, and domestic political opposition toward China and political support for Taiwan in the United States have not been higher since the late 1960s. Moreover, the post-Cold War increases in U.S. arms sales to Taiwan have strengthened the U.S. commitment to defend the island. Chinese leaders also acknowledge that the March 1996 deployment of two U.S. aircraft carriers near Taiwan strongly coupled the U.S. commitment to Taiwan with its commitment to its allies in East Asia. Since then, Chinese leaders have assumed that a war with Taiwan means a war with the United States.[v]

PLA assessments of U.S. military capabilities also contribute to the credibility of U.S. deterrence. Some blustering Chinese PLA authors take heart in the reputed U.S. inability to suffer casualties and argue that China can risk the use of force against Taiwan because it can abort U.S. intervention by sinking a destroyer, for example. Such bluster sells many books in China, but it does not reflect mainstream PLA analysis. Chinese military leaders have criticized these ultra-nationalistic authors and their unrealistic analyses. Faced with the prospect of war with a superior power, professional PLA analysts do study asymmetric warfare. But their writings suggest that the potential value of such strategies is in enhancing China's ability to cope with war against a superior force once fighting begins, not in giving China a deterrent capability against the United States and thus the confidence to risk war with Taiwan.

Moreover, PLA analysts emphasize the critical importance of superior warfighting capabilities in making deterrence threats credible. Indeed, they do not discuss asymmetric warfare against an adversary possessing vastly superior C4I technologies, wartime implementation of asymmetric strategies, and the risk of eliciting overwhelming retaliatory strikes and rapid defeat should deterrence fail. In order to deter, it is necessary to be able to win, not merely to sink a single ship. In this context, the PLA also understands that the United States possesses overwhelming "escalation dominance", so that China lacks the capability to deter U.S. escalation at any level of conflict.[vi]

At the highest level, too, China's limited strategic nuclear capability provides little comfort to Chinese planners. U.S. escalation dominance puts the onus of initiating a nuclear war on China, which would subject it to devastating U.S. nuclear retaliation. But Chinese military leaders have little confidence that China can even launch a nuclear first strike against the United States. China's military literature dwells on the vulnerability of the PLA's few long-range missiles, reflecting concern that the long and overt preparation time prior to launch would elicit a preemptive U.S. attack. China thus lacks confidence that it can use the threat of a nuclear attack to deter U.S. intervention.[vii] Also, because U.S. deterrence of China relies on conventional weapons rather than on nuclear forces, the PLA's strategic analysts argue that it is far more credible than U.S. Cold War deterrence of the Soviet Union.[viii]

There can never be total confidence that deterrence will work. Yet U.S. deterrence of any actual Chinese use of force against Taiwan—outside of a Taiwan declaration of independence—is highly stable. Overwhelming U.S. superiority means that the strategic, economic and political costs to China of U.S. military intervention would be astronomical. U.S. conventional superiority and its strong political commitment to Taiwan mean that the credibility of the U.S. threat to intervene is very high. In an insecure world, the U.S. deterrent posture in the Taiwan Strait is an unusually secure one.

Why Taiwan Will Not Declare Independence

While the United States deters China from using force so long as Taiwan does not declare independence, China deters Taiwan from declaring independence. Thus, following Lee Teng-hui's 1995 visit to the United States and the simultaneous increased momentum of Taiwan's independence movement, the mainland increased the deployment of m-9/DF-15 surface-to-surface missiles in Fujian province. The M-9 lacks terminal guidance capabilities and, thus, precision targeting, as well as significant destructive capability. Nonetheless, it can create havoc in Taiwan's economic and political systems. Mainland military writings emphasize the deterrent role of random missile attacks against a shifting selection of targets on Taiwan.[ix] And, there is no defense against Chinese missiles, for an effective missile defense capability is many years off. Moreover, even should such technology be deployed, Chinese deployment of additional missiles could saturate and overwhelm it.

China plans a similar deterrent role for its conventional military forces. The mainland does not need to be able to carry out a strategically effective air assault or a tight naval blockade against Taiwan for the threat of such actions to deter Taiwanese political ambition. Chinese leaders understand that such actions can have a devastating psychological effect on Taiwan's economy and undermine the island's relations with its major trading partners. The mere threat to use them against a declaration of independence, bolstered by large-scale military exercises and deployment, is therefore a powerful deterrent, and low-level wartime implementation could coerce Taiwan to accept early defeat.[x]

Complementing China's missile deployments and its limited air and naval capabilities is the credibility of its threats. Taiwan's leadership knows that China's failure to respond to a declaration of independence would challenge its international reputation, affecting border security and independence movements around its periphery. In March 1996, despite the risk of U.S. intervention, the PLA launched M-9 missiles into coastal waters within the vicinity of Kaohsiung, Taiwan's major port city, to underscore its will to oppose moves toward independence. These actions were very risky, but they enhanced China's credibility in using force to oppose Taiwan's independence.

Taiwan's interest in preserving the political status quo reflects more than PRC military deterrence. Taiwan's economic prosperity depends increasingly on cross-strait stability. As China's economy has continued to grow and Taiwan's labor costs have increased, Taiwan's economy has become more integrated into the Chinese economy. Its high-technology industries have begun to move offshore to China, so that its export-led economy and future economic growth are increasingly dependent on a stable political relationship with the mainland. Moreover, since late 2000 Taiwan has experienced a significant economic downturn. Unemployment is higher than ever before, the stock market has lost nearly 50 percent of its value, and the New Taiwan dollar reached a 32-month low in early June. The result of Chinese growth and Taiwan's relative decline is that business confidence on Taiwan has reached a five-year low and business elites increasingly recognize China as their long-term hope for continued profits. Consequently, Taiwan's business elite pressures political leaders to keep relations with China becalmed. As these trends continue, especially after Taiwan and China enter the World Trade Organization, Taiwan's ongoing incorporation into the mainland economy and its economic dependence on it will discourage provocations from Taipei.

Taiwan also has critical political stakes in cross-strait stability. Its democracy is young and fragile and has yet to develop a tradition of cooperation across party lines. Its society continues to suffer from a deep fissure reflecting conflict between those born on the mainland and arrived after 1945 and those born in Taiwan. This fissure has contributed to intense partisan politics which, in turn, have undermined Chen Shui-bian's ability to develop a coherent economic recovery policy. They have also undermined voter confidence in Taiwan's ability to contend with mainland pressure.[xi] It is far from clear, therefore, that Taiwan's democracy could long survive intensified mainland-Taiwan conflict.

Taiwan clearly retains an ambition for sovereignty and the associated membership in the United Nations and other international organizations. But, similar to Beijing's demand for unification, this is a demand for face, not a vital interest. U.S. intervention could defeat a Chinese offensive, but Taiwan would nonetheless lose all that is worth defending—its very impressive strategic, economic and political successes. Taiwan's satisfaction with a very favorable status quo and the great risk in challenging Chinese interests combine virtually to guarantee that there will be no declaration of independence—and this is not to speak of U.S. opposition to such an initiative. This reality is reflected in both Taiwan's public opinion polls and in the outcome of the 2000 presidential campaign. Since 1997, support for independence has never exceeded ten percent in government-sponsored opinion polls; the norm is less than six percent. Thus, pro-independence candidates risk appearing reckless should they call for a declaration of independence. Although Chen Shui-bian won the 2000 presidential campaign, he was the beneficiary of a three-way race in which the candidates opposed to independence divided the anti-Chen vote. That he polled less than 40 percent of the vote reflected in part voter apprehension over his prior support for independence.

Beijing's interest in Taiwan's continued formal acceptance that it is part of China is therefore not as much at risk today as seemed to be the case two or three years ago. For the first time in many years, it is confident that "time is on China's side." This is reflected in reduced expectations that China will have to go to war to arrest a trend toward Taiwan independence. Indeed, China has retreated from the February 2000 Taiwan White Paper threat to use force if Taiwan resists unification negotiations "indefinitely." Foreign ministry officials no longer raise this condition; when pressed, they respond that "indefinitely" is a "long time." Thus, while China is deterred from initiating a major war, Taiwan is deterred from doing that which would elicit China's use of force in the first place.

The U.S. Stake

The U.S. aim in cross-strait relations ought to be to re-inforce these offsetting strictures and to make sure that its well-intended efforts to prepare for war do not destabilize a constructive status quo and unnecessarily set back U.S.-China relations. This should not be too difficult.

One advantage in achieving this aim is the fact that the United States does not possess inherently vital security or political interests in Taiwan's strategic role in international politics. U.S. security would not be affected by either China's unification or Taiwan's independence. Thus, every U.S. administration since that of Richard Nixon has declared that the United States does not favor any particular outcome of the mainland-Taiwan conflict, only that it be resolved peacefully. This interest enables the United States to be content with a situation in which neither

Taiwan nor China is fully satisfied with the status quo but both prefer peace to war.

What, then, should the United States do, and what should it avoid doing? First, the United States must continue its effort to maintain the capability and the credibility to deter Chinese use of force against Taiwan. In other words, the United States must hold up its end of the triangle of deterrence and dissuasion. Useful in this regard would be U.S. research and acquisitions strategies that maintain Chinese doubts that asymmetric strategies are enough to deter U.S. intervention. Such efforts should seek to protect the U.S. regional presence through the enhancement of C4I capabilities. U.S. defense planners should also consider how forward deployed arsenal ships can complement the role of aircraft carriers in deterrence, insofar as greater reliance on precision munitions and reduced exposure of U.S. soldiers to attack will enhance the credibility of the U.S. threat to intervene.

But the United States should not abandon its policy of ambiguity regarding intervention in a mainland-Taiwan conflict. Abandoning the present ambiguity would not enhance deterrence or stability, but it would impose a cost on the United States. President Bush got it right on April 25 when he said that Washington would do what it takes to help Taiwan defend itself, but also that the United States opposes a declaration of independence.

Ending ambiguity by clearly stating that the United States would not defend Taiwan in the event of a declaration of independence may clarify the U.S. posture, but it would not make deterrence of such a declaration any more effective. Taiwan is deterred by the credibility of PRC retaliatory threats, regardless of U.S. policy, because the United States cannot defend Taiwan against Chinese missiles or from the economic and political costs of even a limited war. Moreover, clear opposition to Taiwan's independence would be politically controversial in the United States, undermining the fragile domestic consensus on Taiwan policy and making it even more difficult for the White House to cooperate with China.

But neither should Washington abandon ambiguity by threatening intervention against the mainland's use of force under all circumstances. China cannot be deterred in the unlikely event of a Taiwan declaration of independence and it is already deterred from challenging the status quo by U.S. capabilities and commitments. Additional clarity would not enhance deterrence or cross-strait stability. But an unconditional U.S. commitment to defend Taiwan would undermine the U.S. ability to cooperate with China. It would affect mainland assessment of U.S. intentions, creating greater suspicion of the United States and reduced interest in cooperation.

Above all, the United States should not exaggerate the fragility of the cross-strait political or military balance. Stable deterrence across the Taiwan strait means that Washington can refrain from destabilizing initiatives intended to prepare for war and enhance Taiwan's security. The U.S.-mainland balance enables the United States to limit arms sales to Taiwan without undermining

Taiwan's security. U.S. arms sales to Taiwan contribute only marginally to deterrence or to Taiwan's security. What really deters the mainland is not Taiwan's military but the U.S. military. Thus, with the important exception of ensuring Taiwan's air superiority, U.S. arms sales to Taiwan are not a major factor in the security equation. This is especially the case concerning the transfer of theater missile defense technologies to Taiwan. Rather than seek a panacea in an uncertain technology, the United States should have confidence in the strength of its overall deterrent capability and, thus, avoid unnecessary, provocative and destabilizing arms and technology transfers.

Similarly, enhanced U.S.-Taiwan defense planning and coordination will neither aid deterrence nor affect the outcome of a war. Overwhelming U.S. superiority deters unprovoked Chinese use of force. It also enables the United States to incur minimal casualties, so that the Pentagon would prefer to fight a war over Taiwan alone. Washington would demand that Taiwan's forces stand down, sparing the United States the need to manage the complexity of cooperating with Taiwan's relatively ineffective military and risking casualties from friendly fire in a very tight theater. On the other hand, determined U.S.-Taiwan military cooperation will eventually elicit costly mainland opposition. Despite recent U.S. efforts to alleviate the stress in U.S.-China relations and China's evident interest in minimizing U.S.-China tensions, Chinese civilian and military leaders appear to be increasingly concerned over the direction U.S.-Taiwan defense ties.

As sturdy as the status quo in cross-strait relations is, it can be disrupted by unwise diplomacy that threatens the status of the 1979 U.S.-China strategic understanding. The policy changes emerging in the new administration have the potential to harm the interests of both the United States and Taiwan. Such policies will increase suspicion of the United States in Beijing and strengthen the hands of politicians who oppose Chinese cooperation with the United States.

That would be unfortunate. U.S. interest in cooperation with China is not limited to managing the Taiwan issue and avoiding war. U.S.-China cooperation contributes to stability on the Korean peninsula by enhancing Chinese incentives to constrain North Korean ballistic missile proliferation and nuclear weapons development, and by encouraging Pyongyang to pursue dialogue and peaceful unification with Seoul. It also contributes to stability in the Middle East and the Persian Gulf by encouraging China not to proliferate weapons and delivery systems to regional antagonists. It enables the United States to take advantage of China's market to enhance U.S. economic growth and the competitiveness of key U.S. industries. And it enables the United States to encourage political reform in China through economic, cultural and educational exchanges. Increased tension over Taiwan jeopardizes all of these interests without contributing to stability. Moreover, the greatest cost of conflict would be borne by Taiwan. Its security, prosperity and democracy would all be at risk should U.S.-China relations deteriorate seriously.

Rather than repeat the mistakes and subsequent retrenchments of past administrations, the Bush Administration should adopt the novel course of maintaining continuity with the China policy of its predecessors. It is still not too late.

NOTES

[i] Andrew J. Bacevich, "Different Drummers, Same Drum", *The National Interest* (Summer 2001).

[ii] See Michael O'Hanlon, "Why China Cannot Conquer Taiwan", *International Security* (Fall 2000).

[iii] See, for example, Liu Yijian, *Zhi Haiquan yu Haijun Zhanlue* ("Command of the sea and strategic employment of naval forces") (Beijing: National Defense University Press, 2000), pp. 103, 120–1, 144–5, 147–9.

[iv] Zhang Wannian, *Dangdai Shijie Junshi yu Zhongguo Guofang* ("Contemporary world military affairs and Chinese national defense") (Beijing: Junshi Kexue Chubanshe, 1999), pp. 150–1. Also see Zhu Xiaoli, *Junshi Geming Wenti de Yanjiu* ("A study on the revolution in military affairs") (Beijing: National Defense University Press, 2000), pp. 171–8, 185–91.

[v] Shi Yinhong, "Meiguo dui Hua Zhengce he Taiwan Wenti de Weilai" ("U.S. policy toward China and the future of the Taiwan issue"), Zhanlue yu Guanli ("Strategy and management"), No. 6 (2000); Ye Zicheng, "Zhan yu He, Jiaogei Taiwan Dangju Xuan" ("War and peace, give the choice to the Taiwan authorities"), Huanqiu Shibao, October 22, 1999; author's interviews with Chinese government policy analysts.

[vi] Jiang Leizhu, *Xiandai yi Lie Sheng You Zhanlue* ("Modern strategy of pitting the inferior against the superior") (Beijing: National Defense University Press, 1997), pp. 180–92; Chen Zhou, *Xiandai Jubu Zhanzheng Lilun Yanjiu* ("A study of modern local war theories") (Beijing: National Defense University Press, 1997), pp. 149–56.

[vii] Wang Houqing and Zhang Xingye, eds., *Zhanyi Xue* ("Science of campaigns") (Beijing: National Defense University Press, 2000), pp. 162, 168–72.

[viii] Yao Yunzhu, *Zhanhou Meiguo Weishe Lilun yu Zhengce* ("Postwar U.S. deterrence theory and policy") (Beijing: National Defense University Press, 1998), pp. 162, 168–72; Wang Qiming and Chen Feng, *Daying Gaojishu Jubu Zhanzheng: Junguan Bixu Shouce* ("Winning high-technology local war: A handbook of required readings for military officials") (Beijing: Military Friendship Literature Press, 1997), pp. 405–7.

[ix] Wang and Zhang, eds., *Zhanyi Xue*, pp. 252–3.

[x] Wang and Zhang, eds., *Zhanyi Xue*, pp. 409–10; Wang Wenrong, *Zhanlue Xue* ("Science of strategy") (Beijing: National Defense University Press, 1999), pp. 252–3.

[xi] See the line chart of Taiwan's Mainland Affairs Committee on polling from February 1997 to March 2001, New York Times, July 8, 2001; *Far Eastern Economic Review,* July 12, 2001, p. 48, and August 2, 2001, pp. 19–21.

21

China's Hollow Military

*Bates Gill and Michael O'Hanlon**

How good is China's military, and how much should the United States care? There are ample grounds for addressing these questions. In 1995, and then again in 1996, the People's Republic of China (PRC) splashed missiles off the Taiwanese coast. It also reinforced military facilities on the Spratly Islands, which China claims although they are hundreds of miles from its shores. More recently, the PRC has undertaken a steady build-up of short-range missiles opposite Taiwan—hardly, it seems, a benign development, particularly when considered alongside President Jiang Zemin's presumed goal of reuniting Taiwan with the Chinese mainland during his tenure in office. And now these questions have been given a new urgency by the espionage allegations contained in the Cox report.

The PRC, then, has demonstrated a number of intentions and aims that warrant close American attention. The ongoing dispute over Taiwan, for example, is ripe for troublesome misperception. Chinese ambitions toward the Spratly Islands do not converge with U.S. interests or, for that matter, with those of nearby countries. The PRC continues to criticize harshly America's global alliance system and its assertive foreign policy. More generally, Beijing appears poised to translate its growing economic power into greater military strength and geopolitical weight, as indeed a Chinese defense white paper acknowledged last year.

* Bates Gill and Michael O'Hanlon are senior scholars in the Foreign Policy Studies Program at The Brookings Institution, where Gill runs the Center on Northeast Asia Policy Studies.

This essay first appeared in *The National Interest*, No. 56 (Summer 1999).

Despite all of the above, we believe that the recent clamor over China's strategic ambitions is greatly overblown. Most of the Chinese aims that run counter to U.S. interests are in fact not global or ideological but territorial in nature, and confined primarily to the islands and waterways to China's south and southeast. In addition, Beijing has recently taken a number of steps to cooperate with the United States on security matters: signing the Chemical Weapons Convention and nuclear test ban treaty, terminating its assistance to nuclear facilities in Pakistan, pledging to cut off ballistic missile transfers to Pakistan as well as nuclear and anti-ship cruise missile trade with Iran, and quietly restraining the North Koreans. Moreover, China is plagued by enormous socioeconomic problems, whose solution requires maintaining good relations with the world's major economic powers—and with the United States in particular.

That said, our main focus in this article is less on the PRC's intentions, always subject to change in any event, than on its military capabilities. An enormous gap separates China's military capabilities from its aspirations. The PRC's armed forces are not very good, and not getting better very fast. Whatever China's concerns and intentions, its capacity to act upon them in ways inimical to U.S. interests is severely limited, and will remain so for many years.

To begin with, consider some basic facts: China remains a developing country, with per capita income levels—even after twenty years' growth of historic proportions—only about one-tenth those of the West. China's living standards trail even those of American adversaries such as Iran, Yugoslavia and pre-Desert Storm Iraq. It faces enormous challenges in its agricultural, environmental and banking sectors, which its arteriosclerotic central government is ill-equipped to address.

Looking at these facts, the new commander-in-chief of U.S. Pacific forces, Admiral Dennis Blair, has declared that China will not represent a serious strategic threat to the United States for at least twenty years.[i] In almost every respect, China's armed forces lag behind the U.S. military by at least a couple of decades; in many areas they even compare poorly with the "hollow force" that the United States fielded in the immediate wake of the war in Vietnam.[ii] And, on matters ranging from the professionalism of its officer corps and troop morale to training and logistics, China's military is in even worse shape than that.

An Empty Threat

China wields by far the world's largest military, with 2.8 million soldiers, sailors and airmen—twice the American number. (The United States is number two; the only other countries with more than a million active duty troops are China's neighbors—Russia, India and North Korea.) Yet China's military was a full million people stronger in the 1980s—before PRC leaders recognized that its size actually worked against their aim of developing a modern force. Raw size is deceptive. Two million of China's soldiers serve in the ground forces, where their primary responsibilities are to ensure domestic order and protect borders—not to project power. Then, too, the Pentagon estimates that only about 20 percent of those ground forces are even equipped to move about within China. A still smaller number possess the trucks, repair facilities, construction and engineering units, and other mobile assets needed to project power abroad.[iii]

In China's ever expanding defense budget, which has grown by more than 50 percent in real terms over the course of the 1990s and is to increase 15 percent this year, there is also less than meets the eye. Much of this year's increase represents compensation to the Chinese armed forces for divesting themselves of their many business operations, which sapped China's military readiness. Even with these increases, China's announced defense budget will still only total about $12 billion, less than 5 percent of the U.S. figure.

Of course, that $12 billion figure does not capture all Chinese military spending. It does not include spending on foreign arms purchases, nuclear weapons development, most of China's military research and local militias. Nor does it account for subsidies to China's ailing defense industries, or administrative costs such as demobilization and pensions. Taking these additions into account, and adjusting for purchasing-power parity effects—admittedly a difficult and imprecise business—China's actual defense expenditures are generally estimated at somewhere between $35 billion and $65 billion a year.[iv] But these are still modest numbers—especially for such a huge military. Even at the higher estimates, China spends less than 25 percent of what the United States spends on defense, while supporting a force twice as large.

This basic disparity will not change anytime soon. First, as noted, China faces enormous economic challenges that limit its ability to fund a military expansion. Second, even if China begins to close the gap with the United States, it starts from a position of marked inferiority. The United States owns a "capital stock" of modern military equipment valued at close to $1 trillion; China's corresponding figure is well under $100 billion. As such, one can see why a recent study concluded that the Chinese military would have to increase spending on hardware by $22-39 billion annually for ten years to wield a force capable of significant power projection.[v] Further, this estimate does not take into account the additional investments that would be required to man, train, deploy and sustain such a modern force. China is in no position even to attempt this scale of effort.

Weapons and Training

As Congressman Barney Frank has sardonically observed, China did recently acquire its first aircraft carrier. But it then immediately anchored it in Macao and transformed it into a recreation center. So much for the next great hegemon's efforts to launch a blue-water fleet by the turn of the century.

More detailed assessments of Chinese military capability and readiness tell a similar story. Consider China's combat air force. Though roughly equaling the aggregate air power numbers of the United States, China's air forces include only a few dozen so-called "fourth generation" combat aircraft and only a couple hundred "third generation" aircraft. The rest rely on 1960s or even older technology. By contrast, all of the U.S. Air Force, Navy and Marines' 3,000-plus fighters are fourth generation models. China's projected fourth generation arsenal in the year 2005 is expected to include perhaps 150 fighters—by which point the United States will have purchased 300 "fifth generation" aircraft.[vi]

Two additional factors render an even bleaker assessment: supporting equipment and overall military readiness. First, as a recent Pentagon report observed, the PRC's air forces possess minimal aerial refueling capabilities, poor surveillance aircraft and a behind-schedule program to acquire airborne warning and control planes.[vii] Second, and as another Pentagon report describes, the electronic warfare capabilities of the PRC air force are "extremely limited by western standards."[viii] Programs are underway in China to improve certain specialized capabilities, such as the use of space, long-range precision strike, and other "strategic dimensions of warfare."[ix] But the PRC continues to have trouble modernizing its forces. What passes in the literature as "capabilities" are often better understood as long-term aspirations.

As for the caliber of China's military manpower, it is hard to be more damning than the Pentagon's most recent report on PRC military capabilities. It acknowledges that Chinese troops are generally patriotic, fit and good at basic infantry fighting skills, but then goes on to say:

Ground force leadership, training in combined operations, and morale are poor. The PLA is still a party army with nepotism and political/family connections continuing to predominate in officer appointment and advancement. The soldiers, for the most part, are semi-literate rural peasants; there is no professional NCO [non-commissioned officer] corps, per se. Military service, with its low remuneration and family disruption, is increasingly seen as a poor alternative to work in the private sector.[x]

China's military training is elsewhere assessed as getting better, though still weak, particularly as concerns joint service operations.

With respect to the hardware on which those troops rely, the Defense Intelligence Agency expects that, by 2010 or so, perhaps 10 percent of China's overall military will have acquired "late Cold War equivalent" heavy equipment and become reasonably proficient in employing it. Even that will leave them twenty years behind the American curve—and the remaining 90 percent of the force more obsolescent yet.

Projecting Power

So much for an assessment of China's overall military readiness. Some would argue that this type of analysis misses the point in any case. Many American analysts contend that while the United States should not fret too much about China's traditional military power, it should recognize that Beijing, having watched the Gulf War on CNN, might utilize "asymmetric warfare" to threaten American interests in the Taiwan Straits and the South China Sea. By employing advanced cruise missiles, sea mines, submarines, imaging satellites, anti-satellite weapons, computer viruses and other specialized weaponry, China would wage "local war under high-tech conditions" in a manner that exploits American vulnerabilities.

There is a kernel of truth in this concern—militaries, after all, routinely seek to exploit the weaknesses of their adversaries. But it is only a kernel. To defeat Taiwan, for instance, China would need to land enough troops on the island to overcome Taiwan's quarter million-strong ground forces (plus some fraction of its 1.5 million man reserve force). But currently China cannot even move a quarter million soldiers overland into Mongolia or Vietnam. What is more, this type of power projection is precisely the type of operation that future military technology may render even more difficult.

The sum total of China's amphibious transport capacity (about 70 ships) can move 10,000 to 15,000 troops. Its airborne transport may carry 6000 more.[xi] True, China could utilize fishing vessels and cargo ships, and tap its civilian air fleet, for an operation against Taiwan. But all of these vessels, military and civilian, would be fiercely attacked before they reached the island. Making matters worse for China is the fact that there are only a few suitable beachheads on Taiwan where PRC forces could land.

Even if only half of Taiwan's fleet of nearly 500 combat aircraft survived an initial Chinese assault with missiles and fighters, the remaining aircraft could wreak enormous damage on an amphibious armada. The surviving planes would carry enough weapons that in theory they could sink almost the entire amphibious armada in a single sortie. Although Taiwan's air force may not yet have large numbers of anti-ship missiles like the U.S. Harpoon in its arsenal, it could inflict a fair amount of damage with its own Hsiung Feng 2 anti-ship weapons[xii]—and would probably be provided with weapons like the Harpoon fairly quickly. Taiwan also possesses highly effective air-to-air missiles, which would pose a serious threat to Chinese troop transport aircraft.

Things get even worse from the Chinese standpoint. To quote the Pentagon again, "China's C4I [command, control, communications, computers and intelligence] infrastructure cannot support large scale, joint force projection operations at any significant distance from the country's borders." Granted, Taiwan is only about one hundred kilometers from the mainland (though many PRC aircraft would have to operate from several hundred kilometers' distance, given constraints on the capacity of individual airfields). But even if the distances involved are not great, the operation would be enormously complex, as China would need to destroy Taiwan's air force, sink its fleet, deceive its ground forces about the armada's primary objective—and do all of these things after Taiwan was fully aware that hostilities were imminent, since a major and largely visible build-up of Chinese forces would already have taken place. Nor could China rule out the participation of American forces. Even if the United States did not put its combat assets in harm's way, it could provide Taiwan all-weather day-night reconnaissance and targeting data from spy satellites and aircraft.

Bizarrely, after making many of these arguments in its own report, and further concluding that Beijing is making few efforts to improve its lift capacity, the Pentagon's 1999 report on the PRC-Taiwan military balance concludes that, absent third-party intervention, China could probably carry out a successful amphibious assault by 2005. The basis for reaching this conclusion, however, is either unstated or unpersuasive.

China could plausibly blockade Taiwan—at least well enough to cut commerce severely and extract a steep economic price from Taipei. Here, the same technical realities and trends working against a Chinese amphibious invasion of Taiwan might actually work in the PRC's favor. Surface vessels in confined waters are already quite vulnerable. If anything, they are becoming more so—and China has in recent years vastly improved the quality of its anti-ship cruise missiles.[xiii]

China has a large navy, too, one that boasts some 60 submarines, 50 large surface combatants and hundreds of smaller ships. Of the submarines, three are high-quality Kilo-class vessels purchased from Russia; another five are indigenously produced Han nuclear-powered attack submarines. They do not carry anti-ship missiles at present, but may soon. China's stock of torpedoes and mines, too, is well suited for blockade-style operations. But recall, this is a navy for which a three-ship crossing of the Pacific for its first ever visit to a mainland U.S. port—San Diego in March 1997—proved a huge undertaking. Even so, as Taiwan's navy has only 4 submarines, 36 major surface combatants and about 100 smaller surface combat ships, it might well find itself outmatched by the PRC navy. Or at least that is the conclusion of the Pentagon.

In any cross-strait blockade or naval conflict, Taiwan's main advantage would be air cover, especially if it reacted to a PRC blockade by shutting down its ports that face China and routing ships to its less vulnerable eastern harbors. China, however, could pursue Taiwanese-flagged vessels beyond the range of Taiwan's aircover. Even if the PRC navy suffered huge losses, it could effectively discourage merchant shipping and shut down much of Taiwan's export economy.

These options would not be available to China if the United States intervened. Deploying two carriers several hundred miles east of Taiwan, the United States could, with the assistance of the Taiwanese air force, clear the seas of Chinese warships. U.S. airpower, to use a well-coined phrase, can "do" open water much better than it can ferret Serbian tanks and troops out of Kosovo's woods. American anti-submarine warfare capabilities would be challenged only against China's best submarines, of which the PRC only has a handful. At most a few merchant or naval vessels would be lost on the U.S./Taiwan side before the Chinese threat was eliminated.[xiv]

On the matter of asymmetric Chinese approaches to defeating the U.S. military during a conflict over Taiwan, it is especially important to distinguish China's aspirations from its capabilities. It is true that Chinese writers intend to utilize information warfare and other concepts derived from what American analysts often term the revolution in military affairs (RMA). This approach to countering America's edge in traditional military capabilities undoubtedly has particular allure in a nation that gave the world Sun Tzu. But the fact that Chinese military writers can blend ancient maxims with concepts borrowed from the U.S. RMA debate does not mean they will be able to exploit its principles and technology during a conflict in the Straits. And even if China succeeds in developing one type of asymmetric weapon (e.g., a laser anti-satellite weapon), we will retain other systems that will not be threatened (e.g., radar satellites and surveillance aircraft).

What, finally, are we to make of China's recent missile build-up along the Taiwan Straits? Reportedly, the PRC had deployed 30 to 50 short-range missiles on the Straits by 1996, has about 200 deployed there today, and may triple this package within five years. From their current positions, the M-9 and M-11 missiles, both of which are nuclear-capable, can reach Taiwan.[xv] But, neither possesses sufficient accuracy to strike ports, airfields or ships to great effect. Indeed, they would generally miss their targets by several football fields and almost always by the length of at least a single field.[xvi] Granted, if Beijing unleashed a salvo of hundreds of missiles, it might register a few hits. But with the development of more effective passive defenses in Taiwan, most airfields and ports could absorb a few explosions and either continue functioning or be quickly repaired. Commercial sea traffic might disappear for a while, to be sure—but if China exhausted the bulk of its missile inventory to sink a grand total of two or three cargo vessels, would that really be such an intimidating use of force? It would say more about Chinese weakness than anything else.

Today, both China and Taiwan are modernizing their forces. But Taiwan will surely do so much faster, especially given its high-tech economy, its willingness to purchase weapons abroad, and a modernization agenda that emphasizes capabilities such as precision strike, maritime reconnaissance and integrated air defense. China's armed forces talk a good high-tech game, but possess few of the requisite assets and are redressing their weaknesses at a very slow pace.

As for the Spratly Islands, where China has been constructing facilities of late, Beijing seems mostly interested in the economic potential of the surrounding waters and seabeds. Fortunately for it, the countries nearest to the Spratlys—the Philippines and Vietnam—possess little military wherewithal to challenge its claim to the islands. Hence, China's decision to claim sovereignty over the Spratly Islands, while hardly justifiable in law, is not entirely surprising.

Still, given China's inability to project substantial power very far beyond its borders, the PRC will be able to assert and maintain control over the Spratlys now and in the foreseeable future only if the United States allows it to do so. Washington may in fact decide on such a course, even if diplomatic skirmishes over the islands continue to pit China against formal U.S. allies like the Philippines—provided, that is, that China does not attempt to control the adjacent sea lanes. But the Spratlys could prove a costly prize for Beijing. The modest economic benefits accruing would probably be more than balanced by strong political resentment from neighboring states. In that event, the United States might be granted land bases in countries like the Philippines, from which it could patrol and expand its own influence in the region.

The Scandals

For all of the fear and suspicion aroused by illicit transfers of U.S. military technology, they have not fundamentally shifted the strategic balance between China, Taiwan and the United States. While their impact will not be trivial, neither will it be catastrophic.

Consider first the question of nuclear espionage. A native Taiwanese scientist, Wen Ho Lee, allegedly provided China with information on the Trident II missile warhead, known as the W-88; he may have also leaked computer codes mimicking the behavior of that and other warheads. The United States developed this warhead in the 1980s at Los Alamos, where Lee worked until he was fired earlier this year. The warhead has a yield of roughly 350 kilotons, or about 20 times that of the Nagasaki and Hiroshima bombs—not unusually large for U.S. thermonuclear warheads, but still one of the country's most efficient nuclear devices. Warheads of that power formerly weighed well over 1,000 pounds; the W-88 warhead reportedly weighs hundreds.[xvii] With this powerful lightweight warhead, China could place several warheads on missiles that currently carry only one.

That would not change China's ability to threaten the continental United States, which it has been able to do for almost two decades. Beijing at present has about 20 ICBMs that can reach the U.S. mainland. In addition, it has a nuclear-armed submarine, though the vessel is barely seaworthy and would need to approach within about 1,000 miles of the U.S. coast to launch its weapons successfully. China also possesses some 300 nuclear warheads it could use against U.S. or allied forces in Asia.

While the W-88 transfer will not alter the basic facts of the U.S.-China nuclear balance, it would aid any Chinese effort to counter an American ballistic missile defense system, and could provide the PRC with greater targeting options in the event of a nuclear war. That fact might in turn make Beijing believe it had greater leverage in a major crisis with the United States (though if China really thought in these terms, it probably would have already expanded its ICBM force). Moreover, China, which joined the global test ban in 1996, might never have been able to develop its own lightweight warhead without the W-88 technology.

Still, we cannot be sure of the impact. China appears to have tested a warhead similar to the W-88 design only once.[xviii] The United States typically required at least six to ten tests to obtain confidence in a nuclear warhead.[xix] True, if China obtained an already proven design it might require less. But nuclear warheads are highly complex devices. For example, the manner in which a warhead ages can affect its performance. Also, warheads that have been chilled or heated or violently jolted during trajectory may not detonate.[xx] All the weapons blueprints and computer codes in the world cannot substitute for a properly tested and robustly built warhead. China might not wish to devote large amounts of resources to the construction of a warhead that it may not fully understand.

The Hughes/Loral scandal may be the most significant of the recent cases. As part of their work in launching satellites on Chinese carrier vehicles, these companies may have helped China correct a problem in its guidance systems for their strategic rockets. Any technology transfer that increases the accuracy and reliability of China's rockets and missiles will surely aid its ICBM force and its efforts to place military satellites in space. Here too, though, we must be cautious in our conclusions. After all, we still do not know exactly what information was transferred; the former U.S. commander of Pacific forces, Admiral Joseph Prueher, for one, appears not to believe the data was of great import. Even if China's launch capabilities do improve slightly as a result of the transfer, its fledgling satellite program is rudimentary and will likely remain so for years to come.

The Cox Committee has raised serious concerns about improvements in Chinese military capability. Still, enormous uncertainties persist, for acquisitions do not translate automatically into new capabilities. That at least was the conclusion of the CIA's damage assessment, which determined that "the aggressive Chinese collection effort" has not yet resulted in the modernization of its deployed strategic forces. The reality of America's enormous strategic nuclear advantage—U.S. nuclear warheads outnumber China's by a ratio of about 15 to 1—will remain a powerful deterrent in the face of any foreseeable Chinese strategic rocket modernization.

China's military is simply not very good. The majority of its members serve in the ground forces, but so lack in transport and mobile logistics assets that they are more aptly described as internal security personnel. Their training ranges from spotty to poor. Moreover, the armed forces remain plagued by poor pay, nepotism and party favoritism, and attract few of China's brightest citizens.

The PRC's power projection capabilities, too, are constrained by huge weaknesses—especially in areas such as aerial refueling, electronic warfare, command and control, and amphibious and air assault assets. China owns considerably less top-level military equipment than medium military powers like Japan and Britain; it owns even less than smaller powers such as Italy, South Korea or the Netherlands. Nor has it embarked on a concerted effort to purchase sophisticated new weapons. Though some analysts estimate China's military budget to be as high as $65 billion a year in purchasing power terms, the resources it devotes to acquiring modern weaponry are akin to those of countries spending $10-20 billion a year on defense.

The numerous defects of its military establishment notwithstanding, China is a rising power that could one day significantly challenge the United States and its allies in East Asia. But that day will not come anytime soon; it will be at least twenty years before China can pose such a threat. Why it would wish to do so, even with a strong military, remains an open question.

NOTES

[i] Paul Mann, "Spy Charges Jeopardize China's Trade Status", *Aviation Week and Space Technology*, March 15, 1999, p. 26.

[ii] Ronald N. Montaperto, "Reality Check: Assessing the Chinese Military Threat", Defense Working Paper No. 4 (Washington, DC: Progressive Policy Institute, April 1998), p. 10.

[iii] William S. Cohen, "The Security Situation in the Taiwan Strait", *Report to Congress pursuant to the FY99 Appropriations Bill* (Washington, DC: Department of Defense, 1999), p. 11.

[iv] The higher number is the latest U.S. government estimate. The U.S. estimate is similar to the World Bank's, whereas the IMF and the International Institute for Strategic Studies in London come in at the lower end of the range.

[v] Bates Gill, "Chinese Defense Procurement Spending: Determining Chinese Military Intentions and Capabilities", in *China's Military Faces the Future*, ed. James Lilley and David Shambaugh, (M.E. Sharpe, 1999).

[vi] Lane Pierrot, *A Look at Tomorrow's Tactical Air Forces* (Washington, DC: Congressional Budget Office, 1997), p. xiv; Office of Naval Intelligence, Worldwide Challenges to Naval Strike Warfare (Washington, DC: Department of the Navy, 1996); and Lane Pierrot et al., *Planning for Defense: Affordability and Capability of the Administration's Program* (Washington, DC: Congressional Budget Office, 1994), p. 22.

[vii] Cohen, op. cit., pp. 6, 13.

[viii] William S. Cohen, "Future Military Capabilities and Strategy of the People's Republic of China", *Report to Congress pursuant to the FY98 National Defense Authorization Act* (Washington, DC: Department of Defense, 1998), p. 8.

[ix] See Mark Stokes, *China's Strategic Modernization: Implications for U.S. National Security* (Colorado Springs, CO: Institute for National Security Studies, October 1997).

[x] Cohen, "The Security Situation in the Taiwan Strait", p. 11.

[xi] Cohen, "The Security Situation in the Taiwan Strait", p. 9; and "Future Military Capabilities and Strategy", pp. 15-16.

[xii] Duncan Lennox, Jane's Air-Launched Weapons (Couldson, UK: Jane's Information Group, 1998), analysis tables.

[xiii] Bates Gill, "Chinese Military Hardware and Technology Acquisitions of Concern to Taiwan", in *Crisis in the Taiwan Strait*, ed. James Lilley and Chuck Downs (Washington, DC: National Defense University, 1997), pp. 117-20.

[xiv] See Tom Stefanick, *Strategic Antisubmarine Warfare and Naval Strategy* (Lexington, MA: Lexington Books, 1987), pp. 33-70, 155-80.

[xv] Bruce Dorminey, "Chinese Missiles Basic to New Strategy", *Aviation Week and Space Technology*, March 8, 1999, p. 59.

[xvi] Robert G. Nadler, *Ballistic Missile Proliferation: An Emerging Threat* (Arlington, VA: System Planning Corporation, 1992), p. 15.

[xvii] Thomas B. Cochran et al., *Nuclear Weapons Databook, Volume I: U.S. Nuclear Forces and Capabilities* (Cambridge, MA: Ballinger Publishing Co., 1984), pp. 31-6.

[xviii] Carla Anne Robbins, "China Received Secret Data on Advanced U.S. Warhead", *Wall Street Journal*, January 7, 1999.

[xix] Robert Standish Norris and Thomas B. Cochran, "United States Nuclear Tests", *Working Paper NWD 94-1* (Washington, DC: Natural Resources Defense Council, February 1, 1994), p. 12.
[xx] Christopher E. Paine, "The U.S. Debate Over a CTB", *Working Paper NWD 93-5, rev. 2* (Washington, DC: Natural Resources Defense Council, 1993), p. 26.

22

China's Military: A Second Opinion

James Lilley and Carl Ford

In the preceding article ("China's Hollow Military"), Bates Gill and Michael O'Hanlon write that "China's military is simply not very good." We think they got that half right. China is no military superpower and will not acquire that status for some years to come. But measured in terms of its capacity to challenge key U.S. allies in East Asia, China's capabilities have grown exponentially. That is the point; the authors miss it.

Gill and O'Hanlon assert that because China presently has a limited capacity to attack, say, Manhattan, it is therefore "severely limited" in its ability to act upon its "concerns and intentions." But in setting up such a straw man, it is the authors' arguments, not the capabilities of the People's Liberation Army (PLA), that are severely limited. It is China's burgeoning ability to challenge U.S. interests in East Asia, not the danger it poses to the continental United States, that threatens to draw America into a military confrontation in the years ahead. Indeed, one need only look back three years to the Taiwan Strait crisis of 1996—when thousands of U.S. military personnel stood minutes from military confrontation with communist Chinese naval forces—for a preview of what may lie in the future.

---

* James Lilley is resident fellow at the American Enterprise Institute and a former U.S. ambassador to China (1989-91).

Carl Ford is president of Ford and Associates, an international consulting firm specializing in Asian military issues.

This essay first appeared in *The National Interest*, No. 57 (Fall 1999).

Recently, others have observed that, "Increasingly, political pressures are pushing the U.S. toward a self-fulfilling prophesy: Treat China as if it is inevitably hostile and dangerous, and it is more likely to become hostile and dangerous."[i] Gill and O'Hanlon harbor a similar fear, and it is one that we share. But we believe that understating the potential threat China poses to American interests, as the authors have done, is just as wrong as exaggerating it. Sound policy formulation starts with solid assessments, not false assumptions.

By emphasizing direct comparisons between the defense capabilities of the United States and the PRC, the authors create an artificial and misleading construct. Such comparisons distort more than they enlighten. Few imagine that the People's Republic of China (PRC), either now or in the foreseeable future, could best the United States in an all-out war. Though comforting in the abstract, that reality is not terribly relevant to the challenges at hand. What the Jiang regime gives every indication of striving for is sufficient military clout to achieve its aims in Asia. In the short term, it wishes to intimidate Taiwan sufficiently to bring about unification on Beijing's terms. Accomplishing that entails limiting or closing off entirely Washington's ability to intervene early and with enough force to prevent Taiwan from being overwhelmed. Looking further ahead, the PRC seeks to cow its neighbors and diminish American influence in the region. For these purposes, the PLA is close to being good enough today—and even better tomorrow.

Trends Count

First, it makes a big difference where you fight a war. Beijing would be no match for the United States in the Persian Gulf or off the beaches of Waikiki, but a battle fought in Sichuan province would be a very different matter. The same applies to the Taiwan Strait. Anyone who believes that such a confrontation would be a walk-over for American forces misunderstands the challenges the PLA would pose to U.S. operations near China's shores, and how difficult it would be even for the United States to operate on a major scale so far from home. That Beijing does not presently seek to provoke a military confrontation with the United States, and is deterred for now from lesser military actions in the Taiwan Strait, should not delude anyone into believing that China would not be a formidable opponent on its own turf, or that the PLA is as "hollow" as the authors would have readers believe.

Further, any comparison that depends merely on counting up all our military assets or raw defense expenditures for its persuasive power is almost always wrong. Consider, to begin with, Beijing's defense budget. The government has agreed to increase military spending by almost 13 percent next year. Apologists both inside and outside China downplay that boost by claiming that it still leaves the PLA's level of expenditures far short of the Pentagon's. They also argue that most of the increase goes for improving "living standards" and is therefore not very important. Such statements make for good sound bites, but are seriously misleading. Even those who minimize China's military heft admit that defense spending overall "has grown by more than 50 percent in real terms over the course of the 1990s", as Gill and O'Hanlon state. The authors' protestations to the contrary notwithstanding, these trends are important.

Trends provide a good indication of intentions. Investments of the sort Beijing is making can mean only one thing: China is determined to improve the PLA's fighting capability. While most nations are reducing defense expenditures in the post-Cold War era, China is one of the few doing the opposite. We see the same trend in the PLA's training activities, the theoretical work being churned out by its think tanks and educational institutions, and, most important, in its build-up opposite Taiwan.[ii]

Analysts of the Gill-O'Hanlon school typically claim that these increases in military spending are largely benign, going mostly to meet personnel costs. They argue in this vein knowing full well that personnel and related costs take up the bulk of military budgets in any army. What they neglect to mention is that many of the uses for which these expenditures are intended—the PLA's modernization drive and its stepped-up training activities, for example—will have considerable impact on China's military capabilities.[iii] Across the board, the PLA is engaged in a major spending effort to upgrade weapons and equipment and improve its operational capabilities. According to the Pentagon, these efforts have already enhanced China's ability to project military power. One important example is China's growing stock of ballistic missiles aimed at Taiwan. The quick-strike capability these missiles provide China will only increase between now and 2005.

It is also important to recognize that China never tells the truth about its defense spending. For years experts have considered the publicly released figures to be only the tip of the iceberg. While no one can be certain, since much of the funding is hidden, many estimate that the unclassified budget probably understates real spending by at least a third. In fact, most Western estimates put China's annual military expenditure between 28 and 50 billion U.S. dollars—that is, 4 to 7 times the official figure. Moreover, it is precisely in the areas of weapons acquisition and training—both of which the PLA finances with profits from its sale of missiles and other weapons to rogue nations such as Iraq, Iran, Libya and Syria—that the Chinese are most secretive.

We can, however, observe in general terms China's broad interest in military research and acquisitions. The PLA's programs run the gamut of leading-edge military technology. From multiple missile warheads to stealth technology and the neutron bomb, the PLA is investing considerable amounts of time and money to improve its arsenal and its ability to project power. Obtaining air refueling platforms and airborne early warning aircraft remains high on the PLA's priority list, and it will likely acquire both in the near future. China has also shown considerable interest in improving its naval aviation assets and has discussed the need for aircraft carriers.[iv] And, despite its strident protests over U.S. theater missile defense plans, China has long been working to improve its own missile defense capabilities. As Paul Bracken points out, "Ballistic missiles break down the entire strategy of forward engagement from fixed bases. They are directed at the key vulnerability that Western powers in Asia always faced but that until recently Asian nations could not exploit."[v] Indeed, it is difficult to identify a weapons system or new technology that China's is not hoping to acquire.

Also absent from Gill and O'Hanlon's comparison of U.S. and PRC defense spending is any recognition of the costs and restraints associated with Washington's status as a super-power. Our global military responsibilities have always come at considerable cost. Much of our defense spending, dating back to the Cold War, goes toward maintaining nuclear deterrence for ourselves and our allies. While the end of the arms race brought reduced requirements, we still maintain a massive nuclear capability and the ability to retaliate anywhere in the world. China, by contrast, channels its defense expenditures to much narrower uses.

Apples and Oranges

Gill and O'Hanlon suggest that China's antiquated logistics system would severely limit the PLA's ability to fight a real war, especially one outside its borders. Again the naysayers have it half right. China's logistics system is not very modern, and it cannot supply large amounts of cargo by air or support troops fighting far from home. Then again, it was not designed with such purposes in mind. For that, China would need to add new capabilities on top of its existing system.

In China's far western areas, such as Xinjiang, that is, on a small scale, exactly what the PLA seems to be doing. Worried about the activities of Americans and others in the former Soviet states bordering China, and lacking an adequate road and rail network in the area, the PLA has begun improving its logistics system in the region. While these efforts are just beginning, they could serve as a model for similar operations elsewhere in China.

In any case, the appellation "old" does not always mean "bad", and for the PLA's logistics system "tried and true" offers a more apt description than "outmoded" or "ineffective." Chinese forces depend on an elaborate network of existing supply and support facilities all over China, connected primarily by road and rail. The network can sustain the PLA in combat for extended periods of time over vast geographic areas. While the PLA's logistics infrastructure is best suited for protracted defense of its homeland, it can be adapted to support modest forays outside China. For example, the well-timed 1974 seizure of the Paracel Islands from South Vietnam involved successful amphibious tactics against a weaker enemy, executed with dispatch and overwhelming force.

China's continental approach to logistics differs sharply from the American system of power projection. Comparing the two obscures more than it clarifies. For our system, as it developed during the Cold War, depends on creating sea and air links to anywhere in the world on short notice. While each new crisis poses different challenges for the United States, all, except for those of a minor nature, require forward bases to channel supplies into theaters of operation. Without forward bases, severe limits exist on the size of the force we can deploy and how long our naval air units can remain engaged. China, by contrast, is its own forward base.

Just as "old" is not always "bad", so the PLA's large size, which many point to as proof of its technological shortcomings, is not necessarily a drawback. There are times when bigger is better. For one thing, the PLA's size enables it to mount a defense in depth, a classical continental strategy, and the opposite of the essentially linear defense adopted by NATO during the Cold War. China's strategy substitutes successive lines of forces prepositioned in the most defensible terrain for the qualities of mobility and lethality favored by NATO. True, this puts a premium on maintaining large numbers of troops and requires a sizable land mass. But with each success, an invader—much as Napoleon or Hitler in Russia, or the Japanese in China—will find his logistics tail increasingly vulnerable. There is no reason why a continental defense strategy such as this would not prove effective for the Chinese under modern battlefield conditions. It would be at least good enough to deter the United States or some other would-be aggressor from waging a ground war on the Asian mainland. And in the absence of such a threat, it is hard to imagine subduing China with air power alone.

The Nuclear Dimension

We looked in vain for any treatment by the authors of the nuclear dimension in a confrontation with China. Yet any discussion of China's military capabilities is incomplete without it. Not since the Cuban Missile Crisis has the United States come up directly against another nuclear-armed power. Neither for that matter have any of our opponents been able to bring the fight to the U.S. mainland. While we have proved adept at bringing war to the other side almost without limit, our rear areas and support bases have gone untouched. Not so in the case of a confrontation with Beijing. Were one to commence, we would have to be mindful of the PLA's nuclear capability, regardless of how unlikely its use might be.

Small by U.S. and Russian standards, China's mostly land-based missile force can strike the continental United States from fixed silos in western China. Both the 2nd Artillery (China's Strategic Rocket Force) and the navy field less reliable systems—at least at present. But that is about to change. Two new missiles, the DF-31 and DF-41, are modern solid fuel missiles probably with multiple warheads, and are far more mobile than previous Chinese systems.[vi] Both can reach the United States. The DF-31 was successfully tested on August 2 of this year, a launch with a message for both Taiwan and the United States. The JL-II, another new missile under development, has submarine applications, and should be tested this year as well.[vii] China's submarine force is still mostly a threat in East Asia, but sudden submarine attacks on Taiwan's shipping could prove devastating, as Taiwanese forces lack a modern and effective anti-submarine warfare capability. Nevertheless, the mobility inherent in each of these new systems makes them highly survivable even against our latest and best high-tech surveillance systems.

China's Ability To Take Taiwan by Force

The authors are nowhere more off base than on their assessment of the military threat China poses to Taiwan. Since they wish to conclude that the PLA is a "hollow military" and that "an enormous gap separates China's military capabilities from its aspirations", they make two important assumptions: first, that the FY99 Department of Defense military balance report to Congress is seriously wrong; and second, that the United States would intervene to protect Taiwan.

Let us take a closer look at what the Department of Defense has to say in its report to Congress that Gill and O'Hanlon find so bizarre. They seem to have several passages in mind.

On China's defense strategy and force planning:

In recent years, there has been growing evidence that China's force developments strategy is being influenced, in part, by its focus on preparing for military contingencies along its southeastern flank, especially in the Taiwan Strait and the South China Sea.

On a PRC blockade of Taiwan:

Barring third party intervention, the plan's quantitative advantage over Taiwan's Navy in surface and sub-surface assets would probably prove overwhelming over time. Taiwan's military forces probably would not be able to keep the island's key ports and slocs open in the face of concerted Chinese military action. Taiwan's small surface fleet and four submarines are numerically insufficient to counter China's major surface combatant force and its ASW assets likely would have difficulty defeating a blockade supported by China's large submarine force.

On missile strikes:

Within the next several years, the size of China's SRBM force is expected to grow substantially. An expanded arsenal of conventional SRBMs and LACMs targeted against critical facilities, such as key airfields and C4I nodes, will complicate Taiwan's ability to conduct military operations.

On PLA air superiority:

while the majority of the mainland's air fleet will still be composed of second and third generation aircraft, the sheer numerical advantage of older platforms augmented by some fourth generation aircraft could attrit [sic] Taiwan's air defenses sufficiently over time to achieve air superiority.

On conducting an amphibious invasion:

> The PLA likely would encounter great difficulty conducting such a sophisticated campaign by 2005. Nevertheless, the campaign likely would succeed—barring third party intervention—if Beijing were willing to accept the almost certain political, economic, diplomatic, and military costs that such a course of action would produce.

None of the Pentagon's findings strike us as being out of line. All, except for the implications of the recent missile deployments near Taiwan, have been known and widely accepted by intelligence analysts for many years. Indeed, while Gill and O'Hanlon disagree with the Pentagon's most important conclusions, they cite approvingly those portions of the report that have negative things to say about the PLA.

As the report suggests, Taiwan would face an enormous challenge in defending itself against a determined PRC attack. The island is too close to the mainland and the mismatch in force levels too great for Taipei to hold out indefinitely. Although Taiwan's technological advantages, higher levels of training and adequate preparations would prolong the struggle, defeating China is simply too tall an order for Taipei so long as the mainland is prepared to suffer huge casualties and bear the condemnation of the international community. Obviously, costly mistakes by either side or just sheer luck could change the equation, but in terms of raw capability China emerges triumphant under nearly all plausible scenarios.

The name of the game for Taiwan, then, is deterrence. Taipei's best chance for survival lies in convincing Beijing that the costs of an invasion are prohibitive, and that the island can hold out long enough for the international community, and especially the United States, to come to its rescue. In the first instance, this means maintaining a qualitative edge over the PRC. Here perception is almost as important as reality. Without ready access to high-technology weapons systems, which come almost exclusively from the United States, Taiwan cannot sustain the confidence of its troops or its population. On the other hand, any slippage in quality might persuade Beijing that the military balance had shifted in its favor, or that international support for Taiwan is eroding. In either case, Beijing would be emboldened.

Unless Taipei can prolong the conflict beyond a few weeks, the likelihood that the United States, or anyone else, will intervene declines sharply. Give the United States enough time and it can go anywhere and fight anyone with a high probability of success. Rob us of that opportunity, however, and we will be put at a disadvantage, especially if the scene of the combat is far away and our access to bases is limited. Take the case of North Korea. By any measure that nation is no match for either the United States or South Korea. But U.S. and South Korean military officials alike worry mightily about what could happen between the Demilitarized Zone and Seoul during the first few days of any war, or the consequences such a conflict might have if it should commence when the United States is tied down somewhere else. Thus, the North Koreans, with possibly one or two nuclear weapons against America's estimated six thousand, have been able to blackmail the United States for billions of dollars of aid.

Taiwan, like South Korea, must maintain forces sufficient to convince planners in Beijing that they cannot achieve their military objectives quickly. The PRC's new missile deployments opposite Taiwan make this task increasingly difficult. China's General Staff seems to have recognized that its threats of a blockade, an air war or an amphibious assault have become less and less credible, because such time-consuming operations would provide outsiders an opportunity to weigh in on Taiwan's side. The missile threat bears directly on this question, as any rocket attack would come as a rapid blitzkrieg-like bombardment.

Which is exactly why missile defense figures so prominently in Taiwan's current thinking. Now that the PLA has placed a greater emphasis on conventional ballistic and cruise missiles in its deployments opposite Taiwan, Taipei is reconsidering its need for THAAD and aegis missile defense systems. Both will likely receive a higher priority in future arms sales discussions between Taiwan and the United States, and for good reason.

China, and those in the United States who take its side in its dispute with Taiwan, would argue, of course, that there is a much easier and safer alternative to Taiwan's growing insecurity—concede China's claim of sovereignty over the island. Since Taiwan is a democracy and an overwhelming number of its citizens reject that option, this would only happen if Taiwan's population is sufficiently intimidated or otherwise coerced into doing so. Obviously, the American response to China's strong-arm tactics is crucial. Any lack of resolve on our part sends dangerous signals to both Taiwan and the mainland. Fortunately, President Clinton's deployment of aircraft carriers in response to the 1996 missile firing incident does not appear to have been an aberration, but rather evidence of a new American consensus in support of Taiwan having a say in its future.

This does not mean that Americans want to go to war with China, and we think the authors too quickly count the United States into the military equation. Under any circumstances, becoming caught in a conflict with the PRC is the last thing we want to do. Granted, the introduction of U.S. forces changes the equation dramatically and would prove an almost insurmountable obstacle for the PLA. Much, however, depends on the amount of time it takes us to react and on what forces we commit to the conflict. Then, too, there is the nuclear dimension to think about. In fact, Taiwan depending on the United States so heavily for its defense seems to be the most risky option for everyone.

Better that the island, as envisaged in the Taiwan Relations Act, maintain "a sufficient self-defense capability", and reserve for the United States an important, but secondary, role in its defense. Such a course is the most stable and the least susceptible to miscalculation on Beijing's part. Let the PLA General Staff makes its calculations of peace or war based primarily on what it confronts immediately across the Taiwan Strait, rather than considerations of what might be available by way of the United States.

This approach has the virtue of putting the PRC at the center of decision-making concerning Taiwan's defense preparations, but in the right way. The consistent message America would be sending to China is: "It is up to you. Strong-arm tactics will not work. Military build-ups and other provocative actions, contrary to promoting your interests, will only accelerate and intensify Taiwan's defense effort, its arms purchases from the United States, and sympathy for its cause."

NOTES

[i] Gerald F. Seib, "Another Threat Looms: China As New Demon", *Wall Street Journal*, May 26, 1999.
[ii] William S. Cohen, "The Security Situation in the Taiwan Strait", *Report to Congress pursuant to the FY99 Appropriations Bill* (Washington, DC: Department of Defense, 1999).
[iii] Ibid.
[iv] Shen Zhongchang, et al., "21st-Century Naval Warfare", in *Chinese Views of Future Warfare*, ed. Michael Pillsbury (Washington, DC: National Defense University Press, 1998), pp. 261-74.
[v] Bracken, *Fire in the East* (New York: Harper Collins, 1999), p. 48.
[vi] Richard D. Fisher, Jr., "China Increases Its Missile Forces While Opposing U.S. Missile Defense", *The Heritage Foundation Backgrounder*, No. 1268, April 7, 1999.
[vii] James Kynge and Stephen Fidler, "China's Submarine-Launched Missile To Be Tested", *Financial Times*, June 3, 1999.

23

China's Military: Take 3

*Bates Gill and Michael O'Hanlon**

Let us begin by thanking Ambassador James Lilley and Carl Ford for driving home an important point in their article, "China's Military: A Second Opinion": any conflict over Taiwan would be of the utmost seriousness regardless of what one thinks of the conventional military balance in the region. No one who read our first article ("China's Hollow Military") should be led to believe otherwise. The potential for enormous losses in Taiwan and southeastern coastal China; the lasting geopolitical harm resulting from the embitterment and ostracization of the world's most populous state after such a war; and the slight but real risk of nuclear escalation are all extremely worrisome, even if the People's Republic of China (PRC) were to prove unsuccessful in invading or blockading Taiwan.

Lilley and Ford are also right to emphasize that China has been trying to improve its problem-plagued military. And they are surely correct that PRC forces need not equal the capabilities of the U.S. military to pose a significant risk to American interests in East Asia. We made these points too, but it is worthwhile to have them reinforced. On a number of other points, however, Lilley and Ford plainly misrepresent our argument. On others, they overstate China's military prowess, or commit precisely the error we warned against: equating Beijing's aspirations with its actual capabilities.

* Bates Gill and Michael O'Hanlon are senior scholars in the Foreign Policy Studies Program at The Brookings Institution, where Gill runs the Center on Northeast Asia Policy Studies.

This essay first appeared in *The National Interest*, No. 58 (Winter 1999/2000).

Beginning with budgetary matters, Lilley and Ford imply that we understate China's true level of defense spending. But, while they note that most Western estimates put the PRC's annual expenditures between $28 billion and $50 billion, we had put the range between $35 billion and $65 billion. The authors make a great deal of China's revenues from arms sales and the possibility that these could help the PRC modernize its military capability "off-budget." But recent analysis by the Congressional Research Service puts the gross revenues of such sales at no more than a few hundred million dollars per year. Moreover, independent research in books edited by Ambassador Lilley himself shows that little, if any, of the net profit from these sales is reinvested in PLA modernization.

Our essay went on to note that China's defense expenditures, while fairly impressive in aggregate, translate into a low level of spending per troop. China has provided particularly few resources in areas that soldiers know to be critical in warfighting—such as logistics, maintenance and training. Hence the title of our article, "China's Hollow Military"—with its implication that while the PRC's armed forces may be impressive on paper, their quality is mediocre and their fighting abilities limited.

Employing quantitative measures, we point out just how badly China's military equipment lags behind that of the United States. As Lilley and Ford rightly emphasize, China need not approach parity with American armed forces to cause serious trouble in a crisis or war. However, China trails the United States by a factor of well over 10 in its inventory of modern defense equipment, by that same 10:1 ratio in defense research and engineering, and by as much as 50:1 in areas like modern fighter aircraft. In addition, major U.S. friends and allies in East Asia—Japan, South Korea and Taiwan—all possess much more modern militaries than does the PRC. Notably, from 1991 to 1998 alone, Taiwan outspent China in foreign weapons purchases by a factor of nearly 4:1; if we factor in foreign weapons currently in the pipeline, the ratio increases to about 7:1. Unfortunately, Lilley and Ford's essay did not get into such levels of detail.

Lilley and Ford did spend a fair amount of time discussing how well China's military could defend its own territory. We agree, and fail to see the danger in that. In fact, we were trying to highlight the difference between the total of China's armed forces—2.8 million strong, roughly twice as large as those of the United States—and the number that could operate abroad in places such as Taiwan. The latter number is, and will remain, far lower.

In that regard, Lilley and Ford demonstrate a surprising reluctance to engage in analytical exchange. We stated that China would have great difficulty transporting more than 20,000 troops at a time across the Taiwan Strait—many of whom would probably be sunk or shot down en route—and that they would face an active duty Taiwanese force of 250,000, backed by 1.5 million reservists, once they arrived. Which, if any, of these numbers do Lilley and Ford contest? Which do they consider irrelevant? And what historical analogies, or analytical arguments, can they invoke to assert that a force lacking air superiority can assault a small beachfront when its well-armed opponent knows it is coming? To claim that because China is a bigger country it must ultimately prevail seems at best simplistic.

Then, too, while China's old but large air force, and growing missile force, might hit some key fixed targets in Taiwan and intimidate civilian populations, they cannot alter the basic nature of these troop-strength comparisons. As was demonstrated by the Iran-Iraq War of the Cities, Iraqi missile strikes during Desert Storm, and the Battle of Britain, ballistic missile attacks may terrorize but they generally cannot subjugate. (That is not to say that we necessarily oppose Taiwanese acquisition of U.S. missile defense systems, should China continue its destabilizing missile build-up on its southeastern coast.)

It is worth recalling that in the great amphibious assaults of World War II—such as Normandy, Iwo Jima and Okinawa—invading allied forces typically possessed local advantages of at least 2:1 in troop strength. They also had sufficient control of the skies to prevent the enemy from reinforcing and to batter the enemy's beached forces with preparatory gunfire. But in any attempted PRC crossing of the Taiwan Strait, it is Taiwan that would enjoy the manpower advantage. While it might not enjoy air dominance, it would probably not cede it to China either—and it would know a great deal about when and where Chinese forces intended to come ashore.

Lilley and Ford ask why we accept a good deal of the evidence presented in two Pentagon reports, yet challenge those same reports on the question of Taiwan's defensibility. We believe the Pentagon did a good job in acquiring data and reaching narrow military judgments, but erred in its overall assessment. Put simply, it got the trees right, but missed the forest. The Defense Department often relies on opaque models to assess military engagements, models that are typically far less reliable than the data entered into them. We were all reminded of this in Desert Storm, a case in which the Pentagon's models proved to be further off the mark in predicting casualties than most independent estimates performed by scholars armed only with hand calculators.

Lilley and Ford are on firmer ground in their discussion of the blockade scenario. In this case, as we noted, Taiwan might well require U.S. help. We think they are wrong to assume that the United States would simply stand by and watch Taiwan be blockaded, but one can still ask if the United States should adopt such an arms-length policy. What, for instance, are the pros and cons of current policy versus that of selling Taiwan all the arms it seeks—and possibly acquiescing in Taiwan's acquisition of at least a latent nuclear weapons capability—while declaring that the United States would never fight on Taiwan's behalf? In short, what is the case for allowing Taiwan to become, in effect, an Asian Israel? We think that this policy option, however attractive on the surface, would increase rather than decrease the risk of war between China and Taiwan.

So let us close where we began—by acknowledging the danger of a war between the PRC and Taiwan. We doubt seriously that China would use nuclear weapons against the United States should it participate in such a war, given the logic of deterrence and the overwhelming power of the American nuclear arsenal, but acknowledge that this would be the most serious standoff between nuclear powers since the Cuban Missile Crisis. However much we might fear such a scenario, China would have at least as much to dread. And the United States does not have a history of backing down, or of deserting friends and allies, in the face of possible nuclear threats.

Lilley and Ford are correct that conflict between nuclear powers is a dangerous prospect. But they are wrong to suggest that the nuclear danger trumps China's overwhelming conventional disadvantages. If and when the PRC considers its options for taking Taiwan, those conventional military disadvantages will weigh heavily in its thinking, and that, in the end, is a very comforting thought.

24

Balance, Not Containment:
A Geopolitical Take from Canberra

A.D. McLennan[*]

The pages of *The National Interest* have abounded in recent months with analyses, prognostications, predictions, and arguments over what to do with and about China. Robert Zoellick argued persuasively for the need to rebuild a bipartisan consensus on U.S. policy toward China, and both he and Paul Wolfowitz have urged that such a consensus take as its touchstone the recognition that the problem is one of accommodating the rise of a new power (the Wilhelmine Germany analogy), and not that of containing an implacably hostile imperialism (the Stalinist postwar Soviet Union analogy). It is hard to deny, too, the good sense of recognizing the essential tension between China's rush toward economic development and its ossified political system, a tension that Henry S. Rowen and others maintain will be resolved in the end in a relatively benign way, in favor of democracy. And it also makes sense, as Bruce Cumings has suggested, for Americans to understand the historical—and, in some cases, the very subjective—origins of their own images of China before setting off to propound U.S. interests in Beijing.

Less persuasive, however, are some of the means advanced to achieve these goals. Zoellick's argument, for example, that the ASEAN Regional Forum (ARF) could effectively engage China on regional security issues takes insufficient account of China's zero-sum view of international relations—a view generic to

[*] A.D. McLennan, an Australian intelligence and diplomatic official, was deputy director-general at the Office of National Assessments, Canberra, during 1981-90.

This essay first appeared in *The National Interest*, No. 49 (Fall 1997).

East Asia. It also underestimates the damaging collateral effects that might attend such an "engagement" policy line, especially on the U.S.-Japanese alliance, and especially bearing in mind the skill that China has demonstrated in manipulating multilateral security diplomacy to its strategic advantage.

That said, it does not follow that if a policy of "engagement" has its problems, a policy of "containment" must be flawless. The language that has arisen to discuss U.S. China policy is itself seminally misleading; both "engagement" and "containment" arguments usually assume that the Sino-American bilateral relationship is so central that it will, in future, control all major regional outcomes. This is not so. The Sino-American relationship will be the main factor in the game, no doubt; but U.S. policy toward China, as with policy toward any major power, must fit into a larger picture in which Japan, Korea, Russia, Vietnam, Indonesia, and other states will inevitably play a part. In this essay I shall examine this dynamic and consider what such a fit involves, for even the advocates of a containment strategy, simple in principle though it may be, are obliged to begin with a realistic awareness of Asian complexities.

China's Strategic Opportunity

To understand where China is going we might start by remembering where it has been. Several stages distinguish the development of China's foreign policy since 1949. First there was Beijing's alliance with Moscow. Then came the Sino-Soviet split, which led China to pursue a revolutionary foreign policy directed against both superpowers. Then followed the Cultural Revolution, during which China had barely any foreign policy at all. By 1969, Beijing was on the brink of a war with the Soviet Union that it could only have lost. As the chaos of the Cultural Revolution gave way to a new internal balance, China redefined its relationship with America to oppose a formidable expansion of Soviet power. In the Cold War's final two decades, China played a major part in defeating Soviet designs. It tied down Soviet forces in the Far East and outmaneuvered Hanoi and Moscow by countering Vietnam's invasion of Cambodia, where the Soviet Union had sought to outflank China and to challenge America's position at the junction of the straits linking the Pacific and Indian Oceans.

With the collapse of the Soviet empire, China entered a new stage in its foreign policy, one as yet without a name. But named or not, it is clear that China is a major beneficiary of the Cold War's outcome. The collapse of the Soviet Union has removed its main strategic threat, and in doing so has also removed its strategic dependence on America. At the same time, Beijing has embraced the transition to capitalism under party control, unleashing the economic energy of its people and far outpacing the social dynamism of its Russian neighbor. Largely as a consequence of all this, China is feeling its oats. Already identifying itself as one of the world's two most powerful nations, China foresees its economy soon overtaking that of the United States in sheer size. It is obviously eyeing a larger place in the sun, and its rise has captured the imagination of political cognoscenti all over the world—an achievement that, by itself, contributes much to the élan of Chinese assertiveness.

Not all is smooth sailing, of course. Domestically, China's economy is spread unevenly between south and north, coast and interior. Agriculture, having once led the way, now lags, and this, together with the increasing withdrawal of the state from the industrial sector of the economy, is generating unprecedented labor dislocation and internal migration. These phenomena, in turn, are deepening the strains on China's national unity, strains that reflect problems of size, regional and ethnic differences, and a historical propensity to fragment. Finally, with Deng Xiaoping's death, contests for power may test the political system to the utmost.

Already that political system, still led by the Communist Party, lacks legitimacy—as must be the case when economic success is achieved by embracing capitalism, and when, until recently, foreign policy success was achieved by siding with the premier capitalist state against the premier communist one. As has been widely observed, this void makes nationalist appeals and demonstrative firmness in foreign policy important in sustaining the party's hold on power. It also tends to raise the stature of the People's Liberation Army (PLA), which, unlike the Soviet army, has always been more the partner than the servant of the party.[1] The PLA is a logical instrument of national assertion. While China does not harbor any vast territorial ambitions, it does entertain some, mostly expressed in irredentist terms linked to historical claims and past "unequal" treatment. Other nations, indeed, did take advantage of China's weakness, none more brutally than Japan. In doing so, they hurt Han pride and sense of superior civilization. Now, with the tables partly turned, China expects redress of historic grievances and demands "respect."

Context matters. The end of the Cold War and the political successes of NATO during it resolved long-standing issues of international security in Europe—contests over hegemony and the balance of power that underlay both world wars and the Cold War. But this happy outcome has no parallel in East Asia, where the glue of common strategic interests no longer binds the United States and China. Relations among major European countries today are more predictably non-violent than they were before the Second—or indeed the First—World War; the same can simply not be said about Asia. Rather, an uneasy equilibrium persists among China, Japan, and the United States. Weakened Russia is an interested onlooker and would-be player. Tensions focus especially on the Korean Peninsula, Taiwan, and the South China Sea.

The larger question in all this is whether the resolution of one set of problems critical to international order must give rise to another set of problems, just as the strategic consequences of the Second World War produced the Cold War. As far as Europe is concerned, the short answer is no, it need not. But in East Asia it might—and if Beijing uses force to achieve its aims at home and abroad, it will. If it again brutally puts down any domestic challenges to the party's power, and if abroad the leadership should decide to resort to force, and to sacrifice

Chinese lives in huge number in an effort to achieve strategic goals and causes driven by raison d'état, a direct link will again have been made manifest between absolute power and a ruthless foreign policy. Then we will have a real problem on our hands, one all too familiar from the experiences of the last sixty years.

Is there any evidence for fearing such an outcome? Yes, there is some.

Muscle Building

The collapse of the Soviet Union freed China from immense strategic pressure on its northern border. It also liberated the PLA from the Maoist "people's war" doctrine—defense by depth and density of population in lieu of firepower. China is developing smaller, more professional forces with greater mobility and striking power, both typical goals of force modernization generally. Its improvements in military capability have not come at the expense of economic development—a common trade-off in many circumstances. Rather, they have been a dividend from the PLA's own very extensive commercial activities.

China no longer looks north strategically, but south and east to its maritime boundaries and land borders. It accords high priority to modernizing its maritime capability, to moving from a "brown-water" coastal defense to a "blue-water" ocean-going navy. A continental power's decision to go to sea signals strategic warning. China's efforts are not on the scale of the Kaiser's naval building program or Soviet naval expansion under Admiral Gorshkov, but they do represent a shift in gear that is hard to ignore. They reflect a change in strategic mentality consonant with other indicators of growing regional strategic ambition.[ii]

China does not need maritime strength comparable to America's to dominate its immediate east and south, where it can exploit the chain of offshore islands and straits to strategic advantage. That chain, which stretches south from Japan to the Philippines, separates China's coast from the broad Pacific. The Philippines plus Kalimantan (Borneo) turn the South China Sea into a funnel that leads to the critical junction of straits in and around Singapore, waterways that connect the Indian and Pacific Oceans. This island barrier continues eastward through Indonesia and down the east coast of Australia—which explains the intensity of fighting during the Pacific War to control New Guinea and Guadalcanal.

For China, the offshore island chain is strategically double-edged. In the hands of others it could bottle up China's navy, but in Chinese hands it offers a screen for exercising power. China has developed capabilities to force and defend the straits separating the islands off its coast, including combined-arms skills coordinating action by ships at sea with air cover by modern Su-27 aircraft acquired from Russia. China has practiced surge deployment of warships through the straits into the wider Pacific, and it is acquiring Soviet-design Kilo-class attack submarines that will give it a reach sufficient to create a strategic buffer at sea several hundred kilometers broader than what it has at present. This represents a major technological jump, pointing to future advances that should concern the U.S. Navy.

As well, China aims to build aircraft carriers that can accommodate nuclear-capable aircraft, and it has long sought to perfect a nuclear missile-armed submarine that would bring it closer to effective strategic parity with the United States. This potential problem, however, should not be exaggerated; it would take until around 2015 for China to acquire an aircraft carrier battle group, and only after spending billions of dollars. At present, the U.S. Navy can get close enough to China, without much peril to itself, to do whatever it need do. Such a circumstance will not change soon, notwithstanding China's probable desire to increase American costs and risks, and to thereby devalue the assurance and deterrence functions of the U.S. Navy with respect to its Pacific allies.

Nowhere is China's strategic design feared more acutely than in Taiwan. China's maritime power capabilities much reduce Taiwan's capacity to defend itself unaided, and have encouraged the United States to provide Taiwan with defensive weapons, including Stinger missiles. Of China's external claims, Taiwan also has the sharpest political edge. It is an issue in which the PLA has a major stake and that easily arouses national chauvinism; going soft on Taiwan would undermine any contender's claim to power in Beijing. China represents Taiwan as an internal affair in which no outsider has a legitimate voice. Its ambassador for disarmament, no less, announced that its pledge against first use of nuclear weapons did not apply to the recalcitrant province.[iii] China's claimed right, in effect, to nuke itself underlines its realpolitik approach to the world, as did its military intimidation of Taiwan's 1996 elections, aimed at discouraging aspirations to independence. Beijing also warns others not to accord Taiwan de facto recognition or access to arms, thus seeking to isolate Taiwan and force it to negotiate from weakness. China's approach to Taiwan resembles a sort of Asian Munich option: It aims at recovering its own "Sudetenland" by threat of force to which others acquiesce through fear of war. To Beijing, of course, Taiwan represents a potential U.S. bridgehead on China's coast.

China also claims most of the offshore islands and reefs in the South China Sea on historical grounds that others find dubious and that littoral-state claimants contest. Were China unilaterally to enforce these claims successfully, it would gain control of the food and hydrocarbon resources of the South China Sea, and achieve a strategic dominance that would affect the security of all littoral countries and the critical junction of straits near Singapore. Not least among the interests that would be put at risk would be the flow of oil from the Middle East on which Japan and Korea depend.

This threat is not merely theoretical. China has twice used force against Vietnam over the Paracel Islands. Its seizure of Mischief Reef in 1995 reflected a southward advance into the Spratly Islands. The terms of China's formal ratification of the UN Convention on Law of the Sea and the map of baselines it issued aroused much apprehension. Jakarta, for example, feared that these Chinese claims threatened Indonesia's sovereignty with respect to the Natuna Islands, its northernmost territory in the area. While China's claims predate Vietnam's withdrawal from Cambodia, the Soviet collapse and the surrender of its bases at Cam Ranh Bay, and the closing of U.S. bases in the Philippines, those events undoubtedly encouraged Beijing to see a strategic vacuum in the South China Sea and exploit it.

China's assertiveness is not limited to strictly Asian neighbors, but extends as well to its Pacific ones. In the lead up to the Australian prime minister's visit to China in March 1997, Beijing brought pressure to bear against strengthened U.S.-Australian security cooperation on grounds that bilateral security links are now both passé and inappropriate—a song the Chinese sing, as well, in multilateral security forums. The point registered none too subtly was that Australia would pay a price in its relations with China. Beijing's target was the U.S.-Australian alliance.

ASEAN's Response

The ASEAN countries—until recently comprising Indonesia, Malaysia, Thailand, the Philippines, Singapore, Vietnam, and Brunei—have been at sixes and sevens in responding to Chinese pressure. Some are disposed to be accommodating, others more resistant. For reasons of history, propinquity, and bulk, China looms over Southeast Asia. The regional countries know that, unlike Western states, China will never go away. Each has economically significant Chinese minorities, except for Singapore, where Chinese form the majority. ASEAN's progress has moderated fears of conflict among its member states, but it has not abolished them, and it certainly has not provided the kind of cohesion capable of balancing China. The organization's recent expansion to include Laos and Burma will dilute further its cohesiveness in this respect, as will the inclusion of Cambodia, if in the extended aftermath of the July 1997 Hun Sen coup that country is eventually brought in.

Fast growing economically, the ASEAN countries are modernizing their forces and becoming better equipped to counter maritime threats. At this stage of the game, their difficulty in relation to China is not military but psychological imbalance. Though they may not welcome it, several Southeast Asian countries seem disposed to accept the inevitability of dominant Chinese influence. Burma's friendless military regime needs China's support, as does a Thailand that fears Vietnam. Cambodia's leaders appreciate that China's backing is essential to preserving independence. Lee Kuan Yew displays an acquiescent attitude toward China, and he and the Singapore government seem vulnerable to Beijing's clever flattery. Malaysia's Prime Minister Mahathir, militantly anti-Western, declares that China has invaded no country and that Southeast Asia has no need of U.S. military protection.

Indonesia and Vietnam are less pliable. The aforementioned terms of China's ratification of the UN Convention on Law of the Sea prompted Indonesia to stage a military exercise of unprecedented character in defense of the Natuna Islands. (Malaysia's forces helped with preliminaries.) Indonesia's conclusion of an out-of-character security agreement with Australia in 1995 also reflected its concern, as well as its skepticism concerning the security benefits conferred by ASEAN. Last June, in a remarkable policy reversal, an official Indonesian defense review proposed that ASEAN should assume a security dimension. The context in which it did so related the proposal to China's claims and activities in the South China Sea. It reflects Indonesia's sense of isolation, brought about by tensions with the U.S. over human rights and with the EC over economic issues (instigated by Portugal and Japan), as well as rising internal political problems bearing on the presidential succession. Such U.S. pressure on Indonesia contradicts America's strategic interests and plays into China's hands.

To a degree unique among the ASEAN countries, Indonesia is well disposed toward Vietnam, whose will to resist Chinese pressure is undoubted. But abandoned by the Soviet Union, and with suspicious neighbors that dislike its communist regime, for the time being Vietnam is otherwise pretty much isolated.

Despite Indonesia's efforts, ASEAN itself is manifestly incapable of coordinated military action at present, and it will be awhile before that can change, even if there should develop a will to do so. Even its success at coordinated security diplomacy over Cambodia required cooperation with China, legitimizing Beijing's voice in regional security affairs. Further, the ASEAN countries seek to manage their security relations with external powers through the ASEAN Regional Forum, which includes China. In doing so, they run the risk of China's taking advantage of the ARF to divide and rule, as well as to foster anti-Western sentiment. While China is generally suspicious of multilateral organizations, it seeks whenever possible to exploit them for diplomatic advantage.[IV] In this case China coyly denies that the ARF is a mere "talk shop", even as it urges the virtues of "common security", a term recalling the sort of model Soviet diplomacy designed to dilute and render ineffectual all possible opposing coalitions.

The AEAN countries are clearly not strong enough by themselves in any case to call the tune with the great powers. This was evident in their handling of China's seizure of Mischief Reef. Doubtless a test by China, it is unlikely that it would have occurred were U.S. bases still operating in the Philippines. With difficulty, ASEAN developed a coordinated approach that was put to China in a limp "official dialogue." China toyed with this approach as it sought to pick off the ASEAN countries one by one with offers to settle differences bilaterally. The Philippines, meanwhile, has tried to draw in the United States to support its claims in the area, so far to no avail. ASEAN's Southeast Asian Nuclear Weapon-Free Zone is yet another dabble at collective security aimed at China, but it is one that could rebound to its great disadvantage if its realization had the effect of restraining the United States rather than China. The ASEAN countries need U.S.

power to counter that of China, and, for geostrategic reasons, Washington depends on nuclear weapons far more than does Beijing. Indeed, this dependence would increase should the mobility of American maritime forces and their capacity to deploy forward in the Western Pacific be curtailed for budgetary or other reasons.

China, in contrast, practices minimum deterrence. It has just sufficient forces to deter nuclear attack and, as noted, it is modernizing those forces. Because of its mass and weight, China can afford to give assurances against first use of nuclear weapons. Indeed, in light of current imbalances favoring Russia and the United States, complete nuclear disarmament would suit China well given its large numbers and readiness to accept heavy casualties in conventional conflicts. So China enjoys the best of both worlds: Its nuclear weapons reinforce its regional power and influence, but it does not need to say so. ASEAN's regional Nuclear Weapon-Free Zone, therefore, plays to Chinese strengths.

Strategic Disjunction

If the South China Sea nowadays presents opportunities to drive a Chinese knife through butter, in the case of the Koreans and Japanese the Chinese are dealing with East Asian hardheads much like themselves. Moreover, the U.S.-Japanese treaty remains the cornerstone of security in East Asia, both affording the United States a reliable base and cocooning Japanese power in ways that limit regional sensitivities. Japan's considerable naval strength contributes to regional security, and Japan facilitates the large U.S. military presence in East Asia, at sea and on land, a presence that is vital to sustaining a stable balance there. In times of peace, U.S. power does not compel, but it deters and reassures, reassurance being a function of military power that is often neglected but never insignificant. Its effectiveness depends on strategic mobility and nuclear weapons.

America's alliance with Japan and its military presence in the Western Pacific strengthen U.S. security. Historically, the ocean buffers that have afforded America its ultimate physical security have impelled U.S. interest in events on the distant shores of both the Pacific and Atlantic Oceans. America is a Pacific power today not just from habit, but also from need—a need, it is worth emphasizing, that has far more to do with bedrock security issues than with commerce. Increased trade consequent to East Asian economic growth both reinforces and complicates U.S. interests in the Pacific, the complications arising mainly from the domestic political influences touched off by the vested interests of business and labor lobbies. But for Washington, China's assertiveness and the perennial dangers of the Korean Peninsula are still the most likely immediate causes of tension and threat in East Asia.

Changing circumstances present new opportunities for U.S. policy—and new risks. Central to both is the post-Cold War strategic order in the Western Pacific. China and the United States now represent the defining poles of power there. Geostrategically natural adversaries, opposition to the Soviet threat made them allies of convenience. That adhesive having dissolved, clashing political values and opposed security interests underlie their differences today. Mutual economic interests alone are unlikely to override those differences. Indeed, bilateral economic tensions could make things worse.

China resents America's global reach. China would likely be content were the United States to concede its dominant influence in East Asia in return for China's accepting U.S. hegemony over the Americas and leading influence in Europe. But U.S. interests could not admit such a bargain. This bloody century has cast America in the role of "off-shore balancer", the only power capable of intervening decisively in conflicts over the balance of power in Europe and Asia that jeopardize both U.S. security and the stability of these regions. Displacing Britain as the leading maritime power, America also succeeded to Britannia's role, and its capacity to add (or withhold) its weight remains the determining factor with respect to the global balance on which America's own security depends. This plain fact—that America is the balancer, and that it is nowadays only China that may need to be balanced against—defines the geostrategic disjunction that underlies U.S.-Sino tensions over Pacific security. This core strategic reality has nothing to do with human rights, balance of trade deficits, espionage, fundraising improprieties, or the suppression of Christian missionary work—absolutely nothing.

How has the United States managed the Sino-American strategic disjunction so far? At the outset, the Clinton administration floundered over foreign policy generally and, with Warren Christopher at State and Anthony Lake at NSC, it looked dangerously like a Carter administration re-run. But its foreign policy performance did improve. Specifically with respect to policy in the Pacific area, one can note the following milestones:

• Defense Secretary William Perry's February 1995 recommendations on Pacific security policy, issued in the authoritative "U.S. Security Strategy for the East Asia-Pacific Region";

• Secretary of State Christopher's reminder at the ARF meeting following the Mischief Reef incident (and since repeated) that the Philippines is a "core ally" to which the United States has continuing security treaty obligations;

• America's display of overwhelming naval power in reaction to China's missile drills directed at Taiwan's 1996 elections;

• The U.S.-Japanese joint declaration during President Clinton's April 1996 visit to Tokyo, which committed the parties to collaborate in promoting regional and international security on the basis of their bilateral treaty, and the U.S. commitment to continue deployment of about 100,000 troops in the Pacific;

• President Clinton's November 1996 statement in Canberra, en route to the APEC leaders' meeting in the Philippines, which emphasized China's critical importance to future regional security; the centrality of America's "core alliances" with Japan, the ROK, Australia, the Philippines, and Thailand; and the need to build new regional security architecture through ASEAN in order to reduce further tensions in the South China Sea. The President's language was carefully hewn, and warrants close attention. He said: "The direction that China takes in the years to come, the way it defines its greatness in the future, will help to decide whether the next century is one of conflict or cooperation. The emergence of a stable, an open, a prosperous China, a strong China confident of its place in the world and willing to assume its responsibilities as a great nation is in our deepest interest." Though widely interpreted as an olive branch, these remarks effectively cast on China the onus of choice.

In short, and despite many early stumbles, by the end of its first term the Clinton administration had re-established a sense of responsible continuity in Asian security policy. Its earlier emphases on human rights on one side and trade issues on the other had given way to a focus on more traditional, and more fundamental, political and security concerns. That is all to the good, for serious difficulties remain in fashioning future policy toward East Asia.

One difficulty has to do with resolving conflicting pressures on U.S. policy and overcoming contradictions among the White House, Capitol Hill, and the professional bureaucracy, including the military. While this problem is not unique to democracy, it is harder to manage because political processes and bargaining are more or less unconcealed. But a second difficulty is balancing the competing claims of Korean and especially Japanese security interests against each other and against those of the United States with respect to China.

The North East

Three security concerns trouble Japan: China's use of force in pursuit of its interests; Japan's strategic priority for partnership with the United States as opposed to China, even though China will always be "there" while the United States might not; and the reliability of Japanese domestic political support for its U.S.-tilted security policy.

For much of this century, Japan has sought security through alliance with distant maritime powers, first Britain and, since the Second World War, the United States. Japan did so in the former case to cover its tail in pursuit of its own expansionist designs on the mainland; in the latter case, it has done so in apprehension of threats to its security posed by great powers on the Asian mainland. Reliance on U.S. strategic protection since the Second World War has served Japan's interests well. Its own limited defense efforts have muffled regional and domestic concern about revived militarism, while enabling Japan to get on with economic development. Still, Japan has not been supine; its naval power, in particular, contributed much to containing the Soviet threat in the Far East and usefully complicated Soviet strategic planning writ large.

The Cold War's end has disturbed Japan's strategic certitude. It is having to pay more for American strategic protection. The declining domestic acceptability of the U.S. force presence is causing discord. And Japan's responsiveness to pressure to become more active in international security affairs, such as UN peacekeeping missions, remains domestically sensitive. But a Japan that aspires to membership in the UN Security Council is obliged to accept wider international responsibilities. More centrally, any serious loss of confidence in U.S. strategic protection would pose an awful dilemma for Japan—essentially, whether to knuckle under to China and so lose control of its destiny, or to develop the military clout required to secure its international interests, which would inflame regional tensions and arouse domestic resistance.

China is adept at making the Japanese squirm about the Second World War and at extracting what are in effect reparations for it—though those reparations assist Japanese economic penetration of China. China is ambivalent toward the U.S.-Japan security treaty. Ideally, Beijing would like to see Japan reduced to dependence on China; but at the same time a Japan dependent on U.S. strategic protection is preferable to a well armed loose cannon. Beijing's problem with the security treaty is that it denies China paramount influence over Japan and affords the U.S. standing in regional security affairs. Since no one knows exactly what Japan would do on its own—whether it would remain militarily weak and diplomatically pliant, or grow strong and assertive—it may well be that China's counsels on the issue are divided. Or China may see the security treaty as reassuring in the short term while hoping for the recision of U.S. military power from the Western Pacific in the longer run.

As for now, the United States has sought to reassure Tokyo of the certainty of its security commitment while encouraging Japan to play a greater part in regional security. China has criticized Japan for planning to use its forces in a regional role instead of, as in the past, for "inward-looking" self-defense. Meanwhile, having dropped Russia from its list of primary threats, Japan continues pointedly to develop its naval, air defense, and intelligence capabilities, and is undertaking a wider range of international security consultations. Such actions reflect hedging on Japan's part, not just against China's growing capabilities and ambitions, but also against the possibility that its importance to U.S. security might slip relative to China's claims, requiring more self-reliance in defense matters on its part. For without reliable U.S. support, Japan would face a worrisome range of strategic uncertainties. Reflecting history, Korean feelings toward Japan are visceral and a unified Korea could prove hostile, while worst-case proliferation could see both Koreas join Russia and China as nuclear-armed neighbors of Japan. As well, Japan depends on oil supplies that mostly transit sea lanes that could become vulnerable to Chinese maritime power.

While Japanese interests and power force Sino-American relations into a triangle, Korea forces them into a quadrangle. The Korean problem is particularly good at exposing the limitations of thinking about strategic matters in bilateral compartments. For should the United States wish to "engage" China, then it should seek to give China entrée to and influence over a Korean settlement. Should it wish to "contain" China, then both Japanese and even Russian participation in Korea should take pride of place. But could Korea be "settled" diplomatically without China? Could China and Japan ever agree to terms for a Korean settlement? These are important basic questions for U.S. policy, and yet they seem rarely asked or discussed. This is a measure of how poorly the true geopolitical shape of the region is reckoned in Washington these days.

In the long run—or not-so-long run—economic decline or political changes to accommodate reform might "solve" the North Korean problem before much serious thought is brought to bear on consequences and policy options. Economic difficulties have reduced North Korean military readiness and, to that extent, the level of threat it poses. Unwillingness to follow China's example and accept the political risks of economic change have increased North Korea's isolation. Seoul holds most of the cards in the reunification game and, practicing democracy with Korean characteristics, it more or less lurches from success to success. Desperate circumstances are forcing the North into dealing with its enemies, most reluctantly even with the South, while also engaging in a version of nuclear blackmail. Although starvation looms for as many as five million people, the Pyongyang regime seems determined to maintain its monopoly of political power.

China's diplomatic recognition of the ROK underlines how far it has abandoned North Korea, where its influence is limited in any event. Seoul, although increasingly able to defend itself, still relies on U.S. military support, including nuclear deterrence, greatly complicating any aggressive calculations that Pyongyang may entertain. For its part, North Korea has long sought to deal directly with the United States on a basis that excludes the South. That Seoul's interests in managing the North Korean nuclear issue are not identical with Washington's could cause bilateral strain. Indeed, this is already the case.

The larger issue, however, comes back to the United States and China. The idea of bordering on a Korea unified on Seoul's terms is anathema to China. China demands a major say in any Korean settlement, including withdrawal of U.S. ground forces from the peninsula. A unified Korea without U.S. troops could still maintain strategic connections with the United States, but they would be more distant and less convincing.

Russia, too, would like a say in the terms of a Korean settlement, given the vulnerability of its Far Eastern territories. Russia seeks to preserve what influence it can, including its role as an arms supplier, but it would wish to do so only to the extent that it could without adversely affecting its relations with China and the United States. Perhaps feeling that U.S. dealings with the North over the nuclear issue have been insensitive to ROK interests, Seoul has made gestures toward Russia even as it has begun to coordinate intelligence with China in the event of a sudden collapse of the North Korean regime.

Japan, because of its strategic vulnerability and considerable economic stake in Korea, has great interest but not much influence there—mostly the legacy of a caustic history. Strategic cooperation between Japan and the ROK is minimal, though both are American allies that host large U.S. forces.

Influenced by the German experience, Seoul fears hasty reunification. Probably none of the actors wishes it except North Korea, and then only on its own (unattainable) terms. As in years past, containing tensions is the sensible priority and that means maintaining a balance of forces sufficient to check North Korea. The historical record suggests that allowance should be made for unpredictability in Korean affairs, not least the North's penchant for bizarre violence.

Creating a New Equilibrium

China expects to become the dominant power in East Asia. It probably aspires as well to replace the United States at the top of the world hierarchy of power. It is already the second most powerful country and believes that in due course it will surpass the U.S. economy in absolute size. This will feed Han chauvinism and self-regard, which are liable to be particularly hungry for sustenance after more than a century of abuse and humiliation.

Such ambition is misconceived. Despite its recent economic progress, backwardness and overpopulation are huge obstacles to modernity that will weigh China down for decades—probably for generations—to come. Potential conflicts in the Western Pacific are not of Cold War dimension. They are not global in their range as those with the Soviet Union were, and they do not threaten world war. But they do point to competition for power and influence, and so too to strategic tensions. How should those worried by China's actions and ambitions respond?

On both sides, "containment" naturally comes to mind. Containment was a desperate policy adopted by the United States and its allies in the face of Stalin's trying to reap the strategic rewards of victory in 1945 in ways that risked world war. China's manifest ambitions pose no such threat. Because the scale of threat is insufficient, a policy of containing China would be disproportionate and would fail to garner support. But China accuses all who urge a firm response to its challenging behavior of planning containment. This is a clever defense, apt to muddle the thinking of adversaries and observers alike—just as accusations of "isolationism" against those who would be more selective of overseas commitments is clever but inaccurate. That said, the Chinese are abetted by many commentators in the United States, and China's leadership may well genuinely believe that the United States is developing a containment option. While it would risk antagonizing China, such a conclusion would help if its effects were dissuasive. Policy needs to ensure China's appreciation that unilateral action that fails to respect the legitimate interests of others will incur uncomfortable penalties and risk self-defeat.

This principle is easily stated but difficult to implement. No two countries will agree precisely on the nature of the problem. All have interests to prosecute and foreign policy is often hostage to domestic imperatives. Notably, what burden is U.S. opinion prepared to accept in support of foreign policy goals that, in the absence of a clear and present danger, can appear both abstract and lacking in urgency? Will Japan pull its weight? Should it do so, or would that scare others? Given their history, can Tokyo and Seoul collaborate for mutual security ends, even minimally? Do the alliances of both with the United States provide enough cement between them? Policy coordination is difficult to achieve and sustain. Striking the right balance between incentives and penalties, force and persuasion, and maintaining effort over time are all great challenges. China will take advantage of any weakness and disunity on the part of those opposed to its ambitions.

And yet, though long experienced at playing from weakness, China too has exploitable problems. Some are dangerous, especially those involving internal political tensions and Taiwan. While presenting opportunities, they need careful handling. Socialist ideology is dead in East Asia, and capitalism triumphant—though not yet democracy. As even the optimists on this point freely admit, capitalism affords no guarantee that democracy will flourish and autocracy abate; and even if it does, a wave of Asian democracy in itself is no guarantor of regional peace. Establishing and sustaining a stable power equilibrium remains the key to peace and security, and removes any need to think in terms of containment. But unless a stable balance is attained, there is no prospect of China and the United States working cooperatively and successfully to assure Asia's peaceful future.

NOTES

[i] The title PLA comprises all of China's armed forces, not just its ground forces. The point is significant because of the priority that the navy and air force command in terms of military modernization.

[ii] Felix K. Chang's "Beijing's Reach in the South China Sea", *Orbis* (Summer 1996), provides an illuminating analysis of the development in China's maritime power policy.

[iii] As reported in *The Straits Times*, August 6, 1996.

[iv] See Thomas J. Christensen, "Chinese Realpolitik", *Foreign Affairs* (September/October 1996), pp. 38-9.

Part 5

History and Historiography

25

Communist Crowd Control

*George Walden**

In the midst of the Cultural Revolution I once drafted a telegram from the British Mission in Peking, or what remained after the Red Guards burned it, suggesting that Deng Xiaoping was dead. It seemed a reasonable conjecture. The no-neck monster, as we diplomatic juveniles called him, had not been seen in public for some time, was portrayed in the wall posters we read as a leading capitalist-roader, and had begun featuring in caricatures at the wrong end of a rope. Plus we had procured a Red Guard newspaper containing a celebratory account of his actual death by hara-kiri. Getting hold of those newspapers was an operation in itself, so there was a tendency to overplay what was inside them. I suppose I was infected by a scoop mentality, and there were scarcely any pressmen left in Peking to confirm or contradict my words. Meeting Deng some years later, as principal assistant to British Foreign Secretary Lord Carrington, I inspected him for signs of simulation, but he seemed the genuine thing. No one else could smoke that much, or hawk and spit with such vigor.

Are The Tiananmen Papers genuine? With China, you never know. Even the endorsement of some of America's most respected sinologists is not conclusive. Van Meegeren's forgeries of Vermeer were accepted by the leading art historians of his day because they were designed to fill gaps in their knowledge,

---

* George Walden's first-hand account of the Cultural Revolution is included in his memoir, *Lucky George* (Allen Lane, 1999).

This essay first appeared in *The National Interest*, No. 64 (Summer 2001). It was a review of Andrew J. Nathan and Perry Link, eds., *The Tiananmen Papers* (New York: Public Affairs, 2001).

295

despite the fact that the women in them bore a curious resemblance to Marlene Dietrich.

Like those art historians, we want this material to be genuine, in our case for moral reasons. Moralism infects our behavior toward China more than toward the erstwhile Soviet Union, in Britain to compensate for our colonialist misdemeanors, in the United States because the history of American attitudes toward China is one of recurring evangelical hope followed by disillusion. This account of the Tiananmen massacre shows the hard men of Peking in a poor light, and when it is republished in Chinese and makes its way to the mainland, it could do much to strengthen the reformers' hands. That is why the anonymous leaker leaked it in excerpts designed to tell a story rather than as entire original documents. We must be especially wary of good intentions.

Enough caveats: if this is a forgery it is brilliantly done. To me, as to the editors, the voices in these extraordinary documents ring true. As I read the records of Chinese Politburo meetings and secret police reports, mentally I was comparing them with the documents now available from the Soviet period, notably in *The Road to Terror* (1999) covering the Moscow trials, but also later. For all the grim similarity of the Russian and Chinese official press, in private all communists do not speak alike. The Russian voice is a compound of ideology and gangster inflections, of Marxism-Leninism and mafia-speak, whereas the Chinese voice, while retaining a certain formality, is less intellectual, more pragmatic. If the subject were not the life or death of millions one might sometimes call it homespun. That is the timbre of some of the secret documents the Red Guards were fed by their Maoist mentors and reproduced in posters and leaflets, and in that sense, for me The Tiananmen Papers brought back old times.

Deng's voice is especially persuasive. At the start of the occupation of the square the position of this eighty-five year old indestructible was equivocal. At one point he insists, disarmingly, that he is not all that conservative for his age, and in Chinese terms it is true. The tough survivor of many a battle with Mao exhibits Hamlet-like qualities before resolving to do the deed. I know it is frowned upon to ascribe human attributes to Chinese leaders, but something of the enormity of turning the People's Liberation Army on the people seeps through these pages. If the army were a mere killing machine in the Party's hands, why did eight generals at first decline to follow orders? And why did Deng spend so much time rationalizing with himself? There are no reports of Stalin doing that.

In one of his soliloquies Deng tries to persuade himself of the necessity of repression in the interests of the world community. If he fails to keep order in China, the result could be civil war, with hundreds of millions of refugees flooding Asia and destabilizing the world. From a Chinese leader these are novel sentiments, a kind of communist internationalism, style nouveau. This philanthropic line was later to prove persuasive with many an Asian brother, not to speak of Western statesmen such as Sir Edward Heath.

My only doubt about the authenticity of Deng's voice arose fleetingly when he says something that summarizes his world-view so neatly that one wonders for a second whether it has been cooked up to tickle our palates: "Of course we want to build a socialist democracy, but we can't possibly do it in a hurry, and still less do we want that Western-style stuff. If our one billion people jumped into multiparty elections, we'd get chaos." And of course it is gratifying to hear him insist time and again that whatever happens there can be no return to the policy of isolating China from the world, which he rightly sees as the root of many of its problems.

Listening to these legendary figures talking is like seeing waxworks come to life. Sometimes their caricatural aspects are confirmed, sometimes not. Any reader who imagined that Chinese communist leaders are cloned in the cradle will be disabused. The range and interplay of characters—which is to say the human element—is greater than we might have thought. And doddery though some of them are, their antiquity is not always the problem. The youngish but widely disliked Politburo member Li Peng, an adopted son of Zhou Enlai, conforms satisfyingly to his reputation. A pernickety ideologue when it came to doing down Zhao Ziyang, the general secretary who wanted to compromise with the students, he plays on Deng's fears of disorder on the scale of the Cultural Revolution to nudge him toward a crackdown. And when, fearing they would all wake up under house arrest, Deng succumbs and orders martial law, Li Peng insists his every word is gospel.

Though the Party "Elders" all curse and revile the "tiny minority of counter-revolutionaries", Wang Zhen is the only one who is consistently vitriolic: "These people are really asking for it. . . . These kids don't know how good they've got it! When we were their age we lived in a forest of rifles and a rain of bullets. . . . No appreciation!" For all his malign intent, here at least this barnacled eighty-one year old, the old salt of the Party, is speaking no more than the truth. The students come across as moderate and sophisticated, but the effect of their actions is to make China's gerontocrats feel they have been backed into a corner. And when he complains of the soft life of youth, and their lack of gratitude, Wang Zhen, like any irascible father, is factually correct. By 1989 there was more freedom and prosperity in China than at any time since the 1949 revolution. And, naturally, the students and their supporters wanted more.

As the French Revolution, or for that matter the fall of Soviet communism, confirms, it is often when things are gradually improving that expectations grow exponentially and patience snaps. The logic is to dam up those expectations by curtailing freedom, and, despite their lip service to Deng's policies of reform and opening up, that is what Wang Chen and his fellow brutalists wanted to do.

Yang Shangkun, the president, a year older than Wang Zhen at eighty-two, emerges as a prudent figure. He is initially averse to force and balks at appointing Li Peng as Party chairman when Zhao Ziyang is on the way out for having failed to persuade the students to call off their demonstration. Zhao Ziyang himself, alas, appears to have been ineffectual, as well-intentioned people caught up in crises often are, and the tears he shed over the hunger-striking students inspired as much disgust in his more coarse-grained colleagues as they did surprise in the West. Yet despite his failure Zhao's analysis remains, as they say, correct. The hardliners insisted that reform (a highly relative term in their usage) could only proceed in an atmosphere of stability. Zhao insisted that without democratic reform there would be perpetual instability.

But Deng was convinced that instability would result from anything approaching democracy, Western-style. So the discussion in the Party turned and turned in a vicious circle; the only way out the leaders could see was to crush the students. The Greek tragedy aspect of the affair emerges with somber clarity. Given their fears that everything they had fought for all their lives (a powerful, proud, independent new China to them, a communist tyranny to us) was under threat, and given the tenacity of the students, for the old men of Peking there could be no halfway house. The same was true of the means of repression. For them, killing was the only way. For communist autocrats, crowd control has no meaning. Water cannon and riot police are democratic appurtenances, insofar as they assume that demonstrations that may get out of hand are allowed. Logically enough, China had neither. (It is interesting, however, that, when martial law was first declared, a last-minute attempt was made to equip the troops with batons, and at that stage they were ordered not to open fire on the students even if they came under attack, for example, from Molotov cocktails.)

Are we now in a more pacific stage of China's development? Some things have improved since 1989. Yet the very words used by the regime to dismiss this book—"Any attempt to . . . disrupt China by the despicable means of fabricating materials and distorting facts will be futile"—are so redolent of its catastrophic Maoist legacy that they suggest we have not come all that far since the government displayed the "counter-revolutionaries" it rounded up on television being browbeaten by soldiers for the delectation of the masses. It is high time things moved forward, and I would like to think that this will be a salutary book. Though the events are different in nature, my hunch is that these revelations could cause an intellectual ferment in China reminiscent of that which followed Khrushchev's 1956 Stalin speech.

The pity is that we are so often wrong on China, and confuse our hunches with our wishes. So we must allow for the opposite. As I read I tried to imagine how a middle-aged provincial Chinese—China does not consist entirely of Beijing students—might react. Far from being indignant and appalled, might he not sympathize with Deng's dilemma? Might he not admire him for giving Zhao Ziyang a chance and overlook the fact that, though Deng gave the order that "no one must die in the square", he and those about him knew what they were doing and were probably not unhappy at the prospect of a few deaths elsewhere, *pour encourager les autres*? And should our middle-aged Chinese be one of those who has profited from the new prosperity and relative freedom, might he not nod when he comes across Deng's warning about multiparty elections quoted above, and be wary of sowing luan—confusion—which is instinctively associated with the Cultural Revolution, even though that was the result of the Party making war on the people?

The answer, I suppose, could be that students and intellectuals might be stirred by the book, but not to the point of challenging the Party, if only for lack of popular support. More interesting is the possibility that its appearance might spark new thoughts of reform in high places. We are so in thrall to the myth that Reagan and Thatcher simply blew down the walls of the Soviet Union with a blast of their trumpets (if only we'd thought of it sooner!) that we forget the ferment among the more sophisticated senior party folk that antedated Reagan and eventually threw up Gorbachev. The fact that *The Tiananmen Papers* were compiled by a high-ranking Chinese official reminds us that the party whose general secretary was once Zhao Ziyang is capable of evolution, if only with the Burkean intention of self-preservation—though more likely with the aim of maximizing the country's wealth and power.

But this is divination, which this enthralling book inspires. Meanwhile, the regime's potential for viciousness is not in doubt, any more than the need for the West to keep up pressure for reform. If our policy is directed less at China than at our own gratification, we can cite the harsh side of *The Tiananmen Papers*—the paranoia about the West, the thuggish words about the students, the official murders and subsequent arrests—as conclusive evidence that the regime can behave in a repulsive fashion and ignore the rest. The trouble is, we knew that already. So what does this book change?

The Tiananmen Papers should help our China policy mature. The game of counterposing fearless democrats ready to "stand up to China" to sinocentric softies in the State Department or to the Foreign Office mandarins was fun in its time, but it has had its day. In Tiananmen, the crisis of a system, all that was unavailing. Nor is "standing up for democracy in China" a moral policy of itself, since true morality cannot be divorced from practicality. Indeed, it can be immoral if the grandstanders are more concerned with their own *bella figura* than with the fate of the Chinese people, or the results on the ground of the policy in question. I have no problem with a tough stance toward Beijing provided the fruits are clear, but China is a standing temptation for vainglorious politicians.

How far was the last governor of Hong Kong, Chris Patten, a notoriously self-regarding fellow, concerned with securing practical and lasting benefits for the Hong Kong people, and how far with re-launching his career after his rejection by the British electorate? And is President Bush responding to an increased threat, or playing macho politics? The competition he speaks of is implicit in the West's relations with China. How clever is it to force it to the surface, thereby inflaming nationalist sentiment among the Chinese people—a boon for Beijing's hardliners—not to speak of the risk of driving the Russians and the Chinese back together, and European and American policy apart?

Moralistic gesturing did nothing to help the students in Tiananmen Square and will help no one in the future. A truly ethical policy is incompatible with populist stances that dismiss anyone who knows anything about the country as kowtowing lackeys by definition. It means finding workable ways to advance Chinese democracy, alongside our legitimate interests, and staying the uphill, winding course. For all that they record a tragic setback, *The Tiananmen Papers*, a book whose very appearance gives hope, should encourage us to persist. God knows we are going to have enough trouble dealing with a more wealthy and powerful yet still aggrieved and resentful China without antagonizing it further, to no apparent purpose.

26

China and the Historians

Charles Horner[*]

Throughout the second half of the twentieth century, the study of modern China was informed by a "master narrative" whose climax was the founding of the People's Republic of China (PRC) in 1949. All roads seemed to lead to Beijing's famous Tiananmen Square and Chairman Mao's proclamation of China's new order. Of course, the historian cannot but tell the story this way, for he surely knows that this is how China's political struggles during the first half of the twentieth century resolved themselves. In this respect, the student of modern China is not much different from his fellows who are interested in other parts of the world; no matter any historian's claim that he seeks to understand the past on its own terms, his work is always conducted in full knowledge of how things actually turned out. He becomes a determinist de facto, reading consequences back into causes, even as he struggles against it.

And yet new interpretations, re-interpretations and syntheses do appear. Sometimes, without anyone's planning it or even desiring it, the rewriting and reworking of history can provide a new framework for the consideration of contemporary questions. When the subject is a relatively exotic place like China—whose story is not very well known to begin with—the time lag inherent in this process will be that much greater than normal, and a change in the focus of even the attentive public will take that much longer. To this, one must add the ladylike and gentlemanly pace at which the study of China progresses, a reflection

---

[*] Charles Horner is a senior fellow at the Hudson Institute. During the Reagan and Bush administrations he served in the Department of State and the U.S. Information Agency.

This essay first appeared in *The National Interest*, No. 63 (Spring 2001).

of the difficulty of the subject matter, but also a legacy of the careful, deliberate and unhurried way in which the Chinese themselves have studied their own history. And again, we must remember that conditions inside China during the past century and a half have hardly been conducive to the Western or Chinese study of the country's modern history. Inside, chaos and political repression have inhibited the work; outside, foreigners have been constrained by these obstacles—and by a few of their own making, as well.

This said, during the past twenty years, at least three important trends in the investigation and presentation of modern Chinese history have been altering our view of contemporary China—and will therefore influence our stance toward it. There has been, first of all, a profound and revolutionary change under way in interpreting China's last dynasty, the Qing (1644–1912), with important implications for our understanding of the very meaning of even fundamental terms like "China" and "Chinese." There is also a comparable revisiting of the history of the first half of the twentieth century, focused more on comprehending both the complex China and the "greater China" we see before us today, rather than the Maoist China that monopolized our vision for so long. And there is a demographic change in progress: the previously dominant position of non-Chinese sinologists in the study and teaching of China around the world is gradually shrinking as greater numbers of Chinese, whether inside or outside of China, whether citizens of China or of other countries, become involved.

Manchus and Chinese: Whose Great Enterprise?

In February 1912, Prince Chun, the regent acting on behalf of his five year-old son, the emperor of China, executed an instrument of abdication whereby the last Chinese dynasty came to an end. The Qing ("Ch'ing" in the older system of Romanization) dynasty had begun in 1644. It was not the creation of Chinese at all, but the work of a hitherto obscure inner Asian people, the Manchus, who had gradually come to prominence beyond the Great Wall. In the traditional Chinese sense of things, the Manchus' decision to attempt "the Great Enterprise"—that is, the conquest of all of China—was momentous, but far from unprecedented. Non-Chinese dynasties—dynasties of conquest, as they are styled—had governed China for about half its history. The one most familiar to us was created by the Mongols, whose dynasty was known to the Chinese as the Yuan (1260–1348); the emperor of China during Marco Polo's visit, Kublai Khan, was one of these Mongol rulers, a grandson of Genghis. Between the collapse of the Mongols and the ascendancy of the Manchus, China had been governed by the wholly home-grown Ming dynasty, whose rule began in 1368 and lasted for some 275 years.

The decay and decomposition of the Ming house, and how its empire was acquired by the previously unheralded Manchu invaders, is one of the great tales of Chinese history. It is the stuff not only of legend and literature. Chinese resistance to the gradual consolidation of Manchu rule throughout the country created a powerful political tradition of its own, for the Manchu ascendancy raised fundamental issues of loyalty and legitimacy for common folk and elites alike. The relatively tiny number of Manchu outsiders had to perfect a complex strategy of co-optation and intimidation, and then develop a governing style that would hold together their hard-won holdings. How they did this, who owed what to whom, and how to reconcile the initial grand successes of the seventeenth and eighteenth centuries with the catastrophic collapse of the nineteenth century—these issues of historical analysis have informed the debates about Chinese politics for the past century and a half.

How "Chinese" was Manchu-era China? That is the nub of the matter. Some Chinese who turned against the dynasty at its end for its failure to fend off the onslaught of the Western barbarians concluded that the country had been betrayed by the Manchus. They argued that, whatever their degree of "Chinese-ness", the Manchus were of a different race, and, therefore, were willing to collaborate with white imperialists against the interests of the Chinese as a people in order to protect "China" as a Manchu imperial possession. This racial aspect of things also served in some ways to further discredit the entire Confucian imperial idea as inherently opposed to the interests of the Chinese as a people; it fed the argument for junking the imperial system itself and substituting a modern republic in its place. The curious combination of revived racial consciousness (stoked by the "Social Darwinism" of the late nineteenth century), recollections of Ming dynasty loyalism, and different strands of Western political thought all came together in the anti-dynastic, pro-republican movement of the late nineteenth and early twentieth centuries, famously led by Sun Yat-sen.

On the other hand, there was no denying the greatness of prior Manchu achievements. These had been known throughout East Asia, and also to literate Europeans from the reports of Catholic missionaries who had actually witnessed and described with great insight and detail the last days of Ming rule, and who had then over time gained important positions in the Qing court. Western sinology began here, and it was the inspiration for the West's future fascination with *chinoiserie* in all its forms. The sixty-year reign of Kangsi (1662–1722) and the equally long reign of his grandson, Qianlong (1736–96), are arguably the most successful political tenures in the history of the country—perhaps even in the history of the world. The Chinese themselves once knew about the expansion, prosperity, regional hegemony and cultural efflorescence of Qing-era China, and were proud of it and their own role in it. While that memory was dimmed by subsequent humiliations and disasters, the more the Chinese have recovered from the shock of Western intrusion, the more prepared they have been to acknowledge Qing achievements.

Nor has it been so hard to square this particular circle. For many years, received historical interpretation had attributed Manchu successes to "sinicization", that is, to a long-established process whereby various aliens became "Chinese." Among Chinese, it was thus possible to have it both ways—that the

Manchus were both "Chinese" and "not Chinese" at one and the same time, depending, of course, on how the country was faring under Manchu tutelage.

This is not a debating point or a merely theoretical matter; it is a fundamental geographical one, a nation-defining one. The Republic of China that replaced the Qing dynasty was pleased to include in the new country all of "China", that is, all of China proper as the Manchus found it, plus the doubling of the size of the realm as they left it. For China as we know it is more or less China as the Manchus created it. To the historic Han core of the country they added Manchuria, Mongolia and Tibet—as well as Xinjiang, an additional 600,000 square miles (more than three times the size of France) of "new territories" in the far northwest. Indeed, the western half of the country today is sparsely populated, and by non-Han Chinese. It is these peoples—Turkic Muslims in the northwest, Buddhists in Tibet, for example—whose place in today's People's Republic of China is highly problematic. The place of Taiwan, another Qing addition of the late seventeenth century, is of course even more contentious.

There is a growing argument among historians about what history as such can teach us about these issues. The traditional way of imagining "China"—culturally coherent in its "sinicization", politically coherent in its "Confucianism", governmentally coherent in its "mandarinate", and geographically coherent as "one country"—is now challenged by new notions, the results of careful re-examination of the Manchu era and the theory and practice of Manchu governance. Indeed, the rise of "Manchu studies" is in itself a powerful indicator that China as we have known it need not be China at all.

To try to condense two decades of academic debate among a relatively small number of well-informed specialists will probably disconcert all parties to the discussion. On the other hand, our purpose here is well enough served by rather arbitrarily referring to but two of the many relevant works of scholarship that have appeared in the past two decades. In this way, the argument can be more conveniently bracketed.

About fifteen years ago, Professor Beatrice Bartlett of Yale, taking advantage of greater access to China-housed archives in the wake of the post-Mao liberalization, analyzed a parallel set of Qing-era governmental records, these written in the Manchu language, not in Chinese. This allowed her to argue for a different way of understanding the system of imperial governance; Manchu rulers were quite self-consciously neither "Chinese" nor the captives of a venerable Chinese-dominated bureaucracy. Instead, they had an agenda of their own and knew what they were doing to implement it.

This notion of a Manchu self-consciousness could, of course, be analyzed in various ways, and one comprehensive analysis will serve to form the other bracket to the argument. The analysis appeared at the end of the twentieth century in the work of Professor Pamela Crossley of Dartmouth.[i] In her view, there was a well-wrought Manchu imperial ideology that departed in many ways from the inherited Chinese one. In particular, the emperor himself, though he may have displayed a sinified face to his Chinese subjects, did not pretend either to himself or to his many other, non-Chinese subjects that he was Chinese. The enlargement of the empire was therefore not understood at all as the enlargement of China, but, rather, as the accretion of ever more and diverse holdings within a Manchu imperial portfolio. Thus, the emperors did not, on principle, pursue the sinification of newly acquired possessions, but instead respected their traditions and often represented themselves as somehow belonging to one or another of those diverse traditions rather than to the Chinese one. Indeed, the various parts of the Manchu empire developed a loyalty to the emperors seated in Beijing precisely because they viewed them not as the embodiment of an expansion of Chinese influence, but as something quite the reverse: For these outliers, the Manchu emperors were a bulwark against Han domination, not the agent of it.

Is this how it "really" was? The question remains unsettled, but the argument by itself has already given us a new way of looking at the governance of "China" at the time of its greatest size, wealth, power and standing in the world. It is a way of comprehending the governance of this vast land mass that presupposes a genuinely cosmopolitan outlook, one that is tolerant and ecumenical and, most of all, successful. Translated into the language of contemporary politics, it implies something akin to federalism, devolution and pluralism, new political words to be sure, but now legitimated by the splendors of a great historical epoch. It thus becomes possible to imagine a high tradition of political thought and practice, properly understood, that can be placed at the service of the requirements for the effective governance of a modern state of growing wealth, power and standing. Indeed, it also becomes possible to argue that this newly rediscovered model of "tolerance" and "diversity" and "decentralization" may be the only effective template for a twenty-first century system that can hold China together and preserve its civil peace.

How Modern Is Modern?

Just as close scrutiny of the details of a now-defunct imperial system can yield a new understanding of the "traditional", a comparable re-examination of the first half of the twentieth century invites us to consider a new understanding of the "modern." In one sense, the received view of the meaning of Chinese modernity tracks the ensuing life of that forlorn child whose throne disappeared in 1912. In due course, he became the subject of a highly regarded and commercially successful film, Bernardo Bertolucci's The Last Emperor. In one of its scenes, the former Son of Heaven expresses to his British tutor a desire to be part of the modern world that His Majesty knows exists outside the walls of the Forbidden City, though he is weak on the details. He wants to learn to drive a car and to dance the two-step. His first empress suggests that their initial intimate encounter be adjourned with a handshake—as a "modern couple" might end their first date. He learns to play tennis.

We now know, of course, that neither the last emperor nor his country would experience modernity as a series of such leisurely and pleasant experiences. Rather, both lived through the chaos of warlordism and economic collapse, then of protracted and destructive war with Japan, then the resumption of civil war between Nationalists and Communists, then imprisonment in a Maoist madhouse. The last emperor died in 1967, after "reigning" as Japan's puppet in Manchukuo, then spending the years between 1945 and 1959 under Soviet house arrest and in a Chinese prison camp, and finally ending up tending plants in a Beijing botanical garden.

To return to Beijing (better, Shanghai) today is to wonder whether things have returned to square one. It is too simple-minded to say that the country has somehow wholly reverted to its pre-communist modus operandi and overall affect, and yet the communist China supposedly gestating in the preceding two centuries of "modern China" is not much in evidence either. Viewed narrowly as an issue in China studies, it is certainly fair to say that, beginning in 1950, what we wanted to know about was the origin of the PRC. Thus, things that happened between 1900 and 1950 mattered to the degree that they prefigured the Maoist victory and its social and political vision. But today nothing remains of any of that, and whatever the claims put forward for it at the time, nobody nowadays pays any attention to the earth-shaking potential of Chinese communism.

Yet, if today's China is no longer what it was assumed or projected to be even twenty-five years ago, what then is it? Where did it come from, and how did it get here? These are the questions that lie beneath a slow-motion revolution in the academic study of the first half of China's twentieth century. Though perhaps not yet so far advanced in a technical sense as the newer approaches to Qing history, recent reworkings of the story of "Republican China" (1912–49) now lead to a new, and perhaps happier, ending. It used to be that we were taught to regard this era as nothing but an exercise in futility, a series of false starts, an odd sort of opera buffa, albeit with a cast of millions in misery. Now we are encouraged to see the teens, twenties and thirties as a fertile seedtime, with advances in politics, commerce and culture that prefigure the China—and the Hong Kong, the Taiwan and the Singapore—we see today.

As in the "imperial" case, it is a disservice to the range and volume of "Republican" studies since 1980 merely to pick (even if not quite at random) representative samples. But to take just one example, it used to be widely thought that Chinese foreign policy and especially China's diplomacy during the 1920s and 1930s was close to nonexistent and, by and large, irrelevant. Harvard's William Kirby points us in a dramatically different direction, drawing our attention to the deep origins of contemporary China. In Kirby's summation, "The story of Chinese diplomacy in the Republican era is one of stunning accomplishments from a position of unbelievable weakness." The new Republic took only a shaky title to a huge piece of real estate:

No Chinese empire had been so big for so long as the Qing realm of the Manchus. The first decade of the twentieth century was full of portents of its dissolution. But the amazing fact of the Republican era is that this space was not only redefined as 'Chinese,' and as the sacred soil of China, but also defended diplomatically to such a degree that the borders of the PRC today are essentially those of the Qing, minus only Outer Mongolia. The Qing fell, but the empire remained. More accurately, the empire became the basis of the Chinese national state. This was perhaps the greatest accomplishment of Republican diplomacy.[ii]

Kirby also notes that the Republic was successful in recovering the country's internal sovereignty, so that the PRC inherited a state unencumbered by extraterritoriality, foreign concessions and the like. He also praises the skill of the Republic's diplomats in maintaining between 1912 and 1945 an intricate pattern of international alliances and affiliations within a constantly shifting—and always dangerous—international environment.

China's contemporary strategic situation, of course, is not what it was then. What gives the history of the Republic's diplomacy relevance to the present day, however, is its style and complexity. After all, during its first twenty-five years, the PRC had a narrow range of international relationships, especially so-called institutional relations. Much of its energy in foreign affairs was consumed in those peculiar intra-Communist International relations of the old communist world, reflective of the old "two bloc" strategic balance. But the situation of today's China is far more complicated, and its international operations far more varied and intricate—not only on the plane of formal diplomatic relations with dozens of countries, but also with "global" bodies of many kinds. The Republican era thus has new relevance, and will probably earn a new status in Chinese eyes before very long.

If we are able to see things differently from the commanding heights of high politics and grand strategy, the view from the bottom up is also under revision. For one, there is a renewed interest in and a growing appreciation of China's early Republican experimentation with a variety of forms of democratic self-government and local administration. Indeed, many of these preceded the founding of the Republic. In the last days of the Qing dynasty, provincial assemblies and debates therein about political theories—inspired by developments in Meiji Japan, Bismarckian Germany and even post-1905 Romanov Russia—held out the possibility of a constitutional monarchy in China that might have transformed people from subjects to citizens.

For another and more encompassing example, Professor Wen-hsin Yeh of Berkeley, in reflecting on the history of modern Shanghai (China's most important and cosmopolitan city then and now), provokes us to reconsider one of the central conceits of the Maoist view—the "surrounding of the city by the countryside"—understanding it not merely as a metaphor for a tactic of guerrilla warfare, but as a shorthand way of expressing the overcoming of Shanghai's Western-derived reaction and decadence by the revolutionary and modernizing forces of "scientific socialism."ⁱⁱⁱ Yet Shanghai, once a symbol of everything bad that the world had done to China and, worse, a major weapon that served Western interests against Chinese ones, is on balance better seen as something else entirely—the incubator and disseminator of the creatively modern. The false starts and blind alleys, irrelevant because they did not lead to 1949 and all that, have a powerful saliency today. They demonstrate a Chinese capacity to comprehend everything included in the contemporary definition of modernity, whether in politics, economics, science or, especially, culture.

In retrospect, and with the benefit of the hindsight provided by the two decades between the demise of Maoism and the consolidation of Dengism, we should not be startled by such a role reversal between the "proletarian" countryside and the now "globalized" city. All politics may be local, but all history is no longer localized; instead, it can be fitted into a re-evaluation of China's larger cultural history in recent times. After all, the "modern" in modern Chinese art and literature was itself once regarded as inseparable from Chinese political radicalism; but the political radicalism is now gone and still the cultural history remains.

That history has of late become a subject for the method of contemporary "cultural studies", and its technique and jargon have been applied to the material. In the general understanding of this obscurantist vocabulary, such cultural studies are supposed to reaffirm a left-wing view of things. However, even if that were once its intention, when applied to *materia sinica*, the result has been something else again. Taken together, these efforts have not only rediscovered a trove of neglected cultural materials, they have returned us to an older way of looking at China's culture, placing it well above political sectarianism. To invent some lingo of one's own that derives from "postmodernist" argot, the influence of modern Chinese cultural achievement is seen increasingly as universalizing, cosmopolitanizing and de-ideologizing.

The tyranny of politics, which seemed to have killed the Chinese literary renaissance of the 1920s, is now without apologists. The final verdict was delivered by China's first Nobel laureate in literature, Gao Xingjian, in his lecture accepting the prize in Stockholm on December 7, 2000:

> Chinese literature in the twentieth century time and again was worn out and indeed almost suffocated because politics dictated literature. Both the revolution in literature and the revolutionary literature alike passed death sentences on literature and the individual. The attack on Chinese traditional culture in the name of the revolution resulted in the public prohibition and burning of books. Countless writers were shot, imprisoned, exiled or punished with hard labour in the course of the past one hundred years. This was more extreme than in any imperial dynastic period of China's history, creating enormous difficulties for writings in the Chinese language and even more for any discussion of creative freedom.

Politics is no longer in command. The regime in Beijing today is waging at most a rearguard action against Chinese cultural creation on the Chinese mainland, and the regime, with due allowance for its intermittent brutalities and crackdowns, is losing. Moreover, it is without sway over cultural creation in greater China and among Chinese all over the world, and is, in any case, unable to insulate the mainland from the effects of that creation.

Sinology as a Chinese Vocation

For the past four centuries, the study of China has been an international undertaking with non-Chinese having the dominant, though not the exclusive, influence over the world's perceptions of the country and its history. This has been especially true since the mid-nineteenth century, given the enormous difficulties that the collapse of civil order and the subsequent Maoist brutalities presented to any Chinese who might be interested in learning about their own tradition. Those of us outside the country had to develop a kind of self-reliance, relying more on ourselves than we might have had times been more "normal." For example, in the United States the professional study of China and the university teaching that derived from it were initially and importantly the work of American missionaries resident in China and, later, their China-born sons. C. Martin Wilbur (1909–97) and A. Doak Barnett (1922–99) are representative examples, though, in citing them, one should not gloss over the enormous influence of Chinese scholars based at universities in the United States from, say, 1930 on. After all, these men were old enough to be among the last to receive classical Chinese educations, yet still young enough to be Chinese pioneers in earning doctorates from American universities.

Beyond their role as China scholars, Americans of backgrounds similar to that of Wilbur and Barnett also filled important positions in the U.S. Foreign Service. Most of the so-called "old China hands" were China-born, and that influence was felt even after the reopening of the U.S. embassy in Beijing in 1979, as if a kind of restoration had occurred. The man who had closed the embassy in 1949 was J. Leighton Stuart, a prominent China-based Presbyterian educator who was president of Yenching University when General George Marshall sponsored his appointment as ambassador. Since the post was reopened after "normalization", three of the ambassadors who served there were China-born: Arthur Hummel, Jr., J. Stapleton Roy and James Lilley.

The establishment of the PRC, and especially its deep isolation from the Western world in general and the United States in particular, destroyed the human linkages that had dated from the mid-nineteenth century. The sociology of American sinology also changed, tracking larger changes in American higher education and its new post-World War II meritocracy. Just as the student bodies in the Ivy League became less predominantly old-line Protestant, so too did the field of China studies, sometimes establishing new ties between ancient intellectual traditions. Back in 1992, for example, the late Benjamin Schwartz, professor emeritus of Harvard and one of America's greatest sinologists, noted that, "Some of the most meaningful encounters between the Jews and China have occurred only in recent years, as the number of scholars of Jewish origin who are interested in both traditional and modern China has grown significantly."[iv]

Predictably, the transformation of China from a crumbling place in need of patient American tending into a leading-edge revolutionary state bent on supplanting American influence everywhere transformed the nature of America's interest in the place. Students at Harvard and Yale, once drawn to China as a country ripe for religious and political conversion by America, now became interested in the connection between the advent of the People's Republic and other great upheavals in world politics. And the interest changed once again as "China policy" became linked to "Indochina policy" and the controversies surrounding the latter.

Beyond the political, the younger students of the older China scholars had a profoundly, indeed decisively, different educational experience. They were studying China at a time when Americans did not go there. Instead, they would go to the British enclave of Hong Kong and peer into the mists on the other side of the border. Or they would go to Taiwan, not yet the economic success it later became and, for all the claims of the rump Nationalist regime established there, a backwater so far as things Chinese were concerned—still showing more the legacy of fifty years of Japanese governance than the fifteen or twenty of Nationalist rule.

The graduate students of today travel throughout China in search of dissertation fodder, and the China they see is different from anything their teachers could have imagined. In a sense, the transformation of the past two decades, from 1980 to the present day, resembles the startling changes in China between, say, 1940 and 1960. At the least, it all takes some getting used to. Another change has been the enormous movement of young Chinese through the American university system. They now number in the hundreds of thousands, initially directed mostly to the sciences, then to business and management, and then into the study of China itself. These young Chinese from the mainland have joined the many tens of thousands from Taiwan and other places in the Chinese diaspora who have also studied in the United States. And the academic successes of Chinese-Americans have quickly become legendary.

So far as China studies are concerned, there is already an observable trickle-down effect. Even a cursory look at the faculty rosters in university and college catalogues shows how the study and teaching of China in the United States is increasingly the province of people who—in one way or another—are Chinese, who are connected to China and the Chinese world and things Chinese, just as older American scholars and teachers had personal ties to China of one sort or another. Of course, we have had a comparable experience in how we came to our understanding of imperial Russia, the old USSR and Eastern Europe, in that many of our greatest scholars were products of those places, either born there (Adam

Ulam, Richard Pipes) or "first-generation" children of émigrés. More interesting still, several Americans prominent in the conduct of U.S. relations with that part of the globe—Henry Kissinger, Zbigniew Brzezinski, Madeleine Albright—were born in the old world.

But that was the twentieth century, and it is hard to predict what the repetition of that pattern in China studies and diplomacy might imply for the twenty-first. For those whose "old world" is in the East and not in the West, the differences cannot be inconsequential, even if it is hard to compare how a product of the collapse of the Hohenzollern or Habsburg empire has thought about America's connection to his ancestral home to how a product of the Manchu empire might come to view his own such connection. This kind of inner speculation must now inevitably engage those upon whom important responsibilities are devolving by the day—another episode in the endless meeting between East and West.

NOTES

[i] The best summary of the issues and the literature is provided by Evelyn Rawski, herself an important pioneer in this work. As incoming president of the Association of Asian Studies (AAS) she devoted her presidential address to the subject, and it was reprinted as "Reenvisioning the Qing: The Significance of the Qing Period in Chinese History", *Journal of Asian Studies* (November 1996). The work of Bartlett discussed here is *Monarchs and Ministers: The Grand Council in Mid-Ch'ing China, 1723-1820* (Berkeley: University of California Press, 1991). The seminal book by Crossley is *A Translucent Mirror: History and Identity in Qing Imperial Ideology* (Berkeley: University of California Press, 1999).

The debate about all this is growing in intensity, and is not without some irony. A generation ago, the most eminent and knowledgeable authority on this era, Professor Ping-ti Ho, began the debate with a ground-breaking article about Qing achievements, "The Significance of the Ch'ing Period in Chinese History", itself based on his own presidential address to the aas in 1967, and published in the association's journal later that year. For this, he was roundly criticized by some of his confrères for being too sympathetic to the Manchus, and worse. From his retirement, however, he rejoined the discussion more than three decades later, publishing "In Defense of Sinicization: A Rebuttal of Evelyn Rawski's 'Reenvisioning the Qing'", *Journal of Asian Studies* (February 1998).

But, then, China is an old country and the relation between the Han and the non-Han has figured in China's understanding of itself for a very long time—as Benjamin Elman instructs early on in his monumental *A Cultural History of Civil Service Examinations in Late Imperial China* (Berkeley: University of California Press, 2000).

[ii] Kirby, "The Internationalization of China: Foreign Relations at Home and Abroad in the Republican Era", in *Reappraising Republican China*, ed. Frederic Wakeman, Jr., and Richard Louis Edmonds (Oxford: Oxford University Press, 2000), p. 183. Originally printed in *The China Quarterly*.

[iii] See Wen-hsin Yeh, "Shanghai Modernity: Commerce and Culture in a Republican City", in Wakeman and Edmonds, op. cit. Professor Yeh is also the editor of a fascinating eleven-essay anthology on the larger subject, *Becoming Chinese: Passages to Modernity and Beyond* (Berkeley: University of California Press, 2000). As for the modern and postmodern, one should read a book by Professor Xiaobing Tang of the University of Chicago, *Chinese Modern: The Heroic and the Quotidian* (Durham, NC: Duke University Press, 2000), and not be misled by the lingo.

[iv] Jonathan Goldstein, ed., *The Jews of China: Historical and Comparative Perspectives* (Armonk, NY: M.E. Sharpe, 1999), p. 333.

27

Mao in History

*Ross Terrill**

Early one morning in the summer of 1972, John King Fairbank, my senior colleague among Harvard's East Asia faculty at the time, phoned to ask if I would look over a draft article for *Foreign Affairs* summing up his first trip to China since the 1940s. The piece was fairly indulgent toward Mao's regime. Over lunch that day, I said to Fairbank, "This trip to China must have been moving." He nodded and said, "Well, you know, I've been on their side ever since 1943." In Fairbank's draft I queried the sentence: "The Maoist revolution is on the whole the best thing that has happened to the Chinese people in many centuries." The dean of American Sinology, to whom I owe much, stuck with it. But he added the words: "At least, most Chinese seem now to believe so, and it will be hard to prove otherwise."

During the first decades of Mao's China, a time of American self-confidence and strong sense of purpose spurred by the World War II victory, U.S. Sinology for the most part took on an "idealist" rather than a "realist" orientation: hopeful about social progress, benevolent in its view of human nature, open to strong leadership. Since America was the chief bastion outside China of contemporary China studies, this buoyant, progressive mindset influenced the worldwide image of Mao Zedong. True, during the first years after 1949 Mao was viewed in a totalitarian framework as a junior Stalin, but within a decade this view

*Ross Terrill is a research associate at Harvard's Fairbank Center and visiting professor at the University of Texas at Austin. His latest book, *The New Chinese Empire*, is forthcoming (Basic Books, 2003).

This essay first appeared in *The National Interest,* No. 52 (Summer 1998).

gave way to a more open-minded one of the Chinese leader as a flexible Asian communist. The Sino-Soviet split in the early 1960s and the subsequent Nixon opening to China of 1971-72 further softened Mao's image.

While he was serving as President Nixon's national security adviser, Henry Kissinger, back at Harvard in January 1971 for a dinner with international affairs faculty, remarked that whereas in the Kennedy and Johnson administrations "Dean Rusk used to compare Mao unfavorably with Hitler, in this administration we compare Mao favorably with Hitler." A small change, strictly speaking, yet a large change in political-philosophical terms.

Even after Mao's death in 1976, Sinologists, influential Americans like Nixon and Kissinger, and many leaders of the Democratic Party tended to defend the rationality and sincerity of the Chinese leader's attempts at social engineering, while acknowledging his excesses and errors in the Great Leap Forward (communes, backyard steel furnaces) of the late 1950s, and the Cultural Revolution (Red Guards, book burning) of the late 1960s. Distilled through U.S. Sinological research, the popular image of Mao in the West—until the 1990s—was less bleak than those of Stalin and Hitler, which were more shaped by the "realist" approach of European political science. It took most of the Deng Xiaoping era (1979-97) to make Mao look really bad.

American Sinology was traditionally more idealistic, too, than Sinology pursued in Taiwan. Among American scholars there was well into the 1960s a tenacious expectation of unity in the Chinese Communist Party (CCP), against mounting signs to the contrary and in the face of evidence collected by China scholars in Taiwan that Mao was in tension with his top colleague, Liu Shaoqi, and other senior figures. As a student embarking on China studies, I adopted some of this idealism—modified by Australian skepticism—and my early writings lacked realism about Chinese politics. During the Cultural Revolution, American analysts were more inclined than those in Taiwan to see idealistic impulses behind the Red Guard turmoil. In general, from 1949 onward American Sinology focused on what made communist China tick, while Taiwanese analyses focused on cracks in the edifice of the regime.

The loss of life during Mao's Great Leap Forward was estimated by Richard Walker, a leading anti-communist scholar of the 1960s and 1970s, at 1-2 million. As a graduate student at Harvard in the late 1960s, I remember John Fairbank scoffing at Walker's "extreme views" about sufferings during the PRC's first decade. Some indulgence toward Mao's errors by Fairbank and others stemmed from resentment at Senator Joseph McCarthy's potshots at China specialists. Still, the picture we now have of the Great Leap Forward, based largely on documentary sources available within China, is much bleaker than that suggested by the hardest of anti-communists in the 1960s. A thorough 1996 study, *Hungry Ghosts*, by the British journalist Jasper Becker, puts the loss of life at 30 million.

China specialists during the 1960s and 1970s could see a number of evils and injustices in China; if pressed, few of us would have denied that China harbored tens of thousands of political prisoners, or claimed that the former Defense Minister Peng Dehuai—who questioned the Great Leap Forward—got a fair go from Mao in their confrontation of 1959. Yet an intellectual fascination with the gyrations of Chinese communist politics operated to restrain our judgment. This tendency toward a hands-off objectivity was reinforced by the existence of polemicists who did only evaluation, wielding totalitarian theory crudely or taking a purely moral stance toward Chinese communism.

Who would have guessed at Mao's death in 1976, or even at the tenth anniversary of his death in 1986, that by the twentieth anniversary in 1996 much of the focus on Mao would have shifted to his personal ways—indeed to that most personal of all realms, sexual life? But then Americans of the Ronald Reagan era in the 1980s might not have guessed that a U.S. president elected in 1992 would spend his first months in the White House on the issue of homosexuals in the military, the first weeks after his re-election in 1996 on the issue of sexual harassment in the military, and much of early 1998 defending himself against rumors of sex in the White House.

In 1980, I was criticized in reviews of the first edition of my biography *Mao* for paying too much attention to Mao's personality and personal life. Professor Edwin Moise spoke for many when, in the bibliography of his 1986 book *Modern China: A History*, he recommended my book but warned that it "concentrates too much on details of Mao's personal life." Yet a decade later, in a number of serious works, details of Mao's personal life took center stage. Although my suggestion of the possibility of intimacy between Mao and his "confidential secretary" Zhang Yufeng had been rejected, later revelations turned possibility into certainty. Today, indeed, Mao is as often viewed as a conspirator and lecher as he is as a unifier of China, philosopher of Asian communism, and major architect of the collapse of the communist bloc.

A tendency to believe the best about Mao was not the only reason why Western Sinology was for some years disinclined to see the pathological in him. Another was the absence of authoritative evidence of his willful and mindless ways. By the 1990s the material base for viewing Mao's methods of rule has become much more extensive than it was during his lifetime. More than any other single work in English, it *is The Private Life of Chairman Mao* (1994) by Dr. Li Zhisui that consolidates this new perception in the West. Despite questions one might have about the reasons for Mao's physician's sourness toward Mao and the CCP, the book is the only memoir we have by a close associate of the leader who defected from China and then told his story.[i]

Li Zhisui was an elitist intellectual. Little in his background or the working of his mind suggested sympathy for communist goals. But Mao liked staff members who had been in the West or had a Western education: Li had returned to China from Australia after the communist takeover, seeking to make a contribution to his homeland. When summoned to serve as Mao's doctor in 1954, he demurred on the ground that his "class background" was far from working-class, but Mao told him that "sincerity" was all that counted. Perhaps there was an admirable root to Mao's embrace of the stubborn physician. Sycophancy was the norm in Mao's court, but Dr. Li was a rather arrogant man who sometimes declined to oblige, and something in Mao may have recognized the authenticity of Li's independence of mind. Or perhaps Mao liked the challenge of correcting a wayward intellectual.

The West is in a phase of skepticism about leadership, and it needs China less than it did in the 1970s and 1980s. Both points have affected the discussion of Mao, as they have affected U.S.-China relations. Two or three decades after the death of the last titans of the World War II era—De Gaulle, Chiang Kai-shek, Mao—China studies have become influenced by the anti-heroic lens now typically applied to political leaders. Economists and sociologists, with their focus on structure rather than will, lead the field in China studies. It is revealing that Lucian Pye told us in 1996 that he pulled his punches in his 1976 book *Mao Zedong: The Man in the Leader* in not stating—as he says he believed—that Mao "was probably a narcissist with a borderline personality." By 1996 he felt he could come out with his long-held conclusion. The evidence for Pye's delayed conclusion of Mao as a borderline personality mounts by the year. It includes his youthful loneliness and fascist ideas, the constant psychosomatic illness to which his doctor testifies (Li uses the term "neurasthenia", which is no longer in wide professional use), his treatment of family members, his addiction to barbiturates, his lack of give-and-take with colleagues, and his suspiciousness.

Mental problems were not unique to Mao. The fear and tension of the communists' pre-1949 military and political struggle, and later of the pressure-cooker life within the Mao court, brought on similar mental conditions in scores of people around him. The cause of the anxiety differed as between Mao himself and his underlings. Mao felt a gnawing anxiety that people around him might be secretly disloyal. The underlings were simply afraid of dismissal, banishment, or death. Dr. Li goes so far as to say, "In time, I came to regard neurasthenia as a peculiarly Communist disease."

Here are Mao's words to Dr. Li just after his encounter with Khrushchev in 1958 on the problems of the Taiwan Strait and dealing with the United States:

> Khrushchev just doesn't know what he's talking about. He wants to improve relations with the U.S. Good, we'll congratulate him with our guns. Our cannon shells have been in storage for so long they're becoming useless. So why don't we just use them for a celebration? Let's get the U.S. involved, too. Maybe we can get the U.S. to drop an atom bomb on Fujian. Maybe ten or twenty million people will be killed. Chiang Kai-shek wants the U.S. to use the bomb against us. Let them use it. Let's see what Khrushchev says then.

Indeed, these words, if seriously meant as Dr. Li took them to be, are those of a borderline personality.

A second example shows the problem of the influence of drugs that Mao's doctor saw as early as 1958:

> Even as he spoke about sending me to inspect the people's communes [crown jewel of the Great Leap Forward], Mao was falling asleep and his speech was slurred, his voice nearly inaudible. He had taken his sleeping pills just before we started eating and had brought up the idea of the investigation in the midst of that half-awake, half-asleep euphoria he entered as the drug began to take effect. I was not sure whether his suggestion was real or part of a drug-induced dream.[ii]

There were an increasing number of pivotal moments after 1958 when Mao may well have been mentally or physically unfit to make the decisions he did. One of them, documented by eye-witnesses still living in Beijing, was crucial to relations between China and the United States.

It was 1971 and, after much discussion, a decision had just been made in Beijing not to invite the American ping-pong team to visit China. Premier Zhou Enlai had sent a message to Japan, where the American team was traveling, regretting China's inability to receive the Americans. But one night a heavily drugged Mao had second thoughts. At midnight on April 6, he looked again at the document containing the foreign ministry's recommendation not to invite the American sportsmen—already approved both by Zhou and himself. In "drowsy, slurred speech" he asked his nurse to phone Wang Hairong, the trusted aide at the foreign ministry, to reverse the decision. The nurse, without either a tape recorder or anyone to advise her, was in a quandary. Possessed of doubts, she nevertheless decided to phone Wang Hairong. The American ping-pong players were invited; Kissinger and Nixon soon followed. History made a turn.[iii]

Everyone who came in close contact with Mao was shocked at the anarchy of his personal ways. He ate idiosyncratically. He refused to brush his teeth, offering as his excuse that tigers with excellent teeth did not brush theirs. He became increasingly sexually promiscuous as he aged. He would stay up much of the night and sleep during much of the day; at times he would postpone sleep, remaining awake for thirty-six hours or more, until tension and exhaustion overcame him. He was the consummate outlaw, "without law and without God." Said Dr. Li to me when I showed him around the Harvard campus in 1994: "Three words did not exist in Mao's dictionary: regret, love, mercy."

Yet many people who met Mao came away deeply impressed by his intellectual reach, originality, style of power-within-simplicity, kindness toward low-level staff members, and the aura of respect that surrounded him at the top of Chinese politics. It would seem difficult to reconcile these two disparate views of Mao. But in a fundamental sense there was no brick wall between the personal and the public Mao.

Early in Mao's career of cavorting with girls—despite the proximity of his longtime wife Jiang Qing—some provincial leaders made the mistake of supplying him with sophisticated beauties of mature years and artistic accomplishment. Mao turned them all down; for his private moments he did not want famous actresses and singers, but inexperienced peasant maidens one third his own age.

One pretty young woman, Cui Ying, who worked in the office of secretaries in Zhongnanhai in the late 1950s, caught Mao's eye. While dancing with him, we learn in a memoir published in Beijing, she took the opportunity to complain about the unjust labeling of good people as "rightists" in the leftist campaign of 1957. A strict boundary had been crossed. Cui Ying's body was needed, but not her mind. For heaven's sake, she might quote Mao outside Zhongnanhai. Suddenly, one afternoon before an upcoming dance party at which she was to see Mao again, she found herself terminated as a staff member.[iv]

Mao's turn to young women was connected with the decline of trust in the men around him. Sex became an avenue to a oneness that no longer existed in the councils of party and state. The limitation was that Mao could achieve oneness (whether sexual or philosophic) only with innocent young men and women who adored him, or with staff members and junior colleagues who accorded him total loyalty. "What Mao thought, I thought", said his doctor. "It was not that I had contrary opinions that I had to suppress or keep to myself. Mao's opinions were mine. The possibility of differing with the Chairman never crossed my mind." It need hardly be said that any attempt to translate such oneness to the institutional and public life of a nation of six hundred million people—a *da tong* ("great unity") based on personal feelings—was an impossibility, and to essay it was to court disaster.

The real shock in the "personal" revelations of *The Private Life of Chairman Mao* was less moral than political: Mao did not believe a lot of what he proclaimed in public. We find it in small matters and in large. He sang the praises of Chinese traditional medicine, but when it came to his own health he used Western medicine. The Soviet Union disgusted him even as he lauded it for public consumption; he said good things about America while telling the Chinese people that America was the embodiment of evil.

Perhaps Mao did not "mean" some of the things he said in private. Perhaps he was like Richard Nixon, who ranted about Ivy League types and Jews, yet never took action against these sub-groups and went on hiring them in substantial numbers for the White House staff. Yet the two cases are not the same. In the cold light of day, after an evening of uttering stress-reducing threats, Nixon could not easily take action to reduce the influence of Ivy League types and Jews; he was President of a country with laws, a vigorous Congress, and a free press. But when old Mao murmured a judgment for or against a person or a policy, the staff member who heard it set in motion steps of implementation. In a democracy, the individual psyche of the top leader is simply not reflected in public policy as it is in a communist dictatorship.

Thus, the wife of Liu Shaoqi was about to be executed in 1969 when Mao, giving final review to the papers on her case, scrawled, "Spare her the knife."[v] She lives on to this day. One day a male guard touched one of Mao's girlfriends on the buttocks; Mao had the man sent to prison and no one at Mao's court ever heard of him again. So it went; Mao's whim was the law of the land.

The "late Mao" was different from the early and middle Mao. He had not always been vain, insincere, vindictive, arrogant, or duplicitous. In middle age, to take examples from the testimony of his most impressive secretary, Tian Jiaying, Mao was not immodest. When commended for his opening speech at the Eighth Party Congress in 1956, he said, "Do you know who wrote my speech? A young scholar—Tian Jiaying." The Mao of 1949-50 read all of the many letters that reached him from the general public. By 1966 he did not even deign to address the general public; at Tiananmen Square as the Red Guards gathered before him, he merely raised an arm and gave a glassy smile. The Mao of 1950 could cry over the suffering of individuals from the grassroots, but the Mao of the Cultural Revolution did not. Tian Jiaying could testify that Mao changed, for the change wrecked Tian's career and ultimately led him to kill himself.[vi]

To gain perspective on Mao's career at the summit of power in China, one may imagine a Ronald Reagan who not only ruled for the eight years he was elected to office, but also long previously (when a Democrat) and long afterwards (when afflicted with Alzheimer's disease). This approximates the span and subjective variation of Mao's decades-long "reign" in Beijing. Mao's career evolved through an embrace of universal individualism (as a youth), to a phase of belief in Soviet-inspired proletarian progress (in the early 1920s), to peasant revolt (late 1920s), on to war communism (in Yanan), socialist building (the 1950s), disillusion with the results of socialism (from the late 1950s), a philosophical and moral coarsening (1960s), and a final return to a highly subjective individualism (1970s).

It would be nonsensical to say Mao did not change his views and ways over this spectacular lifetime, no less than it would be to say that the Reagan of the White House years was to be equated with the victim of Alzheimer's disease living in retirement in California. But given the Chinese system, most of the different "Maos" were part of the single until-death political rule of Mao.

Hence the more we learn about Mao the person, the more we are driven to analyze the system over which he presided. Because he exercised power for so long, and held it until he died, Mao's personal doubts and decline were translated into gyrations of the Chinese state. Intrigue was unleashed. Uncertainty—the oxygen of Mao's court—turned colleagues and staff into fearful conspirators. The imperial-plus-Leninist system acted as a magnifying glass, giving a huge dimension to each quirk of his personality. But in the service of what vision of history and society did this personality enlist itself?

There was a sharp dualism to Mao's political ideas. His political methods and his notions of how China related to the non-Chinese world probably owed more to Chinese traditions than to Marxism-Leninism. There was little about the modern world—other than Marxism—that Mao knew well; he reached into Chinese tradition for his instinctual knowledge. Yet Chinese tradition did not provide Mao his goals. These came from the social engineering arsenal of Marxism-Leninism-Stalinism. In its fullness, this meant nothing less than the refashioning of the Chinese spirit away from balance and nearer to polarization, away from harmony and nearer to struggle, away from private values and toward the collective values of an Eastern Sparta. The mismatch between goal and method caused many of the tragedies of the Mao era. The clashes between the two began long before the spectacular problems of the 1960s and 1970s, but they intensified as Mao used stratagems from the old novels Dream of the Red Chamber and Journey to the West to prosecute the heightened Marxist class struggle of the Cultural Revolution. As his subjectivism soared, "class" meant little more than a way to demarcate friend and enemy of the moment.

It is surprisingly common for Western scholars of China, still today, to assume that social engineering could have worked if the conditions were correct and it were properly done. I will cite here not extreme cases, but excellent scholars from the pages of *The Politics of China 1949-1989*, which is based on the recent monumental Cambridge History of China, whose points of view are widely representative. My own first two books on China[vii]—much earlier volumes—reflect the influence of this same standpoint; my recent ones do not.[viii]

Frederick Teiwes says of the state dominance over society that issued from the Three- and Five-Antis campaigns against anti-socialist elements in the early 1950s: "As a result, CCP leaders had achieved a position where planned economic development was genuinely feasible."[ix] But, surely the twentieth century has taught us that planned economic development is never feasible, "genuinely" or otherwise. We have abundant evidence, most of it from outside China studies, about the disastrous unworkability of the command economy. (One of the best arguments against central planning is Friedrich Hayek's *The Road to Serfdom*, written before Mao's capture of power. Whatever criticisms may be made of Hayek's thesis when applied to Western societies, his title is an apt summation of communist China's journey and travails.) Here, in the social engineering goals of Marxism-Leninism-Stalinism, lay the most profound flaw of the post-1949 Mao.

It is not satisfactory to laud the success of the Mao of 1949-57 and say that, from then on, with the onset of the crusade against "rightists" in 1957 and the Great Leap Forward soon after, he "made mistakes" or fell into "excesses." Kenneth Lieberthal is able to call the regime of the 1950s "a wholly legitimate CCP rule."[x] Whence its legitimacy? Communist rule continued in the 1950s for the same reason that communist rule came into being in the 1940s: the power of the gun. The Marxist self-righteousness that gave Mao a sense of his own legitimacy was cut from the same cloth as the self-righteousness that made him declare half the people around him "counter-revolutionaries."

"The specific reasons for the failure of the Great Leap Forward remained unclear", says Lieberthal.[xi] But if the reasons for the failure of the Great Leap Forward are not clear to us, then nothing Mao did can be clear to us. Not only Lieberthal but other estimable China specialists still write in the 1990s as if a continuance of the Soviet-model years, without the lurch into the Great Leap Forward and the Cultural Revolution, might somehow have led to the achievement of Mao's stated goals. Nothing in the experience of the Soviet Union or Eastern Europe suggests that this is valid.

Harry Harding even implies that the Cultural Revolution might have "succeeded" if it had been fully carried out:

> The flaw in Mao's strategy, in other words, was that he waged only half a revolution between 1966 and 1969. He failed to design a viable and enduring alternative political order to replace the one he sought to overthrow. . . . In this sense, the Cultural Revolution was the second unsuccessful Chinese revolution of the twentieth century [following 1911].[xii]

But a "revolution" in 1966 would have meant the overthrow of the Communist Party, and that was not Mao's intention. Indeed, the Communist Party was his tool for the social engineering that provided the raison d'être for his being in power. No, the "flaw in Mao's strategy" was fully evident in the first half of the "revolution"—he had not even correctly defined his enemy, and the reason was the blindness to reality that social engineering induces.

Recent scholarship has pushed back in time the critical failures of the CCP-in-power. The same process is evident in the case of the Soviet Union, where a previous notion of Stalin "betraying" Lenin's revolution has given way to a sense of Lenin as one with Stalin in his essential social engineering objectives and their concomitant dictatorial political methods—as shown in Richard Pipes' striking 1996 book *The Unknown Lenin*. Mao's crusade against "rightism" began far earlier than the Cultural Revolution, earlier still than the Great Leap Forward, earlier even than the acceleration of collectivization of 1956. The Thought Reform campaign during the Korean War bears the essential marks of the terroristic methods of the Cultural Revolution. The united front tactics by which businessmen were used and discarded in Shanghai in the early 1950s were one with those pioneered in Yanan a decade earlier and practiced in the use and misuse of allies by Mao throughout his communist career.

Perhaps 1949 is the real watershed in Mao's career, and a more important point of demarcation than any dualism in his own character, not primarily because Mao deteriorated personally after 1949 (that mostly came a decade later), but for reasons inherent in "socialist construction." Benjamin Yang in *From Revolution to Politics* (1990) aptly suggests that, prior to 1949, Mao's "revolutionary idealism" was under the control of his "political realism", whereas after 1949 his "political realism" was at the beck and call of his "revolutionary idealism." From his rich pre-1949 experience of the practice of realism, often in struggle against doctrinaire pro-Moscow colleagues, Mao knew the realist language, and he soothingly spoke it from time to time.

Even as the Great Leap Forward soared, Mao reviewed a report from a certain county in Shandong that ended by saying, "the county will attain communism in two years", and scrawled on it, "add a zero [making it twenty] and the country still won't attain communism."[xiii] But, these flashes of realism were but an intermittent restraint on his rampant leftism. They could not be more than that because Marxist social engineering, Mao's chief post-1949 goal, is inherently unrealistic about the human material that alone can constitute the building blocks of a social order.

The flattering Defense Minister Lin Biao cried that Mao had dealt with questions Marx and Lenin had not grappled with. This was another way of saying that Mao—unlike Marx and Lenin—lived long enough into the period of socialist construction to find out that Marxism in practice was a disaster. Do we not grow suspicious when we find Mao saying of Stalin that he confused the people with the enemy, and then Deng Xiaoping saying the same thing of Mao? Does this not go to the heart of the failure and arrogance of social engineering?

Since at least the anti-rightist drive of 1957, Mao fought two phantoms he would never be able to vanquish: the refusal of the Chinese Communist Party to simply be a Mao Party; and the failure of socialism to take on the splendor he expected of it. Mao's war against phantoms began, like a number of the pathologies of the PRC, in the anti-rightist campaign against loyal, uncomprehending Communist Party functionaries. He wanted the blooming of "a hundred flowers" to result in the rebuke and correction of colleagues who displeased him. He did not want the blooming to question the socialist system, much less his own towering role in it.

But the flowers turned out to be weeds. The criticism from outside the Communist Party did not follow Mao's desires by accomplishing the correction within the party that he sought. Moreover, vociferous anti-socialist attacks required Mao to make a tactical peace with senior colleagues of whom he did not approve. In this respect, the anti-rightist campaign may be regarded as the true start of the Cultural Revolution. In between came the rise and fall of the Great Leap Forward and the purge of Defense Minister Peng Dehuai. Mao's vindictive struggle against Peng in 1959 was inseparable from his growing willfulness and his strengthening doubts about the socialist goal.

In the tragedy of Peng, the personal and public life of Mao were conjoined. One of Peng's criticisms of Mao was of his philandering. The connection between the Peng-Mao crisis and Mao's growing appetite for young female flesh was that Mao had become more self-indulgent. This resulted in behavior that heightened his isolation from senior colleagues, and in an obsessive quest for rejuvenation at a personal, as well as a political, level. Death crept nearer, and with it the possibility that people would deliver a harsh verdict on his career after he was gone, especially because of the Leap. Physical decline was not to be denied, but clinging to young women, as the emperors had done and the Daoists prescribed, kept the focus away from Mao's own crumbling body. It was on the ashes of the experiment in social engineering that there arose the neo-emperor's rule that Dr. Li Zhisui and other staff members observed.

"Revisionism" came to be the term Mao applied to the alleged betrayal that produced the double disappointment of the Communist Party refusing to be a Mao Party and socialism turning out less pleasing than expected. But revisionism was an illusion. Mao never clearly defined it; hence, he never found a way to eliminate it. He knocked down revisionists, but never revisionism; nor was it possible to do so. No surprise that Mao changed his target several times, lunging after an enemy that, because it did not exist in a form that could be tackled, had to be re-imagined after each failed attack. In the end, Mao simply said the revisionists were "zombies."[xiv]

Revisionism (in the China of the 1960s) was merely a communist swear word, no more to be taken seriously than the term "social fascist hyenas" once used by Stalinists to describe social democrats. To say Liu Shaoqi was a "bourgeois" who "sneaked into the Party", as Mao's associates did in the 1960s, was on a level with the propaganda of Goebbels. Such lies proliferated because Mao lunged after his two phantoms.

Mao's social engineering clashed with Chinese conditions, his own political methods, and human nature. This problem, evident throughout Mao's mature years, was the major reason both for the instability of policy under his command, and for the inconsistency between his flexible treatment of certain individuals and his ruthlessness toward the welfare of millions.

In assessing Mao's future reputation, as in observing Beijing politics today, it is important to keep in mind the nature of Leninism and to analyze not only how the post-Deng social-political system works, but where its faultlines lie. The single largest question of perspective for Sinology in the post-Deng years is whether Chinese communism is reforming itself or disintegrating. My own conclusion is that the communist era soon will pass, and that when it does there will be an effort in China to distinguish Mao's contributions from the whole box and dice of Marxism-Leninism.

One day in 1950, Mao came upon his daughter Li Na singing a popular song that included the line, "Without the Communist Party there would not have been China." He rebuked her and said the song should say "New China", not "China." In fact the song was based on an editorial in *Jiefang ribao* (Liberation Daily) in Yanan in 1943, which indeed used the words Li Na sang in the courtyard. The word "New" was not there. But after the incident with Li Na the Communist Party was instructed by Mao to change the words of the song.[xv] Mao in 1950 had the good sense to realize that the communist era was hardly the start of civilization in China. Likewise, a future Chinese leader may see the end of communist rule as a less than momentous event in the long history of China.

The popular "good Mao/bad Mao" dichotomy is not persuasive. It does not quite work to cut Mao up into a "successful revolutionary" part (up to the 1950s) and a "disastrous leftist" part (from the late 1950s). One day we may see the emergence of a "good Mao/bad Marxism" dichotomy. Then it will be said that a number of Mao's contributions to China were made against the tide of Marxism and its chief bastion of the time, the Soviet Union: the focus on peasants, the anti-imperialist frame of reference for the revolution, the attack on Soviet socialism, the turn to the West. John Fairbank's indulgent observation in 1972—"The Maoist revolution is on the whole the best thing that has happened to the Chinese people in many centuries"—will be judged substantially true, though not on ideological grounds.

Mao will be seen as a rebel, a graduate of the University of Outlaws, a southern rebel, who like Sun Yat-sen before him went north to overthrow a government. A new post-communist leader of a maritime-oriented China, who may or may not be based in Beijing, will point out that Mao disliked Beijing from his first stay there in the May 4th period, and that in power after 1949 he fled the "northern capital" as often as he could. All his better instincts were those of the peasant rebel from the south, it will be said, not a Marxist Mandarin of the north.

Of course this would be a distortion, as all historical rewrites of the profile of a revolutionary intellectual tend to be. But a drastic reinterpretation of Mao as a patriotic rebel would enable a future leader to reject Marxism in the name of Chinese nationalism, and to claim that the twentieth century brought a slow restoration of China's wealth and power that would have been faster but for the diversion of Marxism-Leninism. When the Chinese Communist Party becomes just the Chinese Party—perhaps not far off—Mao will be buried doctrinally while being saved as a patriot. He will be seen as a valiant latter-day Qin Shihuang, the unifier of China two thousand years ago, handicapped by the un-Chinese doctrine of Marxism.

Yet for now, and as long as the Leninist system endures in Beijing, the pathology seen in Mao's rule enjoys institutional roots beneath the Forbidden City. Today, the retention of power, rather than the pursuit of ideological phantoms, is the motive around which the political process arranges itself. But politics still is theater, and the Communist Party's sense of its own rectitude still makes the populace, not the source of the political process, but puppets for the party's performance of its self-appointed historical role. The proof that Chinese politics remains fundamentally unchanged under Jiang Zemin is that Jiang is being built up as the third of three great CCP figures: Mao, Deng, Jiang. Political reform, on the other hand, would require canceling the notion of a Great Leader, possessing virtue and a doctrine, and towering over party, state, and nation.

The personality of Mao magnified and dramatized the dictatorship in Beijing. Yet it was the goals of social engineering that gave the Mao era its shape and made it tragic. Jiang Zemin's China is traveling down one road in economics and a different one in politics. The marketization of the economy marks a spectacular, historic departure from Mao. But the retention of a Leninist system and the Leninist insistence on the all-knowing wisdom of the Communist Party perpetuates some of the illusions of social engineering. Staying on that road can only lead to a clash between the state and the new economy and society that Deng Xiaoping passed on to Jiang Zemin. On the other hand, if the special right of the Communist Party to be the engineer of Chinese society is abandoned, in one way or another the exciting, turbulent, post-communist history of China will begin.

NOTES

[i] Dr. Li had a motive to maximize Mao's faults and especially his promiscuity. Li's own father was unfaithful to his mother—much to Li's chagrin—and Li felt he was badly treated in Beijing in the years after Mao's death.

[ii] Li Zhisui, *The Private Life of Chairman Mao* (New York: Random House, 1994), pp. 109, 262, 265.

[iii] Lin Ke, Xu Tao, and Wu Xujun, *Li shi de zhenshi* (Hong Kong: Liuwen chubanshe, 1995), pp. 306-8.

[iv] Cheng Yi and Jia Mei, *Mao Zedong shenghuo shilu, 1946-76* (Nanjing: Jiangsu wenyi chubanshe, 1989), pp. 103-5.

[v] *Gongren ribao*, Beijing, December 6, 1980.

[vi] Dong Bian, ed., *Mao Zedong he tade mishu Tian Jiaying* (Beijing: Zhongyang wenxian chubanshe, 1989), pp. 27, 7-8, 9-10.

[vii] *800,000,000: The Real China* (Boston: Little, Brown and Co., 1972); *Flowers on an Iron Tree* (Boston: Little, Brown and Co., 1975).

[viii] *Mao* (New York: Harper & Row, 1980, and Touchstone, 1993); *China in Our Time* (New York: Simon & Schuster, 1992, and Touchstone, 1993); *Madame Mao* (New York: Morrow, 1984, and Touchstone, 1992).

[ix] Roderick MacFarquhar, ed., *The Politics of China 1949-1989* (New York: Cambridge University Press, 1993), p. 40.

[x] Ibid., p. 92.

[xi] Ibid., p. 114. A recent survey of American Sinology's record by Michael Steinberger in *Lingua Franca* (May/June 1998) takes scholars to task—justifiably—for passing lightly over the famine that followed the Great Leap Forward. But Steinberger, in line with the Sinological tradition on Mao that I am criticizing, cites only the empirical failure to listen to the gruesome reports of refugees fleeing to Hong Kong; he neglects the analytical failure to see the inherent horrors in Mao's entire social engineering project—long predating the Leap.

[xii] Ibid., p. 239.

[xiii] *Mianhuai Mao Zedong* (Beijing: Zhongyang wenxian chubanshe, 1993), vol. 1, p. 239.

[xiv] *The Private Life of Chairman Mao*, p. 380.

[xv] *Mao Zedong he tade mishu Tian Jiaying*, p. 4.

28

China Studies in McCarthy's Shadow:
A Personal Memoir

*Richard L. Walker**

Great differences among academics and personal antagonisms in their fields of specialization are common in the best of times. But the 1950s were not the best of times. In what was to become known as the McCarthy era, differences within American university faculties were stark and personal antagonisms often poisonous.

To some extent this was inevitable. Ideological loyalties and attachments formed during the Depression years, and then strengthened by the wartime alliance with the Soviet Union, came into head-on conflict with the attitudes shaped by a fuller knowledge of the real nature of communist regimes and the beginning of the Cold War.

Senator Joseph McCarthy's peculiar contribution to this conflict was two-fold. First, he coarsened and polarized it to an extent that made it extremely difficult to sustain some vital distinctions. One such distinction, drawn most clearly by Sidney Hook, was encapsulated in the title of his book *Heresy Yes,*

* Richard L. Walker was U.S. ambassador to the Republic of Korea during 1981-86 and is ambassador-in-residence at the Walker Institute of International Studies at the University of South Carolina. He served as national President of the American Association for Chinese Studies (1995-1997).

This essay first appeared in *The National Interest*, No. 53 (Fall 1998).

Conspiracy No. The book represented a rational approach that too few appreciated. Another and even more fundamental distinction for academics was that between what was ideologically correct to believe and what was actually the case. Second, McCarthy's behavior—his bullying, his lying, his demagoguery—gave those who had an interest in doing so a perfect opportunity to change the subject. Instead of the extent, nature, and consequences of allegiance to a political party controlled by a foreign totalitarian power being made the proper object of attention, "McCarthyism" could itself be made the central issue. In some ways, McCarthy's cynical and outrageous antics made it as difficult to be a serious and principled anti-communist in the America of the 1950s as it was to be a fellow-traveler.

For several reasons, the effects of McCarthyism were particularly virulent in the field of China studies in American universities. For one thing, the Chinese communists exerted a strong and long-established claim on the sympathies and imagination of a number of scholars. Often (though certainly not always) this was as much romantic as it was ideological. One of the first works in the 1930s to build up the romantic version of Mao Tse-tung and the Chinese communists was the bestselling work of Edgar Snow, *Red Star Over China*. According to this version, Mao and his fellow communists were the austere heroes of the Long March, the incorruptible reformers living in the caves of Yanan, and the dedicated opponents of both the Kuomintang (KMT) and the Japanese invaders—they were men who seemed to be above and beyond ordinary politics. Such uncritical admiration often coexisted with a distaste and sense of guilt concerning past Western behavior toward China. The late John King Fairbank, professor at Harvard and a dominant figure in American post-World War II China studies, spoke for many when, looking back in 1972, he said, "Well, you know, I've been on their side since 1943." Fairbank wrote and talked with consistency about what he called "the Chinese Revolution", in which the communist phase was represented as both ineluctable and as continuous with earlier imperial China. Communist realities were always played down.

As against all this, with the victory of the Maoist party and the proclamation of the Chinese People's Republic on October 1, 1949, China became a major—and ominous—new factor in the Cold War. When the Sino-Soviet alliance was proclaimed on February 14, 1950, concern grew about how the United States could have "lost" China. This became an even more serious political issue after Kim Il-Sung invaded South Korea in June 1950, with Stalin's blessing and with stunning initial success. In his book, Modern Times, Paul Johnson maintains that "McCarthy would have been of little account had not the Korean War broken out. . . . His period of ascendancy coincided exactly with that bitter and frustrating conflict—one might say that McCarthyism was Stalin's last gift to the American people." Certainly this accumulation of events relating to China created within the small and intimate community of America's China scholars a tinder box of recrimination and finger-pointing, giving the normal rivalries and differences within the academic community an unprecedented intensity. This is part of the background for my own story as one of the less typical sufferers from the phenomenon known as McCarthyism.

Following more than three years' active military service in World War II, at the beginning of the 1950s I was a relatively young assistant professor at Yale University, with several publications in refereed learned journals to my credit. Early on, and while he was still riding high, I made my own position on McCarthy clear on several occasions. On one of them, for example, I sent a letter to my colleague at Yale, Professor Robert A. Dahl, a distinguished political scientist who possessed impeccable credentials for working against the Leninists in academe and who eventually was to become president of the American Political Science Association. He had delivered a talk entitled "Congressional Investigations Threaten Academic Freedom." I felt this was an overreaction to what was happening and wrote to him on July 7, 1953. I began, "Let me state at the outset . . . my firm belief that Mr. McCarthy and his tactics do constitute a real threat to democracy on the American scene today." But I then went on to say, "I sincerely believe that the liberals could make a positive contribution to destroying the power of Mr. McCarthy if they would stop building him up through their hysteria."

The hysteria to which I was referring was real enough and was effectively ridiculed by the literary critic, Leslie Fiedler, at the time:

> From one end of the country to the other rings the cry, 'I am cowed! I am afraid to speak out!' and the even louder response, 'Look, he is cowed! He is afraid to speak out!'

Nevertheless, because of such attempts to make some elementary distinctions and the critical positions I took with regard to the new regime in China, some colleagues in the field quickly labeled me a McCarthyist. It was not pleasant, but it was only a foretaste of what was to come.

In the spring of 1951 I received an invitation that was heady stuff for a young academic. I was asked to review Freda Utley's *The China Story* for the *New York Times Book Review*. Utley was a former communist with experiences in the Soviet Union and China. She was a major supplier of information on Owen Lattimore and other Western intellectuals in China to Senator McCarthy. Given the prevailing atmosphere, this meant that the book was a very hot item, and I was given just 750 words to deal with it.

My review noted that it was a "violent tract" containing "bitter invectives and denunciations" and "attack on personalities." But I did go on to say, "Since this is her answer to Owen Lattimore's *Ordeal by Slander* (which had named Utley), it must in all fairness be read by those who have read that volume." Utley wrote me almost immediately to let me know of her displeasure with my review. More remarkable, given the general tone of what I had written, were the messages from several China scholars upbraiding me for having had anything even faintly positive to say about the book. One of them, particularly sharp, was from

Professor Derk Bodde of the University of Pennsylvania. I mention this because I shall have occasion to refer to him later. The New York Times, incidentally, liked the review, and I was quickly asked to do several more.

A few months later, in the early summer of 1951, I received a call from a friend in government and a note from Sol Levitas, the venerable editor of *The New Leader* magazine—a liberal journal of opinion published in New York and supported in part by the International Ladies Garment Workers Union and other trade unions, but clearly anti-communist. They suggested that since the wild charges by McCarthy—that Owen Lattimore and the Institute of Pacific Relations (IPR) represented part of a communist conspiracy—were hurting us abroad, it might be helpful for me, as a younger scholar who had not been involved in the events then being investigated, to look into the issue. The idea was not to investigate Lattimore's political views, but to assess the quality of his work in scholarly terms.

In retrospect I suspect it was naive on my part to think that, given the academic sensitivities of the time, these two aspects could be separated. In any event I undertook the project, in part because I felt it necessary for my own education to learn about past Asian scholarship and some of the central issues. This involved long days in the Yale library that summer and the following fall going through shelf after shelf of IPR publications, especially its two journals *Far Eastern Survey* and *Pacific Affairs*. The second of these, edited for many years by Lattimore, had been a vehicle for some of his own views, including his justification of the Stalin purge trials.

The result was a "special supplement" (their first) for *The New Leader*. Entitled "Lattimore and the IPR", it appeared on March 31, 1952. It was followed in subsequent issues by numerous letters to the editor and by exchanges first between William Holland of the IPR and me, and then between Owen Lattimore and me.

It is not hyperbole to state that the special supplement caused something of a sensation. It also marked me, and I learned very quickly that it was difficult, if not well nigh impossible, to take a detached view on issues relating to U.S. policies in East Asia, particularly on China. In my piece I had argued that the work of the IPR over past decades was of primary importance, that it had provided valuable and useful service over the years, but that Lattimore had failed in his responsibilities as an IPR editor to maintain the integrity of his publication and had misled the organization. His scholarship left much to be desired. I also observed that the same could be said of the McCarran Hearings on Lattimore and the IPR, which were then continuing. I noted that Lattimore had frequently been a polemicist, but that was not to be the issue as far as I was concerned. The fact was rather that the nature of McCarthy's attack against him had made him both a hero and relatively immune to criticism from colleagues, many of whom would admit in private conversation that he was not without flaws.

But after McCarthy's sensational (and absurd) charges that Lattimore had been a key Soviet agent in the United States, anyone who questioned Lattimore's scholarship was considered beyond the pale. I was now one of those, even though my *New Leader* piece was considered balanced and objective by a number of distinguished scholars. Some messages from overseas encouraged me to believe that through translation into several languages in Europe and Asia, the supplement helped some intellectuals in allied countries to soften some of their hitherto harsh assessments of the American scene.

In 1953 I published my book *The Multi-State System of Ancient China*. The reaction from the scholarly world was very good. One distinguished scholar—who shall remain nameless but who will appear in this narrative again in the context of events that happened a few years later—wrote to me, "I wish to send my congratulations. I find it excellent and marvel at the mass of literature you went through to reach your conclusions. This week—twice—I have had occasion to recommend it strongly to my students in Chinese history." Other reviewers praised the volume. Dr. Hu Shih—a distinguished scholar who had served as China's ambassador to the United States during World War II and who had stayed aloof from the contest between the KMT and the CCP—wrote to me of his admiration for the work and called it a major achievement for American Sinology.

During the first half of the 1950s, in addition to being recalled for a short time to active duty with the U.S. Army at the start of the Korean War, I was able to spend time in Japan, Korea, Taiwan, Hong Kong, and Burma, and to interview some of the refugees from Mao's "New China." These were wrenching and moving experiences that contributed powerfully to my increasingly hostile view of the PRC. I was not completely ostracized from the community of China scholars, and in all fairness I note that, supported by Dean Rusk and C. Burton Fahs, who were with the foundation at that time, in 1954 I was able to receive a Rockefeller Foundation fellowship. Even in the most intense periods of division among the China specialists in the 1950s, there were still individuals who insisted on fair presentations from both sides.

My next major book, published in June 1955, was of a different nature. *China Under Communism: The First Five Years* dealt with contemporary rather than more distant events—a trickier and more dangerous project even at the best of times. Hence I was delighted when Professor Edwin O. Reischauer of Harvard gave it an outstandingly favorable review on the front page of the *New York Times Book Review*. After noting that it was "as lucid and revealing a picture of communist rule in China as is possible at this time", Reischauer concluded by advising his readers that, "This is a book which must be read by those who wish to have a solidly based opinion on China policy." Generally favorable reviews also came from Richard Yang, Robert C. North, George E. Taylor, Paul M.A. Linebarger, and C. Martin Wilbur, all of them acknowledged leaders in the China field.

I should note that Utley also reviewed the book. She claimed that I had made a "valiant effort" to fend off the school that had opposed her—the "Lattimore-Fairbank-IPR school of thought"—with a "massive array of facts . . . a 'balanced' and unemotional record so that he cannot be smeared as a heretic." She continued, "He writes in such a pedestrian style that he can rarely stir the reader's imagination, or evoke pity or terror."

Utley aside, gossip from colleagues warned me that an attack was under way and that Mary C. Wright at the Hoover Institution (yes, things were different back then) had been recruited to "do a job" on the book. Her review in the *Journal of Asian Studies* was 180 degrees away from those of Reischauer (one of her teachers) and the others named above. Her attack ended by dismissing the book as "good lunch-club material." It was no surprise, of course, that the reviewer for the IPR journal *Pacific Affairs* found it "long and tendentious and full of asseverations . . . deeply ballasted with opinion . . . loaded with commentary, the sideways and ponderously hostile approach to everything . . . partisan journalism." This review and Wright's were the ones that were to be most frequently quoted in subsequent bibliographies that listed my book.

It may be appropriate here to refer to an informal review that the book was to receive much, much later. In April 1992, at the time of my formal retirement dinner at the University of South Carolina, the then U.S. ambassador to Korea, Donald P. Gregg, wrote a letter that went in part:

Morton Abramowitz was a recent houseguest of mine . . . and we were talking about the amazing changes we have witnessed in Asia over the past few years. Mort recalled that as a college student in the mid-1950s he had read your book entitled China Under Communism. Mort's comment was as follows: 'A lot of people were dumping on Dixie's book at the time but you know what, he was absolutely right.' Mort is an immensely fair-minded man. His comment was wonderful and I hope some day people will say things like that about me.[i]

But that was far in the future. Meanwhile, at a meeting of the Association for Asian Studies (AAS) in Philadelphia in April 1956, John Fairbank, with whom my relations had been cordial and with whom I had debated on public platforms, came up to me and said, "Here's a lady who wants to meet you", and stepped away. "I'm Adele Rickett", she said. I knew of her because of the book *Prisoners of the Liberation*, which she had written jointly with her husband. "I just wanted to meet the person who wrote that horrible book and see whether you're as inhuman as I thought you were."

That's how things were back then. At that same AAS meeting, one of my graduate students at Yale was told that if he wanted to get anywhere in the field, he would have to get away from "Walker and his gang." It was the first time I realized that I was part of a gang, but I already learned that in the atmosphere of the McCarthy era I would not be given the chance to stick by my views and remain above the political fray. Although I had not in any way supported the junior Senator from Wisconsin, I was being dubbed a McCarthyist.

Late in 1956 the Yale history department sent out letters to twelve top scholars in Chinese history asking them to review my credentials for promotion and tenure. This was the first of two years in which such a procedure could be taken. Meanwhile, I had already received inquiries from other universities about my availability, one of which was to lead to my appointment at the University of South Carolina. The dean of Yale College, William C. DeVane, was a South Carolinian and a staunch supporter of mine. He knew of my situation within the profession and followed it with interest. He also knew the president of the University of South Carolina, Donald Russell, a former assistant secretary of state. I was to end up accepting a full professorship at South Carolina even before the initial tenure procedure at Yale could be completed.

The response to the letters from Yale reflected the impact of McCarthyism and how it had polarized the China field. There were no neutral replies: all were either enthusiastically "pro" or emphatically "con." Despite the fact that I had probably the best teaching, publishing, and research record of any of those up for tenure or promotion, my candidacy in that first year was rejected. It was only later that I learned some of the details of the history department's meeting on my case: that in the sharp division the major strikes against me were that I was too anti-communist, that I was more a political scientist than a historian, and that I was "controversial."

Once one has been labeled controversial in the academic world, any evidence will do to validate the description. One of my supporters at that history department meeting had a copy of the euphoric letter, mentioned earlier, that I had received from a distinguished scholar about *The Multi-State System of Ancient China*. Now, in response to Yale's inquiry, the author of that letter stated blandly that to his knowledge Walker had not done any really serious scholarly research in his career. When Professor Samuel F. Bemis, another of my mentors, held the two letters up side by side, one colleague, later to become president at a well-known New England college for women, triumphantly concluded: "That just proves how controversial Dixie is!"

I had been at Yale for eleven years, including graduate work after my service in World War II in the Pacific, and it was probably time to move on. The offer from South Carolina was challenging, though I must report that some of my colleagues at Yale and in the China field considered going there as being consigned to what we call these days, after the Soviet and Chinese experience, "internal exile." They could not have been more wrong. At the University of South Carolina I was able to put my energies into building a program that in less than a decade had achieved national standing. We were able to establish an Institute of International Studies, including a Center for Asian Studies, that attracted visiting scholars from around the world.

At the annual meeting of the AAS that year (1957) most of the China scholars, as had become the custom, met in a Chinese restaurant for a get-together. Normally a regular participant, I did not attend the sessions that year because I was in South Carolina making preparations for an important move in our family life. Two of my graduate students, who subsequently received their doctorates from Yale, attended the meeting and told me what transpired. Following a few toasts and rounds of drinks, Professor Derk Bodde (who was one of the first to apply for the post I was vacating at Yale) rose and announced, "I propose a toast! We finally got Dick Walker!" John Fairbank and others joined in. Ed Reischauer, who had reviewed my *China Under Communism* so favorably and who was to go on to become our distinguished ambassador to Japan, later told me when I visited him in Tokyo that he had been deeply embarrassed and immediately left. My two graduate students, who still keep in touch with me, told me that episode had been instrumental in turning them against the academic profession. They have subsequently had successful diplomatic and research careers with the U.S. government.

In the remaining years of the McCarthyist 1950s I was able to plow my energies into creative activities. I published another volume titled *The Continuing Struggle: Communist China and the Free World*, which was treated in the same manner as China Under Communism. These were, however, good years for me. I was able to join colleagues at the University of Washington to teach in the summer, to travel frequently to East Asia, and to work with a group of young Chinese from Peking University to set up the Union Research Institute in Hong Kong.

This latter group helped me to gather materials dealing with the Great Leap Forward in China, and in June 1959 I published another special supplement for *The New Leader* entitled "Letters from the Communes." These letters, together with those published a year later in another special supplement entitled "Hunger in China", provided moving evidence in first-person terms of the suffering inflicted on the Chinese people by Mao's lunatic Great Leap Forward. As Ross Terrill has recorded elsewhere in these pages, these estimates were scoffed at as "extreme" by John Fairbank and his circle, or dismissed as mere journalism ("Mao in History", Summer 1998). But as we now know, I grossly underestimated the extent of the suffering: instead of the one to two million deaths that I had calculated for the Great Leap, and that had been so contemptuously dismissed as an exaggeration, the now widely accepted figure is thirty million.

The grotesque blindness that characterized many of those on whom the American public depended for advice on conditions in China did not end as the McCarthy period receded. It was just as evident when the next great convulsion—the so-called Cultural Revolution—occurred, and again I was in a position to observe its effects at first hand. In 1971—that is, at the peak of the anti-Vietnam War movement—I was asked by the U.S. Senate Committee on the Judiciary to do a study on the "Human Cost of Communism in China", a companion piece to a similar study by Robert Conquest on the Soviet Union. In this work I drew on official statements and figures from Chinese leaders themselves. Again it created a major stir, with the result that I became more than ever an outcast in the field.

Fortunately, I have lived long enough to have senior leaders in the PRC acknowledge that my writings were on target. During a conference at the Summer

Palace outside Beijing held in 1980, one of the Chinese participants, a retired PLA general who had fought against us in Korea and was now with the Beijing Institute of International and Strategic Studies, approached me. Over a cup of tea he said, "Now, Professor Walker, about that study you did on 'The Human Cost of Communism in China.'" I blanched and thought, "Oh dear." But he continued, "Your figures on the Cultural Revolution's costs were way low!" At least some of those who were breaking away from the Maoist era—which Fairbank had labeled "one of the best things that has ever happened to China"—understood those of us who have never accepted the official line from the Chinese capital.

So much for one China scholar's engagement with McCarthyism. From the perspective of four decades, what can one conclude about that sorry phenomenon? First, McCarthyism had some deeply negative effects on U.S. China studies. It exacerbated personal disputes and personality clashes, and it polluted even such areas as art and literature. It eroded the integrity of some fine scholars who, under pressure or in weakness, substituted emotion for reason. It polarized the field and created real difficulties for those who wished to maintain an objective scholarly position.

Second, by making it easy to discredit serious and informed criticism of what was happening in China, McCarthyism had the unintended effect of moving the center of gravity in scholarship on the subject considerably to the Left. In my view, that made it more often than not spectacularly wrong on the essentials, in much the same way as left-wing Sovietology was wrong about the Soviet Union. If anything, the situation was worse in the case of Sinology, and error persisted longer.

Clearly the excesses of McCarthyism served to legitimize the Fairbank school of thought and its support of the "Chinese Revolution." From his seat at Harvard, Fairbank devoted himself to presenting the Maoist regime as a legitimate successor in an ongoing history of China. With his protégés Arthur and Mary Wright moving to Yale, and with his command of resources from foundations and academic centers, his ability to get this view accepted was formidable. As Professor Richard C. Thornton has summed up:

> For the better part of four decades, Fairbank exercised enormous leverage on the field of Chinese studies: He influenced where and how resources would be expended; helped to train hundreds of students who went on eventually to fill high academic, governmental, and business positions; and shaped American attitudes toward the Chinese Communist regime.

He confidently dismissed those who disagreed with his position as "insignificant"—a class that included, as he confidently asserted in his 1982 autobiography *China Bound*, the group at the University of Washington, as well as myself. In that same volume he summed up his basic approach succinctly: "I was committed to viewing 'communism' as bad in America but good in China, which I was convinced was true." On the same page he also explained the pragmatic nature of his condemnation of communism in America: "I could state the merits of the CCP effectively only if I were anti-CPUSA at home."

Third, McCarthyism destroyed the careers of a number of fine China specialists in the Foreign Service. What happened to Oliver Edmund Clubb and John Paton Davies was a discreditable chapter in the defense of State Department professionals who were rendering honest service to their country. At the same time, the State Department was not as devastated as these individual cases might suggest, or as some academics were later to insist. Distinguished officers such as Ralph Clough, Howard Boorman, and Charles T. Cross were able to continue their service unobstructed.

Fourth, McCarthyism resulted in some, but only a few, academic purges, which are always ugly, no matter the motive, in a society that cherishes academic freedom. The victims were at both ends of the spectrum to which they had been consigned by the intensity of McCarthyist polemics, though only those at one end have received much subsequent attention.

Fifth, as McCarthyism has become a legend and a catch-all characterization of a decade, its strength and impact have been grossly exaggerated. This has had pernicious effects over the years. Thus, for example, was it possible for Professor Edward Friedman of the University of Wisconsin to discuss the so-called Cultural Revolution as "Marxist McCarthyism." And today a colleague of mine still tells his students that McCarthyism was worse for the United States than Stalinism was for Russia. Such statements are ludicrous and morally repugnant. As ugly as McCarthyism was, nobody died because of it, no one went to a gulag, and the total number of people jailed, usually on charges of perjury, did not exceed 140. By contrast, the Cultural Revolution marked the greatest wave of destruction of cultural and artistic treasures, the greatest purge of intellectuals, and the greatest national destruction since the First Chin Emperor beginning in 221 bc. Accurate estimates of the human casualties are still not available, but the figure is probably more than two million. As for the second comparison, according to Russian scholars Stalin was responsible for the deaths of more than fifty million people during the course of his career. Mao Tse-tung was to score even larger.

The McCarthyism label never matched the reality. There were positive developments in China studies even during its worst years. McCarthyism did not send scholars into headlong retreat in fright. Many were able to continue their studies and inspire a new generation of specialists. Not only did some stand up to McCarthy, but major projects, including the National Defense Education Act and new support for China studies from foundations beginning in the late 1950s, made the field remarkably productive. Indeed, the U.S. scholarly community was well prepared for the access to the PRC that came in the wake of the Nixon opening to China. In the end, and as ugly as it was, McCarthyism was not as powerful as the deafening howls from some academics who insisted that they were forced into silence. It was a sorry chapter, but it was neither deadly nor lasting.

NOTES

---

[i] Morton Abramowitz, one of the country's most distinguished diplomats, served as ambassador to both Thailand (1978-81) and Turkey (1989-91). "Dixie" is a nickname of mine that dates from before World War II, when I worked with a college baseball team as a manager and "Dixie Walker" was a nationally known outfielder for the then Brooklyn Dodgers.